"Elections matter for so many reasons – not least for an orderly transfer of power, and for citizens to reflect on, interact with, and directly affect their state institutions. The performance of electoral management bodies can make the difference between an election that is accepted with an orderly transition of power, or an election result that is challenged with ensuing problems of violence or societal instability. This ground-breaking study is the first to give election management the serious scholarly attention it rightly deserves. Toby James' insights on organising elections will provide valuable evidence-based advice for policy makers and election practitioners alike."

– Therese Pearce Laanela, Head of Electoral Processes, International IDEA

"In *Comparative Electoral Management* Toby James provides an in-depth comparative analysis of one of the core administrative functions of democracy. Rich in data and innovative conceptualisation, the book draws on insights from a variety of disciplines to address a topic, the urgency of which is rapidly becoming apparent to citizens the world over. The result is a highly informed and perceptive analysis of how elections are run and how they might be improved."

– Sarah Birch, King's College London, UK

"Toby James demonstrates very convincingly in this major book that electoral management matters a lot for the quality of elections and for how reliable election results are as a reflection of the electorate's intentions. *Comparative Electoral Management* is, therefore, a book that will be of great value for at least three audiences: students of elections, electoral practitioners, and – hopefully – politicians interested in the improvement of the quality of elections and electoral administration in their country."

– Jørgen Elklit, Aarhus University, Denmark

Comparative Electoral Management

This book offers the first comparative monograph on the management of elections.

The book defines electoral management as a new, inter-disciplinary area and advances a realist sociological approach to study it. A series of new, original frameworks are introduced, including the PROSeS framework, which can be used by academics and practitioners around the world to evaluate electoral management quality. A networked governance approach is also introduced to understand the full range of collaborative actors involved in delivering elections, including civil society and the international community. Finally, the book evaluates some of the policy instruments used to improve the integrity of elections, including voter registration reform, training and the funding of elections. Extensive mixed methods are used throughout including thematic analysis of interviews, (auto-)ethnography, comparative historical analysis and cross-national and national surveys of electoral officials.

This text will be of key interest to scholars, students and practitioners interested and involved in electoral integrity and elections, and more broadly to comparative politics, public administration, international relations and democracy studies.

Toby S. James is a Professor of Politics and Public Policy at the University of East Anglia, UK.

Routledge Studies in Elections, Democracy and Autocracy
Series editors:
Pippa Norris
Harvard University, USA, and the University of Sydney, Australia
Carolien van Ham
The University of New South Wales, Australia.

This series addresses the quality of elections, how and why electoral contests fall short of international standards, and the implications of flawed elections for democracy and autocracy. The series is published in association with the Electoral Integrity Project.

Election Administration and the Politics of Voter Access
Kevin Pallister

Electoral Rights in Europe
Advances and Challenges
Edited by Helen Hardman and Brice Dickson

Electoral Integrity and Political Regimes
Actors, Strategies and Consequences
Edited by Holly Ann Garnett and Margarita Zavadskaya

State Capacity, Economic Control, and Authoritarian Elections
Merete Seeberg

Comparative Electoral Management
Performance, Networks and Instruments
Toby S. James

Comparative Electoral Management
Performance, Networks and Instruments

Toby S. James

Routledge
Taylor & Francis Group
LONDON AND NEW YORK

First published 2020
by Routledge
2 Park Square, Milton Park, Abingdon, Oxon OX14 4RN

and by Routledge
52 Vanderbilt Avenue, New York, NY 10017

Routledge is an imprint of the Taylor & Francis Group, an informa business

© 2020 Toby S. James

The right of Toby S. James to be identified as author of this work has been asserted by him in accordance with sections 77 and 78 of the Copyright, Designs and Patents Act 1988.

With the exception of Chapter 1 and Chapter 4, no part of this book may be reprinted or reproduced or utilised in any form or by any electronic, mechanical, or other means, now known or hereafter invented, including photocopying and recording, or in any information storage or retrieval system, without permission in writing from the publishers.

Chapter 1 and Chapter 4 of this book are available for free in PDF format as Open Access from the individual product page at www.routledge.com. They have been made available under a Creative Commons Attribution-Non Commercial-No Derivatives 4.0 license.

Trademark notice: Product or corporate names may be trademarks or registered trademarks, and are used only for identification and explanation without intent to infringe.

British Library Cataloguing-in-Publication Data
A catalogue record for this book is available from the British Library

Library of Congress Cataloging-in-Publication Data
Names: James, Toby S., 1979– author.
Title: Comparative electoral management : performance, networks, and instruments / Toby S. James.
Description: Abingdon, Oxon ; New York, NY : Routledge, 2020. | Series: Routledge studies in elections, democracy, and autocracy | Includes bibliographical references and index.
Identifiers: LCCN 2019027849 (print) | LCCN 2019027850 (ebook) | ISBN 9781138682412 (hardback) | ISBN 9781315545172 (ebook)
Subjects: LCSH: Elections—Management. | Elections—Corrupt practices. | Election monitoring.
Classification: LCC JF1001 .J289 2020 (print) | LCC JF1001 (ebook) | DDC 324.6—dc23
LC record available at https://lccn.loc.gov/2019027849
LC ebook record available at https://lccn.loc.gov/2019027850

ISBN: 978-1-138-68241-2 (hbk)
ISBN: 978-1-315-54517-2 (ebk)

Typeset in Times New Roman
by Apex CoVantage, LLC

Printed and bound in Great Britain by
TJ International Ltd, Padstow, Cornwall

Contents

List of illustrations ix
Preface and acknowledgements xii

PART I
Foundations 1

1 Introduction 3
2 A realist sociological approach 18

PART II
Performance 31

3 Existing concepts and evidence 33
4 Evaluating electoral management performance: the PROSeS framework 59

PART III
Networks 87

5 Electoral management governance networks 89
6 UK electoral management governance networks 104
7 Comparative electoral management governance networks 125
8 International electoral management governance networks 160

PART IV
Instruments 197

9 Voter registration reform 199
10 Centralisation 221
11 Training and human resource practices 241
12 Austerity and financial investment in electoral management 252

PART V
Looking forward 267

13 Conclusions 269

Bibliography 275
Appendix: EMB budget sizes 307
Index 311

Illustrations

Figures

1.1	The performance of electoral authorities in national elections held worldwide in between 2013–2017 and level of democracy	9
1.2	The performance of electoral authorities in national elections held worldwide in between 2013–2017 and GDP per capita	11
1.3	The performance of electoral authorities in national elections held worldwide in between 2013–2017 and region	12
1.4	An inter-disciplinary approach to electoral management	14
3.1	Structure and agency in assessing electoral management performance	35
3.2	The 'fairness' of electoral officials in 41 countries, 2010–2014	50
3.3	Global EMB capacity, as measured by V-DEM 8.0	51
4.1	The PROSeS framework	61
4.2	Completeness of the electoral register estimates around the world in 2017	68
4.3	Voter turnout at parliamentary general elections in the UK and Canada	77
4.4	Estimates of the completeness of the electoral register in the UK and Canada, 1945–2015	78
4.5	Percentage of votes cast that are invalid at general elections, 1945–2015	79
5.1	Percentage of the electoral cycle delivered by EMBs in the ELECT and EMS surveys	91
6.1	Three constellations of actors in the UK electoral management governance network	111
7.1	GDP per capita (current US$) 1960–2016 in the four case studies	126
7.2	Comparing the four case studies by the V-DEM Electoral Democracy Index 1900–2017	126
7.3	The frequency of interactions between EMBs and other actors (1–5, 5 is high)	157
7.4	The percentage of idea source for changing electoral law in the last five years	158
8.1	Frequency of appearances for each speaker	181

x *Illustrations*

9.1	The effects of IER on the completeness of the electoral register	211
9.2	The effects of IER on the costs of running electoral registration	214
9.3	The effect of IER on employee outcomes	216
11.1	The relationship between human resource management and EMB performance	245
12.1	Percentage increases in EMB budget from a non-election year to an election year	256
12.2	Changes in EMB budget size 2011–2016	258
13.1	The direct and indirect effects of electoral administration (and other) reforms	271

Tables

1.1	Foci of study within electoral studies	5
2.1	Three domains of reality in the realist sociological approach	26
3.1	Existing approaches to measuring electoral integrity and management quality	38
4.1	Type of electoral investments needed to ensure high-quality electoral management	63
4.2	The PROSeS matrix for evaluating electoral management	66
4.3	Estimates of expenditure per eligible voter and per vote cast (figures in US$)	81
5.1	Rhodes and Marsh's (1992, 187) typology of policy networks	98
6.1	Potential resources, tactics and weaknesses of actors in the UK network	118
7.1	Case study characteristics	126
7.2	Number of submissions to the NSW JSCEM 2004–2017 by stakeholder type	138
7.3	Comparing case studies by governance network features	153
7.4	Proposed typology of governance networks	154
8.1	Cross-continental organisations contributing to electoral management	167
8.2	The speaker types at four international conference circuits. Values may not sum to 100 because of rounding up	178
8.3	Most common speaker origin	179
8.4	Most common speaker organisation	180
8.5	Most frequent speakers	180
8.6	Potential resources, tactics and weaknesses of actors in international networks	195
9.1	Number of survey responses by job role	205
9.2	Frequency table of themes and sub-themes raised by election officials	206
9.3	Effects of IER on electoral security and the accuracy of the register	209
9.4	The effects of IER on completeness by local authority type	213

9.5	The effects of IER on the completeness of the electoral register and accessibility of the electoral registration process	213
9.6	Measures of workplace conditions and employee experiences	216
10.1	The effects of top-down directions on electoral management during the 2011 referendums	228
10.2	Views of the management structure used for the referendum (%)	235
10.3	The effects of the 2016 directions on electoral management	236
11.1	Median annual pay for UK electoral officials for 2016	247
11.2	Highest qualification for each level of electoral officials (percentage)	247
11.3	Percentage of UK electoral officials with AEA qualifications in electoral administration	248
11.4	OLS model where stress is the dependent variable	249
11.5	OLS regressions where the dependent variable is EMB performance measured by the Perceptions of Electoral Integrity survey	251
12.1	Percentage of government expenditure and public services expenditure spent on elections	257
12.2	Changes in EMB budget size 2011–2016	258
12.3	Sources of EMB revenue	259

Boxes

1.1	Data sources used in this volume	16
5.1	Different types of policy networks identified by the Anglo School	96
9.1	Examples of changed workplace environment as a result of IER	217
10.1	Example directions issued to local officials in preparation for the 2011 referendums, compiled from Electoral Commission (2011a, 2011b)	226
10.2	Example directions issued to local officials in preparation for the 2016 referendum, based on Electoral Commission (2016c, 12–13)	234
13.1	Policy recommendations based on the research findings and new methods from the book	273

Preface and acknowledgements

The idea for this book began, roughly a decade before it was published, in a meeting of electoral officials in Wales. Dedicated officials were collaborating across constituency and local authority boundaries to make unseen, micro-level, decisions necessary to organise forthcoming elections, grappling with the many complex challenges involved. As they did so, it became clear to me that although there were (hundreds of) thousands[1] of books and articles on elections, few had thought about actually organising one.

In the research projects that followed I was fortunate enough to be given insights, which provided lasting memories. These included interviewing a Scottish manager who had decorated a small interview room with multi-coloured Post-it notes. These were from a brainstorming session with her team about what they could do better next time. They were all still there, several weeks on, because she had not had time to consolidate and action them. I recall being told how electoral officials had had a ballot box stolen from a polling station by an angry citizen during polling day because his name was not on the register (fortunately, a rugby-playing poll clerk caught up with him halfway across the park). I remember a lad in his 20s forlornly telling me:

> 'an election is like a rite of passage. They warned me about it. But you never know what it feels like until you go through it.'

In the years that followed, I extended the reach of this book to outside of the UK and was lucky enough to gasp at the mountain of registration applications given to clerks to process in dusty, factory-like conditions in India; be amongst diplomats and delegates clinking glasses and discussing affairs at the fringes of a conference in Tavricheskiy Palace in St. Petersburg, where new international standards on elections were drawn up; listen to the 'war-stories' from experienced electoral officials who had provided electoral assistance in fragile democracies around the world.

These are among the people who keep democracy working and make important decisions about how it should work. The people that run elections matter. Their workplace setting, the people whom they interact with, the resources they (don't) have all matter. In other words, the sociology of electoral management matters. Research must go beyond number crunching data on electoral laws and vote patterns to capture this sociological, 'everyday' dimension of running elections. The more that research on elections can connect to practitioner experience, the better political science, practitioner's knowledge and elections will be.

Doing this is not always easy. It requires the trust and time of electoral officials. It requires research funding. It requires the support and patience of colleagues and family and commonly takes us outside our comfort zone.[2]

I have therefore been exceptionally fortunate on so many grounds and the book would not have been possible without the help of others. They need to be thanked and their contributions made explicit – not just because it's nice to do so – but because they embody the community of people who form the context in which the book was written. If we're going to be vaguely sociological, this matters, because they are part of the story of the book that follows.

Generous financial support was provided by separate grants from the Nuffield Foundation, McDougall Trust, Electoral Integrity Project, University of New South Wales and the University of East Anglia. Organisations to have provided other forms of assistance included the UK Electoral Commission, the UK Association of Electoral Administrators, Venice Commission, A-WEB, Electoral Commission of NSW, Permanent Electoral Authority of Romania, Central Electoral Commission of Russia and Intentional IDEA.

Thanks must go to Pippa Norris who established the Electoral Integrity Project (EIP) back in 2012, and all those who worked with her on the project. This helped to forge a community of scholars working in this area and a global community of friends too. Holly Ann Garnett, Carolien van Ham and Leontine Loeber are chief amongst these and I richly enjoyed the many late night Skype sessions with them working on the Electoral Management Survey which is used in this book. Holly provided lots of helpful feedback on the book and was always a model colleague. Leontine also introduced me to many of the realities of working in the international community and I have learnt much from her.

I owe a debt of thanks to those who agreed to be interviewed, but whose names are kept anonymous. Bite the Ballot and ClearView Research have been a real pleasure to work with and made a middle-aging academic feel like he's hanging out with the 'cool kids' and doing some good. In particular, Oliver Sidorczuk and Mike Sani, Merve Gunduz and Josh Dell were fantastic to work with. Friends at the Nigerian Independent Electoral Commission were a pleasure to teach, but taught me more. Alistair Clark has been a great colleague and friend throughout and Chapter 10 partly draws from a joint survey that we did. I must also thank Fiona Buckley, Rodney Smith, Michael Pal, EIP Fellows, Alan Finlayson, Lee Marsden, Theresa Reidy, David Farrell, Jorgen Elklit, Sarah Birch, Mark Evans, Marian Sawar, Therese Pearce-Laanela, Marten Haalf, Nic Cheeseman, Rafael López-Pintor, Harry Neufield, Staffen Darnolf, Gaël Martin-Micallef and Robert Gerenge, who all helped, perhaps without realising it. Feedback from participants at the successive APSA, ECPR, PSA conferences, and endless EIP and Electoral Management Network workshops helped progress many of the ideas.[3] Taylor and Francis, Oxford University Press and Palgrave have kindly allowed me to include in this book short sections of articles that were previously published.[4]

Administrative and transcription support from Reuben Braden-Ball and George Lankester made a real difference. Ganesh Pawan Kumar Agoor and colleagues at Apex helped to spot and correct many errors in a dyslexic academic's manuscript (the author alone is responsible for all remaining errors).

Happy writers are productive workers. So above all, thank you to Sam, Dylan and Rosa for the continuous support, patience and happy times. They made researching the book in Australia even more memorable. Rosa's random edits to the manuscript such as 'wasonooooooooooooooooooooooooooooooooooooooooooooo ooooooooo…' in Chapter Seven were thankfully caught before publication.

Norwich, Norfolk, UK, March 2019

Notes

1 Millions, actually. Google Scholar returned 2,760,000 results for 'election' as of 31 March 2019.
2 As I was getting a ride from a taxi driver in Chennai from the airport at 3am in the morning who didn't speak English, and who I had to poke to keep awake so that he didn't crash, I did think that perhaps secondary analysis of other datasets would be easier after all.
3 Other workshops included the Australia National University, "The ballot is stronger than the bullet"?: Democracy in difficult contexts, 6 April 2018.
4 Parts of Chapter 2 were published as James (2018). Parts of Chapter 9 were published as James (2014) and parts of Chapter 10 were published as James (2017).

Part I
Foundations

1 Introduction

1.1 Why electoral management matters

In the immediate aftermath of the 2007 Kenyan Presidential election, the country entered into a political, economic and humanitarian crisis. Post-election violence erupted leading to estimates of over 1,000 people being killed by police, criminal gangs and militia groups, and 660,000 displacements, as opponents of President Mwai Kibaki alleged electoral manipulation (CBS News 2008; Kenny 2019). Tensions were deeply rooted in Kenya's political history. The sequence of events surrounding the conduct of the vote count were the immediate sparks for the conflict, however. An announcement from the Electoral Commission of Kenya (ECK) about the result was expected by 10am on Sunday 30 December at the latest, three days after the poll, But there were repeated delays. Rumours circulated that the results were being rigged by the ECK to favour the President (Throup 2008). In its evaluation of the election, the European Union Election Observation Mission (2008, 1) concluded that:

> Kenya fell short of key international and regional standards for democratic elections. Most significantly, the electoral process suffered from a lack of transparency in the processing and tallying of results, which undermined the confidence in the accuracy of the final result of the presidential election.... This overall conclusion is all the more regrettable, since in advance of the tallying process and despite some significant shortcomings in the legal framework, the elections were generally well administered and freedoms of expression, association and assembly were generally respected.

Kenya 2007 highlights the high stakes involved in delivering elections and the consequences of getting it wrong. Kenya's experience was evidence that fragile multi-party systems can quickly fall apart under intense political pressure (Cheeseman 2008). It wasn't a gerrymandered electoral system that was to blame, or the role of money in politics – the traditional sources of concern about electoral integrity. Instead, it was the logistical delivery of the electoral process.

Problems with the delivery of elections are not uncommon and found in established democracies alongside electoral autocracies and transitioning democracies, however. The 2000 US Presidential election infamously exposed shortcomings in

America's electoral machinery with confusing ballot papers, faulty equipment, queues at polling stations, problems with absentee ballots and citizens missing from the electoral registers (U.S. Commission on Civil Rights 2001; Wand et al. 2001). In the UK, at midnight on Friday 7 May 2010, with the result of the UK general election unclear, the BBC News carried the headlines that the election had been marred by widespread errors with electoral administration. Hundreds of voters in Chester were unable to cast a ballot because of an out-of-date electoral register; long queues formed in Sheffield and Leeds leaving voters 'locked out' when polls closed at midnight; polling stations in Liverpool reported that they had run out of ballot papers. Some dissatisfied voters staged sit-ins to protest against what they called 'disenfranchisement' (Channel 4 News 2010). 'It sounds like a disgrace from beginning to end, the way that this election has been handled', exclaimed the BBC's TV presenter David Dimbleby, who was questioning the Chair of the Electoral Commission, Jenny Watson, live on air as the news unfolded (BBC News 2010). Elsewhere, the completeness and accuracy of electoral registers have been questioned in Ireland (James 2012, 185–90) and New Zealand (Downes 2014). Poor ballot paper design invalidated many votes in Indonesia (Schmidt 2010; Sukma 2009) and Scotland (Denver, Johns, and Carmen 2009). Over 1,300 votes were lost in a knife-edge Western Australian Senate recount race (Lion 2013). In the 2013 Malaysia election, election officials were criticised for not shaking the bottles of indelible ink, meaning that some citizens could wash off the ink and double vote (Lai 2013). Most bizarrely, in the small village of Wallsburg, Utah, part-time election officials *forgot* to run the election. Twice. First in 2011, and then again in 2013. To the hilarity of the US media, County Clerk Brent Titcomb said local officials in the sleepy hamlet of approximately 300 residents had forgotten to advertise for candidates: 'They just went on without doing anything . . . close to the election day, they called to ask what they should do' (Associated Press 2013). A local resident commented that 'they got in a whole bunch of trouble' (Smart 2015).

Elections, it is often said, are the most complex logistical event to be organised during peacetime. These anecdotes and examples routinely catch headlines as they are picked up by journalists and quickly circulated over social media, suggest that societies often fail to deliver elections successfully. But there has been relatively little academic attention on the management of elections. This begs the question of whether, if we begin to turn over the rocks and look underneath, we will find fundamental problems in elections up and down the land, even in established democracies? Or will we instead find that elections are generally well run by dedicated, professional and hard-working electoral officials? Are they officials who don't deserve the tough press and populist criticism that they receive?

This book aims to provide some tools and methods to find out and consider what can be done to improve the delivery of elections, which will be of use worldwide. This introductory chapter begins by arguing that the study of the delivery of elections, electoral management, has been fundamentally overlooked in the academic literature. The concept of electoral management is defined and arguments made for an inter-disciplinary approach to the topic. Evidence is provided

Introduction 5

of the considerable variation in the quality of delivery worldwide. The chapter explains why electoral management matters. An overview of the book ahead is then set out.

1.2 Electoral management: the new sub-field

Electoral studies is widely thought to be one of the most established areas of political science (Htun and Powell 2013). There is a major hole in the centre of the study of elections, however. There has been a lengthy scholarship on why people vote for candidates and parties. There have been considerable efforts to understand how electoral institutions such as the voting system, boundaries, electoral finance and voting technologies shape political outcomes (see Table 1.1 below). We know in detail how electoral systems can affect whether people vote, the nature of the party system and who wins elections. There have been many lengthy studies on the funding of political parties and candidates. The choice of methods used to register electors and cast votes has seen significant attention with many studies looking at the effects of voting by post, early voting and internet voting. Elections are not just about designing laws and procedures, however. Once a law or rule has been made, it needs to be implemented. Resources need to be mobilised, staff recruited and motivated, technology designed. *Electoral management therefore refers to the organisations, networks, resources, micro anthropological working practices and instruments involved in implementing elections.*

Table 1.1 Foci of study within electoral studies

Category	Broad scope	Example key works
Election administration	The administrative procedures used for casting votes and compiling the electoral register	Piven and Cloward (1988, 2000), Massicotte, Blais, and Yoshinaka (2004), Wolfinger and Rosenstone (1980)
Suffrage legislation	The criteria for who is legally enfranchised to vote	Uggen and Manza (2002)
Electoral boundaries	The number, shape and size of electoral constituencies	Handley and Grofman (2008)
Electoral finance	The rules for how political parties are funded in elections	van Biezen (2004)
Electoral systems	The formulae for rules of how votes are converted into seats	Duverger (1951), Rae (1967), Farrell (2011), Renwick (2010)
Ballot initiatives and referenda	The circumstances under which referenda can take place on a policy issue and/or citizens can remove an elected representative from office	Parkinson (2001), Qvortrup (2005), Schlozman and Yohai (2008)
Electoral justice	The resolution of electoral disputes	Orozco-Henríquez (2010), Hernández-Huerta (2017)

6 *Foundations*

The management of elections remains chronically under-researched around the world. Given that elections have been conducted in many countries for centuries, this is an extraordinary oversight. As recently as 1999, Robert Pastor complained that he was 'unable to locate a book or even an article on election commissions or their history' (Pastor 1999a, 76). Since then a number of significant reports have been published by international organisations (López-Pinter 2000; Wall et al. 2006), but these do not fully connect to the literature on democratic theory or assess electoral management through academic methods. The 2000 Presidential election rekindled an enormous interest in the choice of voting technologies (how are people registered? how do they cast their vote?) in the USA (Alvarez, Atkeson, and Hall 2012; Atkeson et al. 2010; Gronke, Miller, and Galances-Rosenbaum 2007; Kiewiet et al. 2008), but this research is predominately concerned with evaluating the effects of voting technologies rather than the design of electoral management bodies (EMBs) and the management of *the people* within these organisations. Some work eventually followed on poll workers (Claassen et al. 2008; Hall, Quin Monson, and Patterson 2009). Poll worker studies eventually expanded to reach Europe (Clark and James 2017; Goerres and Funk 2019). Studies also sought to establish whether an EMB with *de jure* independence would positively affect electoral integrity (Hartlyn, McCoy, and Mustillo 2008). Mechanisms have been proposed and introduced in the US, such as the Pew Elections Performance Index, based on Heather Gerken's concept of a Democracy Index (2009a) (but hereto not been evaluated). These recent inroads have marked important progress. However, studies on how elections are implemented have usually been isolated national cases and there has been no cross-national monograph on electoral management.

1.3 Clarifying the terminology

Such an oversight is remarkable because there is an established set of theories and concepts that have been used to subject the quality of other government services, such as schools, hospitals, and social care, to continuous critical review. An inter-disciplinary approach can therefore be taken to the management of elections. Taking electoral studies into other disciplines requires some conceptual tidying, however, because the terms 'electoral governance', 'management', 'administration' and 'regulation' are often used interchangeably or are not differentiated from each other.[1] Scholars from public administration also attach different meanings to concepts such as 'governance' – and have even criticised themselves for giving terms multiple meanings.[2]

Electoral governance is defined here as the broader set of power relationships and actors involved in deciding how elections are organised. The power relations involved in electoral governance cover all aspects of the electoral cycle – from designing an electoral system, electoral justice or polling station design. Electoral governance is therefore about more than electoral management bodies (EMBs) because there is a wider set of actors who will seek to shape the electoral rules of the game. Electoral governance involves *rule-making* – making decisions about which electoral institution designs to adopt. Rule-making can involve proactive rational decision making, but more often involves institutional drift, layering and conversion (Mahoney and Thelan 2010). The drivers for continuity and change in electoral systems (Blais 2008; Renwick 2010) or other electoral practices (James 2012; Massicotte, Blais, and Yoshinaka 2004; Norris and van Es 2016) have been studied elsewhere. *Electoral administration* is just one set of electoral institutions subject to rule-making – the procedures used to allow citizens to register and cast their votes (James 2010a).

After rule-making comes *rule implementation*. Laws and procedures have been made by Parliaments and executives; the role of electoral management bodies (EMBs) and other actors is to apply them. *Electoral justice* is the final stage of the process. This refers to the mechanisms through which electoral disputes are resolved. This dimension therefore usually takes place in judicial venues (Hernández-Huerta 2017; Orozco-Henríquez 2010).

1.4 Implementation involves rule-making and governance

The focus of this book is *electoral management* – the *implementation* of elections. However, implementation also involves elements of *rule-making and electoral governance* too. This claim deserves some further expansion.

Firstly, designing implementation infrastructures brings rule-making questions. Decisions need to be made about who is responsible for implementing elections – should it be one agency, two or more? What role should there be for civil society? Should the agencies involved be independent of political parties and government ministers – or under their control? Each of these decisions is likely to have consequences for the quality of the election (James et al. 2019a).

Secondly, implementation can involve decision making. There is likely to be considerable discretion afforded to middle-level managers in picking an accessible polling station, resourcing the polling stations and motivating their workforce. As theories from public administration show, front-line local officials and managers are involved in *everyday decision making* in running elections (Lipsky 1980). They may need to interpret hand-written voter registration applications, deal with queues that arise at polling stations and manage conflictual situations in polling stations. The way that they deal with the everyday voter matters. A basic continuum can be envisaged from being friendly and pointing out all services available, to being rude, aggressive and perhaps not even replying to an email or call which can make a vital difference to a citizen.

Thirdly, administrative bodies such as EMBs are also strategic and political actors. Legislators do not make laws on elections alone. As this book shows, electoral administrators can themselves be highly mobilised actors seeking to lobby and affect the policy process. Although this is not always the case, electoral officials in many countries lack organisation – this is itself significant. At the same time, it is common for more than one organisation to be responsible for organising an election. There are commonly many organisations working together. This leads to opportunities for positive-sum collaborative forms of implementation and governance. But less optimistically, it can lead to inter-organisational politics, rivalries and disputes. In these systems, each EMB has strategies, tactics and tools that they can deploy. In short, they are embedded into resource-dependent governance structures in which their powers and futures are dependent on the strategies they take.

Electoral management is therefore not a simple and narrow process which should be left for practitioners to consider or consigned to dusty bookshelves as it has been. As James et al. (2019a) set out, it involves:

- ***Organizing*** the actual electoral process (ranging from pre-election registration and campaigning, to the actual voting on election day, to post-election vote counting).
- ***Monitoring*** electoral conduct throughout the electoral process (i.e. monitoring the political party/candidates' campaigns and media in the lead-up to elections, enforcing regulations regarding voter and party eligibility, campaign finance, campaign and media conduct, vote count and tallying procedures etc.).
- ***Certifying*** election results by declaring electoral outcomes.

But, in turn, these tasks require states to have the bureaucratic machinery for at least the following:

- Measuring and monitoring performance.
- Managing and maintaining external and internal organisational relationships.
- Decision-making processes about delivery mechanisms.
- Designing policy instruments to improve performance.
- Allocating resources amongst the stakeholders involved in the delivery of elections.
- Staff recruitment, training, retention and motivation.

1.5 Evidence of variation in electoral management worldwide

This chapter began with examples of problems with the implementation of elections from a variety of countries. Going beyond anecdote, recent cross-national datasets demonstrate systematic global variation in the quality of electoral management, however. Unweighted data on the quality of elections between 1978 and 2004 in electoral observation reports suggest that problems with electoral management are present on the day of elections in 15.2% of elections (Kelley 2011, 13–15). A more recent survey of experts, the Perceptions of Electoral Integrity survey, asked about the quality of electoral management worldwide 2013–2017. A 100-point electoral authorities index was constructed based on whether the electoral authorities were 'impartial', 'distributed information to citizens', 'allowed public scrutiny of their performance' and 'performed well'. The mean score was 65.1 (Norris, Wynter, and Cameron 2018).

Intuitively we might think that problems are less likely in democracies. Freedom of association and broader levels of electoral integrity should provide the environment in which electoral authorities are held to account more readily and this could boost performance. Figure 1.1 presents data on the electoral authorities

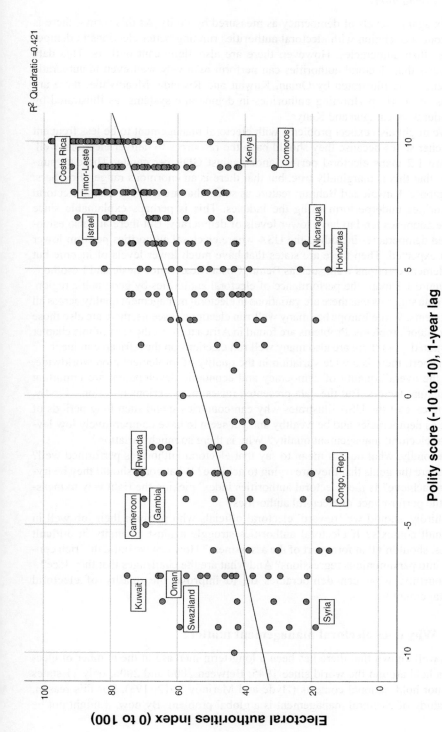

Figure 1.1 The performance of electoral authorities in national elections held worldwide in between 2013–2017 and level of democracy.

Source: Author with data from the Perception of Electoral Integrity Dataset (Norris, Wynter, and Cameron 2018).

index against levels of democracy as measured by Polity. As this shows, there is a strong association with electoral authorities running better elections in democracies than autocracies. However, there are also significant outliers. This data suggests that electoral authorities can perform relatively well even in autocratic systems – as illustrated by Oman, Kuwait and Rwanda. Meanwhile, there are cases of poorly performing authorities in democratic systems, as illustrated by Honduras, Nicaragua and Kenya.

We might also expect problems with electoral management to be less frequent in richer states because they should have the resources to deliver elections well. Figure 1.2 maps electoral performance against GDP per capita. The data suggests that this is marginally true, but that there is an enormous range of outliers. Singapore, Kuwait and Bahrain feature as states that are rich but whose electoral authorities underperform using the indexes. This is perhaps explainable since these countries tend to have lower levels of democracy. But there are also established democracies including the USA where electoral authorities perform lower than expected. Then there are states that have much lower levels of income but implement elections well, such as Benin, Costa Rica, Timor-Leste and Lesotho.

Figure 1.3 maps the performance of electoral authorities by geographic region. The data suggests that there are variations in electoral management quality across all continents. While Europe has many well-run elections, it seems, there are also those with major problems. Problems are found in Africa too – as the start of this chapter illustrated – but there are also many well run elections on the African continent.

In short, there is a wide variation in the quality of implementation worldwide, and the overall quality of democracy and economic development are important contextual factors. But the data presented raises many serious questions. Firstly, as the case of the USA illustrates why can countries spend such long periods of time as democracies and be wealthy and yet seem to have comparatively low levels of electoral management quality? Why is there so much variation?

Secondly, what does it mean to say that electoral authorities performed well? What are the goals that they are trying to achieve? What goals should they be trying to achieve? Is the 'electoral authorities index' picking the right way to measure the performance of electoral authorities?

Thirdly, should we 'reward' electoral officials who perform their job well in difficult contexts? If electoral authorities struggle against adversity in difficult times, shouldn't that form part of the assessment? How can we build this rich context into parsimonious regressions? And what are the challenges that they face?

Fourthly, what can democracies do to improve the quality of electoral management?

1.6 Why does electoral management matter?

It is well known that there has been a long-term increase in the number of elections held around the world since 1945. Between 2000 and 2006, only 11 states did not hold national contests (Hyde and Marinov 2012, 193). For this reason, the study of electoral management is a global problem. By now, it might not be

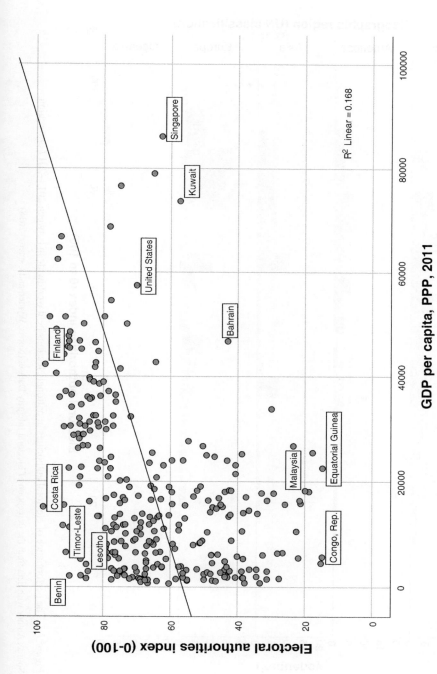

Figure 1.2 The performance of electoral authorities in national elections held worldwide in between 2013–2017 and GDP per capita.
Source: Author with data from the Perception of Electoral Integrity Dataset (Norris, Wynter, and Cameron 2018).

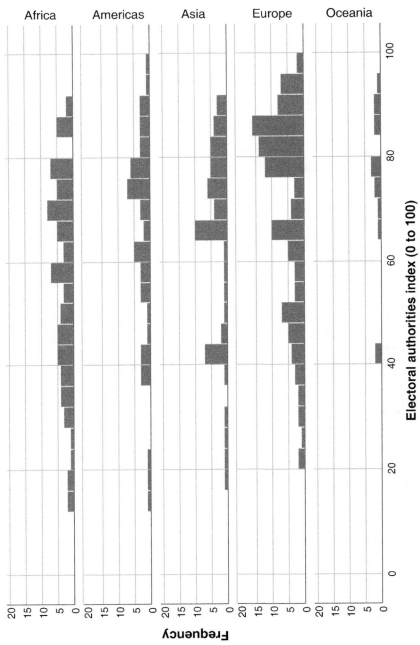

Figure 1.3 The performance of electoral authorities in national elections held worldwide in between 2013–2017 and region.

Source: Author with data from the Perception of Electoral Integrity Dataset (Norris, Wynter, and Cameron 2018).

difficult to realise why such variation in the quality of electoral management matters. But four principal reasons are set out here:

- **Democratic ideals.** As David Beetham set out, democracy is a political system in which there is political equality and popular control of government (Beetham 1994). If an individual's vote is not counted because it is lost in transit from ballot box to polling station, or because of defects in the counting process, then the individual might be denied their democratic right and this equality is undermined. But if errors aggregate to give a systematic advantage to a candidate or party, either through design or mistake, then democratic government is fundamentally undermined.
- **Confidence in democratic institutions.** Defects in electoral management and their widespread reporting can quickly ebb away at public confidence in democratic institutions and we already have some studies to demonstrate this (Atkeson and Saunders 2007; Claassen et al. 2008, 2012; Hall, Quin Monson, and Patterson 2009).
- **Security, peace and conflict.** As the case of Kenya illustrates, situations in which the electoral authorities and the results of elections are not trusted can quickly undermine fragile peace processes. Civil war and conflict may follow – the prospects for democratic consolidation may be undermined (Elklit and Reynolds 2002; Pastor 1999b; Snyder 2013). During times where there are concerns about democratic retreat, there might be consequences even in established democracies (Norris and Inglehart 2018).
- **Public accountability.** There has been an enormous international investment in elections and electoral management around the world, as the professionalisation of elections has been set as a priority by key commissions such as Kofi Annan's Global Commission on Elections (Global Commission on Elections 2012). For example, the European Instrument for Democracy and Human Rights spent approximately EUR€307 million on over 700 projects relating to democracy promotion between 2007–2010 (EIDHR 2011, 8), much of which was spent on electoral assistance. Delivering well-run elections is therefore important to ensure that the public money is spent well.

1.7 Multi-disciplinarity

If electoral management is so important, why did scholars overlook it for so long? One reason is that academics are commonly organised into communities which can be difficult to break down. Scholars might take training in comparative politics, law or public administration – but not usually more than one of them. Professional associations exist with sub-groups such as APSA's organised section on Elections, Public Opinion, and Voting Behavior which was formed in 1994 to focus on research on 'elections, electoral behavior, public opinion, voting turnout, and political participation' (APSA 2018). Or the UK Political Studies Associations Elections, Public Opinion and Parties (EPOP) – but these rarely cross over with other inter-disciplinary groups. Editors of journals that focus on

14 Foundations

elections and democracy may see articles about the management of elections as something that belongs to public administration journals, and vice versa. The barriers for researching electoral management are therefore high at an institutional level. They are also high at an individual level. It requires moving outside of our comfort area and significant additional work reading into other disciplines. The costs of this are high. Workloads in higher education can be demanding. There is a risk of making mistakes if you work in a discipline in which you were not trained. There is a risk that journals will not publish work if it doesn't have 'a home'. However, multi-disciplinarity provides opportunities for new lines of research. It is suggested in Figure 1.4 that at least six sub-disciplines are useful: comparative politics (including electoral studies), political philosophy, public administration, business management, law and computer science. We could even add social policy and sociology. In the aftermath of the 2000 US Presidential election the journal *Election Law* was founded in 2002 to respond to this. Yet much more inter-disciplinary thinking is needed.

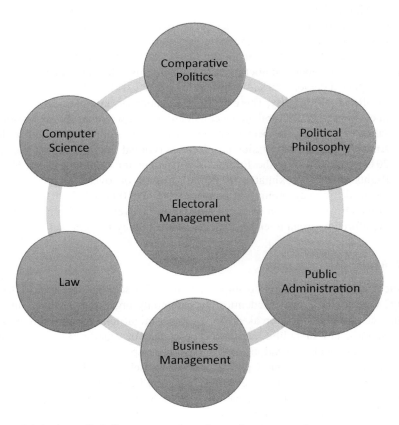

Figure 1.4 An inter-disciplinary approach to electoral management.

1.8 The book ahead

Electoral management is therefore a global issue that requires systematic study. This book, which seeks to advance this, is composed of four parts. The first part is about approach. Chapter 2 sets out a specific methodological approach to the study of electoral management. This is a sociological approach, with its roots in scientific realism. This is quite a deliberate and radical turn away from the positivist-behaviouralist approach which has dominated electoral studies so far. This will need some justification (and maybe a little patience and open-mindedness from the reader). Rather than considering the researcher to be a white-coated scientist who undertakes experiments like a 'natural scientist' we need to recognise that the social world is different. EMB, parties and citizens are all reflexive actors who can change their behaviour in response to our knowledge and the process of generating our knowledge. This has major consequences for the study of electoral management and elections in general – but is rarely explicitly recognised.

Part two looks at performance. How do we know when electoral management bodies are doing their job well? What does failure look like? Performance is often said to be the ultimate dependent variable and we therefore need some considered conceptual definition in the field of elections. Chapter 3 therefore reviews existing measures and concepts of performance as well as reviewing the available data sources. Chapter 4 introduces a new framework for evaluating electoral management based in theories of organisational performance. It argues for thicker, more descriptive comparative evaluations based on multiple sources than has been used to date. This is applied to cases in Canada and the UK so that their relative strengths and weaknesses are identified – and policy prescriptions made.

Part three looks at who runs elections. There is never one single organisation delivering elections: they are delivered by governance networks. Chapter 5 therefore introduces the concept of electoral management governance networks and develops a new typology which supersedes existing typologies of EMBs. Chapter 6 applies the approach to the UK to give a detailed historical account of the emergence there and how parts of this book had contributed towards that, before Chapter 7 contrasts networks based on smaller case studies of India, Jordan and Australia, and comparative data from a survey of EMBs. Chapter 8 demonstrates the usefulness of the governance concept by arguing that a transgovernmental network of actors has emerged since the 1990s with some vertical and horizontal integration. This is undertaken using qualitative interviews with actors, secondary document analysis and data on in-person interactions.

The final section is about policy instruments. Policy instruments are initiatives designed to improve performance or alter the network structure. This might involve changing the organisational structure of EMBs, changing the use and allocation of resources. Rather than taking a rationalist approach, a sociological policy instrumentation approach is taken (Kassim and Le Galès 2010; Le Galès 2016). Subsequent chapters then look at the nature of several

16 *Foundations*

> **Box 1.1   Data sources used in this volume**
>
> - A worldwide survey (consisting of two sister projects: the Electoral Management Survey ('EMS') and the ELECT Survey) of EMB personnel (approx. $n = 2,200$) and EMBs ($n = 70$) (James et al. 2019b; Karp et al. 2016) in which the author was co-investigator.
> - Qualitative interviews of electoral officials in the UK, India and at the international level.
> - Existing public opinion datasets.
> - Secondary document analysis of EMB archives.
> - A bespoke dataset of speakers at international conferences.
> - A bespoke dataset of downloads from the websites of international organisations.
> - Participant observation notes taken from involvement in Parliament and at major international conferences.
> - Auto-ethnography

different types of instruments and the possible causal relationships that they have: voter registration reform, centralisation, human resource practices and austerity.

The conclusion aims to bring together the main lessons and an agenda for future research. Each chapter will provide its own literature review where appropriate and the methods used to research it. However, Box 1.1 above lists the key original data sources that are used overall.

1.9 Contribution

The contribution of this book is therefore to:

- Define *electoral management* as a concept and a new sub-field for political science and electoral studies. A new definition is used in this book which can help to organise future work.
- Develop a *sociological approach to electoral management* in opposition to the rationalist scientific approach which has dominated to date.
- Provide a new framework for assessing electoral management: the PROSeS framework which can be used by future academics and practitioners to identify strengths and weaknesses in any country.
- Develop a new approach to identifying and typologising the delivery mechanisms for elections. Rather than adopting the concepts developed by the international community to date, it introduces the new concept of electoral governance networks.
- Electoral governance networks are the the constellation of actors involved in steering and delivering elections, including the anthropological practices,

beliefs and power relationships between them. A typology of different types of electoral governance networks is set out.
- Develop a new approach for understanding policy instruments with specific evaluations of the effects of new reforms.

These are the key theoretical lessons and contributions. There are also empirical and applied policy lessons which practitioners will be able to take forward into the delivery of elections, which are summarised in the conclusion (Box 13.1).

Notes

1 In setting out the agenda to study electoral governance, Mozaffer and Schedler define it 'as a set of related activities that involves rule making, rule application, and rule adjudication' (p. 5). The term 'governance' is therefore a container concept that involves no activity itself. They claim that 'good elections are impossible without effective electoral governance' (p. 6). Hartlyn et al.'s (2008) much-cited study 'Electoral Governance Matters: Explaining the Quality of Elections in Contemporary Latin America' define electoral governance as 'the interaction of constitutional, legal, and institutional rules and organizational practices that determine the basic rules for election procedures and electoral competition' (p. 74) and then focusses on 'the impact of central institutions of electoral governance – electoral management bodies (EMBs)'. Four types of electoral governance are differentiated depending on the structure of the EMB (depending on the degree of party involvement in the EMB). Elsewhere Ugues's excellent article on citizen views of electoral governance in Mexico is about citizens' evaluation of the Mexican EMB, the Instituto Federal Electoral (IFE). Pastor, meanwhile, often refers to the study of 'Electoral Commissions' as 'electoral administration' (Pastor 1999b). Norris's article entitled 'Conclusions: New Research Agenda Studying Electoral Management' summarises data on the quality of electoral administration (Norris 2019). Her index of 'electoral administration' included whether the electoral authorities were impartial; the authorities distributed information to citizens; the authorities allowed public scrutiny of their performance; and, the election authorities performed well.
2 Kjaer (2011, 104) defined governance as a 'weasel' word.

2 A realist sociological approach

2.1 Introduction

The opening chapter to this book introduced electoral management as a new interdisciplinary area of electoral studies, which has long been overlooked. But how should electoral management be studied? This chapter focusses on the philosophical and methodological framework underlying this book. It will set out a new and alternative realist sociological approach, which is set out in contrast to the mainstream rationalist scientific approaches that dominate other areas of election science – and which underpins the early work on electoral management. Policy makers and practitioners are rarely interested in meta theory of the social sciences. And why should they be? They are rightly interested in applied knowledge that can help them to improve the world they study. Those readers may be tempted to skip forward to Chapter 3. The same temptation is probably still there for the scholar, whose interest in this book is presumably in the subject of electoral management. As one delegate at an academic conference on elections tweeted: 'this is the first recorded usage of deontological at an elections sciences seminar'. 'Don't worry, the coffee is still in plentiful supply' replied another.

If you do skip past, you should take away some key messages. Approaches to political science that are commonly the most highly valued for being 'scientific' e.g. multivariate analysis of cross-national datasets, offer important insights into understanding 'what works' when it comes to improving electoral management (and other political phenomenon). However, they aren't a substitute for contextually specific studies because the meanings that actors give to social practices vary. The effects of social practices on human behaviour can vary by setting. Research therefore needs to be qualitative and case study–driven as well as quantitative. Secondly, political scientists are not rational, objective scientists observing independently of the world they are describing: they are actors within the play they are studying. The process of undertaking and disseminating research can alter the world that is being researched. Thirdly, the knowledge that political scientists generate about electoral management isn't quite as special and as privileged as we might think. It is different to practitioner knowledge, but not necessarily better.

While there are incentives to avoid systematic reflection on the philosophy of the social sciences that underpins the study of elections, our view of our research and ourselves is fundamentally changed if we do. This chapter therefore sets out a realist sociological approach to the study of electoral management, which can be contrasted with the rationalist scientific approach which dominates election sciences and has been used in initial approaches. It is realist because it draws from scientific realism as opposed to positivism as an approach to the social sciences. It is sociological because it seeks to go beyond the analysis of formal-legal systems, which has been the focus of electoral management so far, to look at norms, agency and lived experiences.

The first part of the chapter reviews the existing methodological approaches that have tended to be used in the election sciences[1] so far. The realist sociological approach is then introduced.

2.2 Review of existing literature

What has been written about electoral management so far? Three broad methodological approaches to the study of electoral institutions can be identified and are discussed as they emerged in chronological order. They reflect the broader trends within political and election sciences. In stitching together a rich literature into three parsimonious clumps, there is always the risk of over-simplifying nuanced and significant work. Some parsimony is needed, however, to help to bring order to the literature so that the case for a *realist sociological* approach can be set out.

2.2.1 Formal-legal institutionalism

Formal-legal institutionalism borrows assumptions and methods from 'old institutionalism'. This approach was common in political science until the 1950s and 1960s. Scholarship involved 'describing constitutions, legal systems and government structures, and their comparison over time and across countries' (Lowndes 2002, 90). Exemplar works of the broader tradition include those by Walter Bagehot (1967 [1876]) Herman Finer (1932), Woodrow Wilson (1956) and Nevil Johnson (1975). A premium was put on careful description. It could also be highly normative. In the field of elections, there were many early 'old institutionalist' studies which were historiographical narratives of the institutional changes. In Britain, David Butler (1963) and Martin Pugh (1978), Charles Seymour (1915 [1970]) and Cornelius O'Leary (1962) published narratives of the reforms to British electoral practice during the Great Reform Acts which sought to eliminate corrupt practices, extend the franchise and reform the electoral registration system. There are fleeting mentions of the organisations that were involved in delivering elections. For example, David Butler described how reforms to the electoral registration system involved a transfer of responsibility from poor-law overseers, where it had resided since 1832, to the Clerk of the County or Borough Council as a result of the 1918 Representation of the People Act (Butler 1963, 8). In the US, Joseph P. Harris's (1934) seminal study documented the 'overhead organisations' and 'rank and file' at the time. More contemporary work that describes the structures of electoral management bodies and the historical context from which they emerged include texts on countries including South Africa (Ndletyana 2015), Australia (Kelly 2012) and India (Quraishi 2014).

Cross-nationally, there are very few academic studies which describe how elections are managed and the organisational responsibilities for actors. Information is naturally published by EMBs themselves on their websites. The most useful information describing organisational responsibilities were published by international organisations. A report published in 2000 by Rafael López-Pintor for the UNDP was the first major step (López-Pinter 2000), which was followed by International IDEA's *Electoral Management Design* handbook in 2006 (Wall et al. 2006) – a second version of which was published some years after (Catt et al. 2014). Further reports from international or regional organisations helped to describe how particular EMBs function (López-Pintor and Fischer 2005). Academic studies have increasingly sought to develop typologies based on their institutional characteristics (Garnett 2018). The next chapter will explore this in more detail.

The old institutionalist scholarship has a modern-day successor in election law and legal studies. This research, crudely put, describes laws, interprets the meaning of laws within jurisdictions, provides historical context and normative critique. These studies are therefore couched in a normative tradition – that democratic governance is best, even if it is not explicit. Case study materials are provided from landmark cases that help the law to be understood and the legal powers that different actors have in the delivery of elections (Lowenstein, Hasen, and Tokaji 2001). One important advance is from Michael Pal (2016) who distinguishes the standings that EMBs have in different constitutions. These works all make an essential contribution to the study of elections and electoral management because understanding the legal powers and status of these bodies is enormously important so that we can begin to map variation.

In the broader discipline, formal-legal institutionalist literature has commonly been set up as a Straw Man approach to be knocked down and justify newer approaches, however. The obvious criticism is that describing procedures is helpful in providing information about how things are done, but it doesn't allow the causal effects to be identified in a systematic way. Moreover, *de jure* powers do not always translate into *de facto* powers. New institutionalism was born from a desire to look at institutions other than formal-legal ones: informal norms, practices and cultures are all important (Peters 1999). In the context of this book the design of legal rules and formal procedures doesn't necessarily explain how these practices are experienced on the ground by practitioners, voters and politicians. What challenges do rules create at the implementation stage? What challenges do practitioners face? A further criticism of old institutionalism was that it lacked a focus on causation. More about this will be said next.

2.2.2 Behaviouralism

Problems with old institutionalism laid the way for the emergence of behaviouralism and the 'scientific revolution' in political science. In 1961 Robert Dahl defined behaviouralism as:

a belief that additional methods and approaches either existed or could be developed that would help to provide political science with empirical propositions and theories of a systematic sort, tested by closer, more direct and more rigorously controlled observations of political events.

(Dahl 1961, 766)

There were four characteristics of the new orthodoxy. Firstly, the focus moved from formal institutions to individuals and their attributes, values and behaviour. Formal institutions were thought to be unable to explain political behaviour and outcomes since informal practices mattered. Secondly, earlier approaches were argued to lack the ambition to identify iron laws of human behaviour. This 'grand theorising' would now come from developing theoretical propositions, and routinely testing them against empirical datasets was therefore essential. As David Truman put it: 'a major reason for any inquiry into political behaviour is to discover uniformities, and through discovering them to be better able to indicate the consequences of such patterns' (Truman 1951, cited in Dahl 1961, 767). Thirdly, the new approach would be 'scientific' in that the scholar would not be involved in any moralising, as political philosophers, the other long-established stream of research, had long done. The values of 'how men ought to act is not a concern of research in political behaviour' Truman stated (Truman 1951, cited in Dahl 1961, 768).

Fourthly, although behaviouralism was not reducible to positivism, scholars working within the behaviouralist tradition used an implicit positivist epistemology and ontology to underpin their research. They followed Karl Popper who argued that any theoretical approach should be 'falsifiable' (Popper 1959); that is a theory should be testable against empirical evidence. Researchers should therefore focus on the collection of data from *observable* political phenomena – whether it was at the level of the individual or the aggregate. As Sanders (2010) notes, for both positivists and behaviouralism, a good theory must be (a) internally consistent, (b) consistent with other theories and (c) capable of generating empirical predictions that can be tested against observation. For Sanders (2010, 25): 'The only meaningful way of deciding between competing theories is . . . by empirical testing.'

Fifthly, the methodological tools of choice became large n quantitative studies and a logic of causal inference based in statistics and probability theory. As Goertz and Mahoney (2012) suggest, King, Keohane, and Verba's (1994) *Designing Social Enquiry* provided the exemplar approach. The recommended approach was that scholars identify the dependent and independent variables of interest, and using regression analysis, seek to identify the average effects of one on the other. By collecting data on a massive scale, large n studies had the advantage that statistically significant patterns in political behaviour could be identified. With statistical significance comes 'rigour'. Qualitative research is often discouraged on the basis that it lacks a sufficient number of observations to generate reliably generalisable results. It can therefore only 'promote descriptive generalizations and prepare the way for causal inference' (King, Keohane, and Verba 1994, 227–8, cited in Mahoney 2010, 123) which are less worthy of publication in

22 *Foundations*

higher-profile journals and its findings are given less scientific weighting. As far as it is valued, it is encouraged to focus on observable behaviour, adopt the same causal logic (Mahoney 2010). The availability of 'big data' in the form of social media, electronic newspaper archives, digitalised parliamentary debates provided the impetus for a new wave of quantitative studies.

Behaviouralism not only influenced the study of elections, it was partly born from it. Landmarks books such as *The American Voter* (Campbell et al. 1960) are held up as the archetypical and genre-framing work. Moreover, votes are things you can count. We therefore should not be surprised that the work on electoral management has adopted this approach and quantitative methods might seem natural. Norris (2015b) uses cross-national data on bureaucratic culture, government effectiveness and the formal-legal structure of the electoral management board as independent variables to test for the effects on electoral integrity.[2] Similarly, Van Ham and Lindberg (2015), Hartlyn, McCoy, and Mustillo (2008) and Birch (2011) develop hypotheses and test for the effects of independent variables, including the formal-legal structure of the electoral management board, on electoral integrity using cross-national quantitative analysis.[3] In the case of Norris (2015b) and Van Ham and Lindberg (2015), ordinary least squares regression methods are used to identify the constant and the scalar regressor: the average effect of the independent variables on the dependent variables. Hartlyn and Birch use more advanced regression methods (logit; and random effects tobit model and ordered probit respectively).

These studies use a specific logic of causal inference. If the variables are found to be *statistically* significant predictors of each other, then the conclusion is that there is a causal process. If there is no such mathematical relationship between the data values then there is no causal process. For example, Norris finds that the formal-legal structures of the EMBs are 'not significant predictors of the level of electoral integrity' (2015b, 151) because the beta values for the 'agency model' in her regressions did not reach a sufficiently high level of statistical significance. Likewise, with a different dataset, Sarah Birch reports that 'the variable designating formal electoral commission independence is not significant' (Birch 2011, 121) in determining electoral malpractice, whereas the variable 'representing multiparty involvement in the appointment of EMB members is, however, a significant negative predictor of the quality of electoral administration' (Birch 2011, 121). The practical policy-orientated conclusion is 'that the emphasis of many electoral assistance programmes on formally independent electoral commissions may be somewhat misplaced, as appointment procedures appear to be of greater importance in determining their performance' (Birch 2011, 131).[4]

We can quickly see how this type of research is intuitively of interest to practitioners and policy makers. With the power of established scientific laws, through mass observation, prediction should become possible and future behaviour is therefore identifiable. The likely effects of changes in laws, interventions and treatments can be mapped through statistical models. This type of knowledge therefore becomes a highly useful tool and can be sought after by practitioners looking for expertise. Chad Vickery of the influential electoral organisation IFES expressed his view to scholars of electoral integrity at a Harvard University workshop in 2013:

> I think that it is interesting to listen to the discussion of causality in trying to explain historical events, but for practitioners in the field we need models that are predictive. Explaining what happened five years ago is very interesting, but when I am on the ground and there is an election happening I need to know where there will be pockets of violence so that we can react to it. So I think that models that are more predictive are needed rather than explaining historical events for me, and that is a difficult task, I know.
>
> (Bjornlund et al. 2014, 279)

Behaviouralist work has made important inroads into our understanding of electoral management. The development of hypotheses and testing them using quantitative methods provides more focused arguments about causation than most scholarship within the original legal-institutionalist tradition. The use of cross-national data about legal-institutional characteristics allows analysis to move beyond single cases to a larger number of countries – and even a global analysis. This book uses some of the quantitative methods in subsequent chapters. There are some weaknesses, however. The next section introduces the realist framework and explains how this identifies problems with the behaviouralist approach.

2.3 A realist sociological approach to electoral management

The realist sociological approach to studying electoral management (and electoral institutions in general) is set out here. It is so called because it is premised in scientific realism (Archer 1995, 1998; Bhaskar 1989, 2008; Collier 1994; Putnam and Conant 1990; Sayer 2000, 2010). This is a methodological orientation, built from the philosophy of the social sciences, which 'steers a path between empiricist and constructivist accounts of scientific explanation' (Pawson 2006, 17). It has become established as an alternative approach to political science in the UK (Buller 1999; Buller and James 2015; Jessop 2005; Marsh and Smith 2000; McAnulla 2006; Savigny 2007), although it has had only limited use in the study of elections (the only known exception is: James 2012).[5] There has been more widespread use in international relations (Joseph and Wight 2010; Patomäki and Wight 2000; Wight 2007, 2012).[6] There are a number of key features of the approach.

2.3.1 The nature of knowledge

To begin with the approach has a distinctive conceptualisation of knowledge that differs to the behaviouralist approach. For behaviouralists, scientific knowledge of iron laws generated through academic research is assumed to be the highest form of knowledge. Research on electoral management can and should therefore instruct practice because rigorous, scientific, academic knowledge trumps individual, localised, subjective practitioner knowledge. Yet that assumption is commonly questioned in the everyday experience of a suspicious practitioner. Why would academics know best? Electoral officials deal with elections all day, every day. They have the lived experience of how voters behave in polling stations, how citizens respond to requests to register to vote. Isn't it a big leap to say that the researcher, who often spends their time managing students and completing university administration, should know more, given that their lived experience of elections is watching it on the telly, and sitting behind a computer screen analysing data?

Realists such as Andrew Sayer in fact explicitly claim that it is not the case that this academic knowledge 'can simply be *assumed* to be the highest form of knowledge and that other types are dispensable or displaceable by science' (Sayer 2010, 13). In fact, there are some major problems with how behaviouralists understand knowledge. Crucially, behaviouralists have an over-simplistic model of the relationship between the researcher and what they are researching. Sayer (2010) conceptualises this as the subject-object relationship. Behaviouralists assume that the impartial scientist is entirely separate from the phenomenon that they study. The role of the subject (the researcher) is to document information about the object (the phenomenon under study), and develop explanatory models and predictive forecasts of their behaviour (Sayer 2010, 24). These models can be tested and adjusted through repeated observations. Sayer argues that subjects and objects are bound together in more complex relationships, however. Firstly, subjects have relationships with other subjects. They can only attempt to gain knowledge of the object with the cognitive and conceptual resources available in the language communities (as Sayer puts it) or academic concepts and frameworks (as we may more commonly think of it). Their ability to gain understanding of the object is therefore bounded. Academics use concepts and frameworks in a more heuristic way than they might realise, as 'rules of thumb.' Secondly, objects have relationships with other objects. When non-social objects are studied by those in the natural sciences, they are unaware of the meaning that other subjects attach to them. A non-social object cannot attach meaning to another non-social object. Social objects, however, are different. They will be involved in a process of repeated sense-making with other objects.

Researcher and object as social relations

The realist sociological approach therefore takes the position that we should conceive the learning relationship between the subject and the object not as unidirectional, but multi-directional and iterative. This is because both subject and object are entwined in social relations during the research and dissemination process. Objects may become aware of the meanings that subjects are attaching to their actions and change them. Or objects might learn important information from subjects about themselves and their environment which might facilitate strategic learning. As a result of this, the object might change. It is suggested here that two processes can be identified:

- **The fieldwork process.** In order to gather information, researchers interact with the subject. Let's take the example of the process of organising an interview with a government official. The researcher does not simply take notes from an interview with an electoral official in a hypothetical context. The relationship is social. They write to/email them, giving information about themselves they think the respondent will need to know and may encourage them to reply. They decide how to dress, the questions to ask, the tone of the interview. The interviewee decides whether to respond, makes up a judgement about the researcher, tailors their responses to questions, perhaps decides to leave information out or in. Following the email or the interview, the interviewee may read-up further on what the researcher was asking about and begin to change their practices. In short, they may change their view of the world or change their actions as a result of the research process. This is often thought of as a Hawthorne effect. Social research does not take place in a hermetically sealed environment, however. The consequence can go beyond the experiment into the real world.

- **The dissemination process.** Upon dissemination of the results, objects, which are autonomous agents, may change their behaviour. The subject and object are therefore linked by social relations, even if the researcher does not directly interact with the object or know of this changed behaviour. There are plenty of obvious examples from the field of elections. An analysis and publication of public opinion polling data may make citizens rethink their world and alter their behaviour. They might think that a particular party will win, for example, and change their vote to vote tactically. An electoral administrator may undertake further training for her team, after learning that they will be studied. If researchers identify the strategies that rulers use to rig an election, such as ballot stuffing, rulers may change their tactics and adopt other methods (Sjoberg 2014).

There are two important consequences of identifying these social relations. Firstly, researchers need to reflect on their own positionality when they undertake research. They are not impartial observers, but immediately become actors within their own plays. Researchers should therefore actively d reflect on how their research has changed or become part of the object under study. Subsequent chapters on UK electoral governance (chapter 5), the international community (chapter 8) and policy instruments (chapters 9 and 10, especially) therefore reflect on the role of the research described in the book because it was actively disseminated to practitioners prior to publication. Secondly, behavioural regularities and 'iron laws' can be undone by human agency. Academics might reach conclusions about how electoral integrity can be improved, such as measures to reduce electoral fraud. The transmission of this knowledge to practitioners could, however, alter their behavior and the effectiveness of these reform in the future.

2.3.2 Domains of reality

A further problem with behaviouralism is the focus on pure empiricism. Behaviouralists prefer to focus on what is measurable and observable. Realists, however, stress that there are three distinct domains of reality. The realist sociological approach therefore has a stratified conception of reality. The *empirical domain* consists of the observable experiences that individuals can observe and record. The *actual domain* consists of events, which may often be unobservable to the researcher. The *real domain* consists of the generative mechanisms and causal structures that influence events and experiences but may not be observable themselves (Table 2.1).

Positivist empiricist approaches only seek to measure and quantity the empirical domain of reality and not the actual or the real. If variables are not quantifiable, then they are excluded from frameworks. They therefore do not measure or record any deep structures – often the processes of capitalism, class, race or gender politics stressed by neo-Marxists, feminists or elite theorists.

Legal-institutionalist variables were commonly used in early work on electoral management because they tend to be measurable and observable. But there are many other phenomenon in the domain of the actual and real that might be important. One obvious generative mechanism in the real domain is the desire for personal or political gain by actors. Senior politicians are strategic players who are motivated by a desire to win office either for self-interest or out of necessity to achieve wider goals (Buller and James 2012; Bulpitt 1986; James 2016b; James and Buller 2015a, 2015b). Senior civil servants within EMBs are equally likely to be motivated by career progression, financial gain or prestige, as well as altruistic goals. This mechanism in the real domain will be largely unobservable to researchers because canny actors will naturally be guarded (and perhaps unaware) of their motivations in surveys and interviews. This mechanism will also feed into the events and experiences in the actual domain. These actors will be involved in meetings and discussions in private, away from the eyes and ears of researchers and journalists. An empiricist focus on the empirical realm may therefore miss much of what is important. Social scientists therefore need to use a different set of tools to adjust to this separation between appearance and reality (Pawson and Tilley 1997; Pawson 2006; Sayer 1984). This is not to say that claims should not be tested against empirical evidence, but research can be 'empirical rather than empiricist' (Hay 2002, 252).

A deeper analysis of the sociological mechanisms that influence outcomes is therefore needed. This can help to identify what realists consider the structure-agency relationships underlying social phenomena. The agents under study (whether they are rulers, politicians or administrators) are constrained by the structural context in which they find themselves, but retain some autonomy and free-will. There are a variety of competing ways to describe this structure and agency relationship within scientific realism. The strategic relational approach (SRA) is one of these, developed by Bob Jessop to overcome contradictions in the Marxist analysis of the state (Jessop 1990), but also used by Colin Hay (1996,

Table 2.1 Three domains of reality in the realist sociological approach

	Domain of real	*Domain of actual*	*Domain of empirical*
Mechanisms	✓		
Events	✓	✓	
Experiences	✓	✓	✓

Source: Based on Bhaskar (2008, 47).

2002, 115–34). The SRA involves examining 'how a given structure may privilege some actors, some identities, some strategies, some spatial and temporal horizons, some actions over others' (Jessop 2001, 1223). Actors find themselves in strategically selective environments that favour certain strategies over others as a means to realise a given set of intentions or preferences. There is no level playing field. Strategically selective environments, however, do not determine outcomes because agents are reflexive actors capable of strategic learning. As Jessop put it, they can:

> orient their strategies and tactics in the light of their understanding of the current conjuncture and their 'feel for the game'.
> (Jessop 2001, 1224)

It follows that the actions of agents and the strategically selective environment co-evolve over time to produce a *new* strategically selective environment which might be more or less favourable to the actor(s) under scrutiny. A skilful leader of an EMB might therefore be able to build up the organisational capacity or reputation of their organisation to put them in a better position.

The legal-institutional structures which are the focus of much of the work discussed in the chapter so far are therefore one important structural constraint for actors. Laws setting out roles and responsibilities are important in shaping power, causality and behaviour. The implication of the SRA, however, is that we should be aware of other constraints. These could be ideological or technological. An EMB might be statutorily independent and an electoral commissioner wishing to improve the quality of elections autonomous from government. But they might be working in a cultural environment in which there is intimidation and unprofesionalism.

2.3.3 Context, outcomes and mechanisms

The realist sociological approach conceptualises causation as contextually contingent and partially dependent on reflective agency. Although we should therefore be sceptical about the knowledge that academics create, realists stress that there is causation in the world and academics are therefore important because they have special skills in aggregating individual experiences to identify it. As Sayer puts it:

> There is necessity in the world; objects – whether natural or social – necessarily have particular causal powers or ways of acting and particular susceptibilities.
> (Sayer 2010, 5)

The importance of causation in realist social research stands in contrast with post-positivist interpretivist approaches which try to simply describe, observe and understand the world that they witness (Bevir and Rhodes 2002, 2003; Rhodes 2011). In this respect, it has more in common with the behaviouralist approaches described above. Causation can't be identified or ruled out by trying to observe the regularity of events alone in the empirical domain, however. The non-occurrence of events may be for a variety of reasons, given the complexity of social life and multi-layered nature of reality. The absence of electoral fraud in an election or even a series of elections, for example, does not demonstrate that political parties or rulers would not ever consider using this tactic in the future. The aim is therefore to *understand outcome patterns, sequences and processes rather than outcome regularities*. There are generative mechanisms and the purpose of social science investigation is to identify these. That is to say that we should try to focus on the 'causal powers within the objects or agents or structures under investigation' (Pawson 2006, 21).

To locate some causal mechanisms, a different causal logic is therefore often used to behaviouralists. The retroductive movement involves asking: what must be true for events that we see in the empirical realm to be possible? The process of causal inference is therefore reversed (Belfrage and Hauf 2016). Retroductive arguments therefore progress 'from a description of some phenomenon to a description of something which produces it or is a condition for it' (Bhaskar 2009, 7).

2.3.4 Thicker descriptive, measurement and verstehen

The realist sociological approach stresses the need for greater detail in the measurement of social phenomenon. Realists, like interpretivists, stress the importance of *meaning* that actors give to their actions in social phenomenon and that quantitative social science misses this. Leca and Naccache argue that quantitative analysis reduces the measured object to its measurable, quantifiable dimensions (2006, 637). A citizen might deliberately put a cross in the wrong place on a ballot paper. But why? Is it because they didn't understand the ballot paper? Or did they wish to deliberately spoil their ballot in protest? We can measure – but this doesn't always provide explanation.

We should therefore go beyond (but not completely abandon) quantitative methods. Historical contexts and meanings matter and can be understood through *within*-case analysis of case studies. Process tracing for example, involves 'the researcher examin[ing] histories, archival documents, interview transcripts, and other sources' to see whether a hypothesised causal process is evident between the independent and dependent variables (George and Bennett 2005, 6). Historical case studies are therefore widely used in this book to identify the nature of electoral governance networks.

But in addition to the meanings that we can find in qualitative sources such as transcripts from debates, semi-structured interviews or focus groups – we can look beyond the text. Text alone cannot capture the physicality, the smells of locations, the routine practices that actors have and other cultural products which may be important. It cannot capture the emotions, feelings and thoughts that actors have which go beyond verbal forms, but are a vital part of social interaction. These are important aspects of the social world because they shape action (Rhodes 2011). Ethnographic methods could therefore add considerable value. The German sociologist Max Weber argued that researchers should try to develop a deep understanding of their actors through what he called *verstehen*. More recent political ethnographers, such as Edward Schatz, argue that researchers should immerse themselves in the field by observing their objects. They should also establish a 'sensibility that goes beyond face-to-face contact' (Schatz 2009, 5). As a result, the realist sociological approach to electoral management would value 'thick descriptions' of social practices and phenomenon and not worry if research is not about hypothesis forming and testing. It can could also use autoethnography where the researcher uses their 'personal experience ... in order to understand cultural experience' (Ellis et al. 2011: 273) and reflects on the researchers positionality.

2.4 Conclusions: the consequences of the realist sociological approach

This chapter has argued that, although the substantive focus of this book is on the management and implementation of elections, we would benefit from reflecting on the underlying philosophical traditions and assumptions of the research undertaken. This is important for weighing up the value of evidence collated in support of the claims being made and fending off some criticisms that might emerge about the research validity, choice of methods and the inferences made. However, it also speaks plainly to the value of the whole endeavour of research. What is the nature of the knowledge generated? What longevity will it have? Are the conclusions fixed? What is its value to the real world? These are not small questions.

Previous traditions have made some important inroads into the study of electoral management. More descriptive information about the legal-institutional and constitutional relationships has helped generate new knowledge which was sorely lacking before. Behaviouralist quantitative analysis has made advances in identifying some of the correlations and underlying empirical relationships. However, a realist approach is set out above which has a number of consequences for how we research elections and value the findings:

1. **Contingent causation.** Researchers should strive to identify causal relationships since they have key skills in doing so. However, they should be wary that the knowledge generated is of a particular type. Causation is context-specific and behavioural regularities can be undone by agency as actors become aware of the research. A common misconception is the 'common tendency to think of knowledge as a product or a thing which exists outside of us, which we can "possess" and which is stored in finished form in our heads or in our libraries' (Sayer 2010, 16). Knowledge is socially produced and socially used.
2. **Researcher positionality.** The researcher has to consider their own positionality within the field that they are studying. Social scientists are not independent of their own subject in the way that natural scientists are. Strategic learning can take place amongst academics as well who can better mobilise to use their own research to effect the world.
3. **Structure and agency.** Formal-legal institutions are important, but aren't everything. The strategic relational approach suggests that actors (voters, non-voters, politicians, administrators) have their environment and choices

shaped by institutions, which would include legal institutions. But unlike the legalist approach, institutions should not be the sole focus of our concern. The effects of institutions are mediated by cultural context, the role of other structures and the strategic agency of actors.

4 **The value of description.** Given the stratified nature of reality and the importance of *verstehen* a realist sociological approach should value description as much as causation. There are other forms of knowledge than the predictive iron laws that behaviouralists seek to establish. 'Mere description', as John Gerring (2012) puts it, has significant value.

5 **Mixed methods.** Given the importance of historical context and the need to establish *verstehen*, where possible, a sociological approach cannot be limited to quantitative analysis of cross-national datasets. Methods must be at least mixed, giving equal, if not greater, weight to qualitative, historical and (auto)ethnographic methods. This is not to say that quantitative methods are not useful – and they are indeed used in this book.

Notes

1 The terms 'election sciences' and 'electoral studies' are used interchangeably in this book.
2 With controls for the electoral system, independence of the judiciary, press freedom, wealth, natural resources, degree of globalisation and regional electoral integrity.
3 Also see: (Garnett 2014) (Garnett 2019b)
4 Although Birch (2011: 123–31) does also provide a case study of the Ukrainian election in 2004 to process trace the effects of her variables.
5 There are other post-positivist alternatives to behaviouralism such as interpretivism. See for example, Kirkland and Wood (2016).
6 Within the broad camp of 'scientific realism' there remains debate and diversity. Pawson (2006: 18–19) argues that 'critical realism', associated with the work of Margaret Archer and Roy Bhaskar, stressed that in an open system there are near-limitless explanatory possibilities. It followed that social scientists can simply provide a highly normative and critical narrative to mistaken and popularly held accounts of the world. By contrast, 'scientific' realism (also using the label 'empirical realism', 'emergent realism', 'analytical realism') is more optimistic about the ability of the researcher to judge between different causal explanations in open systems. The term 'scientific realism' is used throughout this book, sometimes shortened to 'realism'.

Part II
Performance

3 Existing concepts and evidence

3.1 Introduction

In the aftermath of an election, there are often considerable arguments about whether the election had been run well. International observers, governing elites, incumbent politicians, opposition leaders and civil society are often at loggerheads about whether the electoral authorities performed well. The consequences can be pivotal. A protracted dispute may undermine confidence in the electoral process or lead a country down a path towards civil war, undermine the stability of government or undermine voter confidence.

So what does a well-run election look like? And how can we confirm it when we see it? These are simple questions. Providing clear and unambiguous answers is much more difficult. There has been a proliferation of possible approaches in recent years, but as Alvarez et al. (2012, 1) recently noted, thinking specifically about electoral management rather than election quality in general, 'currently there is no accepted framework to assess the general quality of an election'. This book seeks to contribute towards the literature on electoral integrity by providing a new framework for evaluating the quality of electoral management, by drawing from theories of public sector management and connecting it to democratic theory. The first task is to clear the ground and consider what work has been done already. The new framework follows in the next chapter.

Part II of this chapter therefore begins by identifying the important philosophical and methodological issues which are involved in evaluating performance and outlines how realism, introduced in the last chapter, can inform these challenges. Part III reviews the existing frameworks that are available and considers their shortcomings. It argues that despite a proliferation in approaches designed to assess the quality of elections that have emerged in the post–Cold War period, a focus on electoral management remains very much overlooked. Part IV considers the range of higher-order principles that could be used to inform an assessment of electoral management. It argues that any such assessment must be connected to democratic theory, since this alone, gives a normative framework for making critical claims. Democratic theory however, needs further development. Part V considers the empirical data sources that could be used to evaluate performance, arguing that all have value, but also some weaknesses. A multi-indicator approach

34 *Performance*

is therefore necessary in which the researcher and analyst but undertake a *qualitative interpretation* of the best available evidence on a case-by-case basis.

3.2 Philosophical and methodological issues evaluating performance

Evaluating the performance of public sector organisations has been a long-standing concern for academics and policy makers. Although assessing the performance of EMBs has only become a relatively recent concern amongst senior policy makers (Global Commission on Elections 2012), there is already a well-established literature on the broader subject of organisational performance (Carter, Klein, and Day 1992; Ostrom 1973; Parks 1984). Organisational performance has always been a concern for governments but it became increasingly prominent under the banner of 'good governance' when Western states implemented new public management reforms and often made development aid conditional on public sector reforms. For scholars, organisational performance has been described as the 'ultimate dependent variable of interest for researchers concerned with just about any area of management' (Richard et al. 2009). However, performance is also a contested concept and there are some difficult conceptual challenges involved in defining and measuring performance.

3.2.1 Objectivity

Firstly, there are questions as to whether we can establish objective measures of performance (Meier, Brudney, and Bohte 2002, 19) or should adopt subjective measures (Brewer 2006). Objective measures might intuitively be treated as the 'gold standard' because of the allure of scientific objectivity. However, the case that performance is socially constructed is strong. For example, assuming that there is a trade-off, should policy makers prioritise voter security or participation? Given that resources are always finite in any polity, should economic efficiency be put ahead of the completeness of the electoral register? As Andrews, Boyne, and Walker (2006, 19) note, if there is any disagreement about what is to be measured, how it is to be measured or the weighting attached to each measure then performance is subjective.

Advocating complete relativism is unhelpful, however. If a realist approach to science is taken rather than a constructivist approach (see Chapter 2), then this ontological position requires us to accept that there is a reality independent of the researcher so there is an objective reality to be measured. The epistemology, meanwhile, requires us to accept that our knowledge can be imperfect and conceptually driven as there are limits to the evidence that the researcher can collect. Pure objectivity may therefore never be possible too. However, through the use of normative theory, as critical realists argue, we can make arguments of what 'ought to be' and use mixed empirical research methods to evaluate elections against these conceptual ideals.

3.2.2 The administrative environment

Secondly, it is important to understand the context in which actors operate when identifying the type and cause of poor performance. Walshe et al. (2004, 201) suggest that in the private sector, some symptoms or causes of failure are 'primarily internal to the organization, such as poor leadership', however, 'others are primarily external and concerned with its environment, such as increased competition, product or service innovation or changes in consumer expectations.' The same is true the public sector (Andrews, Boyne, and Enticott 2006). Shifting demographic trends, for example, place new pressures on education or health care systems. Poor organisational performance can therefore be partly, perhaps even predominantly, determined by an *administrative environment*, or at least, the relationship between the organisation and the environment. The political, economic and social context combine to create conditions under which it may be easier or more difficult for administrators and managers to achieve high performance. The importance of the structure-agent relationship is pivotal to a realist approach, as mapped out in Chapter 2. While we therefore want to evaluate agents such as EMBs we need to be sensitive to the nature of the potentially very challenging, contextual environment in which they find themselves.

3.2.3 Failures of steering and rowing

Thirdly, we need to be aware that the performance of EMBs, as with any public organisation, can be undermined in many ways. We can separate out three different pathways to failures. One pathway is problems in the design of the institutions and organisation. A *failure of steering in electoral management* is therefore defined as *the adoption of practices and strategies that have generated*

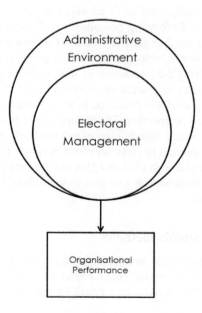

Figure 3.1 Structure and agency in assessing electoral management performance.

36 *Performance*

suboptimal organisational performance in EMBs. These types of problems are system level and exist in the management of organisations. Andrews, Boyne, and Enticott (2006) suggest that common management failures in the public sector are the absence or poor use of indicators, unrealistic aims and goals, weak relations between managers, inadequate relations with external stakeholders and ineffective leadership (ibid. 2006, 276–80). However, as Chapters 5–9 set out, elections usually will involve steering from a variety of actors: Parliaments who design laws, senior managers of EMB who design laws, middle-managers who instruct staff. It follows that failures of steering may come from a variety of quarters.

A second pathway is at the level of the individual front-line worker. They may work in a well-performing EMB, but have 'a bad day' or become demotivated in their work. They might make a simple administrative error or a deliberate malpractice. EMBs might set clear guidelines for processing postal vote application forms, but an individual administrator or team of administrators might not follow these appropriately. In a more deliberate and extreme scenario, they might be attracted to take a bribe. This is a *failure of rowing in electoral management* and is therefore defined as an *error in the implementation of practices and strategies that results in suboptimal organisational performance in the management of elections*. Should these errors accumulate then we may begin to think, however, that they might result from a failure of steering. Staff being demotivated, for example, may be the result of poor human resource management practices. We can therefore clearly see a complex relationship between structure and agency within electoral management organisations.

Unfortunately, failures of steering and rowing are always likely. Managers do not have perfect knowledge and can't be expected to generate optimal performance in all occasions. Reforming procedures is difficult and time-consuming. There is the inevitable need to satisfice. Failures of rowing are equally likely at some point given the vast workforces involved in any given polity. Elections are complex events, involving the interaction of staff, technology and voters. Moynihan (2004) suggests that some accidents and errors are therefore likely at some point, as Charles Perrow (1984) predicted in normal-accident theory. Failures of steering or rowing need perspective. The failure of one individual to their job on election day can be dramatic. Not delivering one batch of votes to a central counting location could be enough to sway an election result. Even if it is not, media coverage of one incident can go viral and give the electors a very disproportionate view of how well elections are run. Our assessments should therefore be sensitive to this type of problem.

3.3 A growth in available methods

The growth of an international community seeking to assess the quality of elections in the post–Cold War period (see Chapter 8) has brought about an expansion of the methods and toolkits that could be used as evaluation criteria for electoral integrity These are provided in the form of practical guides for observing elections and reporting on their quality (Carter Center 2014; OSCE 2010; U.N. Electoral Assistance Division et al. 2005). This has been mirrored by an increasing interest from scholars, with a considerable growth in the range of academic frameworks and datasets that assess electoral integrity. By 2014 van Ham (2014) had identified 23 different approaches in a comprehensive review. Table 3.1 details those identified by van Ham, with some newer approaches that have been developed since. Added to the list is information about the type of data that was collected and the extent to which electoral management featured in the concept and data.[1]

While there are now more frameworks and datasets to assess electoral integrity in more general terms, there are some shortcomings in terms of assessing electoral *management*. Firstly, the main focus is on deliberate partisan rigging or undue influence on the voter. For example, Schedler (2002) famously argued that there is a menu of manipulation from which rulers choose to maintain power. Meanwhile, Simpster was concerned with electoral manipulation, which is, 'a set of practices that includes . . . stuffing ballot boxes, buying votes, and intimidating voters or candidates' (2013, 1). This is directly relevant to the management and implementation of elections. If electoral fraud is happening, then electoral management bodies have a responsibility to act to undertake preventative work. If electoral officials within an EMB are complicit with this, by either stuffing ballot boxes themselves or turning a 'blind eye' then the implementation of democratic elections is clearly failing.

Problems with electoral management do not always occur because of deliberate partisan attempts to subvert the democratic process, however. They might come about through poor management, logistical difficulties, limited resources, error or incompetence. Yet there is little recognition or measurement of this in the frameworks above, and it is often dismissed as being insignificant. In *Electoral Malpractice*, for example, Birch noted that systems of electoral administration can be prone to 'electoral mispractice'. This was the 'incompetence, lack of resources, unforeseen disturbances, and simple human error' (Birch 2011, 26) – but then she moved on to focus again on the deliberate 'manipulation of electoral processes and outcomes' (Birch 2011, 14) and leaves the former category aside.

This was not always so. Elklit and Reynolds (2005b) included a number of dimensions relating to the performance of electoral authorities in their framework. This informed work by Norris et al. (Norris, i Coma, and Grömping 2015; Norris, Garnett, and Grömping 2016) who collected data on various aspects of electoral management including how well electoral authorities performed via expert surveys. Norris noted that elections can be plagued by 'electoral maladministration': 'routine flaws and unintended mishaps by election officials . . . due to managerial failures, inefficiency and incompetence' (Norris 2013b, 568). An alternative framework is developed by Bland, Green, and Moore (2013). Nonetheless, although further interest in electoral management has developed, the focus remains on deliberate political manipulation.

Table 3.1 Existing approaches to measuring electoral integrity and management quality

Author	Concept name	Data sources	Quant or qual	Inclusion of electoral management
Hermet, Rose, and Roquie (1978)	Elections without choice	None	n/a	'The freedom of voters is one criteria which requires being able to cast a ballot free from external influence and have the ballot counted and the reported accurately' (p. 3)
Elklit and Svensson (1997)	Free and fair elections	None	n/a	Comprehensive agenda of criteria, including: Independent commission Impartial treatment of candidates Impartial voter education Access to polling stations for parties, observers and the media Ballot secrecy Ballot paper design Impartial assistance to voters Counting procedures Treatment of void ballot papers Transportation of election materials Protection of polling stations Election results Complaints
Anglin (1998)	Free and fair elections	Electoral observation reports	Quantitative	No overall framework, but the deficiencies in the electoral roll and the absence of secret voting are noted in some elections.
Pastor (1999b)	Flawed elections	*Journal of Democracy* reports	Quantitative	EMB design is set out as an important independent variable towards the dependent variable of 'flawed elections' (where 'some or all of the major political parties refuse to participate in the election or reject the results' p.15). Important aspects include staff training, voter registration systems, distributing voter identification cards, ensuring the security for voters, setting up polling stations and count certification.
O'Donnell (2001)	Democratic elections	None	n/a	None.
Mozaffer and Schedler (2002)	Electoral governance	None	n/a	Outlines the concept of rule application which includes the registration of voters, candidates, parties; the registration of election observers; voter education; electoral organisation; voting, counting and reporting.

Schedler (2013)	Electoral manipulation	International news sources and election observer reports	Quantitative	Electoral fraud, defined as 'the manipulation of electoral administration for partisan advantage at any stage of the electoral process (before, during, and after election day)' p. 198. This includes: voter registration and voter identification; polling station preparation; access to polling stations, voting procedures, secrecy and integrity, polling observation; counting and vote tabulation (p. 415).
Lehoucq (2003)	Electoral fraud	None	n/a	Electoral fraud – such as ballot rigging, vote buying and voter intimidation.
Van de Walle (2003)	Free and fair elections	Election reports in the *Journal of Democracy*	Quantitative	None.
Elklit and Reynolds (2005b)	Election quality	None	n/a	Broad range of performance indicators including perceived degree of EMB impartiality, perceived degree of EMB service quality, perceived degree of EMB transparency.
Calingaert (2006)	Election rigging	None	n/a	Includes voter registration rigging, vote buying, multiple voting, vote tabulation rigging.
Lindberg (2006)	Free and fair elections	News reports and multiple other sources	Quantitative	Not directly measured in the concepts of participation, competition and legitimacy.
Birch (2011)	Electoral malpractice	Election observation reports	Quantitative	Vote buying; voter intimidation; EMB independence; citizens refused voter registration or being registered inaccurately; maladministration of legal disputes.
Hartlyn, McCoy, and Mustillo (2008)	Election quality	Election observation reports, news sources and country experts	Quantitative	Procedural fairness and technical soundness are designated as important, although the key measure of integrity is whether "the major parties all accept the process and respect the results'" (p. 76).
Munck (2009)	Electoral Democracy Index	Electoral official surveys, constitutions, laws, electoral observer reports, news reports	Quantitative	Clean elections: the voting process is carried out without irregularities (but 'elections that might include "technical" irregularities' – are not considered a problem) p. 58. Inclusive elections: the use of the right to vote is not undermined by electoral registration or electoral roll problems (p. 90).

(*Continued*)

Table 3.1 (Continued)

Author	Concept name	Data sources	Quant or qual	Inclusion of electoral management
Davis-Roberts and Carroll (2010)	Democratic elections	None	n/a	International obligations for democratic elections, including the actualisation of the secret ballot; equality before the law; and the absence of discrimination. Separately details the 'professional and impartial conduct of election activities by the election management body' (p. 12).
Kelley and Kolev (2010)	Election quality	Reports from the US State Department Reports on Human Rights Practices	Quantitative	Intimidation; problems in voter lists/registration; complaints about electoral commission conduct; voter information and procedural problems; technical/procedural difficulties; informational insufficiencies; administrative insufficiencies; problems in voter lists; vote processing and tabulation tampering; voter fraud; intimidation.
Hyde and Marinov (2012)	Competitive elections	News media archives, election data handbooks and online election guides	Quantitative	Few, if any, direct measures of EMB performance.
López-Pintor (2011)	Electoral fraud	None	n/a	Corruption and electoral fraud including 'direct action or deliberate inaction by electoral administrators permitting others (such as agents from the executive branch of government or political parties) to interfere with the process' (p. 7).
James (2012)	Elite statecraft	Secondary documents, newspaper articles, interviews	Qualitative	Partisan choice of electoral registration and voting procedures; suppression of voter turnout.
Donno (2013)	Electoral misconduct	Observer reports and news articles	Quantitative	Intimidation of voters on Election Day; violation of the secret ballot; multiple voting; faulty counting/tallying of ballots; certification of fraudulent votes
Simpser (2013)	Electoral manipulation	Observation reports, election handbooks and journalistic sources	Quantitative	Creating obstacles to voter registration; falsifying results; tampering with voter registration lists

Bland, Green, and Moore (2013)	Election Administration System Index	Expert surveys	Quantitative	Voter registry accuracy; polling place accuracy; EMB budget control; voting materials in secure storage.
Coppedge et al. (2017)	Capacity and independence	Expert survey	Quantitative	EMB capacity; EMB independence
Clark (2014, 2015, 2016)	Index of Electoral Integrity	EMB data	Quantitative	Skills and knowledge of returning officer; planning processes in place for an election; planning and delivering public awareness activity; accessibility of information to electors; communication of information to candidates and agents.
Garnett (2017)	Transparency in electoral management	Content analysis of EMB websites	Quantitative	Availability of reports, election results, organisational structure and electoral procedures on the EMB website.
Norris, Wynter, and Cameron (2018)	Electoral integrity	Expert surveys	Quantitative	Elections were well managed; information about voting procedures was widely available; election officials were fair; elections were conducted in accordance with the law; some citizens were not listed in the register; the electoral register was inaccurate; some ineligible electors were registered; some voters were threatened with violence at the polls; some fraudulent votes were cast; the election authorities were impartial; the authorities distributed information to citizens; the authorities allowed public scrutiny of their performance; the election authorities performed well.
MEDSL (2018)	Elections Performance Index	EMB data	Quantitative	A 17-indicator index for the US including residual vote levels, disability-related voting problems, availability of online registration, voter wait time and voter turnout.

42 Performance

Secondly, electoral management is often only a very small aspect of an overall, broader measure of electoral integrity. It is widely recognised that the electoral process involves much more than election day – instead there is an electoral cycle. This includes:

> the design and drafting of legislation, the recruitment and training of electoral staff, electoral planning, voter registration, the registration of political parties, the nomination of parties and candidates, the electoral campaign, polling, counting, the tabulation of results, the declaration of results, the resolution of electoral disputes, reporting, auditing and archiving.
>
> (ACE 2017)

Each aspect is important in and of itself, but also because of its interconnection with others. As the ACE Project continues:

> They are inter-dependent, and therefore the breakdown of one aspect (for example the collapse of a particular system of voter registration) can negatively impact on any other, including on the credibility of the election itself, and thus on the legitimacy of the elected government and the democratisation process of a partner country and its overall development objectives.
>
> (ACE 2017)

As the final column of Table 3.1 illustrates, most approaches are much less than complete when it comes to evaluating all aspects of the elections. Van Ham (2014) noted that some concepts use a single variable to measure all aspects of the electoral cycle. Too much is therefore often compressed into a single data-point as a result. Information about the performance of the organisations involved in delivering elections is crowded out. It is therefore necessary to develop a more comprehensive framework for evaluating electoral management quality.

Thirdly, there is a near universal aspiration to develop quantitative indexes. This reflects the behaviouralist goals set out in the last chapter. Donno, citing King, Keohane, and Verba (1994) in support, claims that: 'Inevitably, small-N or region-specific studies raise questions about broader generalizability. Moreover, there are limitations on how much can be inferred from analyzing a small number of cases' (Donno 2013, 51). Yet this is only one approach to the topic that could be taken. There *is* value in thicker, richer, small-*n* comparisons of EMB performance that describe the contextual environment and consider the points raised in the first section of this chapter.

Fourthly, there are questions about the use of sources for those indices. The validity and reliability of sources of information used in an index are a crucial determinant of the usefulness of that index. This is so essential that the chapter will discuss these below in section 3.5.

3.4 Available conceptualisations of electoral management quality

Given that so little work has systematically sought to assess the quality of electoral management, it is worth identifying a menu of conceptual options. Each is set out in turn.

3.4.1 Democratic theory

One way of assessing the quality of electoral management is to use democratic theory. Normative political philosophy can be used to ask the question: why have elections in the first place? And what should well-run elections look like? International organisations sometimes develop assessments of elections based on whether they fulfil principles. For example, International IDEA has set out seven such principles: independence, impartiality, integrity, transparency, efficiency, professionalism and service-mindedness (International IDEA 2014, 21–5). These principles are intuitively difficult to criticise, but they have not been directly and explicitly drawn from a specific democratic theory. This is necessary since it provides a meta narrative for understanding what we want to achieve when we design elections. Democratic theory should therefore be drawn from.

There are two broad camps of normative democratic theorists that could potentially be used to assess electoral management. One cluster proposes a *minimalist or procedural approach*, where a democracy is said to be in place where particular institutional procedures are in found (Dahl 1971, 1989; Dahl 1956; Schumpeter 2003[1942]). Robert Dahl claimed that democracy is characterised by the 'continuing responsiveness of the government to the preferences of its citizens, considered as equal weights' (Dahl 1971, 1). This required that citizens have unimpaired opportunities to formulate their preferences, signify them and have their preferences weighted equally in the conduct of government (Dahl 1971, 2). Unpacking this, Dahl thought that there were eight institutional guarantees that would be needed for a polity to be considered a polyarchy, the ideal system of government. These included the 'right to vote', 'free and fair elections' and 'freedom of expression' (ibid., p. 3). However, there was too little information here about what a well-managed 'free and fair election' looked like. The same can be said of other minimalist democratic theorists, such as Przeworski, who saw elections as central for ensuring the peaceful transfer of power (Przeworski 1999). These approaches are not therefore useful for assessing electoral management.

The second cluster of normative theorists, who provide the *substantive approach*, criticise the idea of evaluating institutions according to whether they match a pre-determined list, as proposed by scholars like Dahl. David Beetham, for example, argues that doing so provides no rationale for why these institutions should be considered '"democratic", rather than, say, "liberal", "pluralist", "polyachric" or whatever other term we choose' (Beetham 1994, 26). In addition, there is the risk that the analysis becomes 'Eurocentric'. By this, he means that we would potentially be identifying the political systems found in the Western world as 'best' – and then evaluating the rest of the world against this yardstick. Most worryingly, basing assessments on a pre-defined list offers no way of considering how that list could be improved (Beetham 1994, 26–7). For these reasons, a substantive approach is preferred in this book.

Beetham instead encourages us to evaluate democratic institutions by the outcomes that they produce. The concern is whether these institutions fulfil the principles that are essential for democratic rule. Beetham's proposed criteria is whether they achieve 'political equality and popular control'. Crucial to achieving this, writes Beetham, are:

- *Free and fair elections.* This requires a focus on the number of offices that are up for election, the inclusiveness of the registration of parties, candidates and votes; the fairness of the process between parties, candidates and voters; and, the independence of the process from the government of the day.
- *Open and accountable government.* This requires political accountability of the government to the legislature; legal accountability of state personnel to the courts; and, financial accountability to both the legislature and courts. Individual citizens should be able to seek 'redress in the event of maladministration or injustice'.
- *Guaranteed civil and political rights.* These are to include 'freedom of speech, association, assembly and movement' . . . and 'the right to due legal process'.
- *A democratic society.* Civil society should be strong and include a representative media, accountable private corporations, a politically aware civic body and high levels of political participation.

(Beetham 1994, 26–31)

Although these principles sound like those laid out by Dahl, it is the effectiveness of the institutions and procedures in place that should be assessed and not their mere *de jure* presence. Beetham's work has been influential in encouraging Democratic Audits: assessments of the quality of democracy in states around the world. Beetham did not directly link his work to electoral administration and management, nor have many of the Audits that have been based on his work. It therefore holds promise, but requires adaption, which will follow in the next chapter. How can the ideals of political equality and popular control be applied to the management of elections? We should first consider why other approaches are unsatisfactory, however.

3.4.2 Constitutional formal-legal analysis

Electoral management could be assessed by the formal-legal apparatus of EMBs. The evaluation of constitutions is a long-standing field within law and political science (Dicey 1959 [1885]; Lijphart 1999) with data becoming increasingly available (Elkins, Ginsburg, and Melton 2008). This approach neatly maps onto the scholarship using a minimalist or procedural definition of democracy, such as Dahl's identified above. EMBs are usually missing from these analyses, however. They don't feature, for example, in Arend Lijphart's (1999) typology of consensus and majoritarian democracy.

The key criteria often used in formal-legal analysis of electoral management is whether the EMB has independence from government. According to the Venice Commission:

independent, impartial electoral commissions must be set up from the national level to polling station level to ensure that elections are properly conducted, or at least remove serious suspicions of irregularity.

(Venice Commission 2002)

The weakness of many constitutional analyses is that they have often not been mapped onto democratic theory. The normative rationale for some procedures are not therefore fully justified. The empirical effects of particular formal-legal practices are also unclear. As International IDEA (2014, 21) suggests, formal-legal independence is not the same as *de facto* independence. Studies do not always demonstrate that formal-legal independence matters for the quality of electoral administration.[2] As Chapter 2 has already argued, there are lots of non-legal institutions and practices that could affect performance. While an analysis of constitutions is important, they can be therefore only part of the criteria and this approach requires further development.

3.4.3 International norms and standards

An alternative approach to assessing the quality of electoral management is to use international standards as the benchmark. This approach is used by Pippa Norris, who in her landmark trilogy defines electoral integrity as 'contests respecting international standards and global norms governing the appropriate conduct of elections. These standards have been endorsed in a series of authoritative conventions, treaties, protocols, case laws and guidance by agencies of the international community' (Norris 2015b, 4). Most famously, Article 21(3) of the Universal Declaration of Human Rights states that: 'The will of the people shall be the basis of the authority of government; this will shall be expressed in periodic and genuine elections which shall be by universal and equal suffrage and shall be held by secret vote or by equivalent free voting procedures' (UN General Assembly 1948). Since 1948, obligations embodied in international jurisprudence have expanded and international organisations have identified 20 principles for conducting elections that states should be bound by (Tuccinardi 2014). To take one recent example, and of high relevance here, the Venice Commission (2002) has set out a *Code of Good Practice in Electoral Matters*. This recommends that a permanent and impartial body be in charge of applying electoral law. Although formal-legal independence is not necessary in older democracies, the code suggests, this independence is essential when 'there is no longstanding tradition of administrative authorities' independence from those holding political power' (Venice Commission 2002, 10). These organisations, the Code suggests, should include at least one member of the judiciary, have equal representation for political parties and should have some security of tenure (ibid.).

Many of these international standards relate directly to electoral management and therefore could be used in the assessment of electoral management quality in any given jurisdiction. A crucial advantage of this approach is that it might encourage praxis: by pointing out shortcomings in a country's electoral management against international norms and obligations enforceability might be easier. Holding a mirror to an EMB and pointing out what they were committed to deliver gives the international community leverage to demand reform and action. In the corridors of power in the UN, political theory is too fuzzy and less well known to bring agreement about deficiencies in electoral management which might always be contested by the organising authorities or their governments.

There are weaknesses with the approach, however. As Norris herself points out, 'normative authority is understood to derive from the body of human rights treaties and conventions in the international community; not directly from principles of democracy' (Norris 2015b, 4). There is therefore no philosophical guarantee that the international norms themselves are virtuous. If the world order was to shift then we might expect many international norms to shift. At what point do they then cease to be useful in guiding best practice and assessing the performance of EMBs? And how would we know? When there is a clash of ideas, either between states or I(N)GOs about what international best practices should be, how do we arbitrate between them? Without an anchoring against some key philosophical principles, there is also a risk that international norms could be dismissed for reflecting the 'Western' order.

We could add a final weakness. If international norms are used to evaluate elections, then there is no scope for improving international norms. This directly echoes concerns raised by Beetham. Take, for example, the secret ballot, which is seen as an indispensable feature of a democratic election by international bodies around the world. However, it is worth remembering that J.S. Mill criticised the secret ballot (Kinzer 2007; Lever 2007). Claims have since been made that the procedure of secrecy has been 'over-fetishised' as a method of holding elections and other methods can be embraced (Bertrand, Briquet, and Pels 2007). We might ask, shouldn't that standard be subjected to empirical analysis to determine what effect it might have? Simply accepting international norms as the benchmarks for success without an empirical and philosophical argument is an anti-intellectual approach which prevents research and discussion about improving how we conduct and evaluate elections.

3.4.4 Electoral Fraud

The breaking of election laws or other legal regulations within a country could be used to evaluate electoral management. Should electoral laws commonly not be adhered to then the performance of the EMB receives harsh criticism. This is a popular approach in the media commentary of the conduct of EMBs that is also found in academic work. Some studies have sought to estimate or measure the number of times electoral laws are broken (Ahlquist, Mayer, and Jackman 2014), while others, noting the difficulty in measuring cases of electoral fraud, have argued that some voting procedures undermine electoral integrity by having insufficient security provisions (Lehoucq 2003). There are also localised studies of fraudulent practices in particular contexts. Sobolewska et al. found that ethnic-kinship networks in Pakistani- and Bangladeshi-origin communities in England had a 'range of vulnerabilities, which may make them susceptible to becoming victims of electoral fraud' (Sobolewska et al. 2015). In response to findings that fraud exists or there are vulnerabilities to fraud, increased security provisions are advocated, such as voter identification requirements, removing convenience voting provisions such as mail-in ballots or asking citizens for the use of election monitors (Fund 2008; Sobolewska et al. 2015; Kelley 2012; Wilks-Heeg 2008, 2009).

The advantage of this system of evaluation is that it is simple and unambiguous. It self-evidently undermines the democratic value of political equality and popular control of government if a citizen votes many times or if vote rigging brings a candidate or party to power rather than underlying popular support. The approach is commonly defended by legal scholars because it provides concrete instances of injustices. Lorraine Minnitte, in her book, *The Myth of Voter Fraud*, argues that:

> Fraud is a generic term; it lacks meaning outside specific cultural, legal and historical contexts. If we want to find it, study it, and understand it, a broad cross-cultural, translegal, and transhistorical definition of the kind called for by scholars does not take us very far.
>
> (Minnite 2010, 21)

There are some weaknesses in using this as a measure of performance, however. First off, electoral laws vary by country so comparisons are very difficult. Secondly, it prevents a critical evaluation of those electoral laws in the first place. What if the laws of a given locality contravene international standards or democratic theory? For example, Apartheid in South Africa barred millions of people from voting because of their ethnicity. If an electoral official broke that law, and allowed black citizens to vote, should we penalise the organisation in an evaluation of their performance? We should add that EMBs are not usually responsible for making the law themselves. It is therefore unfair to criticise them for the number of cases of electoral fraud if they do not have control over them.

3.4.5 Mass perceptions

Electoral management can be assessed by whether the norms and traditions of a particular country are broken. Different polities may adopt different traditions of democracy. There is therefore a case for assessing the performance of those systems using criteria that are sensitive to those different traditions. Public opinion surveys can be used to ask citizens whether they feel that their elections are well run. This can be thought of as the mass perception approach (Birch 2011, 12). The advantage of this is that there is no risk of the observer imposing Western (or non-Western) ideals upon a society. Yet there are problems too. It makes comparisons between countries difficult because citizens might be assessing elections in different ways. Secondly, it gives up any normative claim to there being a universally

48 *Performance*

accepted best practice about how elections should be run. It is also dependent on citizens' knowledge about electoral management. If they are unaware of problems such as inaccurate vote counting because of a lack of transparency by the authorities then they may rate the EMB highly.

3.4.6 Central compliance

We could evaluate electoral management in terms of whether local officials have complied with the directions of the central organisation. EMBs are sometimes enormous organisations employing thousands or millions of individuals. For example, the 2014 Brazilian elections involved the management of 2,435,303 staff (Toffoli 2016). An essential part of the electoral process is the consideration of whether these officials complied with their directions – a classic principal-agent problem (Alvarez and Hall 2006). Clark, for example, used data on whether UK local authorities implemented the directions set by the Electoral Commission to compile an overall measure of the quality of electoral administration in each area in the 2010 UK general election (Clark 2015).

The advantage of the approach is that This is a useful measure because (a) non-compliance can be a problem within and between organisations – it implies a lack of organisational control and cohesion; and, (b) high levels of compliance suggest that the delivery may be of a higher quality. There are weaknesses, however. Using this approach assumes that compliance with instructions is synonymous with good quality election delivery. Central standards can be poorly designed. In the case of the UK, the standards were actually measuring processes and not outcomes. (James 2013) also reported that officials may deliberately not provide accurate information to game the results of the performance standards. Lastly, internal standards are not usually measured in the same way across countries, if they are measured at all. Comparisons are therefore difficult.

3.4.7 Online transparency and service provision

An alternative approach for assessment is the transparency of the EMB and their online service provision. Holly Ann Garnett (2017) argues that transparency provides democratic control of public institutions. Transparency is essential so that public institutions can be held to account for their performance. Transparency in EMBs, Garnett argues, requires that they are open with their 'decisions actions and data'. She assesses whether a sample of EMBs in 99 countries provide the following five items on their websites to measure transparency: annual or post-election reports, election results, organisational hierarchies, information about the EMB members and the rules/regulations of the EMB. EMBs that are statutorily independent organisations are found to be more transparent, but transparency was not identified as having any effect on citizen's confidence in the electoral process.

It is difficult to argue against transparency being a useful measure of EMB performance. This point is supported by other studies. For Norris (2017c), transparency forms part of a transparency-accountability-compliance nexus. The availability of information alone does not guarantee that it will be used to further electoral integrity. What is also needed are mechanisms for accountability and compliance to ensure that EMBs are held to account and reforms are enacted, Norris argues. Clark and James (2017) also argue that the greater availability of performance information, collected via poll worker surveys, provides a greater opportunity for policy to be evidence-based. Partisan claims from politicians can then be checked and verified.

EMB websites can also be assessed in terms of the quality of services that they provide citizens, especially voters. In an information age, the internet is the vital way in which citizens access government services. King and Youngblood (2016) therefore evaluated voting and election websites in the US state of Alabama. An index was developed to score them according to their levels of accessibly, usability and mobile readiness. Significant deficiencies were found with many websites. The socio-demographic features of a county were thought to be a significant predictor of website quality. In short, both the online transparency and service provision of EMBs are vitally important dimensions of performance that should be studied. They do not, of course, provide an exhaustive system since other aspects of the EMBs work are also important.

3.5 Available data sources for measuring performance

Having considered the variety of higher-order principles by which we can measure the performance of EMBs, we should the consider advantages and disadvantages of using competing data sources to measure performance. The argument here is that there is an increasing variety of sources of information that can be used – all of which have some value. The next chapter will show how they can be used to develop a qualitative interpretation of electoral management quality, but the data source types need to be set out first.

3.5.1 Citizen surveys

Firstly, we could ask citizens of their assessment of the performance of the electoral management body. The most obvious way of doing this would be through online or in-person surveys, although focus groups could also be used, especially for groups of voters who have complex needs e.g. disabled or minority groups. There are some cross-national surveys that have collected relevant data. For example, module 4 (2011–16) of the Comparative Study of Electoral Systems (CSES) has collected data on whether citizens thought the election was administered impartially.[3] Using an earlier module, Sarah Birch (2008) has reviewed data on whether elections were conducted 'fairly' to assess whether formal independence of the EMB affected this. The World Values Survey Wave 6 also asked questions relating to the quality of elections.[4] In 41 countries questions included electoral management–related variables such as whether votes are counted fairly, election official are fair and voters are threatened with violence.[5] Figure 3.2 provides raw data on the percentage of respondents that said that election officials were 'not often' or 'not often at all' fair.

50 *Performance*

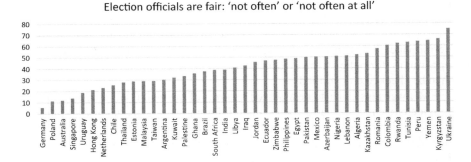

Figure 3.2 The 'fairness' of electoral officials in 41 countries, 2010–2014.

Some electoral management bodies employ polling companies to survey the public as part of post-election evaluations. For example, the UK Electoral Commission undertook post-election surveys from June 2009 to June 2016. It also undertook 'Winter Tracker' surveys of the whole of the UK on issues including the voting and registration process during this time. These included specific surveys on black and minority ethnic communities (Electoral Commission 2017c).[6]

The advantage of this approach is that it intuitively allows the citizen's direct experience to be part of the evaluation. Their voice can be heard and research and the researcher is not dependent on second-hand reporting of information via experts or the media. Using appropriate sampling methods, a representative sample can be sought of the population or specific groups of concern. There are also numerous disadvantages, however. Perceptions amongst citizens does not equate to reality. Citizens may be misled by disproportionate media coverage or claims by partisan actors. For example, a US 2016 survey found that 35 per cent of voters thought that there was a great deal of election fraud in the US (Associated Press 2016); but actual credible cases have been estimated at 31 incidents out of 1 billion ballots cast between 2000–2014 (Levitt 2014). Vonnahme and Miller (2013) have demonstrated that, knowing little about the mechanics of electoral administration, voters take information 'cues' from politicians' public claims.

While questions about the performance of the EMB are beginning to be asked, survey questions about the quality of elections still tend to be about elections in general. Country coverage remains limited and cost is likely to be prohibitively high for individual researchers to run themselves and they are therefore dependent on major projects. Cross-national comparison must also be sensitive to the risk that some questions may have different local meanings. *In what way*, for example, are electoral officials not fair? Nonetheless, surveys of citizens, especially cross-national surveys are useful.

3.5.2 Expert/academic surveys

A second approach is to ask academic experts for their assessment of the quality of electoral management. This method has been used widely to study other political phenomenon across countries such as the power of prime ministers (O'Malley 2007), party and policy positioning (Hooghe et al. 2010; Huber and Inglehart 1995) and evaluations of electoral systems (Bowler, Farrell, and Pettitt 2005). The approach has increasingly been used in evaluating election quality. The Perception of Electoral Integrity Index (PEII) was a survey of experts on 49 indicators in 11 categories. It stated: 'Election experts are defined as a political scientist (or other social scientist in a related discipline) who has demonstrated knowledge of the electoral process in a particular country (such as through publications, membership of a relevant research group or network, or university employment)' (Norris, i Coma, and Grömping 2015, 7). Among the categories are factual questions (e.g. 'postal ballots were available') and judgement questions (e.g. 'the elections were well managed') highly relevant to electoral management. Meanwhile, the Varieties of Democracy (V-DEM) database provides a more limited range of data, but with a much more significant timescale (Coppedge 2014). Experts were asked whether the EMB had 'autonomy from government to apply election laws and administrative rules impartially in national elections' and whether it had 'sufficient staff and resources to administer a well-run national election'. A 5-point scale was used with data covering the entire period of 1900–2017. Figure 3.2 below demonstrates a global rise in EMB capacity.

A final approach using expert assessments is Gary Bland et al.'s *Election Administration Systems Index* (EASI) (Bland 2015; Bland, Green, and Moore

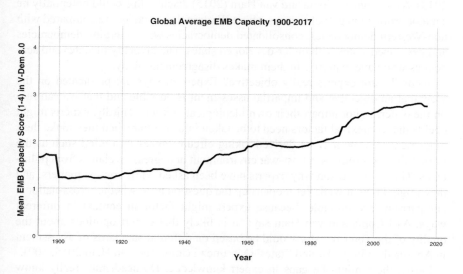

Figure 3.3 Global EMB capacity, as measured by V-DEM 8.0.

2013). The questionnaire includes 48 questions, with 36 of those categorised into a matrix of time points in the electoral cycle and whether they relate to participation, competition or integrity. A Likert scale of 1–5 is used. Experts are defined as 'country and international specialists' who 'may be scholars, for example, former members of national election commissions, leaders of non-governmental organizations, or project directors for international aid organizations' (Bland, Green, and Moore 2013, 366). A pilot study was undertaken with a single expert in 10 countries with a more thorough test in Nigeria (Bland, Green, and Moore 2013). A subsequent study looked at the Kenyan 2013 election (Bland 2015).

The use of expert surveys holds many advantages for undertaking comparative research on electoral management. They allow the researcher to draw from and pool the knowledge and expertise of other researchers around the world. In the age of the internet where survey software is relatively freely available (to researchers in institutions with subscriptions, at least), data can be collected and results disseminated very quickly. Results from the PEI survey from the November 2016 US Presidential election (Norris, Alessandro, et al. 2016) were reaching the popular press before the end of 2016 and informing public debate (Norris, Garnett, and Grömping 2016). Surveys provide options for quantifiable responses that make analysis easier. They are also relatively cheap and therefore more likely to be sustainable (Bland, Green, and Moore 2013, 366).

The use of expert surveys poses important methodological problems, however. To begin with, are the criteria upon which the assessments are made universally clear? Linguistic problems can be avoided by carefully worded survey questions but conceptual terms may be understood differently (Budge 2000; Schedler 2012). As Martínez i Coma and van Ham (2015) discuss, this could potentially be a major problem in global surveys where Western democracies are compared with non-Western democracies, consolidated democracies with emerging democracies and developed states with under-developed states. The diversity of states and academics who have expertise in them makes disagreement likely.

Secondly, are experts really objective? Expert surveys are predicated on the view that an objective and impartial assessment is possible and that we can rely on the expert to not impart their own ideological opinion. Thirdly, experts might decide that contextual factors need to be taken into account when they make their judgement. A view may be derived taking circumstances into mind such as the availability of resources, a post-war environment or aggressive claims from politicians. This is one reason why experts have been asked – this context matters, and they might know it well. Yet it opens up the question as to whether cross-national comparisons are possible, because expert might factor in context in different ways. As i Coma and van Ham say: 'it is likely that expert opinions about the quality of the voter registry would be based on different standards of assessment in Angola than in the United States' (Martínez i Coma and van Ham 2015, 309).

Lastly, there might be gaps in expert knowledge. Do academics really know about electoral management quality? Information about electoral system design is openly available. Experts can easily identify how proportional the system is and whether a partisan process has been used to 'gerrymander' the boundaries. Assessing electoral management, as conceptualised in this book, is much more difficult. It requires knowledge of how laws, procedures and technologies are administered on the ground and how effective they have been. There are few academic studies of electoral management in most countries. 'Experts' to complete expert surveys may have their expertise in other aspects of the electoral process. Bland et al. indeed rely on 'expert hearsay', as they put it, in their own approach. They argue of experts that:

> While none of them may have expertise on every element of the election system, our experience has shown that each will know of weaknesses and controversies from their own work, the local press, and colleagues in the field.
> (Bland, Green, and Moore 2013, 366)

In defence of expert surveys, many of the potential problems have been tested for. Expert surveys tend to be consistent with one another on election quality (Norris 2013a, 2017a). Anchoring vignettes are increasingly being used to standardise the replies (Norris 2017a). With all of these concerns in mind, Martínez i Coma and van Ham (2015) empirically test the validity of expert indices by identifying the extent of disagreement that exists within responses to the EIP surveys Disagreement, for them, implied measurement error. Significant disagreement would suggest that expert surveys could not be used. They found that questions of a factual nature generated less disagreements. Meanwhile, questions which were technical or required information that was not publicly available, including electoral registration, generated greater deviation. Overall, their study gave reason to be optimistic about the use of expert assessments in elections, but some cause for concern for electoral management given that information is not always publicly available.

3.5.3 Observer reports

The evaluation of elections by external observers, as Susan Hyde (2011a) argues, has become a norm in the conduct of elections. A decision by a government not to invite international observers, Hyde argues, is often seen to be a signal that a country is not trustworthy. As a result there is a wealth of evaluation reports of electoral contests publicly available. Researchers have used these to compile cross-national indices of electoral quality, such as Sarah Birch's (2011) Index of Electoral Malpractice.

Observation reports hold many advantages as a source of data. They can provide decades of detailed information about the quality of electoral management which can generate parsimonious indexes. Kelley (2010) is among many, however, to argue that observer reports should not be read uncritically. Observers tend to weight election-day problems more strongly, 'tread more carefully' in states that are important to their donors and non-democratic governments are often less critical in order to 'avoid future criticism of their own regime' (pp. 164–5). Observer reports are useful in comparing an election to international standards or the standards of an I(N)GO, but this is only one set of standards. As noted above, there is no single set of international standards and standards are not necessarily linked to democratic ideals. Lastly, we should add the observations are usually based upon relatively short periods of assessment. A needs assessment mission is usually undertaken several months before an election and longer-term observers can be posted for several months (Bordewich, Davis-Roberts, and Carroll 2019). Yet these are still insufficient amounts of time for a comprehensive review of all the aspects of the electoral process.

3.5.4 Domestic observer reports

A related source of data is election observation reports written by domestic civil society groups (Grömping 2017). Domestic groups may evolve autonomously from civil society – or they might receive international assistance in the short term. Information from domestic civil society observers will have the advantage that the organisation will already have a knowledge of local culture, history and experience which external observers might not have. Their presence in the country would enable them to make observations throughout a longer period of the electoral cycle and give them context and a better understanding of the events surrounding election day. Domestic civil society groups can also publish reports on aspects of the electoral cycle outside of election day. They therefore provide invaluable additional information which can be used to assess electoral management quality.

The disadvantages, however, are that a quick turnaround in staff and a precarious financial position can mean that knowledge can come and go. The research training and background of the authors of the reports may therefore vary, and sometimes be low. The rigour and research quality in some cases might be questionable. Civil society groups are also often established with a mission statement or commitment to a particular cause which can lead them away from neutral findings.

3.5.5 Technical EMB data

Since EMBs run elections, it is self-apparent that they are often best positioned to collect information that is useful for evaluating the quality of electoral management Information can therefore be gathered about how much is spent on running elections and voter registration, the estimated number of people who are on the electoral register and the institutional design of the EMB. Such information is sometimes available on the websites of EMBS or collected for internal processes. For example, the US Electoral Assistance Commission has run a biennial survey of electoral officials, which became known as the Election Administration and Voting Survey from 2014 onwards (US Electoral Assistance Commission 2014). The UK Electoral Commission has publicly made available information about whether local administrators meet the standards that they set (James 2013).

There is a clear case for using such technical data as part of an evaluation. On the surface it provides objective and measurable information about the electoral process. The measures are, in theory, measures of the reality of the performance of electoral managements systems and not the perception of their performance. The data can be aggregated and analysis easily undertaken to identify the determinants of performance (Bowler et al. 2015; Clark 2016). There are dangers, however. The reliability of the information that EMBs publish has to be considered critically on a case by case basis. If they are publishing information on their own performance then we should be aware that organisations do have strategic incentives to publish this selectively. The volume of the information that EMBs publish varies considerably (Garnett 2017). EMBs also have a variety of methods available to them for calculating such technical data so it might not always enable cross-national comparison. However, there a considerable opportunities here to collect EMB data to assess performance. Until recently, there have has been no systematic attempts to collect this information, however, this is beginning to change with new projects undertaking cross-national surveys of electoral administrators (James et al. 2019; Karp et al. 2017).

One particular form of EMB data is the administrative data created by poll workers. For example, Burden et al. (2017) use incident logs created by American poll workers to identify the frequency of problems that occurred in elections between 2008–11. Poll workers are required to complete paperwork known as an 'Inspectors Statement' and part of this asks them to record any incidents that have occurred on election day. An open space was provided in which they are free to describe the problems that occurred. The researchers coded this information to establish that roughly one in a hundred voters expierenced a problem. The most common problem detected in their study was the need to issue a new ballot which might occur because the voter made an error. As the authors state, the figures probably understate the level of problems because not all problems would have been reported (p. 358). Consistent patterns across elections give strength to the reliabaility of the data, however, This certainly provides a useful additional datasource. Unfortunately, such data has not been routinely collected in many countries.

3.5.6 Electoral officials

Drawing from the experience of those involved in running elections themselves provides an alternative way of evaluating electoral management. Public officials are front-line workers with 'local knowledge' who will have firsthand experience of the everyday life of working in a particular setting (Durose 2009, 2011; Lipsky 1980). The academic literature from public administration suggests that the 'top-down' implementation of policies can often face implementation problems and unforeseen consequences (Pressman and Wildavsky 1973; Sabatier 1986). Proponents of 'bottom-up' policy making have long suggested mining the knowledge of 'street level bureaucrats' when developing policies (Hanf and Porter 1978). Borrowing from Yannow, Durose suggests that 'local knowledge' is:

> 'a kind of non-verbal knowing that evolves from seeing, interacting with someone (or some place or something) over time' (Yanow 2004, 12). As implied, this 'knowing' is contextual and refers to a specific setting and reflects 'very mundane yet expert understanding from lived experience' (Yanow 2004, 12). Front-line workers develop their 'local knowledge' from their own subjective interpretations or 'readings' of a situation.
>
> (Durose 2009, 36)

Local knowledge can, therefore, help to foresee implementation problems and the unintended consequences of changes. It can provide detailed information about the reality of running elections, which the public and academics may never be aware of.[7] Scholarship from realist approaches to public policy evaluation, which this book aligns itself with (see Chapter 2), argue that practitioners have unique, real and concrete experience of a programme's effects (Pawson and Tilley 1997, 161). The risk of drawing from the experience of practitioners, however, as Pawson and Tilley argue, is that they often stress the immediate, local and personalised effects of their experiences and may be tempted to overstate the negative consequences to themselves. They often lack the ability to systematically chart, typify and generalise. However, through aggregation, carefully analysing and externally verifying (where possible) the researcher can use the practitioner's insights of the effects of the reforms to draw the 'big picture' (Pawson and Tilley 1997, 161). The effects of 'behind the scenes' reforms are unlikely to be known and experienced by the citizen.

This broader methodology can be used through a range of applied methods. Semi-structured interviews can be undertaken with electoral officials. Semi-structured interviews require the researcher to begin an interview with a set of broad questions or themes that they want the interview to explore but let the interviewee lead the conversation. An alternative to interviews is the use of surveys, where closed questions tend to be used with multiple-choice answers available to respondents. Surveys tends to be quicker. They can be done online to reduce costs and many electoral officials are readily accessible because their contact details are often available online.

Electoral officials, of course, are not one homogenous group. A distinction can be made between studies which focus on middle and upper management officials and those which focus on poll workers. The experience of these two groups, and by consequence, the possible uses of the information that they can provide, varies enormously. Managers can describe the challenges and problems involved in overseeing elections and compilation of the register By contrast, poll workers, the officials who man the polling station and issue ballot papers, can provide insights into what happens on the day of the election. Claims are often made that ballot stuffing, voter intimidation and impersonation has taken place in both established democracies and electoral autocracies. At the same time, it is often suggested that less deliberate problems occur in these places, such as long queues at polling stations, poor ballot design or restricted opening hours. Clark and James (2017) argue that poll worker surveys allow the frequency of any problems and the need for any necessary policy fixes to be established through evidence Some poll worker surveys have been undertaken in the US since 2000 (Alvarez, Atkeson, and Hall 2007; Glaser et al. 2007; Mac Donald and Glaser 2007; Mockabee, Monson, and Patterson 2009; Senecal 2007) but are exceptionally rare outside of the USA (Amegnran 2017; Clark and James 2016b, 2017; Herron and Boyko 2016; Herron, Boyko, and Thunberg 2016).

3.5.7 Researcher ethnography

A type of data that is seriously underused is ethnographical data. Ethnography involves, in its broadest sense, the researcher:

> participating, overtly or covertly, in people's daily lives for an extended period of time, watching what happens, listening to what is said, asking questions – in fact, collecting whatever data are available to throw light on the issues that are the focus of the research.
>
> (Atkinson and Hammersley 1995, 1)

'Data' could include field-notes, transcripts of interviews, photographs, sample objects from the field and videos. It is usually gathered by participant observation, ideally over a long period of time. The origins of ethnography lie in early twentieth-century anthropological studies of small, remote societies such as the Trobriand Islanders and Andaman Islanders (Malinowski 1922; Radcliffe-Brown 1964). The classic positivist criticism of such an approach is that the data is impressionistic, unrepresentative and not objective (see Chapter 2). But for ethnographers, the social world should be studied, as much as possible, in its natural state. By watching and observing, a deeper understanding of cultural practices and belief systems can be identified. It can also be combined with 'doing'. Richard Crossman researched and wrote about the role of a UK Cabinet Minister and backbench MP by *being* one: 'unlike most of my colleagues in . . . parliament, I was an observer as well as a journalist MP' (Crossman 1976, 11). Such insights and insider information are enormously rich information that provides *verstehen*.

It follows that in the field of elections participant observation could also be enormously useful. It does raise ethical issues, however, if it is being collected for the purposes of evaluating electoral management. In this instance, the participant observing switches function to being a performance monitor. What difference is there then between a social researcher and an election observer or a line manager This is out of line with the purposes of ethnographic research, which is to *understand* and not judge. Anthropology is also often wedded to a relativist epistemology that makes judgement difficult. It remains useful, however, because it provides information about the conditions and nature of the election which is

58 *Performance*

not available through other means. Rarely has this been done, with only the occasional use of ethnographic methods in elections (see, for example: Coles 2007).

3.6 Conclusions

Assessing election quality is an inevitably tricky task beset with a range of philosophical and methodological challenges. However, we can't shirk these if we want to have clear conceptual frameworks and logical policy recommendations that we hope will improve the world. To claim that elections are well run or otherwise is a normative claim. Any assessment of the implementation of elections therefore must be tied to normative theory. This chapter has argued that David Beetham's work provides the best starting point for a framework of how we can assess the implementation of elections, but it requires development for the job in hand. The next chapter will look to theories of public management to help provide more fine-grained tools. The chapter has also considered the empirical data sources that could be used to evaluate performance, arguing that all have value, but also some weaknesses. A realist approach must seek to use the best available evidence in a reflective way so that researcher and analyst can give an evidence-based *qualitative interpretation* of electoral management quality.

Notes

1 Schmeets (2002) was included in van Ham's list but excluded here because it was not available in English.
2 However, see: van Ham and Garnett (2019).
3 Variable D5020 – 'How impartial was the body that administered the election law?' Source: www.cses.org/datacenter/module4/data/cses4_codebook_part2_variables.txt
4 Other projects include the Gallop World Polls, Latin American Public Opinion Project and the Afrobarometer.
5 The questions were: V228a How often in a country's elections: Votes are counted fairly; V228d How often in a country's elections: Voters are bribed; V228f How often in a country's elections: Election officials are fair; V228h How often in a country's elections: Voters are threatened with violence at the poll.
6 These surveys were ongoing at time of writing.
7 In one interview, an electoral registration officer recounted the story of how a voter stole the ballot box and ran off across a field with it, only to be caught by a rugby-playing polling clerk.

4 Evaluating electoral management performance
The PROSeS framework

4.1 Introduction

How should we assess electoral management? The previous chapter reviewed the existing approaches that have been developed to measure the quality of electoral management and the sources of evidence that could be used in doing so. It suggested that democratic theory provided an important starting point, however, a more finely detailed approach was needed. This chapter sets out a new comprehensive approach for auditing the performance of electoral management, designed to enable cross-country analysis called the PROSeS framework.

After a review of the rival approaches that are used to evaluate public sector performance in general, five dimensions of EMB performance are set out which are argued to be crucial for achieving democratic ideals in an electoral democracy. The aim is to set out these dimensions, and the sources of data that can be used by researchers to assess whether they are achieved. The UK and Canada are then assessed against the framework so that the utility of the model becomes clear. The concepts and framework also act as founding principles for the remainder of the book.

The model is developed to enable a close comparative study between a small number of cases. A comparison of as few as two countries, the chapter argues, enables useful insights about their comparative performance which take context into consideration. Although quantitative cross-national comparisons involving a large number of cases often much prized amongst large segments of academia, this can lead to a tendency to measure what is measurable and quantifiable rather than what is important. Concepts and measures can become confused and conflated during data reduction processes. The needs of the practitioner looking to improve elections in their own country are put secondary to the need of the researcher looking to create 'rigorous' statistically significant models. Frameworks quickly lose themselves in intangible languages of academese. Where large n data are available and appropriate on some measures, it is used to contextualise individual performance, but not to remove the meaning of individualised cases.

4.2 Approaches to assessing public administration

There are two broad approaches to evaluating performance that are usually used within public administration (Boyne 2002). The first is the 'economy-efficiency-effectiveness' (3Es) model. This prescribes that services should be *economical* in the sense that minimal levels of resources should be spent securing each unit input. *Efficiency* usually refers to the cost per unit of output (e.g. an hour of teaching). *Effectiveness* commonly refers to whether service objectives have been achieved. Given the finite amount of resources available to the public sector, all of these are important criteria and should be part of any model used to assess electoral management.

The second is the 'inputs-outputs-outcomes' (IOO) model, which includes everything present in the 3E model, but also a broader set of criteria that the 3E model overlooks. The efficiency with which *outputs* are created are therefore considered, but so too is the quality of the service. Additional criteria might include the speed of delivery or accessibility for different groups. When the service *outcomes* are considered, it is not just the effectiveness for achieving a single policy goal that the policy maker has in mind. Instead, they should consider the broader *impact* such as whether additional jobs are created in other industries. In addition, the model suggests that we should consider the *equity and fairness* of the provision and whether some groups are likely to benefit more than others.

4.2.1 Going beyond existing approaches

Boyne (2002), however, argues that both approaches remain too limited in their approach for assessing public services for three reasons. Firstly, these models give no value to the preferences of the public. For him, '[s]ervices that are efficient and formally effective may be of little value unless they meet public demands' (p. 18). The responsiveness of public services to the demands of citizens and their representatives should therefore be included in any evaluation criteria. This approach has obvious importance for evaluating elections. Low levels of public confidence in electoral machinery could lead to an erosion of confidence in the democratic process. Equally, if concerns are raised by pressure groups about the quality of electoral management, then this could have profound consequences.

Secondly, Boyne argues that the IOO model is insufficient because it gives 'no voice' to internal stakeholders – the employees of organisations themselves. This is intuitively important because we know, from research elsewhere, that low levels of staff satisfaction can have negative consequences for the likelihood that an individual would quit (Tzeng 2002) but also that organisational outcomes such as customer satisfaction, productivity, profit, employee turnover (Harter, Schmidt, and Hayes 2002).

Thirdly, the IOO approach only considers organisations as service providers. But EMBs are institutions which form part of the democratic state and therefore should be evaluated according to whether they ensure public participation, probity and accountability. Boyne's framework is a significant advance on earlier frameworks for evaluating the performance of public organisations. It provides much added value as an alternative approach for evaluating electoral management. It is therefore adapted here for that purpose.

Drawing from the literature in the previous chapter, the international literature on electoral management and the author's practical experience of dealing with stakeholders, it is argued that there are other areas that a framework based within public administration theory might want to include. In the next section, Boyne's framework is adapted so that it can be applied to electoral management.

4.3 The PROSeS framework for assessing electoral management

This chapter sets out the PROSeS framework to assess electoral management. Figure 4.1 shows that the framework is anchored around the five clusters of process design, resource investment, service outputs, service outcomes, stakeholder satisfaction, which all lead into the realisation of democratic ideals.[1]

As the last chapter argued, we need some higher-order normative principles to appeal to. This is especially important given that this book uses a realist approach – because critical realism argues that research should be critical of the world and be used to improve it. Equally, the book appeals to a tradition within public administration which seeks to bring about 'enlightened prescription' because of 'the symbiotic relationship between knowledge and action, theory and practice' (Evans 2007, 128). The book follows David Beetham (1994)'s focus on a democratic society as one where two key principles of political quality and popular control of government are achieved (see Chapter 2). These principles are then broken down into a number

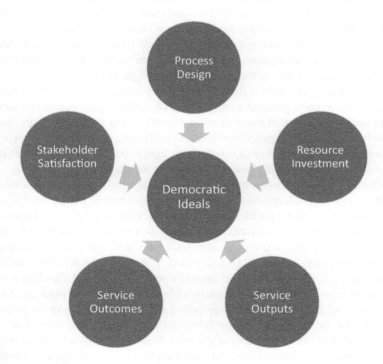

Figure 4.1 The PROSeS framework.

62 *Performance*

of other 'distinct, albeit overlapping, dimensions'. These include the desire for open and transparent government. These are taken as the overarching goals which electoral management is seeking to contribute towards the realisation of.

Achieving any lofty principles, however, requires high-quality public administration. What measures should be used?

4.3.1 Decision-making processes

Firstly, we should focus on the decision-making processes in place in electoral management bodies. This book has argued that electoral officials are public service providers and therefore we should assess them in similar ways to other public services. But if we are trying to achieve democratic values, then these values should run through the decision-making processes inside EMBs themselves. Following Boyne (2002, 19), we should value public and impartiality, participation, probity and accountability in decision making:

- *Public participation* within public services has increasingly been a subject of scholarly interest, as academics have considered how democratisation can take place *within* the administrative state (Kathi and Cooper 2005). Instruments such as elections for public officials, citizen consultations or citizen-led decision making have been piloted (Greer et al. 2014; Kathi and Cooper 2005; Lowndes, Pratchett, and Stoker 2001, 2006; Parkinson 2004). Constitutional Assemblies have been established in some countries involving citizens and have been shown to cause people to change their views and therefore provide some deliberative democracy within public services (Suiter, Farrell, and O'Malley 2014). Public participation has both normative value and instrumental value. The normative value is that citizens have a right to have their voices heard. The instrumental value is that it can improve efficiency and effectiveness but also help to build political communities. We will consider public involvement in decision making in more detail in Part III of this book. There are reasons to be cautious about public involvement in running elections because partisan control of the electoral rules is usually thought to be problematic. However, we should recognise the intrinsic moral value in inclusive decision making.
- *Probity and impartiality* by electoral officials is self-evidently essential. As Boyne describes it, probity involves the 'proper use of public funds and the absence of fraud by politicians and officials' (Boyne 2002, 19). Impartiality requires that public servants do 'not act in ways that advantage or disadvantage the partisan-political interests of any political party, including the governing party or parties' (Aucoin 2012, 179). Electoral officials should discharge their functions without resort to personal gain and should not deliberately give any candidate or party undue advantage. The distinction made in the previous chapter between failures of steering and rowing is useful, however. An individual electoral official may give a candidate or party an advantage by simply following the rules from which this advantage derives. In such circumstances, blame will not necessarily lie with the individual.
- *Accountability mechanisms* for redress should be in place so that if there are suspicions that electoral fraud has taken place, there should be swift, decisive

and accessible methods for investigating and remedying this. This is dealt with elsewhere in the literature on electoral justice and is not therefore discussed in detail here. However, in the management and implementation of the electoral process, there should also be redress for the citizen who feels that their vote was not counted or there were problems at polling stations. A minimal level of service would involve a clear process through which they can lodge complaints and expect a timely response and remedial action. This could be about election day, but also at other stages of the electoral cycle such as with the status of an electoral registration application. Effective electoral justice and dispute resolution will require the accurate collection of information about the delivery of election – so good electoral management will require that that this is collected.

4.3.2 Resource investment

No public service can be provided without resource investment of some kind. Printing ballot papers, paying officials to staff polling stations, hiring helicopters to transfer ballots from remote areas and providing additional security: it all costs money. It is therefore essential that there is sufficient investment in electoral democracy for elections to function properly and democratic ideals to be achieved.

It is helpful to distinguish between different types of costs. The commonly cited categories are based on a report co-sponsored by UNDP and IFES in 2005 called the Cost of Registration and Elections (CORE) (López-Pintor and Fischer 2005), but a slightly different typology is suggested here in Table 4.1.[2]

Table 4.1 Type of electoral investments needed to ensure high-quality electoral management

Sustained investments. Some costs will be sustained throughout the duration of the electoral cycle. An EMB will need to have some permanent officials in place regardless of whether it is an election year. There will be ongoing processes such as voter registration infrastructure (unless it is not a periodic process), the buildings which the EMBs work in and sustained utility costs.
Event-related investments. Some costs will be related to a single electoral contest – the holding of a referendum or election. On the day of the election, there will be additional costs for the officials to staff polling stations, the hiring of premises etc.
Security investments. Some costs will be for security or the integrity of the election. These traditionally have been thought to fall in or around election day, where extra police may be required to secure polling stations. However, threats may emerge at other points. Cyber threats, as illustrated by the alleged Russian interference in the 2016 US Presidential election will need to be guarded against. Security investments may therefore be event-related or sustained investments.
Campaign investments. Some democracies provide candidates or parties with free postage, airtime or resources at another part of the electoral cycle. These will need budgeting for but are separate from the main costs.
Project investments. Most costs are tied to a point in the electoral cycle and are therefore cyclical in nature. However, there is another way in which the timing of some costs should be conceptualised: project time. A major reform might be introduced that may take several years to implement. This may therefore cover two or three electoral cycles and might raise costs during implementation. Projects may also have unanticipated costs which continue into the longer term. Chapter 9 provides a case study of where this happened in the UK.

Chapter 12 provides information on EMB budget sizes in a range of countries. This shows considerable variation – but budget size cannot be used as a direct measure of electoral management quality. For example, if country A spends more money than country B – does this mean that elections are taken more seriously? Or that money is spent less efficiently?

There is some useful literature on best practices in budgeting, set out by organisations such as the OSCE (2015b) and the IMF (2014). Space doesn't permit a full review, but some core principles that should apply to EMBs are:

- *Sufficiency.* As has already been noted, It is important that EMBs are provided with sufficient resources for them to be able to deliver the election or the quality of electoral management can be undermined.
- *Transparency.* Open transparent accounting for the income and expenditure of EMBs is important for at least three reasons. Firstly, it increases confidence amongst stakeholders that money is being spent appropriately. Secondly, it provides for accountability as an EMB can be criticised for the misuse of funds. Thirdly, it allows lesson drawing. EMBs with similar demographic characteristics can compare budgets to see whether they have sufficient funds. This can allow them to lobby for more – or look for ways to spend money more efficiently. Partly for these reasons, financial transparency is a much-prized practice within democracies and banking systems. *The Financial Transparency Code* was devised by the IMF (2014) to set out best practices for transparency which includes the coverage, frequency and timeliness, integrity and quality of information.
- *Sustainability of funding.* Elections are an ongoing process, as the electoral cycle illustrates. Short-term and lump-sum investment may be required to overcome immediate pressures or cash restraint. But it is important that funding is available over the longer term. Donors or overseas governments invest into the electoral process in the short term to get elections up and running but what about the longer term? It is helpful to think in terms of *administrative time* rather than civil time as we more commonly think of it. The electoral cycle usually evolves over a period of around five years. But there are also projects that will require budgets that will take place over a period of time that is different to the electoral cycle. For example, an EMB may decide to change the voter registration process to introduce a new national electoral register but this will take several years. During this time several national or local elections may take place. Sustainability therefore requires thinking about where costs fall with respect to the electoral cycle and ongoing projects.
- *Legitimacy of funding.* Having multiple sources of funding is sometimes necessary to ensure sufficiency and sustainability. Donors such as governments or NGOs may decide to provide direct assistance to the election. Money may even come from private sector sources. Some sources of income could be seen as illegitimate in the eyes of the public and other stakeholders, however. This is most likely to be a problem in transitioning democracies where it could be considered as 'outside interference' or 'Western Imperialism'. The donation of funds from overseas organisations may undermine the electoral process as a result and affect other outcomes.

Evaluating electoral management performance 65

- *Contingency.* Unexpected things happen. Inflation can suddenly change costs, perhaps in response to global shocks such as rises in oil prices or geopolitical stability. Trade unions may mobilise to bring demands for higher wages. Equipment can be damaged through floods, technology may need to be updated and additional polling stations may be needed due to population rises or the building of new housing developments. Risk management plans are therefore essential to ensure that shock rises to costs can be covered.

4.3.3 Service output quality

As all public sector management frameworks suggest, the quantity and quality of service outputs need to be measured. Measuring the quantity of outputs is relatively straightforward. All activities undertaken to register citizens to vote, provide them with voting facilities and count the votes can be quantified. In addition, activities that seek to encourage citizens to register to vote and participate could be included alongside any voter education work. Some key examples are provided in Table 4.2.

However, we need to think further about what good *quality* services would look like. Four criteria are suggested here:

- *Convenience.* In some countries registering to vote and voting is much more convenient for the citizen than in others. Complex ID requirements might be required at polling stations, voting hours might be restricted and EMB websites may provide limited information about how to register to vote. There is an instrumental reason for why convenience matters: it can affect voter turnout. Political science theories of political participation based on rational choice institutionalism have long argued that making voting an easier process will increase turnout since it reduces the costs of participation (Wolfinger and Rosenstone 1980). Although there are limits to rational choice theory (Blais 2000) the effects of calculus is acknowledged in other approaches (Peters 2005). There are also many empirical studies that provide support for this although the effects can sometimes be relatively small (James 2010a, 2011a, 2012). Electoral registration and voting procedures should therefore be convenient as voting provides public good Just as the state encourages greater health care by seeking to develop health care preventative interventions, such as vaccines or taxes on alcohol and tobacco to tilt behaviour, the state has an equal responsibility to make voting convenient to tilt behaviour where possible.

  However, a second argument for convenience is that it has value in and of itself. As a matter of principle, government services should be convenient for the individual citizen. Service convenience is valued within the private sector for example, (Berry, Seiders, and Grewal 2002) and it should equally be so within the electoral process. It is relatively easy to check and compare procedures between states to consider where the electoral process is made more convenient for voters.
- *Accuracy.* Services should be provided without error. When electoral stationery is printed it should be done without misprints. Poll workers should not misdirect voters and counting staff should not miscount votes. Technology,

Table 4.2 The PROSeS matrix for evaluating electoral management

Dimension of performance		Focus
Process Design	Public participation	The involvement of citizens and groups in the design of electoral management processes
	Probity and impartiality	The proper use of public funds and the absence of fraud by electoral administrators
	Accountability	Redress for errors such as miscounting, rejection of paper or long polling queues. Provision of key information on services such as availability of key performance data, financial information etc.
Resource Investment	Transparency	There is transparency in the income and expenditure of EMBs with open access to data
	Sustainability	The electoral processes have stable and sustainable funding arrangements
	Legitimacy	The funding of the electoral process is seen as legitimate by actors
	Contingency	Preparations are made for unexpected events
Service Output Quality	Convenience	The ease by which citizens can register and vote
	Accuracy	Whether elections are delivered with precision and without error
	Enforcement	Rules are enforced
	Efficiency	Cost per unit of production
Service Outcomes	Formal effectiveness	Voter turnout; registration accuracy and completeness; cases of electoral fraud; rejected ballot papers; service denial; violence
	Equity	The distribution of registration and turnout rates by gender, age, race, income, geographical area and other dichotomies
	Diffuse impact	The broader positive and negative side effects such as levels of civic engagement, creation of databases useful for providing other government services
	Cost per unit of service production	Cost per registration and vote cast
Stakeholder Satisfaction	Citizen satisfaction	Citizen satisfaction with the services provided and confidence in the electoral process
	Staff satisfaction	Levels of staff satisfaction
	Stakeholder satisfaction	Satisfaction from parties, media and wider civil society in the electoral process

such as punch card machines or electronic voting equipment, should accurately record the intentions of the voter.
- *Enforcement*. Administrative or legal rules need to be enforced or political equality will be undermined. If polling stations are required to close at 7pm then they should close at 7pm. If polling clerks are required to ask all citizens for voter ID, then they should do so. To do otherwise would undermine the principle of political equality because citizens, parties and candidates would be treated unevenly.
- *Efficiency*. It is often argued that providing electoral officials further resources will lead to better run elections (Clark 2014; James and Jervier, 2017) and, by logical extension, more resources should be provided to improve elections. However, electoral officials, like all public servants, are required to work with finite sources. Just as an unlimited number of beds and nurses can't be provided to hospitals, there are limits on the budgets and number of staff available to electoral officials. The efficiency of electoral services is vital and it is the *optimal* allocation and use of resources that should be achieved and not the maximal. Different definitions of efficiency are useful. Boyne usefully distinguishes between two forms of efficiency (Boyne 2002, 17–18). Technical efficiency is a measure of the *cost of each output*. For example, the cost of providing 300 polling stations can be calculated. However, we could also calculate the *cost of each outcome*. For example, how much was spent on polling stations per the number of people who voted in them.

4.3.4 Service outcomes

Evaluating service outcomes involves assessing the effectiveness of service outputs. What did they lead to? Profit, share value and revenue are usually the key performance indicators of success for private companies. When it comes to the implementation of the electoral process then the following are important:

- *Voter turnout*. Low turnout can undermine popular control of government because low levels of political engagement signal weakened accountability mechanisms. If turnout is disproportionately lower amongst some groups, then it will undermine political equality because the winners of electoral contests might not be representative of the interests of the electorate as a whole. This is one key performance indicator, however, that any EMB has relatively little control over. There are a huge number of factors that determine levels of voter participation (Smets and van Ham 2013). Nonetheless, if we are to assess the quality of electoral management, then levels of voter turnout should be included. Variations between similar polities, and within geographic areas/groups in those polities, may indicate that EMBs could and should undertake action to remedy situations.
- *The accuracy and completeness of the electoral register*. The accuracy of the electoral register has been usefully defined as the extent to which

68 Performance

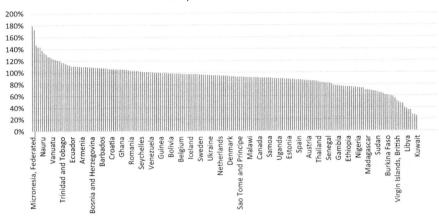

Figure 4.2 Completeness of the electoral register estimates around the world in 2017.
Source: Author based on data from International IDEA.

there are 'no false entries on the electoral registers' (Electoral Commission 2016b, 5). Accuracy is therefore the measure of the percentage of entries on the registers which relate to verified and eligible voters who are resident at that address. Inaccurate register entries may relate to entries which have become redundant (for example, due to home movement), which are ineligible and have been included unintentionally, or which are fraudulent. The completeness of the electoral register, meanwhile, is the extent to which every person who is entitled to be registered, is registered. The electoral register should include all citizens eligible to vote. The reality, however, is that a combination of organisational, demographic and political factors combine to mean that millions of electors are often incorrectly registered or missing from the electoral rolls entirely. This is a major problem because studies of election day have found that many people are turned away from polling stations because their names are not on the register (Clark and James 2017). Calculating the completeness of the electoral register is not easy, however. A simple calculation can be derived by dividing the number of names on the electoral register by the estimated eligible electorate. In many countries, however, there is no central population registrar so population estimates have to be used. The advantage of this measure is that it is quick and easy to calculate (James and Jervier 2017a). Figure 4.2 below uses data on the numbers on the voter registry and the voting age population from the International IDEA Voter Turnout Database, for the last parliamentary election for which data was stored as of December 2017. It demonstrates an enormous variation in implied levels of completeness from 178.9 per cent for the Micronesian 2017 parliamentary election, to 25.4 per cent for the Kuwaiti 2016 parliamentary election. The disadvantage of this measure is that inaccurate or double entries may mask underlying incompleteness. A register might look 100 per cent complete, but 2 million people may have registered twice. Nonetheless, the estimates in Figure 4.2. tell us something: there are problems in Micronesia and Kuwait. If the estimate is above 100 per cent then there are problems with accuracy, if it is below 100 per cent – there are problems with completeness.[3]

- *Levels of electoral fraud.* The ideal delivery of election involves no breaking of the rules by parties, candidates and voters. Electoral fraud, in this sense, is the breaking the legal rules governing the election. Such a definition is limited insofar as the rules themselves may violate democratic principles, as Chapter 2 notes, and a qualitative assessment of the legitimacy of any violation of the laws is therefore required.
- *Rejected ballot papers.* Many votes that are cast at an election are not included in the final result. This could be because voters deliberately spoilt their ballot paper in protest, especially in countries where voter turnout is compulsory or the election itself is controversial. However, eligible and considered votes are often not included. This might be because of poor ballot paper design, misinformation or poor voter education, or faulty stationery/election technology. The highest-profile case was the USA Presidential election in 2000. Across the whole country, 1.9 per cent of votes were invalid (Stewart III 2006, 158) but attention focussed on the state of Florida which effectively decided the contest (Wand et al. 2001). The concept of the residual vote was developed on the back of the American experience to measure 'all ballots cast that did not record a vote. . . . In a mechanical sense, a vote can fail to be counted either because there was no vote . . . on an individual's ballot (an 'undervote') or multiple marks (an 'overvote')' (Stewart III 2006, 159). Rates can be compared across and within countries to identify unusually high rates which might be indicative of problems. An analysis of data from the International IDEA Voter Turnout Database reveals that between 1945–2017 the global mean proportion of invalid votes cast was 2.1 per cent, with a range rates as high as 44.4 in the 1995 Parliament election in Peru. Focussing only on those countries in which voting is not compulsory and are Free, according to Freedom House, Saint Lucia's 1979 Parliamentary election recorded the record high of 19.9. The French 2017 Presidential election was not far beyond with 11.5.[4]
- *Service denial.* Service denial is when an eligible citizen attends a polling station, but is not given a ballot paper. This may often be because they have not completed the necessary paperwork such as registering or have the requisite form of identification. The 'fault' therefore may technically lie with the citizen in an administrative sense. However, there is a burden on

the administrative machinery to make the bureaucracy involved in voting minimal and communication clear. The lines of causation are therefore more complicated and qualitative interpretation might be needed. Polling station incident reports, social media data, poll worker surveys and post-election surveys of citizens can help to identify the frequency, nature and causes of these denials.

- *Violence*. The case of Kenya 2007 demonstrates why we would want, elections to be free of violence (see Chapter 1). While the realisation of democratic values is important, the loss of life is of central importance. Again, violent clashes between competing groups or the sabotage of polling equipment are often outside of the immediate control of the EMB – at least in the short term (Höglund 2009). But these problems also emerge from a political context in which the EMB is involved. In the more conceptual language used in Chapter 2, EMBs are agents within a structural context. No discussion can therefore be had about electoral management quality without a consideration of violence and intimidation.

Effectiveness involves more than an assessment of these measures, however. We should also consider:

- *Equity*. A significant variation in outcomes by gender, ethnicity, disability or other social cleavage also generates political inequality, which should be considered.
- *The diffuse impact* on other government services. If a service has negative effects on other departments by making them inefficient then this matters too. For example, heavy investments in security on election day may need to be met by the police or armed forces.
- *Cost per unit of service production*. Efficiency is also important at the level of the outcomes. For example, what was the cost per registration and vote cast?

4.3.5 Stakeholder satisfaction

Accepting Boyne's arguments for including service *responsiveness* in to measures of success, which were set out above as an important corrective to the IOO model, means that EMBs should be assessed by their levels of satisfaction among stakeholders. The key stakeholders include:

- *Citizens*. Satisfaction amongst citizens is probably the most important. If citizens feel as if the election is not well run then they may come to question the result, or the broader system. Democratic consolidation might be threatened or broader support for the political system will be undermined. Surveys of citizens can be used to ascertain this.

- *Staff.* Levels of satisfaction amongst staff working in EMBs has rarely been considered in the assessment of electoral management. (see: James, 2019) Staff satisfaction matters for instrumental reasons, however. The effects are commonly thought to include improved retention and performance. There are also moral reasons: organisations have a duty of care towards their employees. Surveys and focus groups of workers can be used to research this.
- *Parties and civil society.* Whether political parties, candidates, pressure groups and other non-state actors have confidence that electoral processes are functioning well can have profound consequences for the stability of the system. If political parties decide not to accept electoral results then protests and physical conflict can ensue. Acceptance of the results of elections by losers and the peaceful transition of power is a defining feature of democracy for many scholars (Przeworski 1999). Confidence in the electoral process amongst stakeholders is also important because they are cue setters for the public, who may not know much about the electoral process themselves (Vonnahme and Miller 2013). Any measure of the EMBs' performance cannot be reduced to the views of stakeholders. Politicians might criticise EMBs as a political strategy to excuse their defeat, knowing that the processes are running smoothly. Opposition politicians will often seek to make political capital out of criticising the government's management of the electoral process. Pressure groups have a duty to be critical and incentives to be overly so to grab headlines. As a result of this, it is difficult to separate their real views from their stated views (see Chapter 2 on realism). Nonetheless, it is part of the job of EMBs to build confidence amongst stakeholders, so this remains an important part of the measurement.

4.4 Applying the PROSeS model: comparing Canada and UK

This chapter now applies the framework, summarised in Table 4.2, to the cases of Canada and the UK. An assessment is taken of the overall system of electoral management over the period 2013–2018. Canada and the UK are chosen because they are both relatively stable and mature democracies but with different EMB structures: one centralised, one decentralised. This makes analysing two cases a relatively simple task which is helpful because this is the first application of the model set out above. The focus is on national general elections. The cases were constructed through an analysis of secondary resources including EMB documents, available polling data, news stories and other available information, as set out in Chapter 3. Many documents were taken from the EMB websites in March 2018, which means that the analysis also reflects information available at that moment in time.

4.4.1 Process design

There are few direct ways in which citizens are given an input into the design of the implementation machinery to ensure *public participation*. Both countries are parliamentary democracies and have select committee systems in place. In the

72 Performance

UK, there were occasional select committee enquiries about aspects of electoral management and members of the public are able to submit evidence and have done so. Government white papers also provide opportunities to submit evidence. The Canadian system provides a more direct mechanism for public involvement because the legislation goes through committees, who can propose amendments. Committees can call witnesses to inform their work – and individuals are encouraged to submit written briefs and can even request to appear before a committee (Parliament of Canada 2018). In practice, there is little public participation, however. In the Canadian Standing Committee on Procedure and House Affairs (2017) review of Bill C-23 (that became the Fair Elections Act), 80 witnesses were heard. But these were all expert or NGO representatives. Neither country has any history of providing any deliberative forum for citizens. That said, both Elections Canada and the Electoral Commission have undertaken regular surveys of citizens asking about their satisfaction with the system, which are well cited in their own research work. Elections Canada also set up an Advisory Group for Disability Issues in advance of the 2015 polls consisting of disability advocacy groups (Elections Canada 2018a).

No concerns have been raised about the *probity or impartiality* of electoral officials. While there are occasional cases of electoral fraud (see below), neither country has seen any serious improper conduct by electoral officials themselves – or bias towards any candidate. The OSCE Observation report from the 2015 Canadian Election praised Elections Canada for 'professional performance, impartiality and transparency' (OSCE 2015a, 6). The OSCE raised no concerns in this respect about the UK 2015 general election (OSCE/ODIHR 2015b).

There are mechanisms for delivering *accountability* in both systems, although they are complex, and in the case of the UK, slow, inaccessible and lack transparency. Three organisations were responsible for handling complaints within Canada. Citizens were asked to report problems with the administration for elections to Elections Canada. Complaints about automated calls or online advertising needed to be reported to the Canadian Radio-television and Telecommunications Commission. The Commissioner of Canada Elections was the independent officer whose duty it is to ensure that the key legislation, the Canada Elections Act and the Referendum Act, are complied with and enforced. The Commission had powers to contact the Director of Public Prosecutions who might instigate prosecutions (Elections Canada 2018b, 2018c). It may also, however, draw up a compliance agreement. Whenever the Commission had reasonable grounds to believe that an individual was about to commit or had committed a violation of the Canada Elections Act, it could draw up a voluntary agreement with them so that they take the actions necessary to ensure compliance with the Act (Commisioner of Elections Canada 2018a, 2018b).

The process was even more fragmented and confusing in the UK. The Electoral Commission had a clear complaints page on its website, but it referred citizens to their local authority Returning or Registration Officer for issues relating to electoral registration, voting or polling station issues (with different arrangements in Scotland and Northern Ireland) (Electoral Commission 2018b). Local Electoral

Registration Officers (EROs) and Returning Officers (ROs) can pass on evidence of electoral fraud to the police. The Crown Prosecution Services are then responsible for taking actions. Accountability systems are weakened by the fact that Returning and Registration Officers were exempt from freedom of information requests because they are not a public authority under the Freedom of Information Act 2000. Nor is it clear how EROs and ROs process complaints and no data is available on how many they receive. Meanwhile, the only way in which the result of an election can be contested in the UK was by formal legal proceedings called election petitions. Petitions could be raised by candidates if there an error made by an election official such as the inaccurate counting of the votes, or if there is an electoral offence committed by an opposing candidate or their agent. The petition would then be heard in an open court, presided over by a judge without a jury. The court can declare the election void or another candidate elected (Electoral Commission 2012a, 6–8). The system of raising an election petition, however, was heavily criticised by the Electoral Commission and senior members of the legal profession. Firstly, the system was not seen as accessible or transparent for many candidates wishing to lodge complaints. The initial cost alone of a parliamentary petition was over £5,500. This is especially problematic when unclear electoral law made it difficult for candidates to be certain that they would be likely to be successful. Costs might therefore increase substantially if a case proceeds to a hearing. Returning Officers or the Electoral Commission were not able to bring forward cases on behalf of candidates, despite being well placed to do so because of their knowledge and expertise. Secondly, the process was time-consuming. Complex cases can take nearly two years before a decision is made. Cases where an inadvertent error is made by an electoral official can even take many months for a case to be processed. In the meantime, the declared winner remains in office and there is political uncertainty for the electorate, candidates and parties (Electoral Commission 2012a).

4.4.2 Resource investment

Financially transparent EMBs should publish their accounts openly online. Elections Canada did provide detailed quarterly financial reports online, in order to fulfil legal requirements set out in the Financial Administration Act. The online accounts make the quarterly spending and the annual budget clear; $70.4 million was spent in 2017–2018 (Elections Canada 2017b). Budgeting and expenditure was much less transparent in the UK, mostly because funding is split across so many different organisations (see: James and Jervier 2017b, 6–7). Central government pays for the cost of running an election in Westminster, European and Police and Crime Commission elections, even though local Returning Officers organise the election. For these contests, the amount that the Returning Officer can reclaim (a 'Maximum Recoverable Allowance') is set out in a statutory instrument of Parliament. But how much of this has been claimed has not been routinely published. The costs of running Welsh and Scottish elections have been borne by the Scottish and Welsh Parliaments. Local authorities in England and

74 *Performance*

Wales cover the costs of compiling the electoral register (but it is organisations called Valuation Joint Boards and a Chief Electoral Officer for Northern Ireland in Scotland and Northern Ireland respectively). The Electoral Commission has published the costs of organising referendums for which it is responsible (Electoral Commission 2012c), and has published a one-off study of the cost of electoral administration across the UK (Electoral Commission 2012b) – but there is no routine place to identify costs. Transparency was therefore much greater in Canada, and a general inference might be that transparency is easier when electoral management tasks are centralised into one or a smaller number of organisations. The absence of transparent information in the UK led to newspaper headlines claiming that Returning Officers were receiving 'cash bonuses' (Braiden 2016a, 2016b; Kerr 2016). A parliamentary inquiry followed in Scotland which led to calls for reform (Local Government and Communities Committee 2017). We might therefore also extrapolate that transparency can assist popular confidence in the electoral process.

Both the Canadian and UK systems are relatively robust in terms of *sustainability*. They are both funded by public spending and are therefore not reliant on external actors. However, it is important to note that the UK struggled with a public sector deficit since the financial crisis of 2017–2018. This sent public sector debt to 10.1 per cent of GDP in 2010 (OECD 2017). The central government response to this was to reduce public expenditure, which has placed some uncertainty on electoral officials, especially following the introduction of individual electoral registration (see Chapter 9). Canada has also faced public spending pressures, however, with a deficit persisting from 2009–2016 (OECD 2017).

The Canadian system seems to have better practices in place to cover *contingency*. The Elections Canada financial statements provided statements on risks and uncertainties. The end-of-quarter report for 30 September 2017 included a statement about how the number of electoral events could affect expenditure, but also how a new public sector pay system had made some salaries unaccounted for (Elections Canada 2017b). No such statements were found in the decentralised UK system. It is unclear whether the sharing of costs across so many organisations provides greater flexibility – or makes coordinated and effective planning impossible.

There is no reason for concern about *legitimacy* of the funding for elections in either case, since in both cases it is entirely funded by the taxpayer through public finances.

4.4.3 Service output quality

Convenience is the first assessment criteria for output quality. Voter registration was much more convenient in Canada. UK electoral registration has always been an individual rather than state responsibility. The principle was further embedded in 2014 with the switch from household to individual electoral registration (see Chapter 9). Each citizen was required to provide their National Insurance

Number at the point of registration and their details were checked against a government database before their name was added to the register. Canada also moved from household to individual electoral registration in 1997. However, a system of automatic registration was established at the same time. A National Register of Electors was constructed using publicly held records such as tax agencies, motor vehicle agencies, immigration authorities and local electoral registers. This national database is then used to construct voter registers at the beginning of federal elections and referendums (Black 2000; Elections Canada 2017a). Canadian citizens had an additional level of convenience: they could register at polling stations on election day. In 2015, 777,000 did so – 5.8 per cent of all election-day voters. Elections Canada concluded that: 'This indicates that many electors continue to prefer the "one-stop-shop" approach of registering and voting at the same time' (Elections Canada 2015a, 17). In the UK, citizens had to register 11 days in advance of the election. Many registrations missed the deadline and were therefore presumably citizens (186,000 in 2015, 174,000 in the 2017 election).[5] This is roughly equal to two and a half electoral constituencies – all of whom would have been unable to vote.

Both countries operate online electoral registration. The UK system was introduced in 2014. In Canada it became available on a nationwide basis for the first time at the 2015 general election (Elections Canada 2015a, 15). In both countries it was enormously popular (Elections Canada 2015a, 16). One area where the UK has greater convenience is that it registers 'attainers' – those citizens who will be eligible to vote within the life of a register i.e. 16- and 17-year-olds (but 14- to 15-year-olds in Scotland where 16-year-olds can vote in some elections). Canada did not register 'attainers' because Elections Canada can't legally obtain or store data until a Canadian citizen is 18 (Elections Canada 2015a, 15, also see: Garnett 2019a).

The voting process was also more convenient in Canada. UK polling traditionally takes place on a Thursday between 7am–10pm although citizens could register in advance for a postal vote. There are also options, in limited circumstances, for proxy voting. Pilots were undertaken for advance voting and some electronic methods between 2000–2007, but these were not carried forward (James 2011a). By comparison, Canadian citizens could vote for 12 hours on the day of the election and also opt to vote by mail. Canadians were also presented with opportunities for advanced voting (on the 10th, 9th, 8th and 7th days before election day) (Elections Canada 2019). Where Canadian voting was less convenient was with Voter ID provision. In contrast to the system in Britain (but not Northern Ireland) where citizens need only state their name in a polling station, Canadians had three options. They can either show a single piece of identification with their name, address and photograph on it. Alternatively, they can provide two documents, both with their name, and at least one with their address. A third option involves an elector showing two documents with their name and having another citizen attest for their address (Elections Canada 2015a, 26). The Fair Elections Act 2014 eliminated the use of voter identification cards and citizens 'vouching' for each other (OSCE/ODIHR 2015a, 2).

76 *Performance*

Concerns were raised in Canada about the *accuracy* and *enforcement* of rules after a legal dispute in the electoral district of Etobicoke Centre in May 2011. It was claimed that the result of the election should be 'null and void' as a result of procedural 'irregularities' (Superior Court of Justice 2012). Elections Canada commissioned an independent sixth-month review of the problem of 'non-compliance' with rules and standards afterwards. This involved a nationwide audit of poll documentation. This claimed to show 'that problems associated with compliance in the Etobicoke Centre riding were not unique' (Neufeld 2013, 6). In fact: '[o]verall, the audit estimated that "irregularities" occurred for 1.3 percent of all cases of Election Day voting during the 2011 federal election' (Neufeld 2013, 6).

Elections Canada commissioned Price Waterhouse Coopers to undertake a compliance audit of poll worker practices at the 2015 general election. This found that election officials exercised their powers properly, although there were some inconsistencies in the administration (e.g. record-keeping) for electors who had special procedures – those who registered on the day or had to give an oath (Elections Canada 2015a, 44–6). The UK saw some cases of maladministration hit the news. For example, 1,500 people were unable to vote in Newcastle-under-Lyme in the 2015 general election, in a constituency that saw the successful MP win by only 30 votes. An independent report found that there was 'inadequate performance by inexperienced and under-resourced elections office staff' (BBC News 2017). Similar nationwide audits to those undertaken in Canada have not taken place, however, because the decentralised nature of UK electoral administration means that there is no power or duty of Returning Officers or Electoral Registration Officers to undertake them. It is therefore difficult to get an overall picture. However, it is clear from the cases that problems with electoral management do routinely occur, even in established democracies and that the centralised system in Canada can bring greater transparency by ordering such audits to assess performance.

4.4.4 Service outcomes

When assessing *formal effectiveness* of service, turnout is a good starting point. As Figure 4.3 illustrates, turnout in both countries have seen a long-term decline in parliamentary elections, despite a small recent upward trend in the most recent contests. Turnout is substantially lower amongst younger age groups, however. In the 2015 Canadian elections, turnout was over 20 percentage points lower amongst the 18–24 age group than the 65–74 age group (Elections Canada 2015a, 31). Similar patterns are present in the UK, despite talk of there being a 'youthquake' in participation the 2017 general election (James 2017; Sloam and Henn 2018). There are also disparities by indigenous citizens in Canada (Elections Canada 2015a, 32). Variations in turnout have been documented in the UK by geographical region and professional class (Denver 2015). Turnout at sub-national elections has been substantially lower (Dempsey 2017).

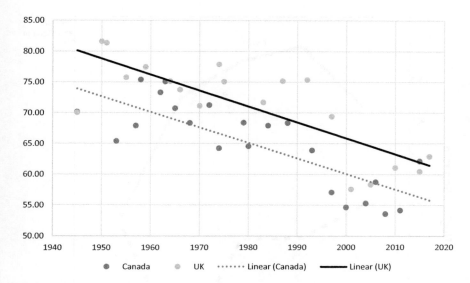

Figure 4.3 Voter turnout at parliamentary general elections in the UK and Canada.

As was noted earlier, there are a variety of factors that shape voter turnout, above and beyond EMBs. However, post-election surveys often ask citizens for their reasons for not voting which is often due to the electoral process. Elections Canada surveys show that half of non-voters didn't participate in the 2008, 2011 and 2015 elections due to 'everyday life issues' such as being too busy, out of town, ill or limited by a disability. Another 8 to 11 per cent didn't participate because of what was defined as 'electoral process' issues such as not being able to 'prove an identity or address, transportation problems, a lack of information about when and where to vote, not being on the voters list or issues with the voter information card' (Elections Canada 2015a, 33). Similar figures were reported after the UK 2017 general election (Electoral Commission 2017b).

Figure 4.4 provides crude estimates of the completeness of the electoral register, calculated by dividing the names on the electoral register by the eligible voting population. In both countries there was a substantial decline after 1945 in completeness. The figure suggests that this was partly reversed in Canada in the late 1990s, however, which was around the time that the National Register of Electors was introduced, suggesting that this was hugely successful at boosting completeness. More precise, but infrequent, studies give a closer picture. The UK Electoral Commission estimated, based on a study which involved canvassing properties to check whether individuals living there were correctly registered, that the December 2015 parliamentary register was 86 per cent complete, and 91 per cent accurate (Electoral Commission 2016b,

78 Performance

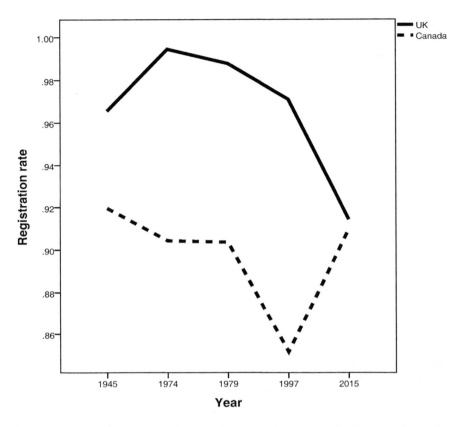

Figure 4.4 Estimates of the completeness of the electoral register in the UK and Canada, 1945–2015.

Source: Author calculations based on data in International IDEA (2018).

6). Elections Canada gave estimates that the October 2015 register was 88.3 per cent complete and 94 per cent accurate (Elections Canada 2015a, 18).[6]

Both countries have therefore had similar levels of performance with respect to completeness. They also exhibit problems with equity. At the 2015 Canadian General Election, only 60 per cent of 18-year-olds were registered, compared to over 90 per cent for other age groups. Likewise, completeness rates were 65 per cent for 18- and 19-year-olds in the December 2015 register, compared to 96 per cent for the over 65s. The Electoral Commission study also provided more detail by revealing the register to be less complete in urban areas (especially within London), amongst recent movers and private renters, Commonwealth and EU nationals, non-white ethnicities, lower socioeconomic groups, citizens with mental disabilities and young people (Electoral Commission 2016b, 8–11).[7]

Evaluating electoral management performance 79

A further measure of service outcomes is the number of *rejected ballots*. Figure 4.5 below shows levels of rejected ballots at parliamentary elections since 1945. Rates have dropped considerably in the UK since the 1950s, leading to very low levels – much lower than in Canada where rates have historically varied, but also been in decline since the mid-1990s. These rates are considerably below global averages. The rejected ballot rates at other types of elections are much higher in the UK where different electoral systems are used.

Both systems have been hit by concerns and headlines about electoral fraud. In the UK, high-profile cases of electoral fraud have caught the headlines. An elected mayoral candidate in London and/or his agents were found guilty of a range of

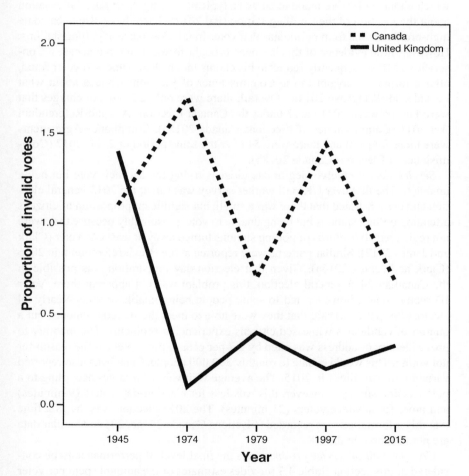

Figure 4.5 Percentage of votes cast that are invalid at general elections, 1945–2015.
Datasource: International IDEA (2018).

offences including personation, postal vote fraud, illegal employment of paid canvassers, bribery and undue spiritual influences (Pickles 2016, 65). Accusations of electoral fraud have become increasingly common since 2000. There was an average of 298 allegations of electoral fraud per year between 2010 and 2017.[8] Despite the headlines and accusations, however, only a small proportion of these led to prosecutions or convictions since most were resolved locally, individuals were acquitted or sufficient evidence was available. In 2017, for example, there was one prosecution and eight police cautions (Electoral Commission 2018a, 7). Less than 1 per cent of polling officials were concerned that electoral fraud had taken place in their polling station at the 2015 general election (Clark and James 2017).

In Canada, international headlines were caught by the Robocall scandal, in which phone calls were made to citizens, typically giving them false information about the location of their polling station (Pal 2017). There have also been some high-profile claims from politicians that voter fraud takes place at polling stations. However, little evidence of this has been brought forward and in one case a Conservative MP subsequently retracted his claims that he had witnessed voter fraud, after a formal complaint to the Commissioner of Elections Canada about what he had said (Wingrove 2014a). Overall, there were only 22 cases of charges that were laid between 2011–2017 under the Canada Elections Act and Referendum Act 2011 (Commissioner of Elections Canada 2018a). Compliance Agreements were more frequent and there were 54 over the same period of 2011–2017 (Commisioner of Elections Canada 2018b).

Service denial involves legitimate citizens trying to cast their vote but being unable to The first ever UK poll worker survey was run at the 2015 general election and demonstrated that there was a small, but significant proportion of citizens attending polling stations but being unable to vote, presumably because they were not registered. Two-thirds of polling stations turned away at least one voter (Clark and James 2017). Similar patterns were reported at the Brexit referendum in 2016 (Clark and James 2016a). Given that election-day registration was possible in the Canadian 2015 general election, this problem was not apparent there. Voter ID requirements, however, led to some people being unable to vote. Nearly all electors (99 per cent) said that they were able to meet the ID requirements, but a quarter of candidates witnessed citizens experiencing problems. The inability to prove identity or address was cited by 2.7 per cent of non-voters as the reason for not voting. This would equate to roughly 300,000 people. Canadians also reported variation in wait times in 2015. The average wait was 12 minutes according to a post-election survey. However, this was less for election-day voters (9 minutes) and more for advance voters (21 minutes). The 2015 election was the first time that this information was recorded (Elections Canada 2015a, 23) and similar data are not available in the UK.

Cost per unit of service production is the final level of performance to be considered in this section. Table 4.3 provides estimates of the amount spent per voter in two general elections in each country that were calculated by the author.[9] Data about the expenditure in Canada was taken from the Elections Canada Annual Financial Statements. Data from the UK was taken from a survey of electoral

Table 4.3 Estimates of expenditure per eligible voter and per vote cast (figures in US$)

	2010/2011		2015	
	$/VAP	$/Votes	$/VAP	$/Votes
Canada	10.51	19.41	13.71	22.07
United Kingdom	5.22	8.57	4.65	7.68

administrators undertaken in 2016 (James and Jervier 2017a).[10] International IDEA's voter turnout database was used to identify the Voting Age Population (VAP) and the number of votes cast at each election. A calculation was made for the cost per person in each currency. The 2010/2011 figures were then adjusted for inflation at the 2015 rate using the respective national bank websites. All figures were then converted into US dollars as of 3 April 2018 using the website www.xe.com/currencyconverter/.

On the basis of Table 4.3, the UK seems to demonstrate a higher level of efficiency. It is also noticeable that Canada saw the costs of running elections substantially rise between these two general elections. In comparison, expenditure *fell* in the UK. It should be noted that arguments have been raised that UK electoral officials have been under-resourced in recent years (James and Jervier 2017a). But it does suggest that efficiency per unit of outcome is higher.

Satisfaction

Neither country features in the World Values Survey and an exactly comparable measure of *citizen satisfaction* is not available, but EMBs have regularly run their own surveys of citizens after each general election that provide reasonably reliable and useful measures. The UK Electoral Commission has also run a 'Winter Tracker' survey, which reports end-of-year confidence levels in the electoral process. Satisfaction levels were generally better in Canada. Taking *registration* first, the UK Electoral Commission surveys undertaken between 2008 and 2016 found that anywhere from 75 to 85 per cent of respondents were satisfied with the process of registering to vote (Electoral Commission 2018c). Satisfaction was marginally higher following Canada's 2015 election, where 88 per cent were satisfied with the registration process that they used (Elections Canada 2015a, 16). This was a major increase on 2008 and 2011. The difference between countries with the *voting process* is more significant. After the 2015 Canadian election, 96 per cent were very satisfied or somewhat satisfied with the voting experience (Elections Canada 2015a, 21). Earlier Elections Canada surveys only asked more precise questions about satisfaction with waiting times, the distance to the polling station and electoral officials, which were all above 96 per cent in 2008 and 2011 (Elections Canada 2011, Appendix 3). In contrast, satisfaction with the voting process varied between 64 and 77 per cent in the UK between 2006 and 2016 (Electoral Commission 2018c). When asked what would increase their satisfaction with the voting process, respondents in 2016 cited more information on the parties and candidates' standing and their policies (31%), a proportional voting system (23%), internet voting (17%), increased security against electoral fraud (17%) and more information on how the voting process works (5%) (ICMUnlimited 2016). Greater convenience might therefore help but there are concerns about electoral fraud, despite the fact that there are few cases. Between 42–45 per cent of people agreed that there could be 'enough electoral fraud in some areas to affect the election result' in the annual 'Winter Tracker' surveys between 2012–2016, although only 7 per cent thought electoral fraud was common 'where I live'. Half of respondents thought that there was sufficient safeguards to prevent electoral fraud, a quarter did not (ICMUnlimited 2016). The problem of fraud is therefore largely a perception-driven one.

In terms of *accessibility*, nearly all Canadian voters (98 per cent) said that it was easy to reach the polling station in 2011 (Elections Canada 2011). Considerable efforts were made to improve accessibility, which included a checklist of 35 accessibility criteria being issued to Returning Officers. Most (96 per cent) but not all of polling places met these criteria (Elections Canada 2015a, 24). Complaints were still made about disability access – with 18 per cent of complaints made to Elections Canada focussing on this (Elections Canada 2015a, 29). A third of voters with disabilities stated that wheelchair signs were not visible (Elections Canada 2015a, 25). The UK Electoral Commission has historically collected less information about disability. However, its report on the 2015 general election found that 5 per cent of people with disabilities were dissatisfied with the voting process. This was higher than 2 per cent for those without a disability. Concerns were also raised in civil society groups (Electoral Commission 2015, 47–8). Efforts to improve accessibility include detailed guidance to Returning Officers – but, unlike in Canada, there is no system to monitor enforcement. Following this, a call for evidence was launched by the Commission asking for information about disabled voter experiences. This brought a wealth of qualitative information with examples such as citizens finding polling stations too narrow or pencils hard to hold (Electoral Commission 2017a). In 2018 a poll worker survey of the local elections found that 14 per cent of poll workers did encounter a disabled voter having a problem completing their ballot paper (Clark and James 2018). Persistent problems therefore seem to exist in both countries.

Information on *staff satisfaction* at the poll worker level is available in both countries, revealing general contentment. Elections Canada collected information about job satisfaction among their poll worker staff in 2016. Most (95 per cent) were content with the working conditions, although officers who worked in the advance poll were significantly more likely to report working conditions were 'not at all good'. Of those who were not happy, the commonly cited causes were a lack of a break, the place of work, the number of hours worked or the complexity of unique cases. Salary and equipment were much less likely to be cited (Elections Canada 2015b). The first poll worker survey in the UK, which was undertaken by academics at the 2015 general election, found staff generally content about their training and administration of the election and their experience of being a poll worker – with 97.9 per cent saying they were likely to work as a poll worker at the next election (Clark and James 2016b, 2017). Data is also available at the middle-manager level in the UK, however, which as Chapter 11 sketches out, did reveal some difficult workplace conditions including stress and a high proportion of staff considering leaving their posts in early 2016, following the transition to individual electoral registration. There has been no similar survey in Canada.

Concerns about voter fraud have been raised *amongst stakeholders* in the UK, often along partisan lines. On the back of a high-profile case of electoral fraud in the Tower Hamlets mentioned above, a Conservative Councillor from the area, Cllr Peter Golds, prominently called for action to stop fraud (Golds 2015). A right-wing think tank published a report claiming that electoral administration 'has long been, and remains, remarkably shoddy' and that 'there remains within the various bodies responsible for electoral administration a culture of complacency and denial' (Pinto-Duschinsky 2014, 6). Left-wing groups such as Hope Not Hate and democratic reformists such as the Electoral Reform Society, Bite the Ballot and parliamentary inquiries, meanwhile, raised concerns about whether democratic engagement was being hindered by restrictive voting practices (Hope Not Hate 2015; James, Bite the Ballot, and ClearView Research 2016; Select Committe on Political and Consitutional Reform 2014; Select Committee on Political and Constitutional Reform 2015).

In Canada, 'for the most part stakeholders are happy, but every once in a while there are storms' (private interview, senior electoral official, July 2018). Most significantly, there were concerns about vulnerabilities for electoral fraud which led to the Conservative government's enactment of the Fair Elections Act, which prohibited vouching and the use of the voter information card as a valid piece of identification. Concerns were then raised amongst civil society groups, academics and parties on the left that this could restrict opportunities to vote. An open letter from 19 professors was signed and sent to *The Globe and Mail* arguing that the Act would 'undermine the integrity of the Canadian electoral process, diminish the effectiveness of Elections Canada, reduce voting rights, expand the role of money in politics and foster partisan bias in election administration' (Wingrove 2014b). A court case was raised to challenge the constitutionality of these changes by the Canadian Federation of Students and the Council of Canadians, but the Liberal government of Justin Trudeau also introduced bill C-76 to undo most of the Fair Elections Act (Bryden 2018). One other area of concern, which diminished over time, was the use of enumerators to knock on doors to register voters. This practice was gradually ended by Canadian EMBs. Elections Canada conducted its last nationwide enumeration in 1997. By October 2017 only Elections Manitoba was undertaking full enumerations because of challenges with costs and the declining efficiency of the tool. Concerns have been raised by some candidates and party organisers that the register was not as complete and accurate as it could be and that Canada should 'go back to the old way of doing things' (private interview, electoral official, 2018). However, these concerns receded over time (Larkins 2017). Democracy Watch, meanwhile, raised concerns about ethics and conflict-of-interest issues; and the National Citizens Coalition has been active on campaign finance roles arguing against an egalitarian law. However, these are slightly outside of the remit of this case study.

4.5 Conclusions

This chapter has sought to develop a new framework for assessing electoral management by developing concepts used to assess public services and apply them to the elections. The new framework, the PROSeS model, has then been applied to the two initial cases in order to demonstrate its utility and tease out problems applying it.

The model has the advantage of identifying comparative strengths and weaknesses of systems across countries, which is sensitive to the quality of information available and contextual circumstances in which electoral officials are functioning. This produces useful academic knowledge about whether democratic ideals are being realised and the quality of public administration. However, it can also be used to inform practice and improve policy. The assessment can be based on the best available evidence and can therefore be undertaken where there are not a large sample of experts, which is a pre-requisite for other approaches.

A UK–Canada comparison reveals many similarities in terms of performance. However, the Canadian system seems to demonstrate clearer systems of accountability in the process design, greater transparency with resource investment, more convenient services, less frequent service denials to voters, and higher satisfaction with citizens. The UK system seems to be delivered more economically and efficiently, has fewer rejected ballots and hasn't exhibited the same accuracy enforcement issues that the Canadian system has – but this might be for a lack of critical examination. A general lesson might be that centralised systems are better positioned to produce more transparency and accountability – but are more costly. Yet further cases and applications of the approach would be needed to generalise in such a way.

There are several potential criticisms of the model that should be taken head-on. The first is that there are too many variables, too few cases – a classic criticism of behaviouralist political science (Lijphart 1971, 686). Can we please crunch this into a single figure to provide more parsimonious country-level scores? As Chapter 3 noted, there are lots of advantages in that – but we miss out on important information about the quality and historical development of electoral management in all of the different areas. Comprehensiveness, detail and context allows policy makers to identify the nature of important problems that are lost in a simplistic score. Researchers are prevented from identifying important underlying causal relationships.

Related, a criticism might be that we have too many dependent variables here – how can we examine all of these? Again, the purpose of the book is to point out the importance of electoral management – and identifying all of the important dimensions is necessary to achieving that task. This is not to stop future researchers picking one aspect of performance as the dependent variable, whether it is the completeness of the electoral register or the extent of financial transparency, and tracing the causal relationships involved. However, a country-level assessment of electoral management should involve an assessment of all of these.

Lastly, surely an assessment of all of the dimensions is unrealistic? How would we find all of the data? Even within this chapter, data is missing on important aspects of performance from two relatively open and transparent democracies. While this is true, the absence of information forms part of the assessment. An approach that is based on a discussion and analysis of whether principles have been achieved is also much more sustainable and transferrable than a method that requires long-term research funding for repeated rounds of surveys to draw out lessons.

The chapter has therefore set out a new broad set of measures to assess performance. The remainder of the book will explore the challenges in achieving this and what can be done to improve it.

Notes

1 Boyne's categories of outputs, efficiency, outcomes, responsiveness and democratic outcome were renamed for simplicity.
2 The term 'investment' is used instead of 'cost' as a rhetorical switch to show the positive importance of this funding to society. The term 'diffuse costs' that was used by IFES – referring to costs borne by other organisations – is dropped because the organisation that pays is not important – they are all costs to the taxpayer. Lastly, it is important to separate out project costs as reforms to the electoral process may involve short-term costs (see Chapter 9 for a case study of this). I am grateful to participants of the workshop hosted by International IDEA to design a new Building Resources for Democracy, Governance and Elections (BRIDGE) module on the financing and budgeting of elections, in Stockholm, November 2017. These collaborative discussions helped to inform some of the work here.
3 The most advanced method for checking completeness and accuracy would include house-to-house enquiries or telephone enquiries to check the completeness of the register against the data collected. This would be the most reliable method but would be expensive and only a sample of households could be checked. Other methods might include comparing the register with other nationally held data such as censuses, health records or private sector information. The downside of these approaches is that they assume that these alternative records are more complete and accurate than the register itself.
4 International IDEA Voter Turnout Database, date accessed 27 February 2018.
5 Data was collected by the author from the Cabinet Office Electoral Registration Dashboard: www.gov.uk/performance/register-to-vote on 30 March 2018.
6 Note that Elections Canada uses the terms 'coverage' and 'currency' rather than completeness. For Elections Canada, 'coverage is the proportion of eligible electors (Canadian citizens aged 18 and over) who are registered'. 'Currency' is 'the proportion of eligible electors who are registered at their current address' (Elections Canada 2015a, 18). The concept of currency is therefore closer to that used by the Electoral Commission, which is used in this book.
7 For more on the UK registers, see: James (2017).

86 *Performance*

8 Calculation based on Electoral Commission (2018a, 6).
9 Both countries held general elections in 2015. Canada's 41st general election was held on 2 May 2011. The UK held a general election on 6 May 2010.
10 This data currently doesn't include the costs of the Electoral Officer for Northern Ireland.

Part III
Networks

5 Electoral management governance networks

5.1 Introduction

The book so far has laid down some philosophical grounds for the study of electoral management and set out a framework for how to evaluate it. Part III of the book now turns to a deceptively simple question: who actually runs elections?

EMBs, of course, play a key role in the delivery of elections and are therefore the key focus of study. However, EMBs come in very different forms, shapes and sizes. The usual distinction that is made is between independent, governmental and mixed systems based on a coding of formal-legal institutions (International IDEA 2014; López-Pinter 2000). This chapter argues that this categorisation system, the premise of much existing research, is of limited use. Firstly, it oversimplifies the number of actors that can be involved in implementing elections. In practice, elections are often implemented by networks of actors rather than one single individual organisation. This might include actors in different government and non-governmental organisations and even the voluntary sector or citizens. Secondly, it focusses on formal but ignores informal relations between actors: how often do they meet? Is there a consensus on policy? Do they have close personal relationships? Thirdly, the formal-legal approach ignores how the actions, strategies and behaviours of key individuals (such as EMB leaders) can affect organisational success and electoral integrity. Managerial and political leadership can be a key determinant of success of public sector organisations.

The chapter therefore begins by reviewing existing approaches to categorising EMBs and the problems associated with them. It suggests that much can be learnt from the policy networks literature. A new framework is then developed to categorise the policy network in a given jurisdiction involved in steering and implementing of elections. The concept of electoral governance networks is introduced which refers to *the constellation of actors involved in steering and delivering elections, including the working practices, beliefs and power relationships between them*. A typology of different types of electoral governance networks is set out on the basis that we countries according to three dimensions: the membership and level of integration; the degree of policy consensus; and, resource distribution and power balance. Subsequent chapters provide case studies from different countries and contexts to identify the type of network in each case. Lessons for those seeking to strengthen electoral integrity are considered in the concluding chapter.

5.2 Categorising electoral management boards: a critical review

EMBs are crucial organisations in the implementation of elections and democracy. The *Electoral Management Design* handbook defines an EMB as an organisation that:

> has the sole purpose of, and is legally responsible for, managing some or all of the elements that are essential for the conduct of elections and direct democracy instruments – such as referendums, citizens' initiatives and recall votes – if those are part of the legal framework.
>
> (Catt et al. 2014, 5).

The classic typology of EMBs was first established in 2000 when a UNDP report classified 148 countries according to whether the government ran elections (a governmental system), the government ran elections under supervision from an external organisation (a mixed system) or whether an independent organisation was responsible for running elections (an independent system) (López-Pinter 2000). This was followed by International IDEA's *Electoral Management Design* handbook (Wall et al. 2006), a second edition of which was published eight years later (Catt et al. 2014) that used a similar typology. EMBs were classified purely on the formal-legal rules regarding their relationship towards government and other actors. The *Electoral Management Design* handbook asked seven questions of these rules such as whether the EMB fully implements elections or is subject to direction from the executive branch, whether it controls its own budget or whether it is required to formally report to the executive branch (pp. 9–11). Subsequent studies on electoral integrity typically use this independent variable to consider the determinants of electoral integrity. EMBs that are statutorily independent from government were frequently held up as the 'gold standard' because they are thought to reduce the opportunities for partisan actors to promote their own interests (Hartlyn, McCoy, and Mustillo 2008; Pastor 1999b; Ugues 2014); however, many other studies describe counter-intuitive results with independent EMBs having a negative, none or very limited effect on electoral integrity (Birch 2008; Norris 2015b).

5.3 The critique

The above typology has been enormously influential and helpful in framing the initial debate. However, it is argued here that there are several key weaknesses, which are explained now.

5.3.1 Inter-organisational complexity and relations

Firstly, it is very common for more than one organisation to be involved in the management of elections. According to the *Electoral Management Design* handbook, an organisation is considered an EMB if it undertakes one of these essential tasks:

a. determining who is eligible to vote; b. receiving and validating the nominations of electoral participants (for elections, political parties and/or candidates); c. conducting polling; d. counting the votes; and e. tabulating the votes.

(Catt et al. 2014, 5)

If these tasks are spread over many bodies 'then all bodies that share these responsibilities can be considered EMBs' (Catt et al. 2014, 5). The handbook notes that there might be even more organisations undertaking tasks relating to electoral administration and management, but are not considered an EMB.[1]

The EMS (James et al. 2019). and ELECT (Karp et al. 2016) surveys provide some data to illustrate how many actors might be involved in delivering elections. The surveys included 10 questions about whether 'your organization is responsible for implementing and/or managing the following tasks.' Responses were merged and coded as 1 for 'primary responsibility', 0.5 for 'shared responsibility' and 0 for 'no responsibility'. A simple overall index of responsibility score was created for each responding organisation by converting the sum of the answers to a 0–100 scale. Figure 5.1 provides a histogram of the responses. It shows that there are some EMBs that do implement a vast majority of the electoral process. The Commission on Elections in the Philippines scored 95, claiming that it had primary responsibility for all aspects of the electoral process except electoral disputes

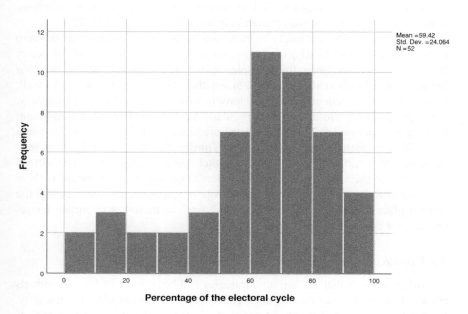

Figure 5.1 Percentage of the electoral cycle delivered by EMBs in the ELECT and EMS surveys.

where it had only partial responsibility. In contrast, there were many organisations that only played a small role. The Norwegian Directorate of Elections scored 5 on the basis that it only had partial responsibility for modifying electoral law.

The focus on the formal EMB also overlooks civil society. In many countries voluntary organisations, political parties and international organisations play a key role in voter registration drives or voter education campaigns, which in effect, often do some of the work of EMBs for them. International organisations can deliver elections in their entirety. The formal-legal approach is therefore problematic because it gives no focus on inter-organisational relations and disputes between all of these actors. Conflict might arise when there are multiple organisations with diverse funding streams, personnel, interests and values. This bureaucratic pluralism requires that these relationships are 'unpacked' since they can have a significant effect on the steering of relations. For these reasons, inter-governmental relations has been a significant sub-discipline in the US and elsewhere (Wilks and Wright 1987, 288–9).

5.3.2 Informal relations

A second problem is that the focus on formal-legal institutions means that there is no coverage of informal institutions: the norms, cultures and the meanings of those institutions. New institutionalism was formed in reaction to an 'old' intuitionalist approach which defined institutions narrowly as 'the rules, procedures and formal organisations of government' (Rhodes 1997, 68). A broader definition and empirical focus emerged so that an institution was taken to mean something as broad as a 'stable, recurring pattern of behaviour' (Goodin 1996: 22).

What informal relations might be important when trying to determine de facto EMB independence? Firstly, *consensus on policy aims and methods*. If actors across organisations agree, for example, on whether reform is necessary, what the priorities of reform should be and/or whether the current system works well, then their statutory independence may have no bearing on their actions. Secondly, *meeting regularity*. Do actors meet regularly to discuss electoral management, keeping it under review? Or do electoral practices go without review for some time? Who are included in such meetings? Thirdly, the *interpersonal connections between organisations*. Do individuals switch positions between organisations bringing with them shared values and beliefs? Fourthly, to what extent is there a *shared broader political culture* on the role of government in society and the 'proper place' of actors within the network? Each of these has important consequences for de facto independence.

5.3.3 Agency and contingency

A third problem is that the actions, strategies and behaviours of key individuals are assumed to have no bearing on organisational success or electoral integrity. Leadership, however, is a key determinant of success of public sector organisations, just as it is in other dimensions of politics. The de facto power that actors have is as much a function of their skilful use of tactics and the development of strategies. Yet, there is no role for this in a formal-legal measurement of EMB structure. A naive EMB might misread the political context and introduce reforms that are unpopular or likely to have the executive stripped it of its powers. The performance of the EMB in delivering elections might be poor. This can undermine its position in trying to shape electoral policy in the future. A leader of an EMB might opt to pursue a risk-adverse strategy to reform for fear of jeopardising their career – or they might be more maverick reform–minded. Individuals matter. Actual power and influence is therefore more complex. Formal-legal institutions are important because they bestow actors with resources. However, the skilful deployment of resources, astute tactics and well-managed implementation are all likely to shape actual power and influence. In short, *outcomes are contingent* on the actors involved in electoral management.

5.3.4 Shifting contexts

A fourth issue is that relations between organisations are assumed to be invariant over time. Studies that treat EMB independence as an independent variable in a quantitative panel analysis, for example, would use a categorical variable with only three possible values (for governmental, independent and mixed). The de facto power of actors can vary considerably over this time, however. For example, socio-cultural practices involved in the decision making and implementation process will change. The effects of changing supplier market structures from monopolies, in which private businesses are powerful, to more competitive markets, are missed. The effects of changes in the availability or use of technological challenges involved in delivering elections will be ignored. Successes and failures in actors' deployment of tactics and resources will lead to ebbs and flows in their power and influence. All of this is data that is lost in a formal-legal approach.

5.3.5 Globalisation

For a long time, the analysis of public policy focussed on decision making and implementation processes within national states. By the 1990s this changed as sociologists pointed out that globalisation had completely reconfigured the nature of the state (Held et al. 2000; Ohmae 1990; Strange 1996). The world had become increasingly interconnected because of the construction of new informational, technological and financial flows. These have combined to develop an intense time-space compression (Harvey 1999). New supranational institutions such as the UN or regional institutions such as the European Union undermined state sovereignty in decision making. Considerable disagreement arose about the extent of these changes. Critics pointed out how some of these transformations were reversible (Held and McGrew 2000; Hirst and Thompson 1999). An alternative perspective stressed regional integration rather than global integration – as illustrated by the growth in regional organisations such as the European Union, African Union, Arab League, South Asian Association for Regional Cooperation and Union of South American States (Hettne 2005).

The globalisation of public policy debate draws attention to how the traditional categorisation of EMBs prevents a discussion of cross-national, regional and international linkages. National EMBs are assumed to be in control of their own internal affairs. The reality, however, might be that there is commonly lesson drawing and international pressure on policy between states. There is a clear need to consider the internationalisation of electoral policy. How are ideas transmitted for good practice in electoral management from the United Nations or other organisations? Claims of electoral irregularities, such as those made by Donald Trump before the 2016 US Presidential election, are beamed around the world. As were accusations made by the CIA, FBI, and National Security Agency (2017) that the Russian government was involved in trying to affect the outcome of the election. A policy change quickly followed in other states with the Netherlands ditching electronic voting machines to maintain public trust (Lowe 2017). The network approach, as will be shown, provides some conceptual space for the presence of these interactions to be identified or ruled out.

5.3.6 *Hollowing out*

The spread of powers upwards to international organisations is not the only way in which national public policy was thought to have changed. Formerly strong West European states have commonly been described as being *hollowed out* in other directions. The advent of New Public Management (NPM) as an academic and ideological blueprint for public sector reform meant that programmes of privatisation were introduced from the 1980s and scopes and forms of public intervention rolled back (Dunleavy and Hood 1994; Hood 1991, 1995; Rhodes 1994, 1997). Osbourne and Gabler's (1992) *Reinventing Government*, which preached the advantages of a small role for government, was influential in the UK, USA and many other parts of the world (Hope 2001). NPM prescribed that government services were best delivered by the private sector and should therefore be 'market tested' or put out to competitive tender. A debate followed about whether NPM improved service delivery (see Chapter 10), but our main concern here is that the number of actors involved in policy implementation quickly expanded.

In the sphere of elections, we can quickly see the relevance. Although elections are not delivered entirely by a private company on behalf of the state, very often, large segments of the infrastructure and technology might be privately owned and supplied (Loeber 2017). This could include election stationery such as ballot papers or voting machines. But it might also involve the contracting out of other activities such as voter engagement programmes. The 'winners' of these contracts are not always private companies. They might also be the third sector. This can open up a new range of questions when we think about issues of *who governs?* A long history of public policy theory suggests that businesses are political actors (Lindblom 1977). There is a risk of oligopolies emerging which can make the state over-responsive to demands of the private sector, especially in the short term. EMBs could then become prone to capture. In states where there is insufficient regulation on the use of personal data, the private sector could use that data for other purposes.

5.3.7 Collaborative governance

By not considering the role of other organisations in delivering electoral management, the EMB typology therefore did not measure whether an alternative approach to public policy implementation is being used to deliver elections: collaborative governance. This involves a deliberate attempt by public agencies to 'directly engage non-state stakeholders in a collective decision-making process that is formal, consensus-oriented, and deliberative and that aims to make or implement public policy or manage public programs or assets' (Ansell and Gash 2008, 544). Collaborative governance is presented by Ansell and Gash as a normative ideal that public agencies should seek to achieve. The aim of collaborating is to take previously adversarial positions and engage in positive-sum bargaining so that cooperative alliances emerge. Managerialist systems of governance involving closed decision-making processes or simply involving limited consultation with groups can be replaced with stakeholders directly involved (Ansell and Gash 2008, 544).

5.4 The policy networks literature

The existing typology of EMBs therefore reduces much of what is important about who runs elections and an electoral governance network model is proposed as an alternative based on the policy network literature. Interest in policy networks has grown exponentially in the past 25 years as it has been increasingly recognised that a greater number of actors were involved in policy making, often as the direct result of new public management reforms (Hood 1991). This had led many to suggest that we live in an era of 'new governance' where the state is often 'hollowed out' of its core decision-making capacities (Rhodes 1997). Since the 1990s, 'policy networks' and 'governance' have probably been guilty of being two of the buzzword concepts. Rod Rhodes (1997) famously cited six possible interpretations of the word 'governance'. Interpretations and usage have no doubt increased substantially since. The purpose of this section is not therefore to provide an exhaustive review — this has been done in detail elsewhere (Berry et al. 2004; Borzel 1998; Klijn 2008; Klijn and Koppenjan 2012; Ramia et al. 2017). Instead, we draw out the key contours of the literature that we can connect to the realist sociological approach set out in Chapter 2 to provide an alternative way for thinking about who is involved in implementing elections.

Tanja Borzel's (1998) distinction between two approaches to policy network theory remains useful. The first tradition is the Anglo 'interest intermediation' school in which policy networks are a way of describing the relationship between the state and interest groups. In short, the question is: who decides policy? The second is the 'governance school' which sees policy networks as a specific method of delivering public services. Rather than services being delivered directly by the state, or markets, they can be delivered via networks. In short, the question is: who implements policy? The two approaches, both of which are useful for our study, are set out, before they are drawn upon to develop a specific framework for analysing the delivering of elections.

5.4.1 'The Anglo School'

The Anglo interest intermediation policy network literature (hereafter 'the Anglo School') began from work on American pluralism in the 1970s and 1980s with scholars such as Heclo and Wildavsky (1974), Heclo (1978), and Ripley and Franklin seeking to describe the relationships between the 'clusters of individuals that effectively make most of the routine decisions in a given substantive area of policy' (Ripley and Franklin 1984, 8–9). This included those in sub-national government, elected representatives in national government, bureaucratic officials in government departments, pressure groups from civil society and private sector actors. As Dowding (1995, 137–8) notes terms such as 'whirlpools' 'sub-governments', 'triangles', 'sloppy hexagons', 'webs' and 'iron triangles' were used to describe different configurations of these relationships.

The starting point for the Anglo literature is that policy making is an exchange relationship in which 'participants manoeuvre for advantage deploying . . . [their] . . . constitutional-legal, organisational, financial, political and informational resources to 'maximise their influence over outcomes' (Rhodes 1990, 303). This exchange relationship occurs within networks which are:

> sets of formal institutional and informal linkages between governmental and other actors structured around shared if endlessly negotiated beliefs and interests in public policy making and implementation.
>
> (Rhodes 2006, 426)

Policy network theorists established typologies to characterise the nature of the network under study. Based on the UK, Rod Rhodes's (1986) early work identified five types of networks, which are detailed in Box 5.1, alongside other types added by later scholars.

Box 5.1 Different types of policy networks identified by the Anglo School

- Policy communities which were characterised by stable relationships, highly restrictive membership, vertical interdependence based on shared service delivery responsibilities and insulation from the other networks, the general public and Parliament.

- Professional networks are characterised by the dominance of one single group dominating the policy process who are able to insulate themselves from other actors – the profession. The UK National Health Service was provided as a key example.
- Intergovernmental networks are based around the representatives of sub-national governmental organisations. These exclude unions but are otherwise broad in their membership with many different types of services involved. They tend to have relatively little vertical integration because the network does not deliver a service itself, but they can bring together actors from a wide range of other actors.
- Producer networks are implied to be those involving suppliers. Here economic interests dominate. There is a heavy reliance on industrial organisations for their expertise and supply of goods.
- Issue networks were defined by a large number of participants, low levels of stability and continuity within the network structure. This was assumed to be the result of a high level of interdependence.
- Epistemic communities were famously identified by Haas as: 'A network of professionals with recognised expertise and competence in a particular domain and an authoritative claim to policy-relevant knowledge within that domain or issue-area' (Haas 1992, 3). These networks are characterised by a shared set of normative and principled beliefs which inform their action; shared causal beliefs derived from their practices about the pressing problems at a given time; shared methodological understandings for weighing evidence and validating knowledge; and a common attempt to influence policy (Haas 1992, 3).

Dimensions of policy networks

Although early work identified descriptive categories of policy networks, Rhodes and Marsh (1992) eventually identified four common dimensions and sought to map policy networks along a continuum according to these dimensions. This allowed them to simplify network types down to two types: policy communities and issue networks (Table 5.1). *Policy communities* described those networks that were more closed. There would be a smaller number of actors and there would be a high degree of consensus on policy. This could be achieved by excluding many possible actors from the network. At the other extreme, a *policy network* would be the more open network. There would be more actors, less consensus, but there would be a great deal of inequality in terms of the resources and power of these actors. Actual empirical cases would most likely exhibit features of both, they thought, and could therefore be placed on a continuum between the two.[2]

Table 5.1 Rhodes and Marsh's (1992, 187) typology of policy networks

Dimension	Policy community	Issue network
Membership (a) Number of participants (b) Type of interest	Very limited number, some groups consciously excluded Economic and/or professional interests dominate	Large Encompasses range of affected interests
Integration (a) Frequency of interaction (b) Continuity (c) Consensus	Frequent, high-quality interaction of all groups on all matters related to policy issue Membership, values and outcomes persistent over time All participants share basic values and accept the legitimacy of the outcome	Contacts fluctuate in frequency and intensity Access fluctuates significantly A measure of agreement exists but conflict is never present
Resources (a) Distribution of resources (within network) (b) Distribution of resources (within participating organisations)	All participants have resources, basic relationship is an exchange relationship Hierarchical, leaders can deliver members	Some participants may have resources, but they are limited and basic relationship is consultative Varied and variable distribution and capacity to regulate members
Power	There is a balance of power between members. Although one group may dominate, it must be positive-sum game if community is to persist	Unequal powers, reflects unequal resources and unequal access. It is a zero-sum game

Criticisms

The policy network literature has its critics. One criticism is that research and analysis would be better focussed on the traditional actors such as Prime Ministers, Parliaments and Presidents. James (2012, 2016b) argues that a focus on meso-level explanations of policy change, such as policy networks, can leave important macro sources of change, notably the influence of powerful hegemonic actors, external to the model. This is especially important in the field of elections given that executives will commonly be seeking to bend the rules of the game to maximise their prospects for successful statecraft, bypassing networks when it suits them. Similarly, Kassim argues that where institutions and actors are given considerable powers and resources, networks become less important. Network theory is of limited value, for example, for exploring relations in the EU because the EU constitution gives actors such as the Commission considerable power (Kassim 1994). In response, it should be noted that executive actors can still be included within policy network analysis. Situating them into networks remains important, however, because executives will often have to focus time on valence issues that will determine electoral outcomes such as the economy, immigration or health care (James 2011c, 2012).

The applicability of the network model outside of democracies could also be questioned because executive actors are endowed with so many resources that their hegemony within networks becomes a foregone conclusion. Clientelistic and autocratic political culture is present in many societies and it is so far unclear whether these relationships can be well captured by policy network theory. Davies et al. (2016), however, apply traditional policy network concepts to Russia. Their empirical analysis shows that governance networks have emerged in areas such as migration, drug prevention and child protection because the state has initiated and established a variety of consultative bodies, grant schemes, multi-agency programmes, and public–private partnerships (Aasland, Berg-Nordlie, and Bogdanova 2016). As might be expected, these networks are asymmetric with tight state control over membership, agendas and ability to affect policy. But in this sense, networks have similarities with those in Britain (Marsh, Smith, and Richards 2003).

A final criticism is that the approach provides a typology of network formations without any causal explanation of how those different arrangements come about in the first instance. It would be better, Keith Dowding suggests, to focus on the strategic actions of the actors as these drive the properties of networks (1995, 2001). The development of a dialectic approach by Marsh and Smith (2000) is designed to tackle the problem flagged by Dowding. They suggest that networks have a causal effect on policy outcomes and future network structures through a three-stage interactive process between structure and agency, which is dialectical in nature. Firstly, critical of approaches that purely focus on the rational strategic actions of actors, or the structures (the network), they claim that both are important. Routinised micro anthropological behaviour of networks can structure member's behaviour, opening up constraints and opportunities. But members of networks are also capable of 'strategic learning' that causes them to change the network structure. Secondly, there is a dialectical process between the network and the context. Exogenous economic, ideological, political and knowledge-led change can cause networks to change, but networks can cause this external environment to change. Thirdly, networks can affect policy outcomes, but policy outcomes can lead to changes in the structure of the network. Typologising and identifying network types therefore matters for considering how policy choices are made, which options are excluded and electoral management performance outcomes.

5.4.2 The governance school

A second approach is to see policy networks as a specific form of governance. Rather than focussing purely on *who decides*, policy networks are conceived as a particular implementation system in the modern era which provides an alternative to hierarchies or the market. It is therefore is a response to developments in the public sector which have emerged over many years such as the introduction of new public management. This reflects that, as Borzel (1998, 260) put it: '[g]overnments have become increasingly dependent upon the co-operation and joint resource mobilization of policy actors outside their hierarchical control.'

In a more recent review Klijn and Koppenjan (2012, 588–9) separate out the histories of this school further. An 'inter-organisational service delivery and policy implementation' tradition emerged from organisational science. Citing the work of Rogers and Whetten (1982) and Hjern and Porter (1981), this approach was principally concerned with how organisations resource share. Each is dependent on other organisations for survival. A separate tradition emerged from within public administration on manging networks – the idea being that networks can be utilised by the state to solve wicked policy problems. Klijn and Koppenjan explain that this approach is closely linked with the development of a more complex (post-)modern network society (Castells 2000).

Research that has roots in these broad schools have noted how networked forms of governance can bring both advantages and disadvantages as a system for allocating resources and managing services. One network formation already mentioned, is collaborative governance. For Ansell and Gash (2008, 544), this is:

> A governing arrangement where one or more public agencies directly engage non-state stakeholders in a collective decision-making process that is formal, consensus-oriented, and deliberative and that aims to make or implement public policy or manage public programs or assets.

They undertook a meta review of 137 cases of collaborative governance to claim to identify the critical variables upon which successful collaboration is contingent. This included the prior history of conflict or cooperation, the incentives that were in place for stakeholders to participate, any power and resource imbalances, plus the leadership and institutional arrangements (Ansell and Gash 2008). Elsewhere, Jessop (2000) warns that while governance was developed as a response to market and state failure, there are causal mechanisms such that can lead to governance failure. The use of partnerships in public policy does not prevent coordination problems – it can introduce new ones.

5.5 A new approach: electoral management governance networks

This chapter has so far identified weaknesses in the basic approaches that were initially developed to typologise who runs elections. The literature on policy networks was then introduced. The argument of this book is that this provides a richer approach to understanding how elections are managed and implemented. But we are left with the challenge – which policy network approach should be used?

'The Anglo School' is helpful in identifying the greater number of actors involved in influencing decision making. The focus on interest-group intermediation seems to be more relevant for explaining *rule making* – a different level of electoral governance set out in the introductory chapter of this book. As the introductory chapter argued, implementation is inseparable from decision making because decisions are always being made about how to deliver services. Yet a focus on the resources, power and tactics of actors would only give us a partially complete answer to the question of who runs elections. The governance school seems more satisfactory in this respect. It allows us to identify delivery systems for managing elections. However, it doesn't have a set of dimensions for identifying network types. A mixture of both is therefore proposed to establish a networked governance approach to studying electoral management.

The new approach involves studying electoral management governance networks which are the constellation of actors involved in steering and delivering elections, including the micro anthropological practices, beliefs and power relationships between them. The approach has five methodological premises:

1 **Define electoral management in functional not institutional terms.** Rather than restricting analysis to the formally named EMB, analysis should include all organisations which play some role in organising elections and consider the whole unit. This analysis would therefore include civil society and state bodies. Just as a biologist would not study an animal that forms part of whole animal in isolation,[3] we should study each contributory part and the whole of the *overall electoral management system*. It is the whole system that concerns us, and not the individual organisation.
2 **Delivery and decision making.** The literature on networks and implementation teaches us that implementation and decision making are inseparably joined as Chapter 1 argues. We are therefore interested in both.
3 **Methodological pluralism.** Cross-national data about the nature of governance networks would certainly be valuable (and is provided later in Chapter 7). But in line with the arguments of Chapters 2 and 3, a richer, qualitative analysis of a smaller number of country-level cases will help to identify the fuller range of actors involved in electoral governance. Process tracing can be used to identify the causal effects of different network types implementing elections in different ways (Collier 2011; Goertz and Mahoney 2012).
4 **Electoral management systems as open polities.** The boundaries of the national state are clearly important as electoral contests take place in defined geographical areas which will shape the range of actors who are interested. However, in an inter-dependent world, there will be international actors interested in promoting the quality of electoral management and undermining it. Suppliers might be multi-national companies. There will also be active policy learning from other jurisdictions as news from overseas elections enter policy cycles. Electoral management works are therefore clearly capable of transcending the national state.
5 **Network identification.** Using the prior premises, research can identify the types of electoral management governance networks for delivering elections

in a given polity by seeking to identify the properties of the network. Drawing from the above literature, three core dimensions are suggested:

a **Delivery partnerships.** What is the *range of the number and type of actors involved in delivery*? Are they small or large in number? Are they local, national or is there some international involvement? What role is there for civil society or even political parties in implementing parts of the electoral process? Are private contractors a prominent and important part of service design or delivery – or are public sector units used? What is *the degree of integration*? How frequently do actors meet? Are there regular meetings with systematic agendas? Do the 'usual suspects' meet in different venues? Or is there no common contact between actors? Relatedly, to what extent is there *vertical integration*? To what extent are the networks connected or disconnected to other countries and the international system? Do they have regular contact with other countries and embark on policy transfer? Or do they remain remote islands in the policy universe?

b **Contestation.** *Is there fierce disagreement on how elections should implemented?* What are the cleavages in those disagreements? Between independent EMBs and the government? Between political parties? Or between civil society and government? Where does class, gender, disability and disadvantage feature in those debates? Or conversely, is there a common consensus – or simply seldom any discussion?

c **Power diffusion.** What r*esources and strategies* are available to actors seeking to shape the delivery of elections? Are there core inter-dependencies or specific strategic weaknesses? Can electoral administrators shape practices or can government dictate how the process functions? On the basis of this, where is the *balance of power*? Does it lie with the government who are able to choose to manage elections in a way that they wish, including for partisan statecraft? Or are there strong checks and balances against this?

5.6 Conclusion

This chapter began by reviewing existing frameworks for identifying the key actors who implement elections. This was developed by the international community of practitioners at the turn of the twenty-first century. It has proved useful up to a point, but it oversimplifies, paints an inaccurate account of who really delivers elections and the dynamics of power relations. It is not surprising that research findings have often produced counter-intuitive results. The chapter has argued that by drawing from the literatures on policy networks and governance, a richer set of concepts can be borrowed to develop a different typology. Three core dimensions are identified as possible ways in which governance networks might vary.

The next chapters will look to explore empirical case studies to examine the following questions:

1 How useful is this governance network model for understanding policy making and implementation in electoral administration and management?
2 What are the causal effects of governance properties on electoral management outcomes?
3 In what ways do governance networks vary?
4 Is it possible to identify different types of networks?

Notes

1 These include organisations that undertake 'other tasks that assist in the conduct of elections and direct democracy instruments such as other registration, boundary delimitation, voter education and information, media monitoring and electoral dispute resolution' (p. 6).
2 Other dimensions have been developed. For example, Waarden (1992) identifies seven dimensions, which leads her to be able to identify four different types (statism, pantouflage; captured statism; clientelism; and pressure pluralism). However, many of these are included in the Rhodes and Marsh framework.
3 In biology, a zooid is a single animal that is part of a colonial animal. Each zooid or polyp plays a contributory role towards the overall colony animal and without each, the overall animal would not function. For example, the Pacific Man o' War is a made up of individual organisms including a float (pneumatophore), the tentacles (dactylozooids) for the detection and capture of food and that convey their prey to the digestive (gastrozooids). Reproduction is carried out by the gonozooids, another type of polyp. (I found out after trying to prevent my kids being stung on Sydney beaches and ended up swotting up with my seven-year-old at the Australian Museum (2017).)

6 UK electoral management governance networks

6.1 Introduction

Opening a seminar on 'Electoral Fraud and Registration' at Kings College London in June 2018, Professor Sarah Birch remarked that: 'Now is an exciting time to study electoral administration and integrity in Britain – major changes are not just being piloted, but being made.' Around the room were 30 participants who shared ideas for how elections should be reformed and their concern about change. Electoral officials from London shared their experience of running controversial voter ID pilots only the month earlier. The Electoral Reform Society spoke about their campaign against the voter ID pilots. One council criticised the Electoral Reform Society for claiming that there was 'chaos' at the pilots that they run when 'there was clearly not' – and this was 'very unhelpful'. Computer scientists introduced arguments for how blockchain and distributive ledger technology could be used to manage electoral registers. Political scientists weighed in with research on electoral registration – in my case, the results of surveys of electoral officials (the research reported in Chapter 10, no less). The Electoral Commission set out the feasibility studies that it would like to develop to modernise electoral registration in the future. Room 1.02 in Bush House, a grand Grade II listed building that formerly hosted the BBC World Service, but now refurbished with slick dark yellow walls and modern sanded floor boards, was for one day the venue to a rich set of ideas and experiences that were flowing about how elections should be managed.

It was not always so. How elections are organised in Britain has often been a topic consigned to the dusty book shelf. Classic texts by David Butler (1963) narrating the early twentieth-century parliamentary debates that led to the 1918 system of electoral registration, have stood collecting dust in many university libraries since, without modern political science applying 'rigorous' methods to the topic. Parliamentary enquiries since have been few in number and light in submissions of evidence from civil society groups. Yet in 2018, the centenary of the 1918 Representation of the People Act that established the electoral registration system, a new community was engaged in the issue of electoral administration and management.

The previous chapter in the book argued that implementing elections is a complex task, in which multiple organisations and actors are involved – in both delivering and shaping ideas about how to deliver elections. To recognise this, a networked governance approach was introduced as an alternative theoretical framework for identifying different delivery systems around the world. This chapter provides a single country case study of the UK 1997–2018 to reveal the transformations in the network properties that took place during this time.

After outlining the methods used, the chapter is structured around the three dimensions of the network framework: network delivery partnerships, contestation and power diffusion. The chapter argues that the UK underwent a major change in the properties of that network. It also provides an insider account of the author's own attempts to shape the network type from 2015–2017 with the formation of an all parliamentary group focussing on electoral modernisation.

6.2 Methods

Process tracing *within* a single case is used in this chapter to describe and identify changes in the nature of the electoral management governance network (Collier 2011; Goertz and Mahoney 2012). Using this method 'the researcher examines histories, archival documents, interview transcripts, and other sources to see whether the causal process a theory hypothesizes or implies in a case is in fact evident in the sequence and values of the intervening variables in that case' (George and Bennett 2005, 6). The chapter therefore draws from a comprehensive secondary document analysis of reports, minutes of meetings and public statements from members of the network. This is complemented with private interviews with many of the actors which have been undertaken over a 10-year period.[1] This chapter was also written by the author providing an insider account. Having researched the nature of the network and presenting it as a conference paper,[2] I set out to try to make it more inclusive and open up opportunities to use my (co-)published research to influence policy and the quality of UK electoral management. This means that this analysis benefits from having seen policy being discussed at a high level in the UK and having experienced some challenges in trying to influence it.[3] As Chapter 2 argues, researchers, especially if they are proactive at trying to bring about policy change, should consider themselves as actors within their own plays. This approach is therefore compatible with the realist approach to social science set out in that chapter. The UK is a useful first case for using the new framework because the author is uniquely positioned to provide a detailed understanding of the case. Inevitable questions about generalisability will follow, but it is the next chapter in which a greater number of cases are introduced, and extrapolation to theory made.

6.3 Delivery partnerships

The making and implementation of elections in the UK has traditionally involved a small number of actors with a very decentralised delivery system. The Representation of the People Act of 1918 gave responsibility for compiling the electoral register to the Clerk of the Borough or County Council. This was to be done through 'house to house or other sufficient inquiry' rather than the use of rate-books or the work of party activity. This took the job from the poor-law overseers and party agents (Butler 1963, 8–9; James 2012). Legal responsibility was later designated to an Electoral Registration Officer. Meanwhile, Returning Officers were responsible for implementation of the poll. Both Returning Officers (ROs) and Electoral Registration Officers (EROs) were local government employees, appointed by local government authorities, but were independent of both central and local government with respect to their electoral duties. A core permanent team then worked in local authorities at the disposal of the ERO and RO to organise the poll and compile the electoral register. In Scotland, the Valuation Joint Boards (Scotland) Order 1985 gave responsibility for compiling the electoral register to another body which was responsible for local tax. A separate Electoral Office for Northern Ireland, appointed by the UK Secretary of State for Northern Ireland, would implement the poll and register in Northern Ireland.

There is no formal codified UK constitution but law has long been made in Parliament in Westminster. The actors involved in designing electoral law for most of the twentieth century were chiefly the Home Secretary, who traditionally held the ministerial portfolio for election law, their civil servants in the Home Office and the Parliamentarians who would approve its passage, present amendments or propose their own legislation. A tradition had been long established for changes to be made through Speaker's Conferences which aimed to reach all-party agreement on reforms to electoral law (private interview, former civil servant, August 2007). Conferences took place in 1916–1917, 1944, 1965–1968 and 1973–1974 when a Prime Minister asked a Speaker to preside over an all-party committee, with members limited to Parliamentarians from the main parties (White and Parker 2009). There was also a tradition for the Home Office to 'carry out a review of electoral practice following every parliamentary general election to take stock of the experience' and consider areas for reform (Howarth 1999, 1). Ministers would circulate election law proposals to an informal group of representatives from rival political parties, in order to achieve consensus. 'There was never any suggestion of a change unless there was all-party consensus', one civil servant suggested (private interview, civil servant, August 2007). In short, relatively few actors were involved in steering electoral law – it was the preserve of parties, civil servants and Parliamentarians.

After 1997, however, there was a substantial thickening in the number and type of actors seeking to steer and deliver electoral administration and management. Firstly, two key non-governmental organisations were established. The Electoral Commission was set up as an independent statutory body on 30 November 2000 to serve as an advisory body with respect to elections. It was given a statutory requirement to report on the administration of elections and referendums. It was also required to keep elections 'under review, and from time to time submit reports' on electoral matters. Its powers were extended in 2006 to set performance standards for EROs and ROs (James 2013). The Chair of the Electoral Commission, however, was legally required to act as the Chief Counting Officer for referendums, with the power to issue directions to EROs and ROs – a responsibility that was not used until 2011. That was also the year that the Electoral Management Board for Scotland was set up by the Scottish Government with 'the general function of co-ordinating the administration of Local Government elections in Scotland'. This would have no direct rule-making ability with respect to elections. However, the Scottish Independence Referendum Act 2013 designated the Convener of the Electoral Management Board for Scotland, Mary Pitcaithly, as the Chief Counting Officer for the independence referendum. The Law Commission, the statutory independent body created by the Law Commissions Act 1965 to keep the law under review and to recommend reform, also decided in 2011 to undertake a project that would propose consolidating electoral law, thereby providing input into the policy process (Law Commission 2011).

Professional organisations became more proactive. The Association of Electoral Administrators (AEA) was a non-partisan body founded in 1987 to represent electoral administrators. Prior to its formation, electoral officials rarely met. Occasional county-level meetings across authorities, training events organised by the then NALGO Education Department or the South West Provincial Council, and the organisation of referendums were the exceptional occasions when some did (Association of Electoral Administrators 2015b). By July 2015, the Association had 1,857 members, the majority of whom were employed by local authorities to provide electoral registration and election services (Association of Electoral Administrators 2015a, 7). The AEA developed a suite of professional training courses and qualifications for electoral administrators and held annual conferences. By 2017, it held net assets of approximately £3million and employed 55 people (AEA 2017). In addition, SOLACE (the Society of Local Authority Chief Executives and Senior Managers) was the representative body for local government senior strategic managers, who often were also the ROs and EROs, and provided training for its staff and held conferences, often in competition with the AEA.[4]

A greater number of central government departments became involved. Whereas elections were once solely the preserve of the Home Office prior to 1997, a series of governmental re-structures and departmental splintering meant considerable fluidity in the governance of elections. In June 2003, the Department for Constitutional Affairs was set up and given overall responsibility for the Constitution including elections. In May 2007 it was renamed the Ministry of Justice and given some responsibilities from the Home Office. In May 2010, a Coalition government was formed and Liberal Democrat leader Nick Clegg was appointed Deputy Prime Minister as part of the Coalition Agreement. This agreement involved responsibility for elections shifting from the Secretary of State for Justice to the Deputy PM and the Cabinet Office for many aspects of constitutional affairs including the speeding up of the implementation of individual voter registration (Gay 2013). There was also a rapid change in the minister responsible for elections.[5]

There has been new parliamentary interest in electoral administration and management. Labour and Liberal Democrat backbenchers have been proactive in introducing bills and amendments into the Commons and Lords.[6] Chris Ruane, a Labour backbench MP elected 1997–2015, was an 'absolute fanatic on registration' (private interview, Sam Younger, 2011) while Lib Dem peer Chris Rennard was a persistent questioner in the Lords. At least five select committee reports were published from 1999–2015 on this policy area (Home Affairs Committee 1998; Howarth 1999; Select Committe on Political and Consitutional Reform 2011, 2015; Select Committee on Political and Constitutional Reform 2015). The Howarth Committee was the first of these, established by the Home Secretary, Jack Straw, to undertake 'a fundamental re-examination of our electoral process' with the committee chaired by a minister to 'reflect the importance' of its remit (Howarth 1999, 1–2).

After 2005, one senior judge played a key role in advocating policy change. Richard Mawrey gained media attention after he served as an election judge and ruled two local government elections in 2004 invalid because of extensive manipulation of postal votes. His claim that there was 'evidence of electoral fraud that would disgrace a banana republic' caught the headlines (Bowcott 2015; Stewart 2006). Mawrey continued to be prominent in the media, claiming that postal voting should be scrapped (James 2014b).

Civil society became much more active in seeking to steer and contribute towards the delivery of elections. Civil society organisations were not routinely part of the Speaker's Conferences on Electoral Law. Organisations such as the National Union of Students, pressure groups, disability groups and academics increasingly gave evidence to parliamentary select committees to lobby for changes in electoral law, however, during the 1997–2018 period. The involvement of civil society organisations in *delivering* elections is especially notable. A pressure group organisation called Bite the Ballot was founded by a former school teacher in 2010, who was frustrated with the levels of political apathy among his students. Bite the Ballot was initially run 'in coffee shops', but after support from the Electoral Reform Society, the Hansard Society and James Palumbo of the entertainment business, the Ministry of Sound, it quickly grew. It ran civic education sessions, provided resources for those wishing to teach young people about politics, developed registration apps and widgets for use on websites, used celebrities to promote voter registration and led voter registration drives across the country. In 2014 it organised the first ever UK National Voter Registration Day, in co-ordination with a supermarket, schools, the National Union of Students and many other organisations. This received widespread media attention, political support and claimed to have registered 35,000 new voters. In 2015, Bite the Ballot claimed to have registered 441,500 electors over the course of a week with a repeat event. It was widely reported that the group was much more economically efficient than the Electoral Commission's attempts to register voters via information campaigns. Partly in response to these claims, the Cabinet Office provided funding for a range of civil society groups to raise voter registration rates in the run-up to the 2015 general election. Bite the Ballot also lobbied the government for legislative changes for more expansive voting and registration procedures, with the support of Members of the Lords (Bite the Ballot 2014; private interview, Bite the Ballot official, 24 July 2015).

They were not alone. The Electoral Reform Society (ERS), who had campaigned since 1884 for electoral system reform, suffered a setback in 2011 when a referendum on whether to adopt AV for elections to Westminster was lost. The organisation undertook a review to 'take stock' and decided to 'broaden out their focus to the democracy field'. They therefore organised a roundtable in October 2011, inviting stakeholders to discuss the impact of the introduction of individual electoral registration (IER). From that meeting onwards the organisation campaigned for reforms to electoral registration and collaborated with other civil society organisations such as 38 Degrees to organise voter registration drives (private interview, ERS official, 3 April 2015). The work of these organisations was self-initiated, but in the run-up to the 2015 general election, the government did spend £4.2 million funding five voluntary organisations to promote electoral registration and engagement in under-registered groups including the disabled, homeless, young and homemovers (Cabinet Office 2015). Bite the Ballot itself did not receive initial funding but was later given money, two weeks before the registration deadline (private interview, Bite the Ballot official, 24 July 2015). Webroots Democracy was also launched in 2014 by Areeq Chowdhury. At the age of 21, Chowdhury had only just graduated but set up the group to campaign for internet voting after he was studying the relationship between the internet and political participation as an undergraduate at university. The group describes itself as a 'voluntary, youth-led think tank' with the aim to help 'modernise, enhance, and future-proof democracy in the United Kingdom.' The team also included recent university graduates, including from 2016 Oliver Sidorczuk shortly after he left his role as Advocacy Coordinator at Bite the Ballot (Webroots Democracy 2018).

Lastly, private sector interests have mobilised to influence electoral law, as will be discussed below. Credit reference agencies were thought to take interest in the sale of the electoral register for commercial purposes, but then became involved in a proposed data-sharing agreement with the Electoral Commission, brokered by Bite the Ballot. ICT companies would commonly have representatives at conferences held by the AEA in order to sell their products. They would also have an explicit policy presence speaking in favour of the use of technology in the voting process. Technology that they were selling.

And then there were the academics. Interest rapidly expanded, from a standing start. No academics formed part of the Home Office Working Party on Electoral Procedures that became known as the 'Howarth Committee' that reported in 1999 and shaped the RPA 2000 (Howarth 1999). Sarah Birch and Bob Watt wrote an article in *Political Quarterly* 2004 arguing that remote voting posed a threat to the secrecy of the ballot (Birch and Watt 2004) and sought to influence public policy with it (Essex University 2014). Stuart Wilks-Heeg subsequently began to write on the topic after being commissioned to write a report on the 'purity of elections' by the Joseph Rowntree Reform Trust (Wilks-Heeg 2008). The commissioning of that work was therefore a result of the electoral fraud cases. The Electoral Commission subsequently advertised for an ESRC-funded Placement Fellowship at the Electoral Commission on the 'The State of the Electoral Registers' which Wilks-Heeg was awarded, and led to the publication of the two reports on the completeness and accuracy of the electoral registers in Britain (Electoral Commission 2010a; University of Liverpool 2014; Wilks-Heeg 2012). Alistair Clark meanwhile began to write on the topic, after examining a PhD thesis at the University of Newcastle written by Judy Murray on US electoral administration reform from the early 2000s (Murray 2012) and the problems that had occurred at the 2007 Scottish parliamentary elections. Michael Pinto-Duschinsky, who had previously written on party finance, wrote a report for the right-wing think tank policy exchange in 2014 criticising the Electoral Commission (Pinto-Duschinsky 2014). For my own part, my interest started in 2000 when I wrote an undergraduate dissertation on the UK electoral pilots in 2001 (following the suggestion of my supervisor Dr Keith Alderman – because, as he told me, 'a dissertation on electoral system reform would be very boring... everyone has done that'). That dissertation was updated and published many years later (James 2011a). I started a PhD thesis on comparative electoral administration in 2005 and undertook further research that is partially detailed in this book. I was initially inspired by the work of American scholars and campaigners Frances Fox Piven and Richard Cloward (Piven and Cloward 1988, 2000) who argued that racial and economic inequality could be more easily addressed if everyone voted, and that electoral administration had been designed to prevent this. There was a memorable image of them standing with campaigners behind Bill Clinton as he signed the 1993 National Voter Registration Act. Could academic research achieve the same in Britain?

What was the nature and frequency of all of the actors? Interaction between the newly thickened array of actors varied. Borrowing from neo-statecraft, at the apex of the British political system is the court – a close-knit clique consisting of the Prime Minister and their most inner advisers (James 2016b). Cabinet meetings take place on a weekly basis but it is unlikely that electoral management was commonly discussed at the highest level – yet this is where executive interests are asserted when they feel threatened or advantage is perceived (James 2010b, 2012, 2016c).[7]

The most regularised meetings instead took place within a national *core tripartite system* of government civil servants, the Electoral Commission and professional representatives. The level and continuity of interaction between these actors increased dramatically over the case study. When the Electoral Commission was established in 2000, the argument was raised as to whether it should be running elections. Sam Younger as Chair decided to reach out to the electoral community. They undertook a review of the 2001 General Election, and their report on that was 'the start of a major engagement with returning officers and electoral administrators on issues of electoral administration' (private interview, Sam Younger, 8 April, 2011). Interactions became increasingly regular thereafter and regular working groups were eventually set up. The first of these was the Elections and Registration Working Group that was initially constituted for the 2009 European parliamentary election and was continued for the UK parliamentary general election in 2010 and the 2011 spring electoral events. This was succeeded by an Elections, Referendums and Registration Working Group (ERRWG). The core membership consisted of officials from the Commission, the AEA and Regional ROs.[8] These were initiated by the Electoral Commission with the aim of the Commission receiving advice on the development and content of its guidance for electoral officials, including the

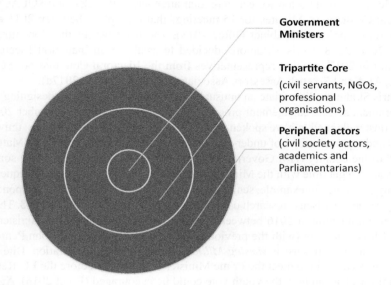

Figure 6.1 Three constellations of actors in the UK electoral management governance network.

performance standards. It was also designed as a forum for electoral officials to articulate their needs and pro to provide a link for communication between the software and print suppliers, the Commission, Cabinet Office and electoral officials (Electoral Commission 2012d). It quickly became a useful forum for electoral practitioners to share best practice and embed these into the Electoral Commission's guidance. A UK Electoral Advisory Board was set up in 2013 to give a more permanent presence to these groups (Electoral Commission 2013).

The Cabinet Office also set up some working groups. An Elections Policy and Co-ordination Group was established in 2011, with the aim of meeting every six to eight weeks:

> to oversee and co-ordinate the development of electoral policy and legislation.... [It will] ... consider the implications of proposed changes to legislation and funding arrangements on the electoral process and act as a forum for the coordination of electoral policy across Government, including identifying strategic high-level operational issues and risks.
>
> (Cabinet Office 2011)

Membership included representatives from seven different UK government departments, the Welsh Government, the Electoral Commission, the Scottish EMB, a range of ROs and the AEA. Meanwhile, government civil servants and the Electoral Commission were also regular attenders at the AEA and SOLACE's Annual Conference. Minutes for 15 meetings that took place between 2011 and 2013 were published (Cabinet Office 2013). The Minister for the Constitution from 2016–2018, Chris Skidmore, decided to establish an inaugural Electoral Summit in 2017, inviting representatives from the Electoral Commission, SOLACE, AEA and Scottish Assessors Association (Cabinet Office 2017a).

Chris Skidmore did initiate an unusually high level of outreach in designing the government's voter engagement programme. Between May and September 2017, the Minster claimed to have spoken to a wide range of civil society groups, universities and representatives of under-registered voters during a 'Every Voice Matters Tour' of the country (HM Government 2017, 52–3). Pressure groups were sometimes able to get time with the Minister and Cabinet Office in response to requests. For my own part, for example, senior civil servants in the Cabinet Office responded to my request to discuss research on the funding of elections in March 2018. There was also a meeting in 2016 between Bite the Ballot, myself, and the minister of state Chris Skidmore (with the previous ministers Chloe Smith and John Penrose in attendance) to discuss a *Missing Millions* report on voter registration. Bite the Ballot was called in to meet the Prime Minister immediately before the EU Referendum for ideas on how the youth vote could be encouraged (Elgot 2016). Again under Skidmore, the Cabinet Office held a roundtable in 2017 to listen to disability rights campaigners making the case for greater accessibility in the electoral process (Cabinet Office 2017b). None of these were decision-making venues, however – they were carefully managed information gathering and publicity opportunities.

A *periphery of civil society actors*, academics and Parliamentarians were meanwhile actively engaged in the broader network – in an increasingly, but not entirely, connected way. Parliament is an obvious, central venue. Peers have permanent positions in the Lords and although MPs' tenure is fixed – many have long periods in office. Parliamentary procedures such as debates, opportunities to ask questions, the passage of legislation and internal parliamentary party meetings provide regular opportunities to discuss electoral management. Select committee enquiries, meanwhile, provide the venue in which Parliamentarians can come into contact with civil society groups who submit evidence. During the 2010 and 2015 Parliaments, the Political and Constitutional Reform Select Committee provided important venues for interaction under the Chairmanship of Labour MP Graham Allen with enquiries launched in 2011 on the introduction of individual electoral registration (Political and Constitutional Reform Committee 2011) and in 2014 on voter engagement (Select Committe on Political and Consitutional Reform 2014, 2015). Earlier notable enquiries include the ODPM: Housing, Planning, Local Government and the Regions Committee on postal voting (2014) and individual electoral registration (2005). Other venues exist in Wales and Scotland (for example, see: Local Government and Communities Committee 2017).

Parliamentary meetings can have a more informal setting. Bite the Ballot established an All-Party Parliamentary Group on electoral registration.[9] This group made collective submissions to Parliamentary Select Committees, making suggestions for legislative reform. Parliamentarians from that group introduced legislative amendments in Parliament, with Bite the Ballot providing a campaign (private interview, Bite the Ballot official, 24 July 2015). Having previously met Mike Sani and Oliver Sidorczuk of Bite the Ballot when giving evidence at the PCRSC, and then interviewed them for future research, I proposed the setting up of a new All-Party Parliamentary Group on Democratic Participation in the Autumn of 2015, aware of the previous success that the group had had, when I did the research for this chapter. The group was formed and held an AGM in November 2015. Bite the Ballot would act as the secretariat, the former Conservative minister responsible for implementing IER, Chloe Smith MP, was elected as the Chair. Co-chairs were recruited by Bite the Ballot to ensure that all parties within Parliament were represented – the only all-party group at the time.[10] The group would have three areas of focus. Electoral Modernisation was one and I assumed the title of Lead Fellow for this area. An open meeting took place in March 2016 to gather ideas for improving voter registration rates, given concerns about under-registration, with representatives from civil society and the APPG. These were consolidated into a report that I co-authored with Bite the Ballot, detailing 25 proposed short- and long-term reforms, called *The Missing Millions* (James, Bite the Ballot, and ClearView Research 2016). Meetings followed between myself, some APPG co-chairs and Bite the Ballot to coordinate the campaign for the *Missing Millions*. The APPG continued for three and a half years (at the time of writing).

Rooms in Parliament were also booked by civil society groups (via supportive Parliamentarians) to hold roundtable discussions to focus on a campaign issue. Taking one example, in November 2017, Webroots held an expert panel–led roundtable in Parliament to respond to its report on the Cost of Voting. The report argued that internet voting could reduce the amount of money spent on elections (Webroots Democracy 2017). Chaired by Anna Wallace, Political Relations Director from PriceWaterHouse Coopers, respondents included a pro-internet voting MP, Mike Summers from Smartmatic and myself. A month earlier, Webroots held a policy roundtable at PWC in London to gather input into the report, with Angela Holden from the AEA, suppliers and myself giving feedback and ideas. A raucously young and supportive audience made of MP's staffers, Webroots volunteers and some electoral officials cheered on the arguments in a grand committee room.

Civil society groups also meet outside of Parliament. A range of pressure groups came into contact to discuss joint activities and campaigns over electoral registration, following the introduction of the 'Lobbying Bill'[11] in 2013. Prior to that, although it may be that there is just st not the institutional memory to record it, there was little evidence of collaboration. The Lobbying Bill would impose restrictions on third-sector campaigning and lobbying and threatened their shared interests. Organisations worked together to 'give a rapid response' given how quickly the government was pushing the legislation through. Having established that forum, it was used as the basis to also discuss electoral registration (private interview, Electoral Reform Society official, 3 April 2014). Further collaborations followed. Hope Not Hate drew together civil rights groups to support its own campaign against individual electoral registration, taking input from Bite the Ballot, Electoral Reform Society and Unlock Democracy (Hope Not Hate 2015).

Ad-hoc advisory groups were often formed. The establishment of an Advisory Group to the Law Commission's Review of Electoral Law, between 2013–2015 created the opportunity for four academics and four third-sector representatives to express views, although the remit of that project was limited to consolidating and not changing electoral law. When former party chairman Eric Pickles was appointed as Anti-Corruption Champion, he requested electoral fraud to be made part of that brief. A seminar was held in December 2015 at the British Academy to gather information from participants to inform the eventual report (Pickles 2016). This included the Electoral Commission, journalists and members of the judiciary who had encountered fraud, representatives from SOLACE, the AEA and representatives of political parties. I was one of four academics to have been invited. There was no broader civil society engagement.

Interactions have so far been discussed at a national level. Local and regional clusters of electoral officials also formed networks, very unevenly across the UK. In Scotland as was noted above, the Electoral Management Board was created in 2011, to 'the general function of co-ordinating the administration of Local Government elections in Scotland'. Beyond that formal role, it more broadly connected electoral officials in Scotland. An eight-member board included Returning Officers and Electoral Registration Officers, but also had advisors from the Scottish Government, Electoral Commission, SOLAR and AEA. The Board typically met eight times per year between 2011–2018 in Edinburgh (Electoral Management Board of Scotland 2018). Likewise, London had a network of electoral officials. The AEA had 11 long-established regional branch meetings for members.

6.4 Contestation

Having rarely been considered an initial consensus about the steering and implementation of elections emerged shortly after 1997, but increasingly broke down. Following Labour's victory in the general election, there appeared to be a considerable agreement about the need to 'modernise' electoral law, since the legislative architecture was commonly described as 'Victorian'. As noted above, the Electoral Commission, having been set up in November 2000, undertook a review of the 2001 General Election and consulted widely amongst the professional community. The Chair of the Commission at the time, said that they encountered considerable:

> 'pent up frustration . . . from all sorts of quarters about things in the electoral arrangements. Mostly niggles, I mean something that was not absolutely fundamental. But large numbers of niggles, everything from the nominations process to the absent voting arrangements to the registration process to the design of ballot papers. Huge number of things.
> (private interview, Sam Younger, 30 May 2007)

There was a strong common consensus that the 'modernisation' of elections involved making it easier for citizens to register and cast their vote. The Howarth Committee's proposals included rolling (as opposed to annual) registration, flexible methods for absentee voting and pilots for innovations such as electronic voting, extended voting hours and all-postal elections. Two other Select Committees reached similar conclusions (James 2012, 137–40). These proposals formed the basis of the Labour legislation. The Electoral Commission positively evaluated the pilots that took place and stressed that: 'At the heart of our thinking is that we must pursue the path of making voting easier and more convenient for a twenty-first century electorate' (Electoral Commission 2003b, 3). It outlined an agenda for future easier voting procedures including the proposal 'there should be a statutory presumption that all local elections be run as all-postal ballots unless there are compelling reasons why an all-postal ballot would be inappropriate or disadvantageous for a group or groups of electors' (2003a, 24). The author understands that one prominent Labour Minister saw this as 'the answer' to voter turnout problems and capable of increasing 'turnout by 10% overnight' (private interview, former civil servant, 8 February 2007).

The Electoral Commission also set out an agenda for preventing electoral fraud such as the proposal for individual, rather than household, electoral registration (Electoral Commission 2003b) which was supported by the AEA. Early Labour ministers were not persuaded, however. Instead, the government pushed ahead and used all-postal elections in the European parliamentary elections 2004, on a much larger scale than the Commission had advised. A high-profile case of electoral fraud in Birmingham in 2004 changed the political environment, however. The judge presiding over the case publicly criticised the introduction of postal voting on demand and caused widespread media concern, especially amongst the right-wing press. Further subsequent criticism came from international observers (Council of Europe 2008; Office for Democratic Institutions and Human Rights 2005, 1), academics (Essex University 2014; Wilks-Heeg 2008) and the Committee on Standards in Public Life in 2007. A select committee also investigated postal voting (ODPM: Housing 2014) – pushing for security reforms. The government accepted the case for some security measures, so long as turnout was not affected, and had prepared individual registration as part of its Electoral Administration Bill. It reversed course, however, after Chris Ruane led Labour backbenchers to voice concerns about the impact on registration levels. The government instead legislated to introduce powers for the Electoral Commission to set performance standards for EROs and ROs. Disagreement followed here too. Rival parliamentary parties argued about whether the focus of the standards should be on maximising registration or reducing electoral fraud.

After Gordon Brown became Prime Minister in 2007, the government conceded the case for implementing IER, but legislated to only introduce it on a voluntary basis initially. In 2010, the Coalition government came to power and quickly introduced legislation to 'fast-track' IER implementation before the 2015 general election (Deputy Prime Minister 2011). The Select Committee on Political and Constitutional Reform (2011), headed by Labour MP Graham Allen, decided to undertake a pre-legislative scrutiny of these proposals. At the inquiry the legislation received support from the Electoral Commission, AEA and some academics. The British Youth Council, the National Union of Students and Operation Black Vote and myself (using the research from Chapter 9) warned about the impact on already low registration levels. Criticism was more roundly made on the government's proposals to make electoral registration voluntary by both the Commission, AEA and the select committee report and this was eventually dropped in the legislation (ibid., pp. 8–10). There was little criticism of the government's proposal to introduce online electoral registration and this was implemented in 2011.

While IER was being implemented more calls were made from academics and pressure groups to do more to tackle the problem of under-registration with IER called a potential 'car crash for democracy' (James 2015). These criticisms came to a head in the 2014 Select Committee on Political and Constitutional Reform (2014) on Voter Engagement. Persuaded by academic and civil society actors submitting evidence (go us!), the committee supported automatic electoral registration, encouraged the government to explore weekend voting, further trials of all-postal voting and internet voting by 2020. Many of these reforms were opposed by the Electoral Commission and the AEA, but became the basis of the Labour Party's 2015 manifesto (Labour Party 2015, 63). Meanwhile, outside of the select committee venue, Bite the Ballot, along with other actors, expressed frustration that there was a 'lack of urgency' to tackle under-registration, concerns which were echoed in a right-wing think tank's report, which also criticised the Electoral Commission's track record as a regulator (Pinto-Duschinsky 2014).

Disagreement later raged about the Conservative's next reform to tackle electoral fraud. There had long been concerns within the party that electoral fraud was taking place (Golds 2014). As noted above, the government invited former Conservative Party Chair Eric Pickles to set up an 'independent' inquiry (Pickles, 2016). The Pickles report was broadly welcomed by the government, who announced two days after Christmas Day in 2016 that it intended to pilot voter identification requirements at the local elections in 18 months' time. This was met with a campaign organised by the Electoral Reform Society in the run-up to the May 2018 polls. An open letter was organised with over 40 charities, campaign groups and academics, including myself, warning that the pilots risked disenfranchising vulnerable people (Walker 2018b). Academics claimed that the scheme was 'a solution in search of a problem' (Walker 2018a). One day after the pilots, the Electoral Reform Society claimed that nearly 4,000 people had been denied their right to vote in a 'chaotic, undemocratic mess' (Patron 2018). Chloe Smith, as Minister for the Constitution, claimed the pilots were 'a great success' (Smith 2018b) but the opposition responded that 'it's hard to spin a government project that denied hundreds of voters their democratic rights' (Smith 2018a).

There therefore became a growing fault line of disagreement over whether reforms should prioritise reducing opportunities for fraud or maximise participation. Labour, Liberal Democrat, SNP and Green and civil society groups advocated measures to promote participation. The Conservatives and members of the judiciary prioritised security measures. The Commission and AEA, meanwhile, were in agreement over most main issues. 'The truth is that we are very close to the Electoral Commission in terms of what we ask for' said one AEA official (private interview, 8 July 2011). 'There is very often a commonality of approach' said one Electoral Commission official (private interview, 31 March 2011). There has also been some overlap in personnel between these two groups. The Head of Electoral Administration at the Commission from 2007–2015, for example, was a former Returning Officer and one of the founding members of the AEA. Clashes between them could be found, however, including the role of the Commission in setting central directions at the 2011 referendums (described in Chapter 10).

6.5 Resource distribution and power

Table 6.1 outlines the resources and tactics that key actors have available to them, along with the weaknesses that they might face in achieving their goals. The relationship between the Prime Minister, his/her cabinet and their government departments has been subject to sustained academic attention, and the literature on the core executive in Britain suggests that each has their own available tactics and resources which they can use against each other (Smith 1999). For the purposes of this case, however, they appear to behave as one unitary actor – the prime ministerial court. The executive is unanimously the most resourced and powerful actor in making electoral law since it has the capacity to set the legislative agenda and implement change in Parliament, providing its parliamentary majority holds. It can therefore usually ignore the advice of other actors as it did over IER and voter ID pilots. As one AEA official put it: 'ultimately it is the government who decides what advice they will take' (private interview, AEA official, 8 July 2011). The executive has the power to control some sites of discussion. It flexed muscle to abolish the Political and Constitutional Reform Committee – the committee that had been most critical of it. In establishing the Pickles Committee, a report that was written by a Conservative MP and former Chair, and using the report as the evidence base for policy, the government exercised enormous agenda control.

Central government can be weak at points, however, presenting opportune moments for other actors seeking change. Election administration was not always a high-profile issue, so Prime Ministers will focus time and efforts on salient political issues that win them elections. Frequent ministerial reshuffles can leave them with low levels of knowledge and open to 'capture' by their departmental officials or other actors. Between 2010–2018, for example, five different ministers had the portfolio for electoral law. At the 2015 AEA conference, I watched with surprise to see all questions from the audience of electoral officials being answered by a senior civil servant rather than the newly appointed minister Sam Gyimah. Frequent re-organisations can leave civil servants themselves with low knowledge (private interview, Electoral Commission official, 3 March 2011) such that some AEA officials, who have vast professional experience, complain that it takes time for them to get civil servants 'up to speed.' Ultimately, central government's weakness is that if unpopular decisions are made, then it can be hit at the ballot box. Accusations that the government is 'disenfranchising' electors or gaining electorally from the reforms can therefore hurt it to some extent, but voters will largely vote on other issues.

Table 6.1 Potential resources, tactics and weaknesses of actors in the UK network

Actor	Potential resources and tactics	Potential strategic weaknesses
Prime Ministerial Court	Power to appoint ministers Power to set manifesto and legislative agenda setting Cabinet agenda setting Political support from electorate	Limitations on time and stretch of resources Public criticism
Minister	Availability of department resources Knowledge Political support from Prime Minister and Cabinet, policy networks and/or electorate	Limitations on time and stretch of resources Political aspirations to move on Public criticism
Government Departments	Knowledge Bureaucratic resources Support from minister Support from network	Absence of resources and capacity if they downsize
Select Committee Chairs	Expertise from specialisation and access to information Attention of media through press releases Reputation as 'cross-party' Appeal to MPs Appeal to public	Need to reconcile preferences of different parties within the committee Executive power to dismantle
Electoral Commission	Knowledge of policy area Reputation as an 'independent watchdog' Lobbying of MPs through parliamentary briefings Use of performance standards	No control of elections on the ground – but often blamed for problems Can be abolished by government/Parliament Criticism from the press
AEA	Knowledge of policy area Access to and lobbying of civil servants and ministers Mobilisation of members	Public knowledge and media attention weak Dependent on funding of members
EROs/ROs	Discretion over implementation Access to the media	Limitations on time
Suppliers	Provision of core supplies in an imperfect market	Competition Legal change
Law Commission	Information and advice Appeal to media Reputation for independence	Tradition of parliamentary sovereignty on issues of principle in electoral law Can be abolished by government/Parliament
Pressure Groups	Lobbying of ministers Mobilisation of supporters	Weak funding
Academics	Expertise Authority and reputation for independence Use of blogs, press releases and networking Use of Parliament	Media attention weak Limitations on time Rarely invited to policy meetings

The Electoral Commission's greatest resource is the knowledge of the policy area that it has from extensive specialisation and a reputation for being an 'independent watchdog.' A culture exists within the Commission of valuing its independence from government. When the Commission devised its performance standards, for example, it consulted with the Ministry of Justice but was clear that it would resist a steer because they 'guard . . . [their] . . . independence zealously, so if they had tried to give us a steer we probably wouldn't have followed it' (private interview, Electoral Commission official, 31 March 2011). The Commission's tactics have included undertaking extensive reviews of electoral law, issuing press releases following the publication of reports to get media coverage for its views and providing detailed briefings to Parliamentarians at each stage of a bill's passage. In the briefings, it outlined its position to lobby Parliamentarians. Having given the Commission a mandate to produce detailed reviews of electoral law, there was a view in central government that they could 'draw down what little resource [they had] . . . and leave it with the Commission', which gave the Commission a 'bespoke position of having policy lead on electoral law'. However, things changed quickly when the government began to disagree with the Commission. According to its former chair:

> The reality which has become increasingly clear since is that there is no way that government will give up its prerogative there, and the second we started to developing some policy capacity . . . government began to develop its own resource to track and deal and cope with what we were doing. So I think that the reality was that we were ever going to be long term the policy lead.
> (private interview, Sam Younger, 8 April 2011)

The Commission also faced the political problem that as the public-facing institution for elections, it was commonly blamed for problems, even though it had no power to direct EROs or ROs in elections. Sam Younger and his successor Jenny Watson faced regular calls to resign when problems came to light. The right-wing press were particularly hostile to Watson following problems in the 2010 general election with *The Telegraph* suggesting that 'Miss Watson blamed everyone but herself' (Raynor and Watt 2010) and the *Daily Mail* commonly undermining Watson as a 'quango queen' and a 'left-wing', 'modern militant', who 'earned £100,000 for three days a week' (see, for example: Chapman 2010; Gallagher 2010). The Commission even faced calls to be shut down in 2010 because of the 'fiasco' at a time when the government was undertaking a 'quango bonfire' in order to reduce public spending. The Commission perhaps strategically responded by calling for more powers to direct EROs/ROs for elections too. The broader challenge, however, was that it's long-term existence was always contingent on the government's legislative agenda.

The AEA's key resource was also its knowledge and professional expertise, which it used to advocate change by developing policy positions and circulating these to ministers. Although the organisation publishes its reports and has issued press releases, the focus of their activity has been largely 'behind closed doors' because the 'public are not that interested.' Each report was therefore followed usually by a request to meet the minister to discuss it. It showed a considerable track record of success. The AEA first met in 1988 and 'spent its first few years just deciding what it was going to do with itself' but it deliberately mobilised itself to lobby government in the mid-1990s. The AEA sensed that the Major government was likely to fall and that this presented them with an opportunity to bring about change. The AEA therefore developed a pamphlet with reforms and approached Jack Straw who, when Labour won office, in turn set up the Howarth Commission (private interview, AEA Chairman, 8 July 2007). The AEA continued to invest considerable time lobbying civil servants. When the Coalition government drafted a bill on individual electoral registration in 2011, for example, the AEA concluded that it:

> contains everything we asked for . . . that is largely because we have invested literally days talking to Cabinet Office officials which the Commission were not prepared to do. So we have basically got what we wanted because Cabinet Office officials advise ministers.
> (private interview, AEA Chairman, 8 July 2011)

Organisational restructuring has helped them succeed. Having a single point of contact made them more effective liaising with other organisations. The AEA was also extremely proactive in responding to government consultations and enquiries. As one Electoral Commission source put it: 'they have been influential because they've been very engaged' (private interview, Sam Younger, 8 April 2011). In contrast, SOLACE submitted far fewer responses and this affected its standing in the community for some time. But even the AEA were not always successful. Despite getting what they wanted on many issues, they often describe themselves as battling over the:

> little things in life. The big things will always be that which the Cabinet decides, all you can ever do there is lobby and hope that they listen.
> (private interview, AEA Chairman, 8 July 2011)

Pressure group tactics were similar. Like the AEA and Commission, there have been concerted efforts to change the mind of ministers and influence the legislative process. Briefings, albeit much less regularly, were been developed for Parliamentarians. Ministers have been very regularly approached, for example, by the Electoral Reform Society and Bite the Ballot. The latter were constantly in 'the faces of ministers'. Convinced that reform had to 'come from within' the parliamentary elite, they set up a cross-party All-Party Parliamentary Group on electoral registration, with Lord Kennedy, a former Electoral Commissioner as Chair. Social media was also used. Bite the Ballot organised a campaign called #TheAmendment to support the legislative reforms, with support from academics. TV appearances were regularly made by the group's leaders. Voter registration campaigns had a significant impact. The groups faced significant financial pressures, however, which after the 2015 general election, forced them to commercialise their voter education resources. Although they initially received Cabinet Office funding for their 'Rock and Enrol' project, relations soured when the Cabinet Office claimed ownership of the resources they had developed. Their early legislative proposals were briefed against by the Commission and the AEA who showed little interest in collaborating with them for National Voter Registration Day, as they were 'not impressed' with their registration ideas and 'did not reach out' (private interview, Bite the Ballot official, 24 July 2015).

The private sector had some key tactics. Submissions of written evidence were made to parliamentary committees to protect the use of the open electoral register. According to one AEA source:

> The Electoral Commission, us, others and particularly civil liberties groups are lobbying hard to say it should be abolished, it is a disgrace. The credit reference agencies, the direct marketing people, all the rest of them who use it of course are lobbying against us. They are not lobbying Cabinet Office ministers but they are lobbying BIS, Mr. Cable and his merry men. The Cabinet Office ministers, Deputy Prime Minister included are caught between two very conflicting points of view.
> (private interview, AEA official, 8 July 2011)

Private sector organisations such as Smartmatic also had the financial security to take up speaking opportunities to promote the wider use of technology.

A final group are academics. The most common pathway is the submission of evidence to existing parliamentary committees and enquiries. This can lead to invitations to give oral evidence – which are much more likely to be cited in the final report. The final report, in turn, if it is published close to a general election can shape the party manifestos of the political parties. Submissions that I made to the Political and Constitutional Reform Select Committee (PCRSC) in 2014 in effect shaped the Labour manifesto in 2015. The 'snap' election of 2017 had no such provisions in it. Select committee recommendations can also be taken forward in subsequent government policy, even if it is not directly cited. The piloting of automatic re-registration, for example, was also based on the *Voter Engagement* report (Penrose 2015). Regular blog posts can lead to invitations to speak at practitioner conferences or give advice to groups. It was as a result of this that I was invited to speak to the Electoral Reform Society to advise on policy and participating in a British Academy seminar with the minister in 2011. They also help awareness of the issue to grow amongst the journalists and gain opportunities to be quoted in the press.

Academics can also, however, instigate their own involvement with Parliament by trying to open up new venues for participation. Parliamentarians can be approached to ask questions in Parliament which leads to the minister putting a stated position on record on a policy issue which can then be taken forward. As described above, it is also possible to establish parliamentary groups with civil society actors and Parliamentarians, as I did with Bite the Ballot. Having learnt of their early success, we jointly established a new APPG and published a report called the *Missing Millions* proposing 25 voter registration reforms. Open letters were written by myself and Oliver Sidorczuk from Bite the Ballot, and published in national broadsheets such as *The Times*[12] and *The Telegraph*[13] urging the government to take urgent action. Co-signatures were recruited and ranged on the political spectrum from Nigel Farage to Jeremy Corbyn. The June 2016 letter received signatures from over 80 Parliamentarians. Parliamentary questions were raised by members of the APPG based on the report (e.g. Hansard 2016b, 2016c) and one co-chair of the group organised a debate in the House of Commons on automatic voter registration on 26 June 2016 (Hansard 2016a). Co-authored blogs were subsequently written with Parliamentarians to keep items on the agenda and to support amendments to bills that APPG Parliamentarians proposed or supported. Meanwhile, Bite the Ballot also organised registration drives to boost registration levels. Media work was sometimes undertaken collaboratively. For example, in co-ordination with the BBC, a series of pieces were run on the day of the registration deadline for the Brexit referendum, the encouraging young people to register. For my own part, I appeared on BBC News at 10, just over an hour before the deadline passed. Throughout, informal correspondence with Parliamentarians was vital. Requests for meetings were (to my surprise) usually accepted. Quick replies to emails asking 'is there any research on. . .' helped to build relationships. Co-authoring blogs helped add clout to my otherwise overlooked voice. I write in more detail about the efficacy of my own attempts to influence policy and legislation elsewhere (James 2018). There is always the risk that I might narcissistically overstate my influence. But I think that I have a solid case for having tried to shape the policy network and policy outcomes, as have other academics, who are required to collect evidence of their policy impact as part of the external evaluation of universities (Essex University 2014; University of Liverpool 2014). And yet academics are at a distinct disadvantage. They are rarely invited to core policy meetings making it difficult for them to give input as decisions are made and track policy developments. Other commitments for research, teaching and administration mean that workload can be high – time for policy impact can therefore be crowded out.

6.6 Conclusions

Who manages elections? The original typologies offered three options: government, an independent body or a mix of both. As this chapter empirically demonstrates, the picture is substantially more complex than this and crude formal-legal conceptualisations tell us only so much about the fluidity of decision-making systems and actors involved in delivering elections. This chapter has provided a 'thicker,' qualitative historical study of Britain 1917–2018 to reveal some profound changes in steering and rowing systems. There has been a considerable thickening of the number and type of actors involved. During the life of the case study, professional and non-governmental actors played an increasing role in the steering of electoral governance. After 2010, civil society increasingly sought to influence the steering and delivery though self-made voter awareness and registration drives. There was a broad consensus amongst professional, non-governmental actors (the AEA and Electoral Commission) about the direction of electoral administration and management. This core constellation of groups developed close access to government ministers, but have sometimes been in conflict with civil society actors, who have largely been excluded from the decision-making process. These transformations are missed by only adopting a formal-legal approach. This governance network structure has had important consequences for electoral integrity since it has provided forums for the spread of best practice, greater scrutiny of government policy and strengthened state capacity for voter registration.

Crucial to this more complex understanding of power is an appreciation of political time, which the case reveals as being important. After the Electoral Commission was established in 2000, central government appeared to have depleted resources to act as a policy lead and allowed the Commission to set the agenda. Central government quickly re-asserted control, however; it is therefore clear that power and opportunity fluctuates. Furthermore, the network approach demonstrates the importance of structure and agency in electoral governance, which the formal-legal approach misses. The routinised patterns of behaviour that characterised the network provided a useful framework for the AEA and Commission to influence policy and have their concerns listened to. But the construction of these networks were themselves a result of the earlier successful deployment of strategies and tactics by AEA officials. Similarly, the leadership and strategic action from Mike Sani and Oliver Sidorzcuk of Bite the Ballot brought many successes, but the prevailing structures of governance limited their ability to influence policy.

What type of governance network exists in the UK? This question will be returned to in the next chapter, after we have examined some other systems.

Notes

1 This includes: semi-structured interviews with 74 electoral officials involved in the front lines of elections undertaken in 2011; 12 elite-level interviews with civil servants, members of professional associations, non-governmental organisations and civil society actors over the period 2007–2015 (some of which were repeat interviews); and publicly available minutes and reports from the Electoral Commission, Cabinet Office, Select Committees including written and oral evidence, parliamentary debates, Association of Electoral Administrators, Bite the Ballot, Law Commission, Electoral Reform Society.
2 This was presented at two conferences (James 2015a).
3 My own personal wish to improve policy was partly inspired by the work of Frances Fox Piven and Richard Cloward who wrote seminal books on the politics of electoral administration in the US and were advocates for change (Piven and Cloward 1988, 2000). I had also always been politically active as an undergraduate student, at one point trying to form a student version of Charter 88 at the University of York (and forming/running an environmentalist group between the ages of 7–11, which sold cakes, badges made on cardboard and second-hand toys to parents in the school playground). Of course, any academic who has had the opportunity to speak in Parliament, as I did many times, will find the process addictive. Policy 'impact' also became increasingly important in the UK during the time of the case study as universities are assessed by it under Research Excellence Frameworks. This created many internal university messages that what I was doing was a good idea, and a lingering thought of 'will this get me promoted? Do I want that anyway?'.

4 In Scotland, the Society of Local Authority Lawyers & Administrators was established in 1975, playing a similar role to SOLACE. Meanwhile, the Scotland Scottish Assessors Association was another voluntary organisation formed in the same year which brought together Scottish EROs.
5 Labour Ministers have included Jack Straw, Harriet Harman, Charlie Falkener. From 2010–2018, the ministers responsible for elections were Mark Harper, Chloe Smith, Greg Clark, Sam Gyimah, John Penrose, Chris Skidmore and then Chloe Smith again.
6 Those to have introduced bills and amendments include Baroness Margaret McDonagh, Lord Roy Kennedy, Lord Charlie Falkener (Labour) and Lord Rennard (Liberal Democrats).
7 Cabinet minutes are only put in the public domain 30 years after the meeting.
8 For European Elections was broken into 11 regional constituencies, each with a Regional Returning Office.
9 All-Party Parliamentary Group is a cross-party meeting that has no official status within Parliament that can include Parliamentarians and outside organisations but are held on Parliament's premises.
10 Co-chairs in the first year were Lord Blunkett (Labour), Owen Thompson (SNP), Lord Rennard (Lib Dem), Gavin Robinson (DUP), Liz Saville Roberts (Plaid Cymru), Mark Durkan (SDLP), Danny Kinahan (UUP), Caroline Lucas (Green), Baroness Grey-Thompson (Crossbench).
11 This Bill became the Transparency of Lobbying, Non-party Campaigning and Trade Union Administration Act 2014.
12 *The Times*, 8 February 2016, reprinted on the Political Studies Association Blog: www.psa.ac.uk/insight-plus/blog/silent-growing-crisis-voter-registration
13 *The Telegraph*, 9 June 2016, www.telegraph.co.uk/opinion/2016/06/09/letters-the-failure-of-david-camerons-renegotiations-poisoned-an/

7 Comparative electoral management governance networks

7.1 Introduction

The previous chapters introduced electoral management governance networks as a new theoretical framework for considering how elections are delivered. Rather than simply categorising countries into whether the government or an independent body ran elections, we need to consider the totality of actors and transactions that collectively deliver elections and the properties of those networks. The framework was then applied to the UK to show that, over time, the UK had seen a rapid change in the network structure. The last chapter demonstrated the development of a more diverse range of actors delivering and trying to shape delivery mechanisms, a considerable breakdown in consensus, but power remaining broadly with the executive. This chapter now aims to stretch the framework by providing further short case studies to help understand similarities and divergences between polities. It will then present a new typology based on the cases.

7.2 Case study selection and methods

Three further case studies were chosen with a deliberately diverse set of characteristics so that different types of electoral governance characteristics could be identified. These cases were: India, New South Wales in Australia and Jordan. This follows a maximum variation case approach (Flyvbjerg 2006, 230). The cases mostly cover the same period of time - the first decade and a half of the twenty-first century.

Table 7.1 lists the cases used in this chapter. India was chosen as it provides an example of electoral management using an 'independent model' according to the traditional typologies of EMBs set out in Chapter 6. It therefore provides a high level of institutional contrast with the UK system and should in theory, generate an entirely different network type. It also provides a case of electoral management in a country with lower levels of GDP per capita (see: Figure 7.1). Yet, as we shall see, despite these major contextual differences, there are surprising levels of similarity with the UK in the nature of the network. New South Wales in Australia was added to provide a case study of a federal system. This also provides another combination of variables with an independent body in an economically prosperous state. Jordan was chosen to give an example of electoral management in an autocratic regime. Figure 7.2 maps the differences

Table 7.1 Case study characteristics

Country	Institutional model	Electoral democracy	GDP	Federal
UK	Governmental	Democracy	High	Quasi-federal
India	Independent	Democracy	Low	Federal
Jordan	Independent	Autocracy	Low	Unitary
New South Wales, Australia	Independent	Democracy	High	Federal

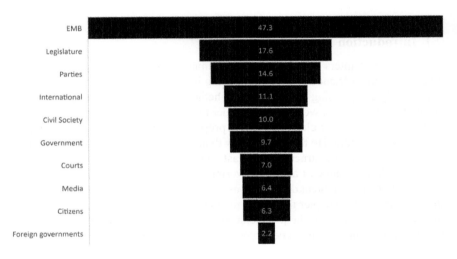

Figure 7.1 GDP per capita (current US$) 1960–2016 in the four case studies.

Source: Author based on data from World Bank, accessed 3 December 2018, https://data.worldbank.org/indicator/NY.GDP.PCAP.CD

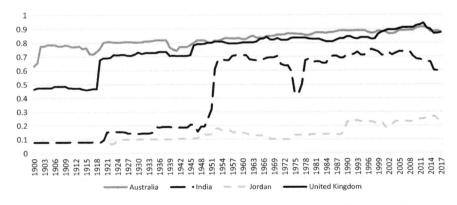

Figure 7.2 Comparing the four case studies by the V-DEM Electoral Democracy Index 1900–2017.

between Jordan and the other cases against the V-DEM Electoral Democracy Index from 1900–2017. Again, the purpose was to search for differences which were undoubtably found, but there were also some areas of continuity.

Cases were researched through a combination of the use of results from the EMS and ELECT datasources, election observation reports, secondary analysis of websites, programme evaluations, news sources and primary interviews. The nature and volume of publications available varied by case. Ethnographic methods were also used in India while observing state elections in 2016 over a two-week period. The name of the state is not provided to ensure anonymity of sources. Interviews were also then taken in a second state that was not holding elections, and further interviews were undertaken with central Electoral Commission of India (ECI) officials in Delhi, alongside civil society organisations. In total 20 interviews were undertaken. Analysis is also constructed using secondary documents made available via the ECI website and officials during the stay, including news releases. The Australian case was researched using analysis of secondary documents from the NSW Electoral Commission website and associated websites, a roundtable interview discussion involving seven key managers from the NSW Electoral Commission (NSWEC) held in their Sydney office on 21 May 2018, interviews with two senior officials from the Australian Electoral Commission and an analysis of parliamentary documents. The Jordanian case was limited to an analysis of secondary documents and interviews with two officials from international electoral assistance agencies. The case studies therefore vary in length and are selected on the dependent variable which is an approach well established in *qualitative* research design methods (Goertz and Mahoney 2012).

7.3 India 2000–2016

India is a federal parliamentary polity that gained independence from British rule in 1947. It has a bicameral parliamentary system with the lower House of the People (the 'Lok Sabha') elected through single-seat constituencies by a simple majority. The upper house, Council of States ('Rajya Sabha'), consists mostly of members indirectly elected by state and territorial assemblies by a proportional representation of the vote. India is broadly a federalised system consisting of 29 states and seven union territories. The Prime Minister is the head of government and is an executive drawn from the legislature. The country has consistently been classified as a democracy since independence (Figure 7.2). With a population of nearly 1.3 billion people (estimated in July 2017), it is world's largest democracy and often noted as being an exception to the theory that democracy requires economic development because it has historically been categorised as a lower-income country. The presence of deep divisions in its society has also made it an important focus of discussion for how democracy can endure (Lijphart 1996).

7.3.1 Network membership and integration

The Electoral Commission of India (ECI) was the permanent body constitutionally ascribed the responsibility for delivering elections in January 1950. The principle that it should be an independent body, free from the political interference of the executive of the day, featured heavily in parliamentary debates at that time (Quraishi 2014, 61–2). The Headquarters are based in a tall red-brick building in the more well kept parts of New Delhi, a one kilometre walk down from Parliament, where, as of 2017, a permanent staff of 300 officials are employed. The organisation exhibited a top-down, hierarchical structure. After being founded, the ECI executive initially only consisted of one Chief Executive Commissioner. Two additional Election Commissioners were appointed in January 1990 and this arrangement remained thereafter until the time of writing. These officials were appointed by the President of India for six years (unless they reach 65) and they could only be removed from office by an impeachment process by Parliament. Deputy Election Commissioners and Director Generals served underneath this. They were appointments from the national civil service selected by the Commission. A third level of management included Directors, Principal Secretaries and Secretaries, Under Secretaries and Deputy Directors. Under their control were seven main divisions (Planning, Judicial, Administration, Systematic Voters' Education and Electoral Participation (SVEEP), Information Systems, Media and Secretariat Co-ordination) (Electoral Commission of India 2018).

At the state level, there was a Chief Electoral Officer (CEO) of State, who was appointed by the central Commission, for each of the 35 states or union territories. Borrowing from colonial terminology, Returning Officers ranked beneath the CEO who were responsible for one of the 672 districts which contained an average of 1.1 million voters (QuraishiPatidar, Jha, and Quraishi 2014, 360). Electoral Registration Officers (EROs), meanwhile, were responsible for preparing the electoral roll for each constituency. They tended to be an officer of government or local government. They were appointed by the ECI in consultation with local government units. A range of more junior positions included Assistant Electoral Registration Officers and Appellate Officers that crossed ECI and local government boundaries (ECI 2012, 10–13).

Further down the hierarchy were electoral observers. Teams of micro-observers were recruited from the broader Indian civil service, but always from outside of the state holding the election. Their role was to report any irregularity in the election back to the ECI including the voting and counting process, violations of the code of conduct, checking of account expenditure tracking of postal ballot papers and appointment of polling personnel. They were provided a training briefing by the ECI, and then strictly prevented from departing until the election period is over. They were required to report to a General Observer. This system has long roots, dating back to the 1951 Representation of the People Act and has meant that India has a domestic rather than international and external system of electoral observation (ECI 2017b; Greater Chennai Corporation 2016).

The structure was top-down by organisational design, but also by culture. As one Chief Electoral Officer diligently told me:

> elections in India are required to work in a particular way, with a single line of management, for everything you have a detailed guideline, detailed instruction. Fortunately for us we have a vast bureaucracy on the ground and almost all of them are aware of the roles and responsibilities (private interview, ECI official, May 2016).

The frequency of interactions at different levels of the organisation depends on the stage of the electoral cycle, however. One Chief Electoral Officer explained how 'our interaction with the central unit is limited during non-election time' but that working groups link together parts of the ECI out of the immediate time of the poll. 'Regular, *regular* working groups . . . ' he told me, 'I think more than 15 or 20, something like that sometimes'. Involvement in these working groups is selective. 'Not everyone is invited or involved', he discreetly indicates (private interview, ECI official, 25 May 2016).

A history of electoral violence means that security forces were more involved in Indian elections than would be common in established democracies (Wilkinson 2006). The ECI could assign state police and military forces to polling stations during an election. The Supreme Court case of 2003, *Janak Singh vs. Ram Das Rai and Ors*, clarified the roles (ECI 2016a, 63–6). As I witnessed the elections in 2016, the ECI were therefore in regular contact with the Central Para Military Forces (CPMF) and Local State Police. Armed forces were required to follow a convoy of vehicles taking voting machines from polling stations to a strong room where they were held until the count begins. Two days after the poll, when the count began in a school, I had to go through a perimeter of rifles and khaki uniforms. The buildings were empty of any evidence of being a school, with only election equipment and police inside. Some were stood down from patrol: crouched and relaxed, trying to find respite from the heat; while others stood alert looking sceptically at me and party agents.

Staff were seconded from other departments of government. In the election that I witnessed, staff from the Income Tax Department and Police Department were recruited and appointed to the Media Control Room. An architectural planner was appointed to help me travel around and visit the various polling stations. On one occasion, he was (understandably) severely late to meet me because there had been floods overnight. He was then called into the front line to help. He hadn't slept all night before coming to take me over to meet the CEO and other senior officials through rain-drenched streets. Meanwhile, an Air Intelligence Unit was set up at the airports by the Income Tax Department to check incoming flights (Greater Chennai Corporation 2016).

By convention, the Commission meets with political parties. This might be a periodic consultation as issues arise, but 'also on the national level on average twice a year', one senior official told me. Most of the time, middle-level party officials attend the meeting – perhaps sending only technical officials to look at electronic voting, for example, but:

> top leaders have also come when the election process is in motion and they come to complain against the other party. Then they come as a big delegation. Top guys, all the people. . .
>
> (private interview, former ECI official, March 2016)

Consultation also occurs at the local level. Local officials are instructed to discuss proposals for polling station locations with representatives from political parties (ECI 2016a, 23). Political party representatives also serve as polling agents on the day of the election. The Electoral Registration Officer is required to convene a meeting of representatives of parties, provide them with copies of the electoral roll and ask them to 'point out any corrections therein and explain to them the need for timely information and submissions' (ECI 2012, 14)

Civil society involvement was traditionally low, but changed as a result of policy instruments introduced by the ECI. The SVEEP (Systematic Voters' Education and Electoral Participation) scheme was introduced in 2009 to address low levels of voter turnout. In the Diamond Jubilee Year of the ECI in 2010, a theme of 'greater participation for a stronger democracy' was adopted and a range of small-scale initiatives launched. A second wave of interventions between 2013–2014 involved top-down directions for local officials to develop state- and district-level plans, which would include representatives from educational institutions, youth organisations and civil society groups. A premium was placed on working with educational institutions to recruit 18- to 19-year-olds into the electoral process. In a later iteration of the SVEEP programme, the ECI planned to incorporate voter education into the school and university curriculum. If successful, this would in effect incorporate the education sector into the delivery of elections (ECI 2013, 2017a, 1–12). States each already had individual examples of collaboration with civil society groups. As one official put it: 'voluntary sector organisations are very useful to us to reach out to the people and getting them on our electoral rolls.' In one major city the CEO used a local theatre group who 'performed a play centred around voting and its importance played across the city'. Each state has its own concept of a state icon such as a celebrity or cricketer who is used to promote voting. MS Dhoni was used in one election. This also reflected how the media is enroled in public engagement activities. The ECI collaborated with state-owned media at the national level by, for example, undertaking voter awareness campaigns with Doordarshan and All India Radio (Electoral Commission of India 2018). A requirement for CEOs to reach out to the electorate via the media was also part of the SVEEP programme from 2013 (ECI 2013).

The commercial sector also became a collaborator. In advance of the election that I witnessed the Liquor Monitoring Committee, responsible for monitoring liquor sales, worked with the ECI to avoid bribery. Under the Representation of the People Act 1951 the sale of liquor is banned during a 48-hour period up to the close of the poll. Hotels, restaurants, clubs, shops and other establishments were to take part and police checks were undertaken across these locations But there is less use of the private sector in the provision of other services – state-owned companies were the suppliers of key electoral materials.

The ECI was also vertically connected as the country plays a proactive role in the international community. The ECI was a founding member of International IDEA (see Chapter 8). An Indian International Institute for Democracy was established in 2011 at an international conference which also marked the Diamond Jubilee celebrations of the ECI with over 30 heads of EMBs from across the world in attendance (ECI 2011a). Training courses quickly follow to overseas electoral officials, as did international visits – the first being a nine-member delegation from the Nigerian Independent Electoral Commission (ECI 2011b).

Yet, ironically, although there was observation internal to the ECI, international observers were not permitted to evaluate Indian elections.

Neither were academics within India part of the network. As one official said 'we could not identify one single academic in India who works on electoral management' (private interview, 24 May 2016), although some computer scientists, as we shall see, were vocal critics of electronic voting machines – and others were proactive in lobbying for reform of laws on corruption and finance in elections.

7.3.2 Contestation

The day after I witnessed the legislative elections, a depression hit the region and months without rain ended dramatically with heavy downpours – 20cm in one day. Through streets sloshing with rain, I was driven through the city to interview the state CEO. His office was in a seventeenth-century building built by the British East India Company on the coast – exposed to winds from the sea. Now it is home to the State Assembly and the government bureaucracy. Parts of the buildings look historic: faded white grandeur architecture that is seeped in history; but there are small puddles of rain in some corridors and, the stairs are wet and slippery. 'Watch your step' my guide told me. Discarded files lay in sodden brown folders in one of the courtyards. Busy officials sat behind each door concentrating on their work. After one of the interviews, a man came from a meeting shouting and pushes a crumpled piece of paper into my hand. He was protesting about the conduct of the election the day before and the piece of paper was a letter, I realised later, detailing his concerns. 'It is his democratic right to be here' said the official who has been my guide.

Contestation about how the election should be run, however, was rare. I asked one CEO whether voluntary organisations sometimes made recommendations about how the ECI or how the elections could be conducted differently or conducted better. He paused and responded

> I see. So the scheme of the elections is quite fixed because there are statutory boundaries which are provided to us, what will be the day, the date, how many campaign dates and all those things . . . what is allowed, what is not allowed.

Political party manifestos were relatively absent of any commitments. For example, the 2014 BJP manifesto committed the party to 'consultation with other parties, to evolve a method of holding Assembly and Lok Sabha elections simultaneously. Apart from reducing election expenses for both political parties and Government, this will ensure certain stability for State Governments. We will also look at revising expenditure limits realistically' (Bharatiya Janata Party 2014). The Indian National Congress focussed on transparency and increased funding arrangements for elections in a short paragraph (INC 2014), but there was no mention in the AIADMK manifesto (2014).

Some civil society organisations were involved in supporting the running of elections (as noted above), but there was historically little organised advocacy from civil society. The development of the Association for Democratic Reforms (ADR) was a key exception. This was formed in 1999 by a group of academics at the Indian Institute of Management (IIM), Ahmedabad, who were concerned about the criminal background of candidates. Using public interest litigation, they asked for the disclosure of the criminal records of candidates contesting elections. Based on their success, the Supreme Court ruled in 2002 and 2003 that it should be mandatory for all candidates to reveal their background prior to the poll by completing an affidavit. The ADR grew in size with a large umbrella of researchers working for it and went on to conduct election watches for state and parliamentary elections (ADR 2011). For instance, in 2018 it gained headlines for revealing that 48 sitting legislators had declared cases of crime against women against them, amid a sharp rise in concern about rape incidents (PTI 2018). It has also taken positions on other issues such as the concurrent timing of elections (Chhokar 2018).

There was some initial concern from within the ECI about whether they should be associated with them:

> They thought we were a bunch of busy bodies. And they thought that we were a kind of trouble creators who disappear over time.
> (private interview, official from the Association for Democratic Reform, 23 May 2016)

But over time connections were made The ECI therefore agreed to give, for example, addresses at ADR conferences. It was better 'having them in your tent pissing out rather than pissing in' one former ECI official said (private interview, 23 May 2016). The ADR also had connections internationally. They were therefore invited speakers to International IDEA conferences in Mexico, and had given advice to like-minded organisations in Bangladesh and Pakistan: 'They want to know what we are doing and how we are doing it' one official told me. The focus of their activity remained within India, however, as the organisation felt that it had plenty to do.

Other smaller, local organisations could be found within Indian cities campaigning on 'ethical voting' – encouraging citizens to not take bribes in return for their vote. On a Facebook page for an event one group wrote that 'there is a disturbingly growing practice of voters demanding/accepting bribes from the candidates,' advertising a panel discussion led by academics. But interviewees throughout my visit did not identify one single organisation that was proactive in disagreeing with the ECI on issues of electoral management and administration.

This is not to say that there were no reforms. Major reforms have occurred, with apparently little opposition. These have included photographic electoral rolls and photo identification requirements at polling stations, and the introduction of voter slips (Quraishi 2014). The one area where there was long-running contestation is with electronic voting machines (EVMs) (ECI 2018b). These were first used on a pilot basis in Kerala in 1982 but were challenged by local candidates. The Supreme Court of India subsequently ruled in 1984 that the absence of any specific law requiring EVMs to be used, meant they could not be used. It was not until December 1988 that Section 61A was added to the Representation of the People Act 1951 to enable use of the machines. In order to try and gain popular trust, the Government of India set up an Electoral Reforms Committee in January 1990, with representatives of political parties, chaired by Law Minister Dinesh Goswami, which recommended that a technical team examine the equipment. Following a supportive report, legislation followed in 1998 enabling a wider roll-out in 1999 to 46 parliamentary constituencies and then widespread use.

There were continued criticisms, however. Research papers from computer scientists have reviewed the security behind the system (Wolchok et al. 2010). In 2010 a special conference convened by the Centre for National Renaissance resolved that the EVMs should provide a voter verifiable paper trail, or the Commission should return to the old paper ballot system. The Janata Party President demanded that an expert committee look into security arrangements. Many computer scientists wrote letters of concern to the ECI demanding reform (The Hindu 2010). Between 2001–2018 tampering has been raised in seven legal challenges in state high courts and one in the Supreme Court of India.

After the 2017 State Assembly election results were declared, several parties also raised questions about the credibility of the system. A meeting was organised with all national and state parties in New Delhi on 12 May 2017, where the Indian Election Commission promised the full roll-out of the Voter Verifiable Paper Audit Trail (VVPAT) for all elections and challenged parties to demonstrate that technology could be tampered with. The Nationalist Congress Party (NCP) and the Community Party of India (Marxist) showed interest and attended the challenge event in June, but did not lodge specific claims (ECI 2018b).

As this issue illustrates, perhaps unsurprisingly with a country so large, civil society criticisms were not usually co-ordinated or connected to each other.

7.3.3 Power diffusion

As a former official put it to me:

> The ECI is the most powerful commission in the world. Anything which requires an act of parliament, we have to depend on the politicians. Everything else we can do ourselves.
> (private interview, former ECI official, March 2016)

Undoubtedly, considerable power resided with the ECI. It had considerable *de jure*, legal independence from the government. As already noted, the appointments were via the President of the state, rather than the Parliament. Since the President was partially a political actor, the appointments were not purely technocratic, but still relatively independent from government. Meanwhile, the. Supreme Court of India has held that where enacted laws did not give explicit provision for how elections should be run, the ECI had residual powers to take action, subject to any other legal provisions (Electoral Commission of India 2018). In terms of finance, the ECI budget is 'finalised in consultation' with the Finance Ministry. There was not therefore complete independence because the financial burden, depending on the type of election, fell on either the federal or state-level government (Electoral Commission of India 2018). Although as one official pointed out to me: 'Our constitution allows the ECI to take the requisite number of resources, whether human, physical or financial for the conduct of elections' (private interview, former ECI official, March 2016).

Decision-making powers included the power to set schedules for the timing of elections, the location of polling stations, assignment of voters to polling stations, arrangement of polling stations and counting processes. Through convention, no one can intervene in the electoral process once the elections had began and the ECI was itself responsible for investigating any irregularities until after the election is over (Electoral Commission of India 2018). It could cancel the election. In Chennai 2016, it first used its power to cancel the polls in two constituencies for the TN Assembly contests following reports of 'inducing electors by candidates and political parties by offering money and other gifts to woo them in their favour' (Phadnis 2016). CPMF and Local Police Forces remain independent bodies – but the power that the ECI wielded is striking compared to established democracies. Section 131 of the Representation of the People Act 1951 gave power to the Presiding Officer to instruct a police officer to arrest and charge any person who is behaving in a disorderly manner at a polling station on the day of the poll. The ECI also had the power to deploy forces on the day of the poll (ECI 2016a, 63–7).

The top-down hierarchical structure was strictly observed with a culture of respect and obedience to commanding officers. A compendium of instructions was issued from the central ECI office on how the election is to be run, which was then cascaded down to sub-ordinate officers. A CEO described how:

> The election is something in which no discretion is given to any one. Everything is documented and instructions are clear for each circumstances, it's clearly laid out.
>
> (private interview, ECI Official, 31 May 2016)

Some officers pointed to minor areas of discretion. As one put it: 'Discreetly, best practices are shared.' Another told me that they could improve some 'local logistics' such as an expanded use of webcasting from polling stations – which might not be done elsewhere.

As an observer, I felt the power of the ECI as forceful. When I was picked up and put into a car, a sign saying 'ELECTION' was added to the back window, akin to a UN convoy The car was able to force its way through chaotic city street life like a knife through butter. TV channels switch to the press statements of the ECI officials, who command immediate attention.

The power of observers offered some internal pluralism within the ECI. Observers have the statutory power under the amended Representation of the People Act 1951 to give instructions to the Returning Officer to stop the counting of votes at any time, should they feel that the polling stations, counting locations or ballot papers are unlawfully taken out of the custody of the Returning Officer, or if there is any accidental or intentional damage or error in the process. After using this power, they must report to the central ECI who will then take 'appropriate directions' (ECI 2017b, 2). The reports of observers would remain confidential, however, and observers were prohibited from speaking to the press, even after the elections were over. They were also only allowed to give their reports to the most senior officials. Appointment is also tightly controlled.[1]

It remained the case that the ECI must conduct elections subject to the laws passed by Parliament. The power of Parliamentarians to reform those laws meant that power diffusion was anything but complete. It was subject to the ebbs and flows of power in parliamentary politics. The decisions of the ECI could be challenged in the Supreme Court of India if petitions were raised. The ECI, however, openly lobbied for reforms and would write to the government detailing proposed reforms (ECI 2016b) and again would write to the Ministry of Law and Justice to follow up on these requests (ECI 2018a). As is noted elsewhere, 'such proposals are often simultaneously discussed in the media in order to bring pressure on the government and encourage public debate' (Catt et al. 2014, 361).

Political parties were anything but powerless, however. The ECI was dependent on their trust and explicit support for the system. They were able to make criticisms of the way that the election was conducted which can lead to change as the case of EVMs shows. The ECI held regular meetings with the parties, them once or twice a year. Meanwhile, the Association for Democratic Reform proved its ability to be influential through media work and taking judicial action.

> I think our greatest strength is our visibility and our impartially. We have never been even insinuated against that we are partial to one party. We are completely non-partisan. We are equally nasty to all parties . . . we guard our neutrality very, very zealously.
>
> (private interview, official from the Association for Democratic Reform, 23 May 2016)

There were periodic committees that had undertaken reviews of electoral practices[2] but the absence of a permanent parliamentary committee limited opportunities for civil society mobilisation such as found in the UK.

7.4 New South Wales, Australia 2004–2018

Australia is a federal bicameral parliamentary democracy. A codified constitution was enacted in 1901 which established six self-governing Australian colonies to form the Commonwealth of Australia. New South Wales is one of eight states and territories. In 2017 it had an estimated population of 7.8 million – the most populated state which covered roughly a third of the entire population (Australian Bureau of Statistics 2018), but a much smaller land area of only 10.4 per cent (Geoscience Australia 2018) with Sydney as the largest city and capital.

7.4.1 Network membership

Australia had a highly federalised electoral management system in which the Australian Electoral Commission (AEC) was responsible for organising and supervising federal elections, but state and local government elections were overseen by a separate Electoral Commission in each state and territory. The AEC was established by the 1983 Commonwealth Electoral Legislation Amendment Act, replacing the Australian Electoral Office (Kelly 2012, 9).

At the national level, the Commonwealth's Joint Standing Committee on Electoral Matters (JSCEM) had a long-standing history of undertaking parliamentary enquiries into a range of aspects of electoral affairs including reviews of federal elections (Kelly 2012, 14–15). For instance, an inquiry into the 2016 federal election recommended that the Australian government invest additional funding to enable the moderation of IT and business systems, additional training for temporary staff and trial the electronic scanning of ballot papers (JSCEA 2017). Federal political parties, however, rarely showed much interest in the management of elections. According to one senior source:

> The parties aren't too worried, even, about deploying scrutineers. They're much more interested in campaigning. . . . They're not worried about the integrity of the process.
> (private interview, with former AEC official, 3 May 2018)

Civil society interest at the broad level was low, with some fringe groups taking an interest in voter identification, mostly on the right of the Liberal Party. Initiatives for reform instead came upwards from the state Commissions. Automatic enrolment involved citizens being added onto the electoral roll using data from other government databases – an initiative that had come from the states.

> It came from New South Wales actually, Colin Barry pushed it and one of his big triumphs was that he got it up and running at the Commonwealth level. It has changed, basically, the model that had been around since 1911.
> (private interview, with former AEC official, 3 May 2018)

Australia was also integrated into international networks. As one of the few countries which had a permanent EMB in the 1990s, it was able to provide electoral assistance overseas. This also structured national networks. There was 'a high level dialogue' between the AEC and AusAID in the Department of Foreign Affairs and Trade. This began with initiatives in Namibia and Cambodia but was consolidated when an amended Electoral Act made international assistance part of the mandate of the AEC. This was the result of significant lobbying from former AEC official Michael Maley, after he and colleagues 'basically drafted the Electoral Act. . . . It wasn't government drafters that were drafting legislation and providing it to the electoral commissioner to have a look at, it was actually the other way around' (private interview, former AEC official).

In New South Wales, the focus for this case study, the central organisation was the New South Wales Electoral Commission (hereafter 'ECNSW'). The Commission approved funding to parties and candidates, maintained the roll of electors and conducted most local government elections. In 2018, the ECNSW consisted of three members appointed by the Governor of NSW. It was led by an Electoral Commissioner (ECNSW 2018). A four-person senior management team consisted of an executive director for elections, funding and disclosure, information services and corporate management (ECNSW 2017, 11).

The Electoral Commissioner was required to report to the NSW Parliament's Joint Standing Committee on Electoral Matters (JSCEM). This Committee could conduct inquires and reports into electoral laws and practices. It was first established in 2004 (JSCEM 2016, 1). It could only look at issues referred to it by either the NSW House or a Minister. The Committee could be established by resolutions passed by the House. Between 2004 and 2018 the Committee undertook 11 such inquires (NSW Government 2018). The Committee was cross-party, but the broader balance of power of the NSW legislature shifted after elections. The Labor Party long held control of the NSW government between 1995 and 2011, winning four terms in office. At the elections to the 55th Parliament, a Liberal-National coalition came to power and retained office at the 2016 elections.

The submissions of evidence made to the JSCEM 2004–2017 enquiries usefully demonstrates the range of other actors involved in the network. Table 7.2 provides the frequencies by stakeholder type based on an original content analysis. Local government is demonstrably a key actor, providing a large volume of submissions. This is no surprise since local government ran some local elections – and there were spikes in their submissions when local government elections were the subject of inquiry, as they were in 2009 and 2012. Equally, while the volume of submissions is high, only a third of local govenment units submitted evidence, suggesting that there is uneven involvement. The Local Government Association of NSW was also a proactive organisation that raised concerns on behalf of the local government units about the quality of delivery of elections and the costs that they were facing (Local Government Association of NSW and Shires Association of NSW 2009).

Suppliers from the private sector were regularly present as witnesses as well as contributors of written evidence. As we shall see, legislation was passed in NSW allowing councils to run elections themselves or appoint a private company to run elections on their behalf, thereby embedding the private sector into the network. The Australian Election Company was one example. The owner and founding President was Richard Kidd who had worked at the Australian Electoral Commission from 1972 to 1998 and privately ran the first outsourced Australian election in Queensland in 2000, before setting up the company in 2006. The company continued to run elections in Queensland before opportunities emerged in NSW (Kidd 2018).

The JSCEM reports reflect a strong and consistent mobilisation from civil society. Pressure groups included civil rights groups such as the Australian Centre of Disability Law and Homelessness NSW, but also business groups such as the NSW Business Chamber which made regular submissions. They did not seem to play a role in contributing towards the running of elections, however.

Table 7.2 Number of submissions to the NSW JSCEM 2004–2017 by stakeholder type

Date of referral	Report focus	Parties	Individual	Academic	Pressure group	Supplier	Local gov	NSW EC	NGOs	Unions	Politicians	AEC	Total
Aug 2017	Preference counting in local government elections in NSW	2	9	1	1	1	8	1	0	0	0	0	23
Jun 2015	Administration of the 2015 NSW election	6	5	1	3	2	0	2	1	2	0	0	22
Jul 2014	Preparations for the 2015 NSW state election	3	0	0	0	0	0	1	0	0	1	1	6
Sep 2012	2012 local government elections	5	4	0	3	2	53	0	1	0	3	0	71
Apr 2012	Review of the Parliamentary Electorates and Elections Act 1912	8	6	0	3	0	0	1	0	1	19	0	19
Nov 2011	Administration of the 2011 NSW election	6	3	1	3	1	0	0	0	0	0	0	14
Mar 2009	2008 local government elections	5	5	2	6	0	49	0	4	3	1	0	75
Jun 2007	Administration of the 2007 NSW election	4	4	1	7	0	0	0	0	0	3	0	19
May 2006	Voter enrolment	1	3	0	10	0	0	0	0	0	0	0	14
Sep 2004	Administration of the 2003 NSW election	5	4	0	4	0	0	0	0	0	2	0	15

A small number of academics made submissions, such as Dr Anika Gauja and Professor Rodney Smith from Sydney University. The most regular participants, however, were computer scientists Vanessa Teague and Roland Wen. 'Elections Analyst' Antony Green, who regularly did media work as an expert for ABC, made ever-present detailed contributions. There were also proactive individual citizens, including professionals writing in an individual capacity. For example, a doctor wrote to a 2012 inquiry to draw attention to how one of their hospitalised patients had been 'denied the opportunity to vote ... because the mobile electoral team were unable to attend to her before the 6pm closing of the polls'. Unsatisfied with the response of the NSW Electoral Commissioner, the doctor wrote persistently to the Committee (Boutlis 2011, 2012).

The reports also show some international connections. The first JSCEM inquiry involved an overseas study tour to Malta, Dublin and New York (JSCEM 2005b). Political parties were ever present – either at a local or state level. Correspondence often came in from staffers. For example, an office manager for a NSW MP wrote to the inquiry on the 2007 election to raise concerns about the number of residents of nursing homes who were missing from the register (Rumble 2008). Even if submissions were relatively low, party representatives were invited to give oral evidence. The ECNSW were usually called as witnesses, even where they did not give written evidence. The national AEC was rarely present – only making one submission.

Some individuals worked for multiple organisations in the network. Mark Ratcliffe, for example, gave evidence as Business Development Manager for Everyone Counts in the inquiry into the administration of the 2011 NSW election, where he worked between 2011–2014, before becoming the iVote Manager the ECNSW and then Director of Electoral Innovation in July 2017 (Radcliffe 2018). To illustrate these connections, when I arrived at the NSW Office in May 2018, one official around the table had just returned from the UK to visit Webroots Democracy only a week earlier, where a former colleague was presenting at Westminster on the NSW work (Brightwell 2018).

There were other forms of interactions, outside of the committee forum, of course. While the national AEC was rarely present, it was regularly connected to the ECNSW, with daily communication at both the junior and senior level. There would be joint role agreements between the state and the Commonwealth to ensure that the process of enrolling electors was done consistently and in a harmonised way. The outsourcing of local elections to the ECNSW also created a system of contract negotiation with local government. Meanwhile, the ECNSW has also historically run NSW Aboriginal Land Councils, bringing in a wider set of connections with stakeholders.

7.4.2 Contestation

The JSCEM inquiries and the government responses to them provide useful detail about the degree of contestation. There were some areas of agreement, which often led to uncontested legislative change. The first inquiry, for example, made the case for legal modernisation. The JSCEM (2005a) noted that the Electorates and Elections Act 1912 had been in place for over 90 years, at that time, and heard representations in favour of modernisation from the State Electoral Office, with which the government agreed. The areas of disagreement are discussed in turn.

Resourcing elections

The resourcing of elections was one common area of concern and disagreement. At the Inquiry into the 2003 election political parties were vocal and in agreement that further resources should be invested. As the Green Party commented: 'The state electoral office does a good job considering its resources, but in our view it is clearly understaffed and the government needs to increase the allocation of budgetary resources (JSCEM 2005a, 8). Independent experts and pressure groups such as the Proportional Representation Society rushed to agree and the Committee recommended further funding.

A debate erupted after the 2008 local elections, however, about where the costs should be borne for running elections. The Local Government Act 1993 had required councils to meet the costs incurred by the ECNSW who ran local government elections on their behalf. However, complaints arose from the local government sector that these costs were rising. One council argued that the ECNSW acted as a 'legislated, price protected monopoly' service provider (JSCEM 2009, 13). Elsewhere, concerns were raised about the '$195 per hour charge out rate used to determine the administration fee charged to councils' (JSCEM 2009, 22). The Committee was not persuaded that a different approach 'would be cost-efficient or necessarily feasible' but agreed that the cost model should be externally reviewed, which was supported by the Labor government. The ECNSW defended the rationale and calculations behind the fee and agreement was reached for better information sharing about the costs (JSCEM 2009, 22).

With a change of NSW government, the new Liberal-National Minister for Local Government supported the right of local councils to run their own elections, should they prefer, and passed this in the Local Government Amendment (Elections) Act 2011. The responsibility therefore lay with the general manager of the council, unless they chose to allow the ECNSW to run it (JSCEM 2014, 6). This legislation was needed, argued the Minister, 'following a significant increase in fees faced by all councils' and cited the Local Government and Shires Association's support (JSCEM 2014, 10). Fourteen councils then ran their own elections in 2012, with 10 outsourcing to the Australian Election Company.

The ECNSW raised concerns about inconsistencies in service provision and suggested that the reforms amounted to the 'the privatisation of the conduct of local government elections' (JSCEM 2014, 9). Some councils insisted that the Commission played an important role in light of the fact that 'arms-length ensures independence, ensures the general manager is not under any pressure by either existing or potential councillors ... when tough decisions need to be made' (JSCEM 2014, 9). Meanwhile, the Australian Election Company argued that it was unfair that the ECNSW was exempt from paying payroll tax, while as a private provider, it had to. This did not create 'a level playing field' in the market to run elections. The ECNSW disputed this (JSCEM 2014, 17).

Voter participation

Concern about voter participation and the completeness of the electoral register arose at many points, with civil society groups pressing the case for reforms that improved accessibility or helped to enfranchise marginalised groups. Voting rights for disabled persons were commonly raised with organisations such as Vision Australia, People With Disability Australia (PWD) and the NSW Disability Discrimination Legal Centre (NSWDDLC) arguing that 'many disabled voters were still unable to cast a secret and independently verifiable vote' (JSCEM 2009, 70). Organisations such as Homelessness NSW suggested that the ECNSW made some simple improvements to its website, such as including the word 'homeless' as a search term (JSCEM 2012, 20). While there was agreement that information should be readily available, there was little agreement from ECNSW and other organisations about how to change voting and registration procedures or how to address these accessibility and related issues to participation. The Community Relations Commission raised concerns about the effects on people from non-English speaking backgrounds who 'already experience difficulty understanding the requirements and processes for enrolling on the electoral roll' (JSCEM 2006, 19).

The JSCEM (2006) report focussed on the completeness of the electoral register following a request from the Premier. The Committee heard concerns about levels of registration among indigenous Australians, people with disabilities, non-English-speaking backgrounds, the young and the elderly. Concerns from civil society were raised about the impact of the Electoral and Referendum (Electoral Integrity and Other Measures) Act 2006 (Cmth) passed by the Commonwealth Parliament which would introduce new requirements for enrolment such as a driver's licence number. The Committee was critical of the change stating that:

> There is a disproportional impact on young people, indigenous people, the homeless and people with disabilities. This has a negative impact on universal franchise.
>
> (JSCEM 2006, 13)

Organisations such as the Youth Action & Policy Association (YAPA) claimed 'that is really concerning how this will impact on disadvantaged young people' (JSCEM 2006, 16), citing data on young people having fewer driver's licences. Similar concerns were raised by the NSW Commission for Children and Young People. The Committee therefore encouraged:

> the SEO to liaise with the AEC on strategies that will increase the level of youth enrolment and also ensure that the new requirements do not leave young people unable to enrol.
>
> (JSCEM 2006, 18)

The introduction of a Smart Enrollment system followed thanks to government funding (JSCEM 2008). This was broadly welcomed with the ECNSW

Commissioner saying that the system 'would enable progressive updating of the enrolment details of electors throughout the year' (JSCEM 2008, 10) while the Committee expressed the view that it 'would be desirable for this project to be finalised as soon as possible, preferably in advance of the next election' (JSCEM 2008, 11). The government subsequently supported this further roll-out with the Parliamentary Electorate and Elections Amendment (Automatic Enrollment) Bill introduced on 12 November 2009 (NSW Government 2009). The scheme was met with criticism from the Liberal group who thought that 'We do not believe that it is the right of the State to put people on the register' (JSCEM 2012, 38). The Committee, however, considered it a 'considerable achievement' (JSCEM 2012, 39).

Internet voting

There were clashes over the eventual deployment of internet voting in NSW. The Committee was not convinced in 2005 that e-voting would be secure enough to be used (JSCEM 2005a, xv). But it was later introduced and then pushed by the Premier of NSW. Some years later the Committee had changed its mind, 'applaud[ing] the introduction of technology-assisted voting which enabled persons to cast their vote via the phone or Internet in the 2011 New South Wales State election' (JSCEM 2012, 40). There was some support for the further roll-out of iVote to local government elections (JSCEM 2014, 59). NSW Labor argued that the system was 'assisting voters' while the Nationals were interested in using it to make voting easier for rural voters (JSCEM 2012, 43–4). Further support came from the Greens and others (JSCEM 2014). There was support from the Liberal government in principle, but the cost feasibility needed to be explored and not until the 2020 local government elections (NSW Government 2014, 7).

Two academics persistently argued that there were security vulnerabilities with the existing system, however, and that the system should therefore be discontinued (Teague and Gore 2015). Their arguments were supported by an Australian IT company but strongly contested by the ECNSW and, unsurprisingly the manufacturer of the iVote system. The political parties raised concerns and supported further security measures, but did not suggest abolition. The Committee suggested that no wider roll-out took place and that an independent panel of experts assess the system ahead of the 2019 election with the system only continuing if these concerns were addressed (JSCEM 2016, 11–12). It also agreed with the academics who sought for the code to be made open access, against the wishes from the ECNSW which the government accepted in principle. Labour, the Greens and the Shooters, Fishers and Farmers Party pushed for further opportunities for scrutiny of the system, but the ECNSW and Committee agreed that there had been sufficient opportunities for scrutiny (JSCEM 2016, 14).

Electronic voting at polling stations was proposed by a series of stakeholders such as Anthony Green, who thought that it would make for easier auditing and reduce queues. The academics that were critical of iVoting agreed that it would be a useful alternative for those who find pen and paper difficult for accessibility reasons. All political parties supported it provided that sufficient security checks could be put in place but the ECNSW raised concerns about cost. The Committee suggested trials which the Liberal government supported (JSCEM 2016).

Postal voting

Postal voting remained another contested area. After the 2007 NSW elections there was support from the Physical Disability Council of NSW to extend postal voting rights to the disabled and from Homelessness NSW/ACT to extend it to the homeless and women escaping domestic violence, which were supported by the Committee. Support from the Labour government led to proposed legislation (NSW Government 2009, 5).

More contentiously, there was also concerns from the ECNSW about rural and remote postal voters who already had postal votes because irregular and infrequent mail deliveries left them with a tight window to vote in. The National Party was especially concerned, since this was their core vote. Both the Nationals and the ECNSW supported the automatic sending of postal voters in order to speed up the process, but the Committee was not supportive and preferred raising awareness strategies (JSCEM 2008, 19–20). The Nationals also pushed for more pre-polling in rural areas, claiming that there were 'simply not enough pre-poll booths to satisfactorily service remote NSW voters who have to travel long distances – hundreds of kilometres, to attend a pre-poll centre' (JSCEM 2008, 21–2). The Labor government subsequently supported this with revised legislation to enable mobile pre-polling (NSW Government 2009, 3). The National Party also pushed for extending the period between the close of nominations and polling day to at least three weeks (JSCEM 2012, 12–13), but met resistance from the ECNSW and the Committee.

Universal postal voting was raised ahead of the 2012 elections, with the NSW Commissioner 'arguing' that cost savings of approximately 15–20% could be made' (JSCEM 2009, 62). Some councils argued that it would increase participation. Yet there was opposition from the Local Government Association President who argued that attending polling stations was the more 'traditional' way, and the Shires Association's Senior Vice President claimed that it ensured that citizens 'have interest in the candidates' (JSCEM 2009, 64). Noting this difference of opinion, the change was not supported by the Labor government. Arguments were raised again in 2014, this time with support from the Australian Election Company and the Local Government Taskforce. The Liberal government therefore agreed to support it in principle on the basis of cost saving and suggested removing eligibility requirements for all citizens in the City of Sydney in the first instance before further work could be done to enable all postal elections (NSW Government 2014, 6).

Fraud

Unlike in the UK, concerns about electoral fraud rarely surfaced. Only after the 2011 NSW elections did the NSW Election Commissioner claim that multiple voting might be a problem and therefore suggested smartphone technology to mark off electors at polling stations (JSCEM 2012, 54). The NSW Commissioner saw no objections to voter identification being brought in, nor did the Christian Democratic Party, but there were concerns raised by Homelessness NSW. The committee suggested that a feasibility study could be undertaken leading to draft legislation for voter ID (JSCEM 2012, 56–7). The NSW Liberal government did not support this measure, however, but was keen on the use of an electronic mark-off system to prevent multiple voting. Over time, the Liberal Party switched position to argue that 'In this day and age people generally have a form of government-issued ID' (JSCEM 2016, 5). But there was opposition from the Labor Party who expressed concern that a large number of voters might be disenfranchised. The Liberal government agreed that it was not necessary since 'it has not been established that multiple voting is a significant issue in NSW' (NSW Government 2016, 3–4). Electronic poll books were trialled, however, in the Sydney Town Hall in the 2015 NSW elections (and in 2012 local elections) and was later supported by the Committee for wider roll-out (JSCEM 2016, 3).

7.4.3 Power, strategies and tactics

Although the Australian system was heavily federalised, considerable power resided with the national government of the day. Major reforms could and would be instigated at the federal level by incumbent governments. As Kelly noted, there were two such waves. The Hawke Labour government, after coming to power in the 1983 general election, established the AEC, but also instigated reforms such as party identification on ballot papers and ballot order decided by lot. A second wave of reforms was introduced in 2006 under the Howard Liberal-Nationals Coalition Government. This included the earlier closure of the electoral roll, tougher voter identification requirements alongside changes to donation disclosures (Kelly 2012, 2–4). Statecraft strategies are therefore viable. Although there is autonomy within NSW for sub-national elections, there are high administrative incentives to ensure that these systems align with national practices so that dual systems are not administered. The NSW JSCEM reported, for example, that the if voter ID was something that the national government was considering then legislation would need to follow in NSW to ensure that a joint enrolment process for registration remained in place (JSCEM 2005a, xxi).

Within NSW, parliamentary politics also remains central. The Premier of NSW was the head of government. They were formally appointed by the Governor of New South Wales, but by convention appointed on the basis of being able to have sufficient support of the majority of members of the lower house, the Legislative Assembly. They therefore assume key powers to push policy forward by proposing legislation. In the case of iVoting, the Premier announced on 16 March 2010 that the 'Electoral Commissioner will investigate Internet voting for visually impaired people of New South Wales, improving their democratic right to a secret ballot' (ECNSW 2016). An amendment to the Parliamentary Electorates and Elections Amendment Bill 2010 statutorily required the ECNSW to undertake this investigation (ECNSW 2010, 1). As one official at the NSWEC put it:

> the Premier of the day basically gave the commissioner 24 hours' notice of a press release saying they're allocating 1.5 million to internet voting for the blind, and that he was going to put a feasibility report request in parliament to report back within two or three months.... We drafted that and it all went, because the Premier just kept saying, 'Keep going unless I say, "Stop,"' so we did.

The feasibility report argued that a 'remote electronic voting system would be of benefit to a broader audience of stakeholders than the blind and vision impaired' (ECNSW 2010, ii). This was sent to the Premier's office in July and tabled before Parliament in September. Legislation was passed to bring it into effect from December 2010 (ECNSW 2016). It was also the Labor Premier, Morris Iemma, who asked the JSCEM to look into levels of voter enrolment in NSW (JSCEM 2006, 11).

The Premier and political parties obviously have an ability to shape parliamentary votes in Parliament, in favour or against legislation. This can have a decisive effect on the power and function of other actors within NSW. The Constitution Act 1902 and the Parliamentary Electorates and Elections Act 1912 provided the legislative framework for many years. The Electoral Act 2017 was a rewriting of this legislation, which altered, amongst other areas, the structure and role of the NSW Electoral Commission, its responsibility to maintain an electoral register and powers to automatically enrol citizens. Decisions made within the executive and political parties in the legislature, to support or block legislation, would be profoundly affect electoral management. In the second reading of the Electoral Bill, Paul Lynch, leading for the opposition Labor Party, stated that they did not oppose the bill and acknowledged that it drew from the reports of the JSCEM 2012 to 2015, on which he served. 'The NSW Labor Party made submissions on the draft bill and a number of those submissions were successful.... The joint committee's intention and the Government's aim in introducing a modernised version of the bill is entirely sensible' (NSW Parliament 2017, 46). Despite the consensus and large cross-party approach on this area, however, there was considerable scope for parties, the NSW government and parliamentarians to take a less hospitable approach. This consensus was not present, for example, in the aspects of the law relating to electoral funding, where Labor criticised the government for leaving the Election Funding, Expenditure and Disclosures Act 1981 'untouched and alone' (NSW Parliament 2017, 46).

The ECNSW had considerable influence. The Constitution Act 1902 and Parliamentary Electorates and Elections Act 1912 gave the Electoral Commissioner the responsibility to administer the enrolment of electors, the preparation of the electoral register and the conduct of elections. They therefore inherited considerable legal power and were provided with administrative power and resource to carry out their functions. As the hearings to the JSCEM testify, the ECNSW was given a front and centre position in the discussions – always drawn upon to present their views and recommendations for reform. This gave them considerable opportunity to influence. Many of their recommendations were approved by the Committee and went on to become government policy.

The format of the JSCEM, however, also provided civil society groups with a previously unprecedented opportunity to present their views and lobby for policy. Civil society views were regularly cited throughout the reports. They were thus given an opportunity to agenda-raise and push for reform. For example, concerns were raised by disability groups at the 2007 election, following a roundtable JSCEM discussion. Based on this the JSCEM recommended: 'That the NSWEC examine ways to allow vision impaired electors to cast a secret ballot, for example, through the use of e-voting and i-voting' (JSCEM 2008, vii). NSW went on to become one of the world leaders in the use of remote voting. The format of the JSCEM also gave greater power to local government stakeholders and the private sector who were able to lobby for change.

The backdrop to the case study was also structural pressure for change. Creeping centralisation, one long term employee of the AEC argued had taken place as a result of changes in information technology:

> I joined the AEC in 1982. Essentially, you had 125 field offices that were feudal baronetcies. They were autonomous at election time, they had unlimited budgets to spend, they made all their own local arrangements. At the centre you didn't really know what the periphery was doing. The offices didn't have computers. They were running, essentially, manual processes for everything.
>
> Little by little, and without it ever being stated in any strategic plan – they've moved from a situation where these officers were feudal lords to where they're cogs in a big machine. Now they have automated enrolment, you have automated election management systems, you have automated results systems, they're all networked together. The role of the divisional officers has fundamentally changed, the staffing levels [in the periphery] have dropped, staffing levels in the centre have increased. There is a lot more structure to it. Along with that, the capacity to know what's going on – at the centre – is much greater. (private interview with former AEC official, summer 2018).

The geographic context provided a further structural context to the debates. The relatively low population density for NSW (and Australia more widely) encouraged a predisposition to explore remote voting options that states with higher population densities might not. As one ECNSW official explained to me in Sydney:

> We are fairly sparsely populated in many parts of the state, which means that some of the areas are enormous. I think two of the electoral districts are famously bigger than the size of Germany after our electoral boundary redistribution in 2013. Some of the logistical challenges can be quite enormous.
> (private interview, NSWEC official, 24 May 2018)

7.5 Jordan 2009–2017

Jordan gained independence in 1946 to become a parliamentary monarchy ruled by King Hussein from 1953–1999. King Abdallah II, his eldest son, took the throne following his father's death. The bicameral Parliament consisted of the Senate ('Majlis Al-Aayan') and the House of Representatives ('Majlis Al-Nuwaab'). Between 1973–2017 it was ranked as 'not free' for 19 years and 'partially free' for 26 years by Freedom House, and had a very low Electoral Democracy Index score from V-DEM.

It therefore provides an opportunity to explore a very different network.

7.5.1 Policy network membership

Prior to 2012, national elections were organised by the Ministry of Interior, while local elections were run by the Ministry of Municipal Affairs. That year, however, the King approved a new law establishing a new Independent Electoral Commission (IEC) to take over national elections. It oversaw its first elections in early 2013 for the 17th Jordanian Council of Representatives. The next year it also became responsible for future municipal and governorate elections (IEC 2018).

Within the IEC, a Board of Commissioners was responsible 'for determining the general policy of the Commission as well as approving all plans and procedures' (IEC undated, 1). This consisted of a chairman and four other members who were appointed by Royal Decree for six years, with the possibility of a renewal of their term. The IEC executive body was the Secretary General, which was appointed by the Board of Commissioners and was responsible for 'overseeing all of the operations of the IEC and executing strategic initiatives' (IEC undated, 1). The IEC had seven directorates: Electoral Processes; Policies and Institutional Development; Communication, Information and Awareness; Information System and IT; Administrative, Financial and Human Resources; Internal Control; and Legal Affairs. The permanent staff size was approximately 100 but up to 50,000 temporary workers were recruited at election time – either from other government departments or on an unpaid basis, including 2,000 poll workers. Local officers are only operational during election time. In the early years of the IEC's formation, permanent staff were seconded by the Ministry of the Interior, but by 2017, the number of seconded staff was limited (Reske-Nielsen 2017, 8). There remained a role for the Ministry of the Interior, however, in providing security and logistics, who would meet with the IEC on a daily basis during the run-up to the election (private interview, electoral assistance official, July 2018).

There was also heavy international electoral assistance. The UNDP, EU, USEA, IFES and ECES all contributed financial assistance and provided technical assistance on a very regular basis. Less often, but still common, has been the provision of supplies, training, advice and logistical and personnel support (James et al. 2019). The government of Jordan requested assistance from the UNDP in November 2011 for support in establishing an independent EMB. The Strengthening Electoral Processes in Jordan (SEPJ) was launched by UNDP

Jordan in May 2012 with a Senior Electoral Advisor (SEA), Ray Kennedy, taking responsibility for the overall management to a project team of consultants and advisors who were physically sharing the premises with the IEC that was being established. The SEA post became vacant immediately after the 2013 parliamentary elections until Maarten Haalf took the position. Larger projects followed from 2012–2018 (Beale 2013; Reske-Nielsen 2017, 3) and a request was made from the Jordanian government and IEC for support to continue (Reske-Nielsen 2017, 5). Some international actors were not always in direct co-ordination with others. For example, UN-Women implemented programmes to increase female participation with the Jordanian National Commission for Women – but 'with limited engagement' with other projects (Reske-Nielsen 2017, 9). IFES took responsibility for most of the IEC's training activities and this took place outside of other projects (Reske-Nielsen 2017, 13). But many international actors shared buildings with each other and the IEC and came to know each other on a personal basis. The organisations all collaborated to establish the IEC and its capacity. An early crucial focus was on supporting the IEC's drafting of '"executive instructions" (EI), electoral regulations, and strategic and operational plans' (Beale 2013, 7) – in effect an operating manual. Support was also introduced to build 'individual capacities through on-the-job training and mentoring, learning by doing, south to south experience sharing, exposure to international best practice and well-targeted study visits' (Beale 2013, 7).

A keen concern was also for the IEC to build relationships with civil society to promote active citizen participation in the electoral process. New channels of communication would be establishing stakeholders, including a formal National Voter Education Committee (NVEC) and a Political Party Liaison Council (PPLC). The latter was important in trying to promote gender strategies to encourage women to vote, take part in parties and become candidates (Beale 2013, 7). The involvement of the UNDP was not only therefore network broadening by itself, but acted as a multiplier to involve civil society groups. It also brought in further government departments since project steering committees were established to involve the Ministry of Planning and International Cooperation. A Public Outreach Advisor was also appointed to link government departments with electoral stakeholders, citizens and the media.

Civil society involvement was also present elsewhere – even if it was relatively sparse and unstructured. Prior to 2011:

> there was almost nothing. There was one meeting in the run up to the 2010 elections between disability groups and the Ministry of the Interior. After 2011, there was dramatic increase.
> (private interview, electoral assistance official, July 2018)

This work included the Communication, Information and Awareness Directorate of the IEC being charged to undertake voter outreach communication work with marginalised communities. In response to the Electoral Management Survey

(James et al. 2019b), the IEC listed other organisations that it was collaborating with. This included the National Committee for Women's Affairs and the Women Solidarity Institute, who had worked to spread public awareness of the importance of the role of women. The latter monitored elections from a gender perspective and reported on the campaigns of female candidates, ran workshops to mobilise women representation in Parliament and raised an awareness of women's rights (SIGI 2018). The National Center for Human Rights also campaingned on broader human rights issues. It was established in 2003 and was in receipt of funding in 2017 from the EU to support increased participation of citizens (NCHR 2017). Meanwhile, a coalition of 50 Jordanian civil society organisations also pooled resources under the umbrella of Integrity Coalition for Election Observation to produce observation missions in 2012 and 2016 (ICEO 2012, 2016). Historically, political parties, although numerous, have been weak with tribal or family connections shaping voting patterns and political opposition restricted. The Muslim Brotherhood had not participated in many elections.

Civil society projects were time-bound, however, meaning that lasting network change would not be inevitable. One early evaluation report noted that the National Voter Education Committee and the Political Party Liaison Council 'were not "institutionalized"' (Beale 2013, 14). The concepts 'did not gain traction' with senior IEC decision makers who demonstrated 'an underlying hesitancy to engage with civil society on a formal basis' (Beale 2013, 20). Liaison officers were identified from political parties, which was a marked step forward, but no formal liaison mechanism with them was established, as of 2013. Nonetheless, the establishment of informal pathways was a noticeable change (Beale 2013, 22). Seven meetings subsequently took place between February 2015 and May 2017, 'to discuss electoral processes and issues, including . . . changes to the electoral system' (Reske-Nielsen 2017, 17).

Jordan's IEC was also involved in vertical networks. The Organisation of Arab Electoral Management Bodies (ArabEMBs) was launched in June 2015 to provide 'a platform for networking and exchanging information and expertise' with the aim 'to strengthen the Arab EMBs capacity, competency, and professionalism' (Badrieh 2015). The body would have six members (Jordan, Iraq, Palestine, Libya, Lebanon and Yemen). The idea for the body was first raised in a session of the European Commission–United Nations Development Task Force on Electoral Assistance in April 2014, following a discussion of approximately 100 participants from electoral commissions in the Middle East and North Africa. Preparatory meetings took place in Spain in June 2014 and Beirut in January 2015 before a charter was finalised in Jordan in 2015 (ArabEMBS undated, 4). Jordan was then chosen to host the General Secretariat of the Organisation headquarters following a secret ballot in January 2015. Dr Emad Al Saiah, Chairman of the Libyan High National Elections Commission, was initially appointed as President with a three-member executive board. An Interim Secretary General, Ms Badrieh Belbisi, was appointed from the Electoral Commission of Jordan (ArabEMBS, undated).

7.5.2 Contestation

Civil society activism was central to spurring political change and restructuring the nature of the governance network. Political opposition strengthened to culminate in widespread protests against the regime in January 2011. Known as *hirak*, these protests were connected to a wider Arab Spring, but were built on Jordanian concerns about difficult economic conditions and corruption. As one widely cited protester put it 'the roots of the Jordanian movement were there before the Arab Spring, but the Arab Spring gave it strength' (Amis 2016, 177). Nervous of repression, the protest was legalist in nature – avoiding direct criticism of the King to focus on a restoration of civil and democratic rights (Amis 2016, 176). Demands were set out for anti-corruption measures, political reforms and 'following subsidy cuts in November 2012, the end of the monarchy' (Carter Center 2013, 6). However, the King responded with a range of reforms aimed at strengthening parliamentary power, the publication of a series of discussion papers on reform and the early calling of the 2013 parliamentary elections so that the Parliament could be a venue for reform. These elections, however, were boycotted by many opposition forces such as the Muslim Brotherhood's Islamic Action Front.

Contestation was therefore at the broader regime level rather than just electoral management – but the establishment of an independent EMB was central to the reformers' demands and was granted as part of the King's reform agenda (Amis 2016). The Jordanian Alliance for Electoral Reform (JAER) formed from civil society organisations from across Jordan to push for reforms. This network included representatives from political parties, trade unions and NGOs. On 7 February 2011, the NCHR held a meeting to discuss recommendations reached in 2009 about the need for reform. The participants set out a reform agenda which included the establishment of an independent electoral commission, 'headed by a prominent public figure or an independent and neutral personality'. Demands were made for the role of electoral observers to be set out in law and assurances requested about the secrecy of the ballot (NCHR 2011).

Following the establishment of the IEC, criticism of election management and calls for reform continued. The Integrity Coalition for Election Observation (ICEO) was proactive at providing constructive criticism of the IEC and proposing more nuanced reforms. Following the 2012 election it declared that many aspects of the contest complied with the regulations, but noted 'violations that took place during registration which were committed by some potential candidates and their agents, sometimes in collaboration with individuals inside registration centers' (ICEO 2012). It called for action to address these problems, and more reforms were called for after the 2016 contest (ICEO 2016). Elsewhere, the Carter Center provided clear international criticism of the 2013 elections, claiming that despite 'important technical advances' there were 'persistent concerns about vote buying, proxy registration, and other problems' (Carter Center 2013, 3) and listed its own proposals for reform.

Evaluations of electoral assistance revealed heated debates too. A failure to take sufficient action to adopt a gender strategy was pinpointed (Reske-Nielsen

2017, 13), suggesting some differences in the importance attached to this between members of the international community and officials in the IEC.

7.5.3 Power diffusion

It is striking that a much more detailed and richer set of civil society actors were present in Jordan than was present in the UK – or India. But this should not disguise how broader political power unquestionably resided with the King. The King had a legislative veto. Although legislation needed to be passed by both houses of Parliament, it required the King's approval. He could dismiss Parliament and did so in 2011 and 2012. Appointments to the IEC were closely controlled and the first three chairmen were former ministers.

Yet there were some signs of IEC de facto independence. The Carter Center noted in its report on the 2013 elections that the commission did not take a position against the boycott of the election by the opposition forces – instead it emphasised that 'it is your choice' and imposed a code of conduct against its own staff. Moreover, it played a proactive role in institutionalising the secrecy of the ballot and combatting electoral fraud (Carter Center 2013, 14).

The provision of assistance from the international community gave this community considerable opportunity to shape electoral management. 'A lot of these things came from the UNDP' suggested one interviewee. There was some consensus in electoral observations of the 2012 and 2016 contests of notable improvements in the delivery of the elections (Reske-Nielsen 2017, 12). External evaluations of the election demonstrated that the assistance had therefore had some success. That more was not achieved by 2013 reflected the fact that, having only been established in 2012, the 'IEC faced the goliath task of preparing for its maiden election while simultaneously attempting to develop an institutional framework from scratch and build staff capacity (Beale 2013, 15).

There was a tightrope to be walked in terms of the sustainability of electoral assistance projects. A 2017 evaluation noted that the UNDP country office had remained responsible for the delivery of the project. Although this had not diminished a sense of 'ownership' from the IEC staff, they did suggest that there could have been more consultation (Reske-Nielsen 2017, 19). After many years of electoral support, the IEC was still 'finding its feet' and questions were being asked about when 'it would graduate'. No exit strategy had been developed and there were fears about the skilled staff leaving. Longer-term support was therefore likely to be needed (Reske-Nielsen 2017).

Electoral assistance providers also found themselves with co-ordination problems. Collaboration and communication was often strong, but there were several instances when 'UNDP and IFES, both based at the IEC, to their mutual embarrassment, discovered that they had embarked upon the same areas of support' (Reske-Nielsen 2017, 20). In sum, the power of the international community to positively influence electoral management according to their goals was contingent on successful co-ordination and management: in political science speak, agency. There remained concerns about the levels of voter turnout, especially amongst

152 *Networks*

marginalised groups, women and youth, suggesting some limitations in the effectiveness of the international community's efforts.

The international community could also shape practices through best-practice sharing. There was significant evidence of lesson drawing from other organisations through the ArabEMBs. Members of the Committee visited conferences organised by the Venice Commission and ACEEEO to 'become acquainted with the way these kinds of organisations perform, the discussions they hold as well as the structure and functioning of the Secretariat' (ArabEMBS undated, 8). During the January 2015 meeting, when designing the ArabEMB charter, the charters of similar organisations such as those of ACEEEO, ECF-SADC and UNIORE were referred to. A Memorandum of Understanding was signed with the Venice Commission in October 2015 setting out the nature of collaboration (Venice Commission 2015; Venice Commission and ArabEMBS 2015). This would involve the Venice Commission providing technical legal assistance in areas relating to legislation and best practices. There would also be collaboration in identifying standards, conducting workshops and training events, undertaking joint research and issuing joint publications (Venice Commission and ArabEMBS 2015). As an example, support for organising the 2nd General Assembly in Tunisia was provided by the UNDP and Venice Commission (Venice Commission 2017c).

More broadly, the Arab Spring illustrated the tentative nature of wider power for any ruler. It was the protests that forced the government to develop a reform strategy including the development of the IEC. The power and resources available to the public should therefore be noted Protesters used a variety of tactics. In Madaba, roughly 50km south of Amman, a small group of activists undertook a first march, focussing on issues of bread and living standards. This was seized on by Dr Khaled Kalaldeh, the leader of the Social Left to organise wider protests. Social media was used by dissidents to brand the Amman march as 'The Jordanian Day of Rage,' a deliberate reference to events in Tunisia (Amis 2016, 172–5). Events overseas, however, provided some political cover for the campaigners and created exceptional circumstances, not likely to be frequently repeated. The King's tactics and resources no doubt would have ordinarily involved the use of the repression of protest. During the first decade of Abdullah II's reign, mobilisation by political parties and professional associations was met with bans on marches, rallies and the use of physical force against them (Schwedler 2003).

7.6 Comparing cases

Having described the nature of four electoral management governance networks, we are now in a position to compare and contrast them against the network properties set out in Chapter 5. Table 7.3 summarises the results.

The governance networks demonstrate very different characteristics in terms of *vertical connections*. Australia and Jordan are both well integrated into the international system. Australia has provided considerable external support. In contrast, Jordan has been 'an importer' – benefitting from the direct support of international organisations, but then becoming increasingly proactive within the

Comparative EM governance networks 153

Table 7.3 Comparing case studies by governance network features

	UK	India	Jordan	Australia
Vertical connections	Low	Low-Medium	High	High
Delivery partnerships	Medium-Low	Low	Medium-Low	Medium-Low
Integration	Medium-Low	Medium-Low	Low	High
Contestation	Medium	Medium-Low	Medium-Low	Medium
Power diffusion	Medium-Low	High	Low	Medium

ArabEMBs. Although there are some individuals from the UK who have interpersonal connections overseas and who may have given training/consultancy, the network has been very isolated. India was less integrated for many years, and prevented external observation of its elections. The establishement of the IIIDEA, however, marked a step towards vertical integration.

All networks have seen a gradual expansion in terms of the range of actors involved in *delivery partnerships*. Civil society actors have been useful in pointing out accessibility problems and encouraging marginalised groups to vote. There has been a greater proliferation in suppliers with a move to full privatisation in NSW and the contracting out of election supplies in the UK. A variety of state enterprises were used in India. While Jordan has not moved to the private sector, the involvement of international actors is notable – and the establishment of the IEC added considerable network pluralism.

All networks also have common *integration* patterns. In each network there is an inner-core of actors who have regular contact with one another. These tend to be key senior officials from the EMB, national ministries and local government who are all involved in delivering part of the election – or for whom the elections are funded. Political parties tend to have some intermediator role. In India they are brought into regular meetings at the national level – but their role is less clear elsewhere. Civil society groups then form the outer periphery. In India, they are barely formed; in Jordan they are restricted, while in the UK and Australia they are proactive at trying to bring change – but restricted in opportunities for involvement. A key mechanism for integration is the use of parliamentary committees. The NSW JSCEM provided a regular platform to bring civil society actors together, as did the UK's Select Committee on Political and Constitutional Reform before it was abolished and the APPG on Democratic Participation established. India and Jordan lacked these venues.

Contestation in the area of electoral management has historically been low or non-existent in the older democracies of Australia and the UK. Procedures established in the nineteenth and early twentieth centuries were left uncriticised and unreformed for a long time. In both cases consensus increasingly broke down, however, and this consensus was broken by committee hearings and increased network integration where new ideas were brought forward. Jordan, meanwhile, presents a case

154 *Networks*

where contestation was most likely silently simmering for some time under repression. India provides a more mixed story of some criticisms sometimes being raised about the conduct of specific polls – but there were also longer run growing concern, if fragmented, about issues such as the use of EVMs.

Lastly, in terms of p*ower diffusion* – there is asymmetry in all cases, but the asymmetry comes in different forms. The more powerful actor remains executive government. The Premier of NSW, the Prime Minister of the UK, the King of Jordan, the Prime Minister of India: each has power over Parliament such that, provided they can ensure party discipline, they can pass the laws to change the system as they see fit. But there are important divergences in micro-dynamics such that if parliamentarians and political leaders are to care little about the minutia of how elections are run – other actors can be influential. EMBs can also become powerful in that context, especially with constitutional provisions. India sees the ECI dominant, for example.

In short, there are striking similarities in structure and trajectories between governance networks in India, Australia and the UK – despite the deliberate attempt to identify divergence cases.

7.7 Proposed governance network types

Can we generalise from these cases to form a new typology to replace the existing one? There are always dangers in generalising from a small number of cases, but detailed case studies provide the opportunity to still suggest contrasting types of implementation governance networks. Five are suggested here, which are summarised in Table 7.4. This an ideal-type typology (Collier, Laporte, and Seawright 2008). Cases may not precisely fit into the categories and may have aspects of each of them. However, the categories are designed to identify contrasting types of network systems.

1 *Closed statist systems*. At one extreme, in closed autocratic regimes, which nonetheless still hold elections, we might expect that there are only a very limited range of actors involved in delivering elections. A desire to have close control over the electoral process, which might only be contests for

Table 7.4 Proposed typology of governance networks

	Closed statist	*Contested statist*	*Mature inter-governmental*	*Asymmetric*	*Pluralistic collaborative*
Delivery partnerships	Low	Medium	Low-medium	Medium	High
Contestation	Low	High	Low	Medium	High
Power diffusion	Low	Low	Varies according to EMB independence	Medium	Medium-high

local or parliamentary seats and not the position of head of state, might lead the regime to have a limited number of actors involved in delivering policy. There would inevitably be little open contestation of the rules and a dispersion of power as a result. A single state-run EMB or government department is involved in the delivery of elections – in a system akin to Soviet-style nationalised state industries. Control mechanisms are therefore top-down. There is a silent consensus because criticism is unlikely out of fear of repression. Of our cases, Jordan arguably fitted this criteria before the Arab Spring. But as the case study illustrates, grievances may exist but not be publicly expressed because of concerns for repression.

2   *Contested statist systems.* Entirely closed autocratic regimes are few in number, because there is often some contestation over policies and politics, even in regimes where leaders have the odds stacked in their favour (Levitsky and Way 2002, 2010). Closed statist systems will therefore be few in number too. Existing within contested autocratic regimes, a contested statist network involves a greater variety of delivery partners because political parties and civil society groups are more proactive in voter registration and mobilisation activity in favour of opposition groups – seeing it as an opportunity to change the government. These governance networks also see a much greater degree of contestation because the delivery of elections is an important site of political struggle as rulers use tactics from the menu of manipulation to rig voter registers and manipulate polling stations. Levels of professionalism within the civil service may be sub-standard with officials likely to accept orders for electoral malpractices. With some degree of political competition and freedom, opposition parties can call foul – and will have much more to call foul about than is the case in more consolidated democracies. Our case study of Jordan during and after the Arab Spring may therefore fall close to this category, as civil society groups lobbied for reforms such as an independent EMB and voter registration reform. Archetypical types might be competitive authoritarian regimes such as Putin's Russia.

3   *Mature governmental networks.* Within this governance network type, elections are delivered by a single state organisation or collection of state organisations. Elections are professionally delivered in a way that follows the rule of law. There is little civil society interest or involvement in how elections are managed because the rules of the game are largely accepted. There is therefore a 'silent' consensus because contestation about the rules of the game, if they exist, tend to focus on other areas such as electoral systems or electoral finance design. This silent consensus derives from a general lack of consideration of how elections are run. It is therefore a different type of silence to that found in closed statist systems where it is silenced by fear. The most that non-state actors are involved in is the provision of contracts by a small number of private sector suppliers. Electoral bodies still demonstrate independence and impartiality – but insulation from civil society might cause policy drift and opportunities for strong government influence over the process. As Chapter 6 details, the UK from 1872 to 1997 provided a perfect example of such a system. Before that, the UK system was more akin to contested

statism, electoral irregularities were more common and the rules of the game were contested as movements such as the Chartists sought to establish the secret ballot (James 2012). Contemporary India also has most characteristics of mature governmentalism since elections are professionally run and civil society influence contestation is low. Yet India has important differences because the EMB rather than the government has many more powers to shape how elections are conducted. In a variant to the mature governmental model – *mature independent network* – the EMB may have some constitutional independence from government and Parliament to shape the conduct of elections. If 'fearless' independence is shown, then this substantially prevents successful partisan statecraft by incumbent governments.

4   *Asymmetric network.* Rather than there being a 'silent consensus' – a variety of actors seek to deliver elections and contest how they are run. Governmental bodies are therefore pressed on policy issues and there are pressures for change. Equally, governmental bodies might be partially reliant on civil society actors to collaborate in the delivery of elections. For example, enabling outreach activities to marginalised communities might require collaboration with gatekeeper organisations. Political parties' contacts might be important brokers in keeping their activists 'in line'. But the distribution of tactics and resources is heaped in favour of governmental actors – often the government, making statecraft possible. The UK drifted towards this model after 1997, as many more actors sought to be involved in delivering elections and shaping how they should be run. We might expect this system to be found within many US states where there are Get Out the Vote campaigns from civil rights groups and political parties – and debates about funding electoral services – but power is systematically asymmetric.

5   *Pluralistic collaborative network.* At the furthest extreme, in this network there is a greater range of state agencies involved in the delivery of elections, each of which has considerable strategies and tactics available to them. These agencies are in regular and open consultation with political parties, civil society and other interested groups who are mobilised to influence policy and also equally contribute towards delivering the electoral process. There is often no consensus on policy – and explicit criticism of the status quo or government policy from civil society and parties who seek reform. The scope for partisan statecraft by the executive is more limited because the networks act as a check on government power. NSW Australia is the closest of the case studies to this model. The availability of a regular, sub-national parliamentary committee provided an important venue for different types of interests to mobilise and be further involved in election delivery. But the ideal type is never likely to be entirely realised, because removing power asymmetries entirely is very difficult.

7.8 EMB interactions with other organisations: a macro-scopic overview

How widespread are these ideal governance networks? Further research will be necessary to fully understand that However, some initial light can be shone on the questions with data from the EMS and ELECT with respect to two questions.

Firstly, data was collected on the frequency of EMB interactions with other organisations. Respondents were asked 'how often does your organization interact with the following entities?' on a 1–5 Likert scale, with a higher value indicating a higher number of interactions. Figure 7.3 provides the mean score for a sample of 30 respondents. Governments appear to be the most frequently cited actor. This is perhaps not surprising given that governments are able to pass legislation in Parliament, have key resources and may issue instructions. Figure 7.3 suggests, however, that academics and civil society groups are less influential. In terms of the network typology, this gives little support for the widespread presence of pluralistic collaborative networks worldwide.

A second question asked in the surveys was about where the ideas for successful reform had come from. Figure 7.4 summarises answers to the question: 'Of the amendments to the electoral law proposed by your organisation in the last five years, roughly what percentage were inspired by the following?' The figure provides the mean percentage for each actor. Top of the list are EMBs – in other words, EMBs think that they are the most influential actors. This is entirely plausible. At the same time, it is also likely that EMBs are more likely to attribute ideas to themselves, partly because for reputational reasons, but also because they are more aware of their own input into the policy process.

What is more striking, however, is that those actors who EMBs interact with most do not feature as highly on this list. Governments are rarely the source of

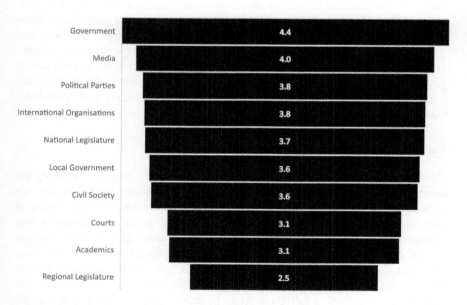

Figure 7.3 The frequency of interactions between EMBs and other actors (1–5, 5 is high).
Source: Author based on data in ELECT and EMS surveys.

158 *Networks*

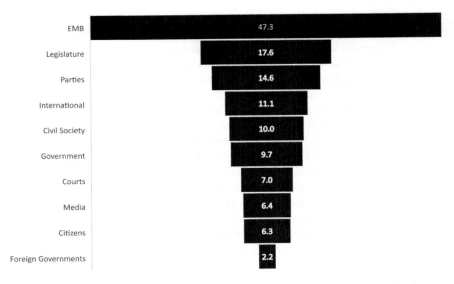

Figure 7.4 The percentage of idea source for changing electoral law in the last five years.
Source: Author based on data in EMS and ELECT surveys.

policy ideas, and even less frequently are the media. Instead, legislatures and political parties are the most influential in driving policy. Civil society and international organisations even surpass governments. There are some limitations in using the figure; it cannot be read as a league table of power and influence since it is rather simplistic – governments may well act as gatekeepers and prevent certain policies. But it does suggest that innovation comes from outside of government, because government might be more preoccupied with other policy issues. It gives support for the idea that networks worldwide are more pluralistic than governmental in nature.

7.9 Conclusions

Over the past three chapters the book has presented a new way of answering the question 'who runs elections?' We have argued that elections are run by governance networks that take different forms within different polities. By looking at four case studies, a new working ideal-type typology for differing networks was provided. Interestingly, in all of the four cases there was a gradual move towards greater pluralism over time: more actors were weighing in to implement elections and shape how they are run. On top of this, some cross-national data was then introduced that suggested that while pluralistic collaborative networks were unlikely to be realised in full, there might be more systems moving in that direction than the old inter-governmental systems than we might expect. Although we should be cautious given the limited number of cases, this suggests quite a profound change in the who runs elections.

Notes

1 In fact, some fear appointment, preferring to remain in their own state. 'Anything but elections,' especially if there is a risk of violence and intimidation in the polling stations.
2 These have included the Goswami Committee on Electoral Reforms (1990), the Vohra Committee Report (1993), the Indrajit Gupta Committee on State Funding of Elections (1990), the Law Commission Report on Reform of Electoral Laws (1999), the National Commission to Review the Working of the Constitution, the ECI–Proposed Electoral Reforms (2004), the Second Administrative Reforms Commission (2008) and more latterly, the Law Commission Report on Electoral Reforms (2015). Each, however, was not followed by legislation (Law Commisssion of India 2015; Ramesh 2011, 1–2).

8 International electoral management governance networks

8.1 Introduction

Who runs elections? The answer provided in this book so far is electoral management governance networks of different forms. But the focus has been on the shape and form of governance networks within national states. Electoral governance networks are no longer nationally bound. This chapter argues that there are interconnected networks that operate at the international level which have vertical connections downwards into many states – but certainly not all. This chapter maps how overlapping networks emerged during the late twentieth and early twenty-first century. These were unprecedented in the history of democracy. This emergence was partly a result of, but not reducible to, the third wave of democratisation and globalisation. The collapse of authoritarian socialism and proliferation of the number of states holding elections generated demands for electoral expertise. Meanwhile, the availability of the internet facilitated knowledge sharing. The emerging networks had an asymmetric geographical involvement with a select few countries acting as home to 'global leadership'. They were based on established inter-organisational and interpersonal connections. The governance networks tended to be limited to governmental and professional actors with civil society groups largely excluded and academic involvement rare, but not entirely absent. Power remained with national states. International actors developed soft diplomatic tools such as the provision of electoral assistance on request, network building and monitoring. In line with the central argument of the book, such influence was contingent on the successful deployment of skill, strategy and agency.

The chapter uses a variety of methods to make this argument. This includes secondary document analysis, interviews with senior and established members of the network and a new bespoke dataset on conference appearances. There has been empirical work on whether particular policy tools are effective (Hyde 2007; Norris 2017b), but no overall theoretical narratives about the nature of networked governance in the international system in electoral management. This chapter attempts to provide this. It begins by reviewing the broader literature on transgovernmentalism and the types of networks that have been identified to date in other policy areas. The methodology is then explained for identifying the type of networks present in the international electoral community. The subsequent sections then profile the membership, degree of integration, contestation and the available use of tactics/resources to actors.

8.2 Globalisation, global public policy and transnational policy networks

It was argued in Chapter 5 that the development of globalisation meant that we could no longer focus solely on national states when thinking about electoral management. Work on interconnected governance in broad terms dates back to the 1970s when a literature on transgovernmentalism claimed that there were 'sets of direct interactions among sub-units of different governments that are not controlled or closely guided by the policies of the cabinets or chief executives of those governments' (Keohane and Nye 1974, 43). More recently, a policy network literature conceptualised networked governance connections in more detail For Stone (2008) globalisation created transnational policy spaces where global public policy could occur. These spaces were called the 'agora' – a concept borrowed from Athenian history meaning 'a marketplace or a public square' (Stone 2008, 20). In ancient times this was a physical place where key social and economic interaction took place. The boundaries of political action were ill defined with political activity taking place within private shops. This blurring, argues Stone, is also present in the modern global public space where there is an 'intermeshed relations of politics, markets, culture and society' (p. 21). The agora is defined by 'relative disorder and uncertainty where institutions are underdeveloped and political authority unclear, and dispersed through multiplying networks' (Stone 2008, 21). Few are directly involved in global politics. International non-governmental organisations, international organisations and internationalised public agencies drive public policy. Policy activity may take place within private associations among non-state actors and the vast majority of citizens are likely to be uninformed about policy crucial venues. Stone argues that the national state is 'not necessarily retreating or declining' but 'reconfiguring with the dynamics of globalization and remains an important or central agent in the agora' (p. 25). Many of the concepts developed to understand public policy within the confines of a national state, she argues, apply to global public policy (such as agenda setting, decision making, policy implementation and policy evaluation). An important process within the agora is the opportunity for policy transfer. This is a process in which 'knowledge about policies, administrative arrangements, institutions etc. in one time and/or place is used in the development of policies, administrative arrangements and institutions in another time and/ or place' (Dolowitz and Marsh 1996, 344; also see: Evans 2004; Evans and Davies 1999). In most cases international organisations lack the organisational capacity, sanctions or authority to implement policy. Options are therefore limited to 'engineering consensus, moral pressure from other states, trade sanctions, and, at the extreme, military intervention' but there are strong disincentives to exercise these options (Stone 2008, 27). Instead, softer options are exercised such as 'exchanging information, coordinating policies, enforcing laws, and regulating markets through increasingly elaborate informal intergovernmental channels' (Stone 2008, 27).

8.2.1 Network types

Typologies have been developed to characterise the nature of different international policy networks. For Stone (2008) these include *internationalised public sector officials* who are nationally based civil servants that are horizontally integrated into transnational networks. In contrast, *international civil servants* are employed by international organisations and therefore do not have the authority within a specific nation-state but will have considerable expertise and access to other key global policy actors. A third group are *transnational policy professionals* which would include a diverse group of 'consultants, foundation officers, business leaders, scientific experts, think tank pundits, and NGO executives who are growing in number, policy reach and professionalism' (Stone 2008, 30–1).

Others to have been traced include *business-orientated networks* such as the Transatlantic Business Dialogue which has market-deepening as its goal. Its activity, however, is sometimes described as covert and is more akin to 'insider groups'. Meanwhile, *transnational advocacy networks* involve actors 'who are bound together by shared values, a common discourse, and dense exchanges of information and service' (Keck and Sikkink 1999, 89). They will then plead the causes of others or defend a cause or proposition. Slaughter (2009) argues that *cross-border governmental networks* commonly form. These are governmental officials who work together to exchange information and collaboratively tackle problems – and this is cast as a positive development. Elsewhere *knowledge networks and epistemic communities* are sometimes argued to have emerged to give 'scholarly argumentation and scientific justification for "evidence-based" policy formulation' (Stone 2008, 32).

Rather than looking at network types, Anna Ohanyan (2012) proposes a network institutionalist framework to identify the bridging and associative capacities of NGOs. She suggests that multiple bridging practices exist:

- Mechanistic – where the NGO fosters network partnerships because it is capable of delivering services.
- Regulative – where the track-record of an NGO provides 'predictability of behavior and capitalize on the donors' need to work within established channels of aid delivery' (p. 376).
- Normative – where the donors approach NGOs according to a "logic of appropriateness".
- Mimetic – where NGO relationships are mapped from one country onto another through diffusion.

8.2.2 Asymmetric power

The absence of a sovereign organisation and diversity of interests within the international arena is sometimes argued to foster pluralism (Keck and Sikkink 2014). Work on epistemic networks argues that knowledge is power, and the ability of actors to spread ideas and information can 'prove to be an important determinant of international policy coordination' (Haas 1992, 3). Actors with such resources may therefore have more influence over policy in the international domain than in national states where executive control of a government's legislative agenda limits external influence (James 2016b).

However, many other writers point to the strategic selectivity of the political terrain (Jessop 2005). Just as the analysis of interest group activity at the national level teaches us that some actors are more endowed with resources than others, the same is true at the global level. Phil Cerny deliberately draws from classical theories on neo-pluralism to understand the transnational level (Cerny 2010). Neo-pluralism famously claimed that amongst all other groups business has a privileged position because the state is dependent on it to generate jobs and businesses make key decisions about investment and employment (Lindblom 1977). Similar imbalances can be found within transnational forms of governance. Cerny writes that new transnationally linked interest and value groups have mobilised and 'are coming to dominate a growing range of crosscutting, uneven yet crucial, transnational political processes' (Cerny 2010, 4). As a result, they are crystallising their influence into webs of power as they are involved in processes 'of politicking – of pursuing their collective interests and goals, of seeking to influence and control policy making' (Cerny 2010, 19).

Meanwhile, it is commonly argued that there is a democratic deficit within world politics (Moravcsik 2004). The inequality and lack of accountability within systems of global governance have commonly been subject to strong normative critique. Social scientists have sought to redress this by advocating systems of global government of some sort (Held and Koenig-Archibugi 2004).

8.2.3 Existing work on international electoral networks

The literature on international networks has not been connected to electoral governance or management. Some researchers have assessed the effectiveness of the tools used by the international electoral community such as electoral observation (Debre and Morgenbesser 2017; Kelley 2012) and electoral assistance (Borzyskowski 2016; Lührmann 2018; Norris 2015a) using cross-national datasets. There have been some descriptive accounts of the development of the international electoral community in academic scholarship (Carothers 2003), but also in the grey literature published by I(N)GOs themselves (ACE 2018b, 2018c). Cordenillio and Ellis (2012) provide a helpful descriptive account of the role of regional organisations in elections. There has also been scholarship on the development of cross-national organisations such as the Venice Commission and OSCE, and their broader impact (Galbreath 2007; Galbreath and McEvoy 2013; Hardman and Dickson 2017; Hoffmann-Riem 2014) in the context of a broader literature on international organisations (Pevehouse and Borzyskowski 2016). Despite this early excellent work, there has been no attempt that the author is aware of to link developments in the electoral field against a governance or policy network framework. This chapter seeks to address that gap.

164 *Networks*

8.3 Methodology

To establish how the nature of international policy networks have evolved from 1990 to 2018, the theoretical framework will be used from Chapter 5. This asks: who are the network members? How integrated is the network in terms of frequency of interaction, inclusion and continuity? Is there policy consensus? And what is the distribution of tactical resources and power? Ten semi-structured interviews were undertaken with senior past or present members of some of these organisations asking them these questions during 2017 and 2018. By way of background, the author was present at three international conferences in Europe and Africa in 2016, 2017 and 2018. This was not for the purpose of researching this book, but it provides helpful background understanding about the nature of the events and the networks. Actors were identified through a literature review of academic and grey literature, reviewing conference agendas and through interview snowballing. They are anonymously cited in this chapter using the principles of 'deep background' on the basis of the political sensitivities of some of the topics and organisations involved. This is an appropriate methodology because the book takes a critical realist approach that focusses on underlying mechanisms which are not always observable (see Chapter 2).

The chapter also makes use of the Database of International Electoral Expert Speakers (DIEES) 1.0. This is an original dataset established for this book which collected information on the speakers and presentations at regular international election conferences. Conference agendas were collected via website searches with follow-up requests for missing data. The speakers, their affiliation, country of residence and paper titles were recorded. This provides an original way to view the nature of the network. It helps to identify who the most frequent actors were at an individual, country and organisational level. It also provides a unique insight into the sources of ideas and expertise about elections and the possible sources of policy transfer. A criticism of this data is that it only records observable political behaviour, rather than unobservable political phenomenon (Lukes 2005). Many meetings and presentations would have taken place behind closed doors. There is no evidence from the dataset that conference attendance led to policy change or transfer. However, the qualitative interviews address this gap.

The interactions described are also at the *elite* level. They involve the most senior officials of organisations and take place in flush locations in some of the most illustrious cities and locations around the world (with travel usually paid for by the conference organisers or the delegates' employer). This is only a partial view of the network because interactions may (or may not) take place at a more meso-level of organisations. But the identification of an elite network and frequency of these interactions is an important step in identifying organisational linkages.

8.4 Members and type of organisations

8.4.1 National governments

National governments have played a critical role within international networks. Attempts to shape the management of elections overseas have their antecedents in US foreign policy – predominantly beginning from around the middle of the twentieth century (Carothers 2003). A major trigger was the US strategy of promoting democracy to defeat the Soviet Union. Increasing the number of democracies, the logic was, would increase the number of US-friendly governments. Providing foreign aid to the 'developing world' was therefore a key component of American foreign policy from the 1950s. This was initially through economic aid and strengthening public administration. The view from Washington was that economic prosperity in Latin America and Third World states would build a middle class and lead to democratic governance. This indirect approach to democracy promotion became more direct over time. In 1966 the US Congress sponsored Title IX of the Foreign Assistance Act 1961 to tilt assistance towards 'the encouragement of democratic private and local government institutions' (cited from: Carothers 2003, 23). Programmes included civic education initiatives to promote democratic values and voluntary participation (Carothers 2003, 19–27). Confidence waxed and waned in the 1960s and 1970s. The 1980s saw President Reagan's idea for a centralised democracy assistance programme initially fail, but the US government eventually established the National Endowment for Democracy (NED) – an alternative bipartisan idea from Congress, described in more detail below. This would be a private, non-profit foundation that would make grants to support democracy around the world. Other initiatives included the USAID funding of the 1982 constituent assembly elections in El Salvador and the dispatch of Americans to observe the process. Two years later USAID also paid for a voter registration system and computers for the presidential election in the same country. Democracy assistance then boomed again in the early 1990s after the fall of the Berlin Wall and the break-up of the Soviet Union. Initiatives included the setting up of a Support for Eastern European Democracy (SEED), passing the 1991 Freedom Support Act and the Defence Department initiating a Cooperative Threat Reduction programme (Carothers 2003).

Much of this architecture remained in the early twenty-first century. The State Department continued to deal with high diplomatic judgements about democracy assistance as part of American foreign policy, with the Bureau of Democracy, Human Rights and Labor playing the specific role. Under President Obama, the 2013–2017 US State Department and USAID's combined mission statement was to 'shape and sustain a peaceful, prosperous, just, and democratic world and foster conditions for stability and progress for the benefit of the American people and people everywhere' (US State Department and USAID 2014, 1). USAID continued to act as the development aid delivery organisation and provide support for democracy-related projects around the world, much of which is on elections. The election of Donald Trump as president on an 'America First' platform, however, put overseas electoral assistance's future in question (Rogin 2017).

Narratives of overseas government interest in electoral assistance are often histories of the US electoral assistance such as that written by Thomas Carothers (2003). The role of other governments are only silently mentioned in as far as cross-national organisations such as the UN, OAS or OSCE are discussed (see, for example: Bjornlund 2004, 20–30, 53–93). Many other countries also saw democracy and electoral assistance as part of their development or foreign policy missions. A Freedom House evaluation of the work of 10 states and the European Union in democracy support 2012–2014 picked Sweden as the strongest of the select cases (Calingaert, Puddington, and Repucci 2014).[1] During this period Sweden provided bilateral election support in countries including Kenya, Mali and Somaliland. Major investments were made to Zimbabwean civil society groups and Sweden became the largest investor in the Zimbabwe Election Support Network. This worked to train local election observers and promoted women's and youth participation. In addition, Sweden was headquarters of International IDEA (see below) and provided approximately 50 per cent of its total budget (Calingaert, Puddington, and Repucci 2014, 4). Some other governments did little. Brazil, Japan and South Africa, for example, were identified as doing the minimal amount in the same report. States including Russia, China, Saudi Arabia and Iran were meanwhile identified as taking active efforts to *discourage* democratic change among their neighbours (Calingaert, Puddington, and Repucci 2014).

8.4.2 Cross-continental organisations

The end of the twentieth century saw a significant rise in organisations were working across continents to contribute towards the management of elections in one or more countries, as Table 8.1 shows. The UN had been an overseas electoral assistance organisation as far back as the 1940s, with the signing of Article 21 of the UN Declaration of Human Rights and the first UN observation of elections in the Korean peninsula. But substantial work did not commence until the 1960 and 1970s with the Trusteeship Council assisting or supervising roughly 30 electoral events. Major electoral missions began to be organised by the 1980s and early 1990s such as Namibia in 1989 which involved the supervision and control of the electoral process (ACE 2018c).

There was a watershed moment in 1991, however, when the General Assembly introduced Resolution 46/137 on Enhancing the Effectiveness of the Principle of Periodic and Genuine Elections. The 1989 Namibia operation was pointed to by many interviewees as being pivotal. It was a large-scale operation which was perceived to be a success and this re-affirmed member states' commitment to electoral assistance as it gave them confidence that it could make a difference. An organisational framework for providing electoral support was established. The General Assembly endorsed the Secretary-General's view that the UN should 'designate a senior official in the Offices of the Secretary-General to act as a focal point, in addition to existing duties and in order to ensure consistency in the handling of requests of Member States organizing elections' (United Nations 1991, paragraph 9). This focal point would be a 'first among equals' (private interview, UN official, 2 June 2017) amongst UN organisations, supported by the Electoral Assistance Division of the Department of Political Affairs of the United Nations Secretariat. It would advise on the design of missions and projects, provide the 'institutional memory', maintain a single roster of experts, be responsible for policy development and provide ongoing political and technical

Table 8.1 Cross-continental organisations contributing to electoral management

Formation date	Organisation
1982	Carter Center
1983	National Endowment for Democracy
1983	National Democratic Institute
1983	Center for Electoral Promotion and Assistance
1985	The Association of Electoral Bodies of Central America and the Caribbean
1987	IFES
1990	Venice Commission
1991	Inter-American Union of Electoral Organizations
1991	United Nations Resolution 46/137
1991	OHDIR
1991	Association of European Electoral Officials
1992	IPA CIS
1995	International IDEA
1996	EISA
1997	Pacific Islands, Australia and New Zealand Electoral Administrator's Network
1997	Association of African Election Authorities
1998	Electoral Commission Forum of the South African Development Community Countries
1998	Association of Asian Election Authorities
2006	ECOWAS Electoral Assistance Division
2013	A-WEB
2015	Organisation of Arab Electoral Management Bodies
	Commonwealth

support to all UN entities (United Nations Secretary-General 2015, 4). However, there remained many other organisations within the UN. The United Nations Development Programme (UNDP) would be the 'major implementing body of the Organisation' outside of peacekeeping or post-conflict situations. Whereas during such contexts, components of field missions would be under the Department of Peacekeeping Operations or 'Department of Political Affairs. Military and police components of peacekeeping missions support national law enforcement agencies in providing security for electoral processes' (United Nations Secretary-General 2015, 4). Meanwhile, the Office of the United Nations High Commissioner for Human Rights provided training and advice relating to human rights monitoring (United Nations Secretary-General 2015, 4) and the UN Entity for Gender Equality and the Empowerment of Women (UN-Women) would be mandated to provide 'guidance and technical support to all Member States, at their request, on gender equality, the empowerment and rights of women and gender mainstreaming' (United Nations Secretary-General 2015, 4). Other organisations included the United Nations Educational, Scientific and Cultural Organization (UNESCO) – the specialised agency providing a role in supporting freedom of the press, freedom of expression and freedom of information, the United Nations

Volunteers programme, the Peacebuilding Fund and, the United Nations Democracy Fund (United Nations Secretary-General 2015, 5). Co-ordination of many diverse organisations would inevitably be a challenge and the Assembly 'repeatedly stressed the need for comprehensive coordination, under the auspices of the focal point' (United Nations Secretary-General 2015, 4).

US foreign policy, noted above, gave birth to four enduring organisations in the 1980s. They would be American-based organisations, but with independence from American government. NED was founded as a private, non-profit foundation in 1983, following President Reagan's address to the British Parliament, and a preparatory study directed by Professor Allen Weinstein who would become the NED President (The Democracy Program 1983). The Carter Center was founded in 1982 by US President Jimmy Carter in partnership with Emory University as a research institute that would connect scholars with practitioners to advance peace, health and human rights worldwide. Early projects included workshops such as *Reinforcing Democracy in the Americas*, which in November 1986 brought together academics along with statesmen such as the President of Argentina and Prime Minster of Barbados (Carter Center 1988). Improving electoral management was therefore only one among many goals, but by 2017 the Carter Center had observed over 100 elections in 39 countries (Carter Center 2016). Meanwhile the International Foundation for Electoral Systems (IFES) was founded in 1987 by Republican political strategist F. Clinton White as a non-profit organisation. It was launched with support from USAID to 'monitor, support, and strengthen the mechanics of the election process in developing countries' and to 'undertake any appropriate education activities which contribute towards free, fair, and credible elections' (IFES 1990, 2). Two domestic election experts who were recruited and become influential were Joe Baxter and Jeff Fischer. As one interviewee put it: 'they became two very central people, who shaped what election administration support would look like.' The National Democratic Institute (NDI) also followed in 1983 with a broader democracy focus on political parties and electoral observation, rather than directly management.

Europe became home to cross-continental organisations as well. The Organisation for Security and Co-operation in Europe (OSCE) began in the 1970s as a vehicle for multi-lateral dialogues between Eastern and Western Europe. The Helsinki Final Act in August 1975 set out commitments on sovereignty, security, respect for human rights, the fulfilment of international law and co-operation (OSCE 1975). Fifteen years later, the Paris Charter 1990 was signed, shifting the format from a series of conferences to an organisation. Permanent institutions were eventually established including a Parliamentary Assembly, Summit and Ministerial Council. Membership would grow to include 57 states from Europe, Central Asia and North America. Associated with this, The Office for Democratic Institutions and Human Rights (ODIHR) was an executive structure set up in 1991 in Warsaw to promote democratic elections, respect for human rights, tolerance and non-discrimination and the rule of law (Oberschmidt 2001; Reif 2000). Although the OSCE could direct ODIHR to undertake special responsibilities, it would otherwise be an autonomous organisation under the control of a Director (Galbreath 2007, 52).

Meanwhile, the Venice Commission, thought to have been the brainchild of the idea of an Italian Minister for European Affairs, was formed following a conference of all 18 Council of Europe members in Venice in January 1990 with states from Central and Eastern Europe also in attendance. Again, the collapse of the Berlin Wall and the end of Communism meant that the members were keen to facilitate democratic transitions. By 2017, the Commission had 61 member states which included 13 non-European members such as Brazil, Canada and New Zealand. The Commission would also include members of state in an individual capacity – mostly members of the judiciary or academics in law. The primary aim would be the provision of legal advice to its members with a view to bringing member states in line with common 'European standards' and international experience in the field of elections (Jeffrey 2001; Venice Commission 2017d; Visser 2015).

Also within Europe, the International Institute for Democracy and Electoral Assistance (IIDEA) was founded as an intergovernmental organisation in Stockholm, in 1995. A declaration of the organisation began by historically situating itself in the third wave of democratisation: 'the world was entering into an age of democracy' (IIDEA 1995, 2). The institute set out its aims to promote 'the advancement of sustainable democracy worldwide and within this context to improve and consolidate electoral processes' (IIDEA 1995, 2). Fourteen states were identified as being behind the project[2] but the declaration noted 'special thanks' to the Secretary-General of the UN for this encouragement and active support. Further member states joined including Benin, Brazil, Canada, Indonesia and Mexico bringing the total number to 31 in 2016. A Board of Advisors included academics and practitioners. The Institute gained observer status in the UN General Assembly in 2003 and an office was also established in Brussels.

One organisation that had been involved in elections for some time was the Commonwealth, a voluntary intergovernmental organisation that consisted mostly of former territories of the British Empire. It had a broader interest in peace and conflict, but meetings between EMBs were organised as far back to at least 1995 (private interview, Commonwealth official, 21 June 2017), when a Commonwealth Ministerial Action Group (CMAG) was set up to deal with serious or persistent violations of the Commonwealth's political values. The Commonwealth established a Commonwealth Electoral Network (CEN) in 2010 to promote best practices in electoral management. The CEN was to be supported by a steering committee of national election commissioners and the Commonwealth Secretariat (The Commonwealth 2017).

8.4.3 Regional associations of practitioners

Regional associations of EMB practitioners followed, with Latin America the pioneer. The continent had been a hive of activity with the Organization of American States (OAS) playing a role in elections since 1962 when support was provided for the Costa Rican Presidential and the Dominican Republic general elections (OAS 1962). The Association of Electoral Bodies of Central America and the Caribbean (known as the Tikal Protocol) was established in 1985 in Guatemala and the

Association of South American Electoral Organizations (the Quito Protocol) was set up four years later in 1989. Following this, the Inter-American Union of Electoral Organizations (UNIORE) was established in 1991 to promote co-operation between these associations under the Tikal and Quito protocols. The Secretariat of the network would be the Costa Rica–based Center for Electoral Promotion and Assistance (CAPEL). Meanwhile the Association of Caribbean Electoral Organization (ACEO) dated back to a 1977 meeting in Kingston, Jamaica, where representatives from 22 states met (Palacio 2003).

In Europe, the Association of European Electoral Officials (ACEEEO) was set up quickly after the collapse of the Soviet Union, with many countries needing to run elections, but they did not have permanent election structures and experience. IFES organised a conference with the Hungarian National Election Office at the end of July 1991 in Budapest where 'participants discussed their experiences . . . [and] political and legal issues' that they were facing (Szolnoki 2016, 7), and this led to the establishment of the association. Initial membership included officials from Albania, Bulgaria, Czechoslovakia, Hungary, Poland, Romania and Yugoslavia, and in the next five years, elections experts from Croatia, Latvia, Lithuania, Macedonia, Moldova, Russia and Ukraine. The newly found organisation resolved to have annual conferences and the first two were held in Hungary in 1992 and 1993 (Szolnoki 2016).

In Africa, a multitude of overlapping organisations were in place by the end of the 1990s. The Electoral Institute for Sustainable Democracy for Africa (EISA) was established in Johannesburg in 1996 as an NGO to oversee 'credible elections, citizen participation, and strong political institutions for sustainable democracy in Africa' (EISA 2018). A small core of permanent staff was supplemented by a collection of local and international experts. The organisation expanded from one office in South Africa to have seven field offices in the Central African Republic, Kenya, Madagascar, Mali, Mozambique, Somalia and Zimbabwe. The initial focus was on South and Southern Africa, but the scope was broadened to work across Africa. At around the same time, the Electoral Commission Forum of the South African Development Community countries (ECF of SADC) was set up in December 1996. The Southern African Development Community (SADC) was a broader inter-governmental organisation, established in 1992 at a Heads of Government meeting to focus primarily on economic development, but also security and conflict preventing (SADC 2019). The first full meeting took place in Cape Town in July 1998 where the aim was 'ensuring that the management of elections in the SADC countries is improved and in building the capacity of election management bodies to fulfil their roles' (ECF-SADC 2017). This included 15 members: Angola, Botswana, DRC, Lesotho, Malawi, Mauritius, Mozambique, Namibia, South Africa, Seychelles, Swaziland, Tanzania, Zambia, Zanzibar and Zimbabwe. The Secretariat was to be based in Gaborne, Botswana (ECF-SADC 2017). EISA provided the ECF with this secretariat and technical services until 2003 when the ECF appointed its own permanent secretariat (ECF-SADC 2008, 4).

Meanwhile, larger pan-African organisations were also proactive. The Organization of African Unity had formed in the 1960s to promote African unity and then undertaken its first work in collaboration with the UN in Namibia's 1989 elections (ACE 2018b). This organisation was disbanded and replaced with the African Union in 2002 with a new vision of promoting African unity, peace, redress remaining problems of colonisation and promote international co-operation. Borrowing UN organisational language and structure, the Department for Political Affairs would be the focal point. The West African organisation ECOWAS also established an Electoral Assistance Division (EAD) in 2006 'to assist the Commission in coordinating support, managing and draw up regional policies in electioneering processes' (ECOWAS 2018). Under the Political Affairs Directorate, the Division derived its primary mandate from the relevant provisions in Article 12 of the Supplementary Protocol on Democracy and Good Governance (2001) (ECOWAS 2018). There was also an Association of African Electoral Authorities (AAEA), born following a conference in November 1994 in Victoria Falls, Zimbabwe. A working group was set up to explore options and was supported by the UN and IFES. An inaugural meeting was held in 2002 in Burkina Faso with 19 members (Tapsoba 2005).

In Asia, the Association of Asian Election Authorities (AAEA) was established in 1998 with 20 Asian countries and India as the founding member (AAEA 1997). The goals included independent and impartial election authorities, the professionalisation of Asian election authorities and the development of resources for election-related information and research (AAEA undated). Around 10 years later, at a meeting of eight country EMBs in Bangladesh, a resolution was also passed to establish a Forum of Election Management Bodies of South Asia (FEMVoSA). Meetings were then held in Pakistan (2011), India (2012), Bhutan (2013), Nepal (2014), Sri Lanka (2015) and the Maldives (2016).

A Pacific Islands, Australia and New Zealand Electoral Administrator's Network (PIANZEA) followed. After visiting a regional meeting in Africa, an Australian Electoral Commissioner returned, saying: 'I think that we could actually do better' (private interview with PIANZEA official, May 2018). Alistair Legg, a Papua New Guinea born official working in the AEC, proposed that a meeting bringing together the heads of electoral commissions in the Pacific be set up. The AEC collaborated with International IDEA and then found some initial funding with the New Zealand Ministry of Foreign Affairs and Trade, and the New Zealand Chief Electoral Office. The group was established at a conference at the Warwick Hotel in Fiji in 1997. The objectives included sharing materials, regular exchange of information, staff exchanges, study tours, technical assistance, and to hold conferences every 18 months to two years (private interviews; Dacey 2005).

Last of all, the Organisation of Arab Electoral Management Bodies (ArabEMBs) was launched in June 2015 to provide 'a platform for networking and exchanging information and expertise' with the aim 'to strengthen the Arab EMBs capacity, competency, and professionalism' (Badrieh 2015). The body would have six members (Jordan, Iraq, Palestine, Libya, Lebanon and Yemen). EMBs directly acknowledged that this was triggered by the Arab Spring. As the founding 'welcoming brochure' set out, many Arab states have recently witnessed demands to democratise elections in the region. In this context, given 'the diversity and range of electoral expertise across the Arab region', there was a 'united goal to enhance the credibility of the electoral process...[and]...reinstate the citizens' confidence in the electoral process, its outputs and management' (ArabEMBS undated, 4). Jordan was chosen to host the General Secretariat of the Organisation Headquarters following a secret ballot in January 2015. Dr Emad Al Saiah, Chairman of the High National Elections Commission in Libya, was initially appointed as President with a three-member executive board. An Interim Secretary General, Ms Badrieh Belbisi, was appointed from the Electoral Commission of Jordan (Badrieh 2015).

While these organisations were international in focus, the Association of Electoral Officials (A-WEB) was set up in South Korea to explicitly be the world's body for EMBs. The organisation was proposed by the South Korean National Election Commission in 2011 (Arirang News 2013) (A-WEB undated). An elaborate launch followed in 2013 where plates were engraved for each member organisation, which were subsequently hung in the headquarters in Incheon, an hour's drive from Seoul. The vision was attributed to Kim Jeong-Gon of the South Korean Electoral Commission, who had worked within the organisation since 1998, having lectured overseas electoral officials through the Korean Civic Education. After some internal resistance from the Korean Electoral Commission, the organisation eventually supported the proposal. Interviewing him on the 24th floor of a high-rise, slick office building, overlooking a regenerating Yeonsu-gu district, I listened as he explained his motivation. Korea had been a poor country in the 1950s and had a military dictator, but was now prosperous and democratic, he explained.

> When I looked around the world, there are so many poorest and military dictatorship countries in the world. They are going through the same difficulties to Korea. I have felt sympathy to these kinds of countries. I would like to help them to overcome their difficulties.
>
> (private interview, 3 September 2014)

Economic growth, he thought, required stability within politics and legitimate elections. He planned and designed A-WEB to help 'all EMBs to be independent and impartial professionals'.

> Most people appreciated my idea, my suggestion, so they told me, especially UN Secretary General Ban Ki Moon, he told me A-WEB is a very timely and creative idea.
>
> (private interview, 3 September 2014)

By 2019, the organisation boasted 111 EMBs from 105 countries.

8.4.4 National EMBs and EMB officials

When the third wave of democratisation bought a gold-rush of states needing to run elections without prior experience, many turned to the permanent national EMBs in countries such as Australia, Canada and Mexico for advice and support. Almost by accident, these EMBs and their staff were afforded a key role in shaping the implementation of elections around the world and became established into lasting networks. As one interviewee put it: 'So, in the early days, there wasn't "consultancy".' Instead:

> it was a lot of word of mouth, but that's where some of the election commissions came in, because there were not that many very strong election commissions in the world who had permanent staff that they could let go on secondments, and so forth. Western Europe had nothing like that. So Canada and Australia came to play such a large role in forming how election administrations would look.

Electoral assistance missions such as the much-cited Namibia 1989 mission forged new relationships between individuals from these agencies that would come to be important in future years, such as Harry Neufield from Canada, and Michael Maley from Australia, for example.

The domain that they were entering was not one in which professionalism was the norm.

> ... we were really creating in many ways a profession. It's not that people hadn't been administering elections for years but it kind of always seemed like something people did by accident and never really put a whole lot of effort into the professionalization part. Now, in the last 10 or 15 years, we've put so much more into the professionalization.
>
> As with most things that start from pretty nearly scratch, that meant that in the early days there wasn't a lot of institutional knowledge, and it was an area for pirates.

From a position where there were limited EMB experience to draw from in 1990, EMBs increasingly sought to be exporters of expertise two decades later. This activity was probably partly linked to attempts to shape the world's perception of these states. For example, the Electoral Commission of India established the India International Institute of Democracy and Election Management in 2011 to organise workshops and conferences to promote better-run elections (see: Chapter 7). 'What you are doing', the Indian Prime Minister told one senior EMB official, 'is national diplomacy' (private interview, April 2016). South Korea established a Civic Institute for Democracy (KOCEI) with regular invitations made to senior academics and practitioners worldwide; and A-WEB followed to provide courses, training and conferences. Many EMBs became hosts and organisers of regional conferences, as the chapter will explain, or undertook other initiatives such as the Romanian Permanent Electoral Authority which became proactive in launching a journal called the *Electoral Expert Review* in 2013.

8.4.5 Other actors

In the 1990s and early 2000s a small community of academics were commonly called upon by practitioner organisations to provide advice and consultancy, such as the University of North Carolina's Professor Andrew Reynolds and Aarhus University's Jørgen Elklit – authors of some of the early academic work on electoral management (Elklit and Reynolds 2001, 2005a, 2005b). Reynolds worked on projects for the UN, IIDEA, the UK Department for International Development, the US State Department, the National Democratic Institute, the International Republican Institute, OSCE and IFES. He also served as a consultant on issues of electoral and constitutional design across Africa and Europe. Elklit was one of the early visitors to the newly founded Johannesburg office of EISA in the mid-1990s (EISA 1997, 8). A further key scholar was Rafael López-Pintor who was called upon to write the influential report on electoral management design (López-Pintor 2000) for the UN and the IFES report on the cost of elections (López-Pintor and Fischer 2005). But this community grew.

> You know, now there are thousands of young people who are willing to be consulted . . . [unlike] in the old days when it was more election commission-based.

The founding of the Electoral Integrity Project in 2012 was a major step forward. The project was launched by Pippa Norris, a Professor at Harvard University who had taken a position at Sydney The project was funded by the Australian Research Council until the end of 2018. It organised workshops which involved academics and practitioners, and hosted research fellowships in Sydney. The project produced many publications and datasets, but also forged a community of scholars to collaborate around the topic of electoral integrity (EIP 2018). As one senior member of the international community reflected, The EIP:

> brought so many people together, and encouraged a kind of order . . . So, that would be a big influence of more recent times in academics entering the field, and being reflective, and finding data, and so forth.

A corollary of the EIP was the Electoral Management Network, founded by myself, Holly Ann Garnett, Carolien van Ham and Leontine Loeber in 2016. We had met through EIP workshops and fellowships and borrowed the workshop format that the EIP had established, involving practitioners from the UN, IFES and many other organisations as participants (EMN 2018). Elsewhere, the Electoral Regulation Research Network was established at Melbourne University, funded by the NSW and Victoria Electoral Commission, under the directorship of Joo-Cheong Tham in 2012 (ERRN 2018). Robert Krimmer founded the Competence Center for Electronic Voting and Participation (E-Voting.CC) which held regular conferences in electronic voting, beginning in 2004 (Krimmer 2018). A perceived global shift towards populism led many within the community to shift their research focus, howeve, when the EIP funding ceased. (Norris and Inglehart 2019).

Private-sector suppliers also operated at the international level. For instance, Smartmatic was founded in Palm Beach County, Florida, USA in 2000 (home to the Bush-Gore controversy) and moved its headquarters to the Netherlands in 2004 and then established an R&D department in Taiwan. It subsequently developed the technology that was used in Venezuela in 2004, for biometric registration in Mexico in 2009 and Zambia in 2010, and internet voting in Estonia (Smartmatic 2018), to give just some examples. There is also an unmeasured, but arguably large pool of private consultants who have previously undertaken work on electoral management and apply for short-term consultancy projects worldwide (various private interviews).

8.5 Integration: frequency of interaction, inclusion and continuity

8.5.1 Qualitative interviews

The qualitative interviews reveal the dynamics of the relationships between actors. There were strong inter-organisational and interpersonal horizontal connections at the highest levels of the networks with a shared sense of community:

> Yes, there is a perception that there's an international electoral community, in which people know each other, and I think that that does reflect a reality. You will certainly find people in the broader development world who will tell you that past elections are a 'magic circle' in that way.

Conferences organised by regional associations of practitioners were a common opportunity for people to meet. Although some individuals and organisations would be meeting for the first time, for many, they were opportunities to 'catch-up' with people that they had shared histories with. Often this might be electoral assistance or observation missions:

> 'People who know each other from ancient history . . .'
>
> 'either we worked together somewhere else, maybe 5, 10 years before. Or we have common friends that can be doing the introduction. So, yes. It's quite a close-knit community as such.'

This allows trust to form as having regular counterparts at other organisations made collaboration easier. However, historical legacies can work both ways:

> Sometimes just because you've been working together previously, doesn't mean that you love each other. It might actually be the opposite.

There are also closed forums. The UN, for example, was keen to maintain an active network of regional organisations such as the African Union or SADC who had 'expressed an interest in developing their own capacity on elections'. One-off meetings could also be instrumental trips with I(N)GOs/IGOs in hope of funding for projects. Major donor countries, interviewees suggested, might be less observable in public forums, but their money underwrote many of the electoral assistance projects. Financial support from governments, as member states of the UN, 'would not always be present in the records in most cases'. Their steer might therefore only be broadly political, giving less direction 'on electoral policy or electoral assistance policy'.

Meetings were also shaped by historical geo-political relationships:

> You have all the usual suspects . . . that is the Nordic countries, Holland, the Germans, the French, and Britain and so on. They tend . . . they meet amongst themselves. Then you tend to have in the last 10–15 years a very closed working relationship between the Brits and Americans, they're sort of on their own. You tend to have more informal, not as constructive, engagement between the first world and the Africans. The Africans at the most will defer to the AUs, and the SADCs, and ECOWAs, so on.
>
> (sic)

Language barriers can reinforce regional differences. Latin American meetings work in Spanish and interviewees thought that the lack of wider usage of Spanish prevented some 'good and interesting ideas' from 'reaching the rest of the world quite as fast as things in other parts of the world do'.

Collaborations on specific projects also brought organisations and individuals together for purposive meetings to forge common histories. For example, in 1998 IFES, International IDEA and UNDESA collaborated to create the Administration and Cost of Elections Project, which was later renamed the ACE Electoral Management Network. The subsequent site would contain, amongst much else, articles, encyclopaedia entries on best practice, electoral news and election calendars.

Online networking also offered other opportunities. Meetings were increasingly possible via Skype for specific projects. The ACE Electoral Management Network, however, was developed to provide an online electoral knowledge network in which questions could be posed and practitioners worldwide could respond.

Connections can be internal to organisations. The UN had an internal policy development forum, meeting two or three times a year, composed of 'anyone in the UN system who thinks or has a role in electoral systems can be part of that'. As a senior UN official explained:

> For our policy development we have a set forum that meets somewhat irregularly which is called a consultative mechanism for electoral assistance, this is the place where all the UN entities who have an interest in electoral assistance to meet on common interests. We don't talk so much about countries but more the global policy perspective on things. So this is where we negotiate and hammer out these policy documents . . . that's our form for the global strategic perspective.

I(N)GO and IGOs had vertical linkages downwards into states where they become electoral assistance providers. For the UN:

> our primary counterpart is the EMB and I would say that in almost all cases we work in that it's the election commission rather than a ministry. . . . Then we often work with legislatures, when it comes to drafting legislation or planning

the electoral system and so forth. We deal with members of the executive branch of government, whether it's foreign affairs or finance because there are issues of international funding and so on.

Domestic civil society actors tended not to be directly connected to international organisations, unless there was a project that specially was based around building the capacity of civil society and domestic monitoring. But there might be indirect linkages through the EMB who may have outreach campaigns. Other I(N)GOs, however, suggested that building links with civil society was an important strategy for exerting influence over EMBs.

There would also be domestic connections to the international community *within* any given country. Donors such as EU, USAID or DIFID may have representative branches in other countries, in addition to ambassadors. At a higher political level there was also high-level engagement by the political leaders and the head of opposition so that messages about good conduct, and acceptance of results, contesting results through legal means could be conveyed to 'create a conducive relationship environment'. There would also be within-country relationships with other electoral assistance providers who might be working alongside each other, co-located in election commission buildings.

8.5.2 International speakers dataset

In order to get a further sense of the frequency of interactions between different types of actors, this chapter now presents original data on a series of major international electoral conference circuits that became established in the late 1990s and early 2000s. Four conference circuits were included. The Global Elections Conference was established in April 1999, hosted by Elections Canada in Ottawa and has tended to be a bi-annual event. OAS has organised the Inter-American Meetings of Electoral Management Bodies since 2003, with the first event held in Panama City (OAS 2010, 1). ACEEEO has held annual conferences in Europe since 1991. The Venice Commission has also held conferences for the European EMBs since 2004 – but to which non-European members were welcome. Content analysis was then undertaken to identity who the speakers were, what organisation they were representing, and where they had travelled from. This provides a unique insight into the interactions in the network. This is not the entirety of interactions, as has already been noted. However, it is an uncharted and important step.

Table 8.2 summarises the percentage of speakers of different types for the conference circuits. There are some notable differences between the conference circuits. I(N)GOs are ever present, but this varies considerably across the circuits. The Global Elections Conferences, first established in Ottawa in 1999, unsurprisingly has a higher proportion of cross-continental representation. I(N)GOs are much less frequently represented at regional conferences of the Americas or Europe – yet they still constitute a quarter of speakers in the OAS and Venice Commission circuits. Speakers from national EMBs are ever present, covering roughly half of speakers in all circuits – but as much as 63 per cent in the case of the Venice Commission conferences.

Table 8.2 The speaker types at four international conference circuits. Values may not sum to 100 because of rounding up

Conference circuit	Number of conferences	Number of speakers	Speaker type (%)									
			Academic	Consultants	Civil society	I(N)GO/ IGO	Judiciary	Media	EMBs	Private	Professional associations	Ministers/ Heads of state
GEO (1999–2016)	7	186	3	0	4	46	1	1	44	2	0	0
OAS (2008–2015)	6	84	1	0	0	26	10	0	55	1	0	5
ACEEEO (2003–2016)	14	293	4	0	1	39	1	0	51	0	1	0
Venice Commission	9	184	7	1	2	25	2	0	63	0	0	0

It is then notable how little involvement there was with other speaker types. Civil society groups are almost entirely excluded from the events. Rare exemptions included Memo98, a Slovakian-based organisation, who were launched with support from NDI in 1998 to monitor the Slovak media (Memo98 2019). Representatives from disability groups such as the European Disability Forum, Down Syndrome Ireland and the National Council of the Hungarian Ethnic Minority were invited to speak on accessibility issues. Academic involvement was also minimal – although it was noticeably more frequent at Venice Commission events with 7 per cent of speakers being academics. Many of these speakers had connections with stakeholder organisations, however. The most frequent academic speaker, Robert Krimmer, was a professor from an Estonian University. He spent time as SCE/ODIHR's first senior adviser, however, on new voting technologies and was an expert for the Council of Europe Ad-Hoc Committee on Electronic Democracy. Pippa Norris appeared once at a GEO conference in 2007 to give a presentation based around her book *Electoral Engineering* – but that followed a period of time serving as the Director of the Democratic Governance programme at the UNDP 2006–2007. There are a very small number of presentations from the private sector, although providers Smartmatic and Accenture were given the floor in some instances. Google and Facebook also presented at a 2016 GEO elections conference. In general, however, it is led by representatives from EMBs at the highest level and broadly closed to other types of actors.

It is notable that some countries and organisations are more commonly featured. Table 8.3 describes the most common geographical origin for the speakers and Table 8.4 the most common organisations. Understandably, speakers from international bodies are very commonly represented and regional bodies' representatives dominate the OAS and ACEEEO conferences. Elections Canada and the Instituto Nacional Electoral Mexico are truly global leaders, however, with speakers found across all the Americas and Europe. The Permanent Electoral Authority of Romania and the Central Election Commission of Russia feature highly, partly because they hosted large Venice Commission conferences in 2017 and 2018 respectively.

Table 8.3 Most common speaker origin

GEO		OAS		ACEEEO		Venice Commission	
Origin	%	Origin	%	Origin	%	Origin	%
International	25	Regional – Latin American	21	International	26	International	12
International – US Based	11	Peru	12	Regional – Europe	13	Russia	11
Africa	6	Brazil	10	Romania	5	UK	10
Mexico	6	USA	8	Mexico	5	Austria	7
Canada	5	Jamaica	7	Hungary	5	Regional – Europe	6
USA	3	Canada	5	Russia	4	Estonia	6
Europe	3	Mexico	4	UK	4	Mexico	6

180 Networks

Table 8.4 Most common speaker organisation

Organisation name	Count
ACEEEO	39
Central Election Commission of Russia	29
IFES	29
International IDEA	28
Venice Commission of the Council of Europe	27
Instituto Nacional Electoral Mexico	24
OSCE/ODIHR	18
Organisation of American States	16
Elections Canada	16
Permanent Electoral Authority of Romania	13

Table 8.5 Most frequent speakers

Speaker name	Affiliation	Count
Jean-Pierre Kingsley	Chief Electoral Officer Elections Canada/IFES President/Honorary Member of ACEEEO	12
Arnis Cimdas	Chairman of the Central Election Commission of Latvia	11
Zoltan Toth	Secretary General, ACEEEO	10
Gregor Wenda	Deputy Head, Federal Ministry of the Interior of Austria	10
Manuel Carillo	Chief of Staff, Instituto Nacional Electoral, Mexico	6
Peter Wardle	Chief Executive, Electoral Commission, UK	6
Kazimierz W. Czaplicki	Secretary, National Electoral Commission, Poland	6
Emilia Rytko	Head, National Electoral Office, Hungary	6
Jeno Szep	ICT Expert, ACEEEO	6
Robert Krimmer	Professor of e-government, Tallin University of Technology/OSCE/OHDIR consultant	5

Equally, it is noticeable that some countries provide little representation. Although the dataset covers the major European conferences over a long period of time, speakers from France and Germany only appear twice each. There is also a within-country dynamic as not all EMBs within a given country are present. The UK features prominently with 35 appearances. These were mostly speakers from the Electoral Commission or academics, however, and only included one speaker from government – the office for E-envoy – not the government department responsible for setting electoral law, which had no representation at all.

There were some, presumably key individuals, who were regularly present. Table 8.5 details the most common speakers. There was a huge variety of individuals with 514 different speakers who gave 746 presentations between them – with many therefore only giving one. Figure 8.1 shows frequency of appearances for each speaker which shows that it was a single appearance for most speakers.

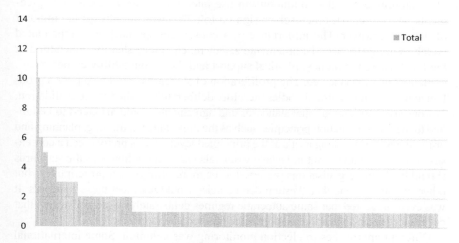

Figure 8.1 Frequency of appearances for each speaker.

Nonetheless, there was a core of some much more frequent participants. One was Jean-Pierre Kingsley, who was the Chief Electoral Officer for Elections Canada (1990–2007) and then President of IFES (2007–2009). Kingsley was therefore influential in setting up with the GEO conference circuit, playing host in 1999.

8.6 Contestation and consensus

Overall the international governance network exhibited considerable consensus about how elections should be implemented. As one interviewee put it:

> At a theoretical/conceptual and even technical level, I think the consensus is pretty strong. Such a consensus is clearly illustrated by the many international documents about international standards as endorsed by all relevant institutions . . . as well as by a myriad of national codes of conduct for electoral officers, parties and candidates as well as monitors.

Within the UN 'all of the policies we have adopted have been adopted by consensus' (private interview, UN official).

The idea that there should be international standards was met with some initial resistance in the early 1990s because some international electoral assistance providers took an approach that was sometimes interpreted as 'West is best' or 'this is how things are done in established democracies'. The laying down of standards could therefore be resisted by states citing arguments about sovereignty and state interference. Over time, however, the major electoral support organisations became increasingly careful to stress that the development of international standards was not the 'activity of a global policeman with a big stick, but the result of a commitment in the community to use international instruments and agreements which countries themselves sign on to'. This was not always the mindset of donors, however. The importance of a consensual approach was appreciated widely among the actual implementers, but much 'more shakily understood at the level where the money, political support and the accountability comes from', explained one interviewee. The proliferation of standards could also pose a problem and some international bodies therefore deliberately pushed for consolidation.

Consensus on international standards and agreements would also tend to be limited to the implementation principles such as the importance of training, planning and professionalism. 'As long as it's at the principled level, there's pretty much a consensus' as one interviewee put it. Debate would also arise about how specific standards should be. Some organisations preferred to be more detailed and prescriptive – but others would respond that Western democracies would not meet these standards. It was even suggested that some autocratic regimes deliberately suggest standards that cover more areas so that the recommendations become more vague.

Different approaches to election monitoring was common. Some international organisations were more likely to criticise the conduct of states than others. During the early 2000s, for example, the AU and SADC observers were suggested to be more likely to be more 'cautious, conservative, and have a state-orientated view than say NDI, Carter Center and the Commonwealth'. Officials might also question the professionalism of other agencies.

The community of electoral assistance providers was generally collaborative. However, there was inevitably inter-organisational rivalry between bodies with the same goals who could be competing for the same revenue sources or political limelight. When International IDEA was established, there were some national states and I(N)GOs who were concerned:

> 'They thought it was trying its way into a field that was already well covered. In fact, IDEA took that on board . . . [and] reconfigured their plans so that they weren't walking on other people's patch. As a result of which, I think they found their niche very nicely. They've become a well-respected organisation.'
>
> 'When IDEA was starting, IFES was furious.'

Equally, when A-WEB was established, some other actors were uneasy about its approach, suspicious that it was set up to support Korean vendors. Inter-organisational disputes within the UN were often claimed to be present and 'intractable turf wars' could develop. The level of collaboration between donors also varied with some more willing to share information than others.

Operational disputes could also break out. One senior interviewee suggested that Carina Perelli, the former director of the UN Electoral Assistance Division between 1998 and 2005, was keen to 'do as much as they could to support the Independent High Electoral Commission in Iraq' following the invasion, but there were concerns elsewhere in the UN about being too involved because of the political nature of the conflict. On another occassion, Perelli criticised the US military forces for distributing material encouraging Iraqis to vote in the elections because it would undermine the Iraqi sense of ownership over the election. Responding to a journalist, she said: 'I'm glad that you reported it, because I'm going to be screaming on the phone in two minutes' (Lynch 2005).

However, despite all of this, differences could dissolve over time and could disappear at an individual level:

> Human beings are very good in this field, many of them have worked for almost all the major organisations. So that helps to create this community of people who are almost more loyal to the field of election administration than they are to the particular organisation who is paying their salary at that moment.

8.7 Tactics, strategies and resources

What are the tactics, strategies and resources available to actors? *National governments* undoubtedly remained the most powerful actor in shaping the way that elections are run. They ultimately shaped the laws that are passed in legislatures, as the previous chapter suggested, and allocated resources on the ground. However, this chapter has revealed how donors and cross-continental organisations – a broad term to cover the I(G)NOs and regional professional associations described above – could affect how elections are run within countries. Academics are also considered. There are other actors that are important. The contracting out and the privatisation of government services has taken place around the world since the introduction of new public management in the 1980s (Hood 1991). This gave private sector vendors an increased role. Data from the ELECT and EMS surveys reveal that of the EMBs to respond, the technology used to run elections was owned by a private company in 26.5 per cent of cases (Loeber 2017). Oligopolistic conditions could easily develop in which the EMB becomes partially dependent on suppliers – especially where they are few in number. However, the focus in the following discussion will be on donor governments, cross-continental organisations and academics on the basis that this gives coverage of many key dynamics in the transgovernmental network.

8.7.1 Donor governments

The ability of overseas governments to shape elections was restricted because their involvement could also taint the legitimacy of the contest in the eyes of the public. Western governments have historically been open to potential criticisms of 'foreign interference', 'Westernisation' or 'Americanisation'. This was recognised from an early point with the NED deliberately set up as an external armslength organisation. It was mandated to:

> provide political assistance to democratic forces in repressive or other sensitive political situations where U.S. Government support, even where channelled through intermediary institutions that were non-governmental, would be diplomatically or politically unfeasible.
>
> (Lowe undated)

Donor governments could instead provide the funds on which most of the electoral assistance and the entire existence of international or regional organisations depend. They had regular funding streams from tax-revenues and democratic mandates from their electorates to give legitimacy to their allocation of funds. This meant that they could shape priorities or pull funds. One guide for electoral assistance agencies, written by an experienced consultant, warned that donors are 'special friends who need to be treated as such through personal relations, effective engagement and provision of unique insider information' (Miiro undated).

Yet there were severe limits on the tactics available to donor governments. Populist backlashes could cause them to change position. The US State Department considered removing support for democracy assistance in 2017 following the election of Donald Trump (Rogin 2017). Changes in the geo-political system also led to declining political support for democracy and electoral assistance. The military intervention of the US and allied forces in Afghanistan and Iraq was widely thought to have created further instability in the region, and increased the chances of terrorism and conflict. The Arab Spring brought some hope for the spread of democracy, but many states slid backwards. As a result, there was an overall mood of pessimism towards overseas democracy promotion amongst policy makers and the public. In Europe, migration crises sucked money away from democracy promotion budgets. The election of Donald Trump marked a shift towards regimes ideologically less likely to invest in electoral management overseas (Norris 2017b).

8.7.2 Cross-continental organisations

There were a variety of tactics that were deployed by IGOs, I(N)GOs and other organisations, such as regional bodies.

Defining standards and developing common policies

One approach was norm building through attempts to define common standards and develop common practices for running elections. As Norris (2014) noted, there was a rich set of international laws, multi-lateral agreements, treaties and conventions that have been published to constitute best practices which began with Article 21(3) of the Universal Declaration of Human Rights (1948). The Carter Center went on to develop a database of obligations (Carter Center 2014) facilitating their dissemination. Cross-national organisations can play important roles as the facilitator of these agreements. Some agreements are binding and might structure the calculus of actors' incentives, but they can also shape what is culturally appropriate Finnemore and Sikkink (2005) suggest that there are several stages to norms shaping behaviour. In the first stage norm entrepreneurs seek to promote these ideas. They are then cascaded out to states and international organisations and networks who become concerned about their legitimacy and reputation. In the final stage these ideas become habit and institutionalised in law, among professionals and in bureaucracies (2005, 898).

Standard setting was a key approach taken by the Venice Commission, who drew up reports and guidance on transnational issues on an ad-hoc basis but also established the *Code of Good Practice in Electoral Matters* (2002). This began as a resolution made by the Standing Committee of the Parliamentary Assembly of the Council of Europe (PACE) in November 2001, and was approved by the Parliamentary Assembly, the Congress, and the Committee of Ministers of the Council of Europe. This code was not legally binding on member states but was a powerful source of influence within the rubric of soft international law. The endorsement by the Committee of Ministers of the CoE, as a senior political group, gave the code particular authority, much higher than its legal status. The code came to be adopted by the European Court of Human Rights as the standards to be used for its judgements after a Resolution of the Parliamentary Assembly of the Council of Europe (No.1320/2003) and in a Declaration of the Committee of Ministers (of 13 May 2004). It was also cited in many subsequent opinions, which began with the ECHR in the 2007 ruling on *Russian Conservative Party of Entrepreneurs and Others v. Russia* (Fascone and Piccirilli 2017).

As Fascone and Piccirilli (2017) argue, however, there were weaknesses and limitations for the code. The Venice Commission could not act alone, as it required other institutions to request an opinion. The countries in question also tended to be limited to consolidating European democracies, usually when the national government itself asks for an intervention. Moreover, although the code is used by the ECHR, there were limitations in its strength. Violations of the code might remain unsanctioned. The code often only stated what already exists in other conventions. The code was often also not cited, such as in cases as *Hirst (No. 2)*. In addition, some of the code is literally 'lost in translation'.

Electoral assistance

Electoral assistance could be provided to countries – or part of the electoral process could be entirely run by an external organisation. The UN, just one organisation that provided assistance, did so following a request from a member state or following a mandate from the Security Council or General Assembly. Types of electoral assistance might have included technical assistance, in which 'legal, operational and logistic assistance ...[was]... provided to develop or improve electoral laws, processes and institutions' (UN 2019), but also efforts to generate a conducive environment through the deployment of security forces, certification or verification of the results, and supervision or the overall management of the election. Information about its work was published in the reports of the Secretary-General to the General Assembly (for example, see: United Nations Secretary-General 2015).

Lührmann (2018) estimated that, between 2007 and 2014, the UN assisted more than a third of all national elections worldwide. She argue that the UN's efforts had mixed effects. The UN's role heightened during particular moments where there was no state capacity, such as Afghanistan in 2004 or Bosnia and Herzegovina in 1996 where, as an interviewee explained:

> it wasn't just a number of advisors sitting at their headquarters, but 100s of people were election officials often paired up with a national counterpart, often with authority to sign off on things and make decisions.

Different approaches could be deployed by I(N)GOS. Some might prefer working:

> more slowly with election commissions in their own countries, on their own reform processes, in a very locally adjusted way, but using international practice to guide them. [Whereas] the IIDEA way was of spreading information more ... to individual practitioners – either through publications, or through websites.

Effective electoral assistance could depend on many factors (also see: Lührmann 2018). There would often be incentives from donors to demonstrate their impact with incentives to have EU or American logos supplied on equipment. But this could have a negative on local ownership of the process and should be avoided, suggested some interviewees:

> Your job is to make your counterparts look good to their populations, to build the credibility of the organisation. You don't want to give the impression that they wouldn't have made it a success without you being there. So you stick in the background.

Defining mandates would be important so that electoral assistance agencies did not overlap in their work. Longer-term work was preferred because:

> if you parachute in five, six, seven advisors close to the election day, not only do you not have enough time to build this rapport, but with so many advisors in one go, the commission feels it's under siege.

Political co-ordination between heads of mission and the ambassadors was important so that there were clear messages and pressures being put on EMBs telling them that it was 'okay, you're allowed to make these kinds of changes'. Connecting to civil society actors could be one very effective strategy at bringing about change too.

> if we want to have reforms within the commission, it's not enough to have an advisory inside, it's also useful to have external pressure, and that is external pressure coming from the political parties or the civil society. And then we, from the inside, can say, 'You know what? You're about to probably be slammed by the observers in these things, you don't want to look bad, but there's things we can do to make you look good without jeopardising independence.

The political challenges delivering effective electoral assistance included historical links between countries. For example, it was felt that it was important that the UK not play a visible role in Zimbabwean elections because of its colonial heritage. Meanwhile, social media also meant that 'inappropriate content' from donors and stakeholders could travel quickly. For example, senior US government officials giving statements about a country could be seen almost immediately via digital technologies. An electoral assistance provider complained that they were 'getting video clips on WhatsApp' of what donor country officials had said while they were on mission. 'That's how quickly it travels.'

Cultural challenges were often present and could be key to good interpersonal relations. Dealing with senior officials had to be done differently in different contexts:

> In some places it's perfectly fine to challenge senior officials even within groups. In others that is an absolute no-no and once you have done that they will never accept you.

The provision of electoral assistance also remained dependent on bottom-up demand. The guidelines for the UN providing electoral assistance, for instance, set out that it can only be provided on receipt of a request from a member state, except where there is a mandate from the Security Council or General Assembly, as might be the case in situations of peace-building (United Nations 1994).

Knowledge building

Organisations sought to build knowledge libraries and share this knowledge to build capacity and establish professionalism. Information libraries and archives were an early focus. One of IFES' first steps after being established was to set up a resource centre in 1989 in Washington, DC, to provide information on electoral systems such as books, file materials, periodicals, posters, videos and other materials. These were used to service the needs of 'IFES staff, consultants, and field officers, election officials, legislators and non-partisan civic groups'. By 1997, it covered 1,500 square feet (Kennedy 1997). Similarly, when EISA was established, early work included setting up an Electoral Education Centre in Johannesburg to house scholars (EISA 1997, 6–7). Hard copy libraries soon came to be superseded by online libraries. The ACE Project was launched at the United Nations in 1998 by International IDEA, IFES and the UNDESA. Over time, the project expanded to include encyclopaedia pages on topics, a comparative dataset of election practices and election statistics, election calendars and other materials (ACE 2018a). International IDEA was among many organisations to develop grey literature documents on best practices. This included influential handbooks such as the *Electoral Management Design* handbook, first published in 2006 (Wall et al. 2006) and then updated in 2014 (Catt et al. 2014).

Training courses were developed for electoral officials. Most prominently, the Australian Electoral Commission (AEC), International IDEA, IFES, UNDP and UNEAD met in Canberra in 1999 to devise the BRIDGE (Building Resources in Democracy, Governance and Elections) project. The thinking was that practitioners should be encouraged to reflect on everything that they wished they had known in hindsight when they first started running elections – and to consolidate that into a curriculum. By 2018, 24 separate modules were developed with 1,437 workshops and 2,047 modules run worldwide between 2001–2017 (Bridge 2019). Attempts were made to develop postgraduate-level courses too. Responding to proposals from Jeff Fischer, a former IFES advisor turned consultant, and Andrea de Guttry of the Sant'Anna School of Advanced Studies in Pisa, International IDEA formed a working group to establish a model curriculum for a master's in Electoral Policy and Administration which was subsequently launched (IIDEA 2014). Academic and practitioner publications were important too to serve as dissemination forums and improve scientific knowledge. NED established the *Journal of Democracy* in 1990 which became a well-cited publication in the field of political science, while the Romanian Permanent Electoral Authority published *Expert Electoral Review* in 2003 on an open-access basis.

Network building

Network building was a further tool to disseminate best practices, knowledge and norms of professionalism. The founders of International IDEA set out the need 'for a meeting-place where . . . varied actors can interact and draw upon each other's experience' (IIDEA 1995, 3). As the chapter has already set out, many newly founded organisations invested in establishing regular conference circuits. Network-building mechanisms were institutionalised by many organisations. NED proposed the International Forum for Democratic Studies (IFDS) as a centre to link 'scholars and practitioners on a regular basis' (Lowe undated). This was launched in 1994 and received funding mostly from private sources, the NED and the US State Department's Bureau for Democracy, Human Rights and Labor.

Networking also had instrumental effects, however. International meetings would strengthen actors domestically. As one interviewee from an international assistance organisation put it, 'the mere fact that you were doing that helped to give some credibility to them.' It gave a sense of togetherness.

> it gave a sense to other election administrators that they weren't alone. That these issues were being dealt with in other places. I think a lot of friendships were made across the countries, as a sense of peer support.

Network meetings were not always successful. There would often be the risk that it would turn into a 'talk-fest' with no concrete actions or 'where people, basically, just went on a holiday and went to a resort.' The bureaucratic burden for participants, such as visas and committee paperwork, could be high and this could disincentive participation. Workshops would work best where those issues were addressed and where meetings were established within the spirit of the local/regional culture. For example:

The Pacific, it's a consensus basis and everybody is equal, you talk about it until everything is resolved and then it's just settled. That's basically our culture. It's informal.

Informal relations would then be important for maintaining the network. One network was maintained by an official spending Friday afternoons phoning up officials from member EMBs.

I would have a list. I'd ring people up and talk to them and say, 'How's it going?'

Legal review

Legal review involved external bodies providing assessments of the legality or compliance of national practices with international or national legislation. The Venice Commission, for example, set up a constitutional 'helpdesk' by legal opinions on draft legislation, or legislation already in force. It also undertook full studies and reports. Opinions could be requested by member states, the Council of Europe, specific international organisations or constitutional courts including the European Court of Human Rights. Draft opinions were submitted to plenary sessions of the Commission and sometimes discussed with sub-commissions with the national authorities. All were checked in terms of their compliance with international standards. The opinions were then published. This could counter-balance the interpretations of constitutions being undertaken by national politicians and institutions. They could also issue subsequent legal rulings with the status of 'soft' international law. Data published in 2017 showed that it had published more than 500 opinions on more than 50 countries and 80 studies. The European Court of Human Rights has referred to these opinions in over 90 cases between 2002–2017 (Venice Commission 2017b, 2017d).

Election monitoring and 'naming and shaming'

Election monitoring involved the external observation of an election by officials from international bodies or other countries and the publication of an evaluation report. Early examples included a 1948 UN supervision and monitoring of elections in Korea and the 1956 Plebiscite in British Togoland (Bordewich, Davis-Roberts, and Carroll 2019); however as time progressed, it become an 'international norm' for observation to take place (Hyde 2011b). The procedures for assessing elections increasingly became consolidated into standardised methodologies and toolkits. Early efforts to write these included the International Human Rights Law Group's *Guidelines for International Election Observing*, funded by the US Agency for International Development (Garber 1994), and the Inter-Parliamentary Union's book on election standards, that Professor Goodwin-Gill of Oxford University was asked to develop (Goodwin-Gill 1998, vii). Eventually many international actors came together to publish a *Declaration of Principles for International*

Election Observation (U.N. Electoral Assistance Division et al. 2005) and multiple methods documents became available for practitioners (OSCE 2010).

A lack of professionalism by monitoring organisations was lamented by Thomas Carothers (1997) before the standardisation of practices had taken root. A flurry of academic studies followed some 15 years later to see whether election monitoring did work (Debre and Morgenbesser 2017). Inconsistencies are commonly found in reports written about the same election by different organisations. In Kelley's analysis of reports between 1984–2004, one third of missions disagreed with each other in their overall assessments (Kelley 2010, 162). There was also a bias towards weighting election-day problems as more important – since these were the most visible to the observers. Furthermore, some IGO member states, Kelley argued, might be less likely to condemn other states in order to avoid future criticism themselves – or might influence IGOs to produce favourable reports (Kelley 2010, 164–5). These problems were reflected in the interviews. As one interviewee put it:

> Problems such as the abuse of incumbency by the ruling party I think was difficult for an intergovernmental body to take on as rigorously given that its shareholders, if you like, are the very governments that I would say are the main problem.

Some organisations, most notably the UN, deliberately avoided public criticism for risk that opposing candidates would instrumentalise the report politically and justify their subsequent action.

Mission success would always be contingent on individuals:

> If you've got relatively small groups of people then a lot can depend on which people are involved in which mission.

A lack of resources prevented longer-term missions or key equipment. 'I can't remember that we ever had an expert on an Observer Mission who was a technology expert,' reflected one interviewee. There could be challenges with the ethnicities of observer groups. Efforts were often made to ensure that European-based observer groups working in Africa were multi-ethnic and multi-national so that the teams were 'ethnically identifiable'.

The publication of an observation report alone could be picked up by the national media and act as a pressure for change, but a follow-up with diplomatic pressure would be the most effective method. 'A bit more muscle' in the follow-up by national governments or I(N)GOs could make the crucial difference as to whether reform occurred. Informal efforts by more junior staff could also make a difference. More formal follow-up mechanisms were established by some I(N)GOs (OSCE/ODIHR 2016). An 'electoral cycle approach' was stressed which involved using non-election years to enact reforms. This could face some pressure, however, since as soon as the election was over, staff and resources might be dispersed away from the EMB back to other agencies. This was specially the case in transitional democracies that lacked a permanent civil service devoted to elections.

Financial reliance

While I(N)GOs had many strategies available to them, most had common underlying weaknesses. The organisations remained heavily reliant on donor government(s) for their sustained activities and work. When NED was established, it was given an initial budget of $31.3 million by the House Foreign Affairs Committee. However, this was roughly halved in FY86–87 as a number of opponents in Congress sought to eliminate the organisation altogether. Support on Capitol Hill grew and stabilised in the 1990s and 2000s – but there remained some attempts to remove funding altogether. Congress continued to play a role in framing NEDs work by, for example, providing special appropriations tied to work in specific countries (Lowe undated).

Donors therefore had to be managed carefully and methods proposed in the community included careful research such as establishing donor calendars, identifying the needs and interests of funders and their organisational requirements, being proactive in asking for funding and keeping donors updated. I(N)GOs were encouraged to ensure that donors are thanked and key staff are well treated. One method was by establishing clubs for donors 'where, senior managers, ambassadors and donor representatives could meet regularly and share information. This could also include a donor bar, special lunches, dinners or breakfast meetings.' Advertising the donations made could help donors feel that their investment is noted and of worth. Mechanisms to boost donations might have included branding them as 'Gold, Silver or Bronze' donors.

Nationally based I(N)GOs meanwhile remain dependent on national politics and shifts in public opinion away from international development agendas. NED faced political challenges over the years from both the left and right in America. The left argued that democracy promotion was interfering in the affairs of foreign states or promoting American foreign policy to the detriment of others. The American right raised criticisms that a 'social democratic' agenda was being promoted (Lowe undated). In Australia, the government was a major contributor to the governance community, but saw major cuts under the Tony Abbot government, which affected what could be done and centred policy more around national interest. Electoral assistance work then had to become more about reacting to events than developing longer-term capacity.

New organisations generate excitement and political interest, but this can quickly wane causing squeezes on funding, an interviewee explained:

> As happens with launching international organisations of any kind, when you first do it a minister, or a senior civil servant, or a senior diplomat turns up, because it's new and exciting. Three years later that mantle has moved on to something else. Then it goes down the food chain, and the second secretary turns up, and then the third secretary turns up. And the money doesn't become quite so much of a priority, and so there's a squeeze on.

International IDEA saw a major squeeze on funding five years after being established. There was an initial founding view 'that multilateral organisations doing good things people should put money into them and let them get on with it' and funding was initially largely covering core costs without being tied to a specific project. But pressures then came from member states to have a practical field side, with a greater proportion tied to specific projects. Further squeezes emerged on core funding as some funding schemes moved to contract-based, competitive tendering. But this added another 'challenge for INGOs and IGOs because member states and stakeholders would develop views about who should be collaborated with on such grants.'

A further difficulty for the I(N)GOs was that it would often be difficult to demonstrate the benefits of their projects. Given the challenge in measuring electoral management quality discussed in this book, and the multitude of factors that can affect it, I(N)GOs might struggle to demonstrate a causal effect to donors.

> [Running elections] is complicated, and sometimes it's hard to tell a complicated story of why this needs to happen. . . . Embassies sometimes are in charge of a pot of money to place towards elections, and there are things that are simple for them to understand, like, women being involved in further education, or something like that; but there are other things that are really important, but that are hard to understand.

Given these difficulties in obtaining money, personal relationships can be helpful:

> I don't know how many times, I'd pick up the phone from xxx and hear, 'Here is something coming along we haven't got the money for, but it sounds like a good idea.' 'I'll go and find some money for that,' I'd say. You make it work that way, which you wouldn't be able to do if you hadn't got a mechanism for cutting through the usual bureaucratic bullshit that you've got to go through if you're going through embassies and all that sort of thing.

Further I(N)GO tactics included putting politicians on the board of directors. National legislators and former national legislators could then be crucial for national agencies trying to protect their budgets because they have the personal contacts within the legislature to protect key resources for them.

8.7.3 Academics

The data presented above (Table 8.2) illustrates how academics relatively rarely featured in EMB conferences. There are reasons for this. As one interview put it:

> Diplomacy works best with some privacy. . . . So it's often the diplomatic instinct to say well this is not something you can study or put into data.

Academics that generate rankings and league tables of countries' performance could undermine diplomatic efforts – and this might dissuade stakeholders to invite them, interviewees explained. They can, however, come to be appointed as key advisors or consultants on research projects which puts them in the room more regularly with key decision makers. Rafael López-Pintor was approached by IFES to write a report on the state of election administration around the world in 1998, which came to be the influential report (López-Pintor 2000). López-Pinor was given roughly a year to undertake the research which was subsequently discussed in a three-day workshop with 'over 50 experts and seasoned electoral managers from five continents' (Rafael López-Pintor, private correspondence, 20 June 2017). The consultative nature of the research project meant that the findings were easily circulated among relevant stakeholders.

Academics have reputations for expertise and independence which could be valuable assets for influencing policy and shaping implementation. Background research about the nature of the policy community and the structure of power itself (as documented in this chapter) can help them develop strategies for influence. Academics usually had a more secure financial basis than international organisations. Universities were multi-dollar(pound) organisations operating with large numbers of permanent personnel and the availability of libraries, media suites and other resources. Income from student fees and government grants could be more reliable than that available in the international community. Yet academic roles were tended to be restricted to:

> 'a positive albeit very limited manner'. The main contribution to election management comes from bureaucratic officers and democracy practitioners while academics provide necessary conceptualisations and some theoretical foundations. This is generally done indirectly through scholarly products (i.e. books, articles and lectures) rather than by direct involvement of academics in the electoral operation field. I have seen very few academics directly involved in operations, which is logical and to be expected in terms of role definition.
> (Rafael López-Pintor, private correspondence, 20 June 2017)

Personal diplomacy and skill would be crucial:

> Academic and other type of intellectuals have mainly one way to influence other people behaviour, that is by showing in a convincing manner that they have control of uncertainty in specific domains. Both, expert knowledge and individual charisma are important, in order to make knowledge acceptable. I have always found that no matter how the good recipes are that you may have to offer to a government, an EMB or other actor, it is the personal ability and tact to present and make your case that what matters most. Of course, one may also affect indirectly the course of action by a document reaching a decision maker, but it is often role of personalities.
> (Rafael López-Pintor, private correspondence, 20 June 2017)

Rafael Pintor-López's experience described above was also unique in that it was responding to a request from international actors to generate particular knowledge for them to then use. Finding a way to influence the international community using research that has been produced without request a prior is arguably more difficult. It is easier to respond to demand, than try to create the demand.

My own personal attempts to influence the international community were to try to foster collaborative research. Following an American Political Science Association conference in 2015, I began to work with Holly Ann Garnett, Leontine Loeber, Carolien van Ham and a team led by Pippa Norris at the Electoral Integrity Project. The project idea was to develop a survey of EMBs and their staff – the datasets that became known as EMS and ELECT and are used in this book. The Electoral Integrity Project developed links with A-WEB to survey many countries, while we focussed on Europe. This was made possible because Leontine Loeber, who had previously worked for the Council of Europe, made introductions with the Venice Commission enabling us to present the project idea at a European Conference of Electoral Management Bodies in Romania in 2016. A survey was designed to be presented for consultation with delegates. The conference formally endorsed the project in the conference conclusions, encouraging EMBs to reply. The following year, we were able to present provisional findings from the survey back to the conference delegates at the 14th European Conference of Electoral Management Bodies, held in the Tavricheskiy Palace, St Petersburg, Russia.[3] Uniquely, the conference was organised around the theme of 'Operational Electoral Management Bodies for Democratic Elections' with the survey findings billed in the conference press-release. Recommendations were made based on the research (disseminated in this book, but also the special issue of *International Political Science Review* (James et al. 2019a, James 2019) that I co-edited.

Many of the recommendations then informed the conclusions to that conference which noted the importance of the research project and endorsed further studies (conclusion 3). The conference also endorsed actions based on the research. These included the promotion of gender equality within electoral management bodies (conclusion 18), encouraging the promotion of recruitment processes based on merit through a rigorous process, job security, career opportunities, employee involvement in decision making, a supportive supervision of staff and a consideration of employee job satisfaction and stress levels (conclusion 17); and underlined the importance of adequate human and financial resources for EMBs to be able to fulfil their tasks (conclusion 5) (Venice Commission 2017a). The project involved endless Skype calls at anti-social times, a large number of emails being sent around Europe asking EMBs to complete the data and some patience. But there is a claim that it made a difference. The conclusions of Venice Commission conferences would not be binding, but could be used by international organisations such as the Venice Commission, OSCE/ODHIR and the European Court of Human Rights in their opinions and judgements on the electoral procedures in the member states. They are also useful to signal best practices in elections all around the world.

Such an opportunity to present in that environment was unique and rare. Suspicion and lack of trust from international actors about academics no doubt exists – and might be warranted. The incentives for academics to be as interested in the policy impact of their research as the ranking of the journal in which they are published are not found in every university or higher education sector. Academics are few in number. Academics are therefore understandably a limited actor in the international field – but there are opportunities for developing strategies for changing how elections are run.

8.8 Conclusion: governmental networks

This chapter has traced a rapid transformation in the range of actors involved in running elections. Attempts to improve the quality of overseas elections, that began with post-WWII American foreign policy, spread in the late 1980s and early 1990s. This was triggered by a combination of the third wave of democratisation that created a demand for knowledge and resources on how to run elections, the development of the internet and broader political dynamics bound up with globalisation. By the 2000s, international networks of practitioners seeking to shape how elections were run and play a direct role in implementing them were found worldwide. This soon became a cluttered environment in which actors were partly in competition as well as collaboration with one another. Power ultimately remained at the national level and the main gatekeepers were national EMBs and governments. However, international actors working through consensus and collaboration developed many soft power tools to affect how elections are run. Table 8.6 summarises the tactics and tools available to different actors. The

Table 8.6 Potential resources, tactics and weaknesses of actors in international networks

Actor	Potential resources and tactics	Potential strategic weaknesses
National governments	Direct control of EMBs Ability to change electoral law	Accusations of partisanship Lack of capacity, resource and knowledge
Donor governments	Regular income stream Democratic mandates Key source of funding for electoral assistance	Risk of accusations of colonialism, Westernisation or foreign influence Populist backlashes against overseas investment
(Cross-)continental organisations	Defining common practices Electoral assistance Knowledge building Network building Legal review Election monitoring and follow-up	Reliance on donors Risk of interfering with sovereignty Inter-organisational rivalries Risk of geographical over-reach Internal divisions
Academics	Expertise and perceived objectivity Research capacity that EMBs lack University infrastructure	Suspicion and lack of trust from international actors about data uses Time commitments
Vendors	Oligopolistic conditions can develop	Competition policy regulations
Private consultants	Historically small pool with extensive expertise	Short-term contracts Expanding pool

dynamic and contingent nature of power meant that implementation owed much to agency. Electoral practitioners acting at the senior level needed to have a rich skill set to be successful, including having:

> not only some idea about the substance [of electoral policy] and . . . capabilities in management and administration . . . but who were capable of acting as diplomats as well, because there was much more direct engagement with member states.

Using a sociological rather than legal approach drawing from interviews, content analysis of secondary documents and grey literature, this chapter hopes to have traced the transformation of this international governance network.

Notes

1 For a detailed evaluation of Australia's role, see: Arghiros et al. (2017).
2 Australia, Barbados, Belgium, Chile, Costa Rica, Denmark, Finland, India, the Netherlands, Norway, Portugal, South Africa, Spain and Sweden.
3 The Tavricheskiy Palace was made home to the Interparliamentary Assembly of the Commonwealth of Independent States. After being in the imperial family, it became home to Russia's first Parliament in 1906 and was then briefly home to the provisional government in 1917 – a hundred years before the EMB conference. It meant that we were on the stage talking about EMBs, almost a century to the day that Lenin was talking about the revolution. As someone with a long interest in that period of Russian history, I was awestruck. Space, unfortunately, does not permit the touristy photos.

Part IV
Instruments

9 Voter registration reform

9.1 Introduction

In the fourth part of this book, we turn to policy instruments – reforms or measures that are introduced with the aim of improving electoral management. Although research on elections had traditionally focussed on voters and electoral system design, the study of EMB design, the polling process and electoral registration has seen increased interest. Mirroring this, highly political debates have often played out in legislative chambers and newspaper editorials around the globe. In the US, attempts to implement voter ID laws have been introduced to combat electoral fraud, but have been characterised as partisan attempts to rig the electoral process by deterring particular voters (Hasen 2012). Estonia's use of internet voting has been held up as an exemplar by advocates seeking remote voting elsewhere in the world, but the system has been criticised at home (Kickbusch 2015). Automatic electoral registration has been advocated in many other countries as a way of building a more inclusive register and democratic system, but has been suggested to undermine the accuracy of the electoral register by resistance governments.

Research that has sought to investigate the effects of using different voting and registration technologies has brought major advances into our understanding of the electoral process. It has left a major gap, however since it has tended to only evaluate the *front-office* effects of reform the direct effect on the citizen's experience. This chapter argues that this approach is therefore limited in its scope. Implementing new voting technologies or electoral registration processes affects many aspects of the electoral process and we should also consider the effects on the people and organisations that implement elections. We should, in other words, be more sensitive to the *back-office* effects of reform. The impact that reforms have on staff and resources and the broader functioning of EMBs are important too since shapes the performance of EMBs as set out in Chapter 4.

Part II of the chapter reviews the existing literature on voting technologies. Part III explains the evolution of plans to introduce individual electoral registration (IER) in Britain and the existing evidence about the effects of the reform is covered in Part IV. Part V explains the methodology. A thematic analysis of interviews with British local election officials was undertaken to identify the likely effects prior to the implementation of the reform. This research was then disseminated prominently during 2011–2018 in the UK – and may have had some effect on implementation. A post-implementation survey was undertaken to identify whether these predictions came true. Parts VI, VII and VIII explains the results. The initial interviews suggested that IER would improve the security of the registration process. However, it was expected to lead to 'spill-over' effects in terms of staff training, recruitment and resource drain. The post-implementation study revealed that the reform did indeed reduce opportunities for electoral fraud and the accuracy of the electoral register. There were some effects on the completeness of the electoral register. However, what was more striking was that there were significant effects on costs of running electoral services and the workplace experiences of employees with significant effects on workload, workplace environment, stress and the propensity of the employee to quit. The chapter concludes by encouraging further research to use the local knowledge of street-level bureaucrats to examine the 'back-office' effects of election administration reforms. It is useful for both academics and policy makers seeking to pre-empt the effects of a policy reform. In other words, it enables bottom-up learning.

9.2 Research on voting technologies

Election administration refers to the 'administrative systems through which the electoral register is compiled, and votes are cast and counted' (James 2010a, 369). There is enormous variation around the world in the practices that states adopt for running elections such as whether there are sanctions for citizens who do not register, the methods through which citizens can register and whether postal voting is available for all citizens or not (Massicotte, Blais, and Yoshinaka 2004). There is a large body of work, largely based on studies of US elections, that seeks to identify the effects of variations in procedures on voter turnout and registration levels. These studies date back to at least the 1930s (Harris 1934), but this research has accelerated over the last 30 years. The seminal work of Wolfinger and Rosenstone (1980) was a key marker. However, the politics of the National Voter Registration Act 1993, the US Presidential election in 2000 and more recent debates about voter identification laws has brought a new generation of studies (see, for example: Alvarez and Sinclair 2004; Ansolabehere and Konisky 2005; Atkeson et al. 2010; Barreto, Nuno, and Sanchez 2009; Wolfinger, Highton, and Mullin 2005). Much of the work implicitly or explicitly deploys a rational choice logic that some forms of election administration create barriers to participation by increasing the 'costs' to the citizen of registering to vote and casting a vote. Individuals will be more likely to register to vote and cast their ballot when it is more convenient to do so (Wolfinger and Rosenstone 1980). Elsewhere, I differentiated between procedures which are 'expansive' i.e. increase participation and those which are 'restrictive' i.e. reduce participation. This was then used to developed a continuum which categorised each of the registration procedures according to their effects on electoral participation (2010a, 378–80). At the same time, there are often concerns about electoral fraud at elections – and some procedures have been argued to make fraud or undue influence on the voter more likely (Birch and

Watt 2004; Wilks-Heeg 2009) or produce lower levels of confidence amongst voters that their ballot has been counted (Atkeson and Saunders 2007). The study of election administration is therefore of vital importance at a time when many states are concerned about declines in levels of electoral participation, mistrust of political institutions or vulnerabilities to electoral fraud.

There are some deficiencies in the literature. The overreliance on studies of US elections is certainly one of these.[1] The ability of US states to choose their procedures, within a framework of federal legislation, has provided a fertile research opportunity for researchers to analyse the effect of variations in practices on levels of participation. These studies have advanced our knowledge of electoral procedures immeasurably. However, one consequence of this is that we know little about procedures which have not been used in any state in the US. One of these is IER (as will be explained below). Further research on this procedure can therefore make significant contributions to our knowledge of electoral procedures and assist practitioners deciding how to run elections.

A second deficiency is that research on the effects of reforms have been limited to analysing the effects on registration rates, turnout and voter fraud. Important as these are, the effects of reform have been restricted to the researcher's existing expectations about what effects reforms might have. This, in turn, is usually shaped by the political science literature. As Sayer (2010, 24) suggests, scholars develop knowledge within the cognitive and conceptual resources available in the language communities they work within. This discourages open-ended attempts to look at the effects of reforms in their entirety. This chapter makes a contribution to redress both of these gaps in the literature – which are both empirical but also methodological.

9.3 Individual electoral registration in Britain

IER was first proposed for mainland Britain by the Electoral Commission in 2003 as part of its electoral modernisation programme, *Voting for Change*, on the basis that it was 'vital to security . . . particularly in relation to absent voting' and other forms of remote voting (Electoral Commission 2003b, 16). The Labour governments were long resistant to introducing IER, however, at least partly because many senior ministers thought that it might affect their 'core vote' (James 2010b, 192). However, the case for IER gained momentum with support from the Select Committee of the Office of the Deputy Prime Minister (2004), the Office for Democratic Institutions and Human Rights (2005, 1), the Committee for Standards in Public Life (2007, 6–7) and the Association of Electoral Administrators (2010). These recommendations came on the back of high-profile cases of postal vote fraud (Stewart 2006) and a report published by the Joseph Rowntree Reform Trust (2008) which argued that the processes for registering to vote and casting votes were insecure and had been proven vulnerable to fraud. Eventually the Labour government conceded to the case for IER and legislated to introduce it on a voluntary basis for those wishing to register after 1 July 2010 in the Political Parties and Election Act (PPE). The Act also mandated the Electoral Commission to evaluate the impact of this change and required Parliament to consider whether it should be made compulsory after a review in 2014. The Coalition government, elected in 2010, sought to fast-track implementation, however, as part of a series of reforms with the stated aim of reducing fraud (Deputy Prime Minister 2011). Some reforms, such as providing an 'opt-out' box so that citizens could choose to not be on the register, were dropped. Those to survive involved a number of simultaneous changes including (Electoral Commission 2016b, 25–7):

- **From household to individual registration.** An annual canvass would take place, usually each autumn, whereby a form was sent to each property listing those citizens registered. The 'Head of Household' would then delete individuals no longer resident at the property and add those eligible citizens who were. This information was then used by Electoral Registration Officers (EROs) to update the register. Citizens living in university or care-homes could previously be registered by the landlord or university administrator – but would now be forced to do so individually.
- **The use of personal identifiers and verification.** Applicants were required to provide their National Insurance Number and date of birth. This information was then verified against the Department of Work and Pensions (DWP) database before they were added to the electoral register. If the individual could not be matched then EROs had some discretion to use other local records to verify them.
- **Two-stage canvass.** Households were still sent annual canvass forms (now called 'Household Enquiry Forms'). However, those citizens who were listed on this form were then sent an individual form asking them to register.
- **Online registration.** Applicants were able to register online for the first time following the launch of a central government website. The submission of an application through this website would be passed to EROs to verify.[2]
- **Funding.** Additional short-term funding was provided by the government to EROs to cover some of the additional costs involved in running elections.

IER was phased in. From June 2014 onwards,[3] new applicants were required to register individually with the personal identifiers before they were added to the register. Existing entries which could not be verified by December 2015 were removed. Approximately 770,000 such names were removed – 1.7 per cent of the total December 2015 electorate (Electoral Commission 2016a, 6).

9.4 Existing knowledge about IER

Most countries operate IER rather than household electoral registration (HER) so there have been few opportunities for researchers to assess the effects of the change from one to the other and their relative merits. Research on this procedure is limited since it consists of various policy reports following its implementation in Canada and Northern Ireland. HER was abolished in Canada in 1997 when a new national electoral register was compiled by Elections Canada. Widespread confusion was reported with the new system when it was adopted for the first election in 2000 and there was some evidence that the new system led to a decline in electoral participation, especially amongst citizens from lower socio-economic groups (Black 2000, 2003). IER was introduced in Northern Ireland after the Electoral Fraud (Northern Ireland) Act 2002 and roughly 10 per cent of the electorate dropped off the register overnight. However, drawing lessons from the Northern Ireland experience is difficult because the annual carry-forward of names was ended at the same time. It was also argued that the names removed were not 'real' people – they were false registrations or duplicates (James 2011a, 47–8).[4]

No other academic knowledge about the effects of IER in Britain has been published, apart from the research described in this chapter which was disseminated during the implementation process. Some pressure groups argued that IER would lead to millions of voters being disenfranchised. Hope Not Hate, for example, claimed in September 2015 that IER could mean that '1.9 million people may fall off the electoral register in December' (Hope Not Hate 2015, 2). This was based on the assumption that all unconfirmed names on the electoral register were real entries and would not be confirmed. Their survey of universities found that many were unaware of the reforms and were scaling down voter registration work because there was no general election that year (Hope Not Hate 2015, 2).

The most complete assessment to date of the impact of IER was that undertaken by the Electoral Commission. The Commission undertook an evaluation of the completeness and accuracy of the electoral register prior to the introduction of IER in 2014 (Electoral Commission 2014b), and then immediately afterwards the transition to IER in 2016 (Electoral Commission 2016b). The methodology involved house-to-house surveys with the aim of checking the accuracy and the completeness of the electoral register. In 2014, 5,000 households were canvassed; on the basis of a 'before and after' comparison of the statistics for accuracy and completeness, the Commission concluded that:

> These accuracy and completeness findings suggest that there was no notable effect on the completeness of the registers from the removal of these entries and that the main impact is likely to have been the improvement in accuracy.
> (Electoral Commission 2016b, 8)

There were some important qualifiers to this. Although there was only a small, non-statistically significant, aggregate decline in completeness, the Commission did report drops in completeness among younger-age groups. There was a drop of approximately 9 percentage points among 18- to 19-year-olds, for example.

The Electoral Commission research has some limitations in its ability to identify causation. It assumes that the introduction of IER was the sole variable to affect levels of accuracy and completeness during this time – there are no controls for other push/pull factors. Policies are not implemented in hermetically sealed environments, however. There are other factors that may cause these levels to change. This was a period, for example, that included a general election in 2015 which was forecast to be close and may have led to a spike in participation. It was also a time when national registration drives were organised by Bite the Ballot (see Chapter 6) which added a considerable number of entries to the electoral register. Concerns raised about IER may have also had a mobilisation effect in increasing registrations. I explain later in the chapter how this research actually played a role in this.

9.5 Methodology

A methodologically innovative approach was taken to evaluating the effects of IER in this chapter. Rather than undertaking an analysis of the electoral registers themselves, which is the most common approach taken (for example, see: Wilks-Heeg 2012, 25–6), the approach here is to use the knowledge of electoral officials themselves. Continuing the conceptualisation from Chapter 3, public officials are front-line workers with 'local knowledge' and first-hand experience of the everyday life of working in a particular setting. Their insights therefore provide a privileged view into the effects of change and they see the effects of reform on the ground in their local areas. Qualitative interviews were undertaken with the local election officials involved in implementing elections by the author in 2011. The aim was to establish the likely effects of IER prior to its implementation. The author undertook interviews with 74 senior elections staff across 41 organisations in England, Wales and Scotland.[5] In most cases these were individual interviews, but in a few cases participants were interviewed in pairs. Urban and rural authorities and different authority types were included. The interviews were semi-structured in order to let the interviewees define the issues. The names of individuals and authorities included in the study were withheld so that the interviewees could speak freely. This chapter then uses Braun and Clarke's (2006, 2012) approach to thematic analysis to analyse the data. Interviews were transcribed and themes identified inductively from the texts. The aim was to identify both semantic and latent meanings. This research process requires the researcher to undertake 'a constant moving back and forward between the entire data set, the coded extracts of data ... and the analysis of the data' (ibid., p. 86). Having generated the core themes from the data, Braun and Clarke suggest using the themes to construct an analytic narrative of any processes at work – in this case, the likely effects of introducing IER.

To identify what effects the implementation of IER had had, a post-implementation survey was put into the field in January 2016 asking officials about the impact of IER in practice. The survey was circulated by email to the official email address for each department and respondents were asked to circulate the link within their team. The survey questions were premised on the interview responses from 2011 with the aim of identifying the frequency of themes and whether the anticipated effects materialised. However, before the survey was sent out qualitative interviews were undertaken with electoral officials in four local authorities to see whether additional questions were required. As a result of these, an additional battery of questions relating to working conditions and job satisfaction was added and will be discussed below. Likert scales were used for the battery and the respondent had the option to also provide qualitative responses which provided considerable additional data. There were 271

Table 9.1 Number of survey responses by job role

Role	Frequency	Percentage
Administrative/Clerical	99	36.5
Deputy Management	27	10.0
Management	95	35.1
Upper Management	21	7.7
Senior/Strategic	29	10.7
Total	271	

responses to the survey. Of the potential 382 local and electoral authorities, 189 local electoral organisations were represented, giving a high response rate of 49.5 per cent. Respondents were asked to pick from a range of job titles and these were coded by the author according to the level of seniority.[6] The composition of the responses by management level were a greater mix than with the pre-implementation interviews (Table 9.1).

Overall, the chapter provides new research on the effects of IER, but also a more holistic understanding of the effects of introducing reforms. This is important since the side effects of reforms can also have indirect effects on the voter's experience.

9.6 Pre-empting the impact of IER

The themes that were raised in the interviews anticipating the effects of IER in Britain are presented in Table 9.2. As Braun and Clarke note, the significance of a theme is not equal in proportion to its prevalence because the aim is to identify the nature of the phenomena, not its frequency. However, it is important to be transparent about how codes are constructed and why their significance is emphasised in the analysis. Table 9.2, therefore, also summarises the frequency of the themes raised.

One theme from the interviews was that IER would *reduce opportunities for fraud and improve voter confidence (T1)*. No respondents claimed that fraud was a problem in their authority, but some thought that it would help to alleviate concerns by removing some opportunities for fraud. According to one:

> I think something needs to be done to reassure the electorate that there is some form of double-checking that, you know, everybody needs to produce a PIN number or a signature for most things they do nowadays.

Others suggested that it was a necessary modernisation of procedures that were now out of date as 'this idea of a household form is from a very, very old fashioned time.'

Concerns were raised about *declining participation rates (T2)*. Some citizens would be reluctant to provide their national insurance numbers because of the

Table 9.2 Frequency table of themes and sub-themes raised by election officials

Theme	Sub-theme	Frequency
T1: Fraud, accuracy and voter confidence		14
T2: Declining registration levels		
	Harder for citizens to register (general)	10
	Citizen concerns about giving out personal identifiers	7
	Citizen concerns about use of personal identifiers	2
	Other citizens and organisations undertaking registration	4
	Young people less likely to register	7
	Students less likely to register	2
	Accessibility issues will arise	2
	Sub-total	*34*
T3: Concerns about increased costs/administrative burden		
	Higher administrative workloads and staff costs	28
	Fear of late implementation	1
	Resources of data-checking	5
	Urban areas especially difficult	2
	New software	3
	Additional stationery costs	7
	Sub-total	*46*
T4: Data issues		
	Data quality from public completion of forms	3
	Data quality arising from public completion of forms	1
	Physical storage problems	2
	Increased transactions	1
	Sub-total	*7*
T5: Spill-overs and displacements on other practices		
	Delayed other reforms	3
	Other changes made in preparation	2
	Cuts anticipated elsewhere to implement IER	3
	Sub-total	*8*

additional task involved in that the national insurance number would not be readily accessible for most – and they might also have concerns about how such information would be used. Other members of households, interviews suggested, were also playing an important role in registering others. Young people and students were pinpointed as groups among whom registration levels would drop the most. University students may have previously have been registered by their university administration, for example.

> I think it's going to be very, very difficult to collect the information from all these people. I've got a 17 year old son, I can't imagine he's going to be the least bit interested in filling in a registration form to be honest.

A third theme was the effect on *local government resources (T3)*. Canvassing individuals would take more time and resources than canvassing households. There would be additional costs involved in postage and stationery. Two local authorities expected that their staff numbers would need to double to deal with the implementation. One had done some initial costing estimates and expected their overall costs to increase by 50 per cent.

> I think the biggest concern now is that all that it's doing is adding to the bureaucracy. . . . Because with the annual canvass, you could do it by household, with individual registration, you've got almost, you know, for every single person some sort of contact with them.

A fourth item was concerns about *data quality and management (T4)*. On the one hand the public were reported to be prone to make errors on their forms. One LEO worked in an authority that had piloted internet voting and reported that some citizens, especially the elderly, had difficulty in providing key identifiers that were necessary for the system to work. According to her:

> [individual registration] is designed by these intelligent people who don't realise how daft some members of the public can be. It's a lovely idea but when I was in authority x . . . [we had to] get them to supply their national insurance number.

The use of personal identifiers would also involve further data-checking tasks by administrators. Data quality issues may arise because of conflicting data between different information systems, respondents thought. New and higher levels of staff skills such as manipulating datasets might be required. Some authorities would require new computer systems to deal with the changes. This would compound problems with resources and staffing.

A final theme was that IER would or had already created a number of *'spill over' and displacement effects (T5)* on the reform of other internal and external processes or aspects of election administration. Often IER was reported to compound declines in registration levels indirectly by affecting other procedures. For example, one authority delayed introducing new telephone, mobile phone and internet re-registration methods for citizens whose details have not changed as a result of IER.

> Our thinking was 'We don't want to introduce something that the public will get used to and then dismantle it.'

In other cases officials anticipated making cuts in other services to compensate for the new additional costs involved in implementing IER. These might include reduced payments for canvassers and public awareness work.

9.7 Negotiating IER

The findings from the interviews outlined above were used by the author to present policy briefings to Parliament about the likely consequences of IER. A briefing was made at the Welsh Assembly in 2011 and a submission of written evidence was made to the Political and Constitutional Reform Committee (James 2011b), which was undertaking pre-legislative scrutiny of the bill. This argued for additional longer-term funding for electoral services and the use of expansive measures such as 'Motor Voter' or automatic registration. Blogs were published in a variety of settings such as with the *Huffington Post*. Concerns were also raised by civil society groups about a potential fall in registration levels. Operation Black Vote, the British Youth Council and the National Union of Students raised similar concerns in their evidence (Select Committe on Political and Consitutional Reform 2011, 12). Meanwhile the Electoral Reform Society held a roundtable about the under-registration (Electoral Reform Society 2011).

The Select Committee report was sympathetic to these concerns noting that the 'introduction of IER carries the risk that people will drop off the register and become disenfranchised, particularly in urban Areas' (Select Committe on Political and Consitutional Reform 2011, 3). Behind closed doors, senior Liberal Democrat peers lobbied for the 'opt out' system to be dropped which the Coalition government eventually agreed to.

The passage of the Electoral Registration and Administration Act made IER a reality. From 10 June 2014 all citizens wanting to re-register or register for the first time had to do so individually and provide national insurance numbers.[7] As part of a transition process, all existing elector details were checked against the government's Department for Work and Pensions database during a 'confirmation dry run'; 87 per cent of records were matched and automatically added to the electoral roll. However, the matching rate varied enormously across the country. It was as low as 59 per cent in Hackney, but as high as 97 per cent in Epping. Those that did not match government records were written to and invited to register. Gradually, the number of unconfirmed entries on the register fell to 1.9 million in May 2015 and then 770,00 by December 2015. Against the advice of the Electoral Commission and stiff opposition in the House of Lords, the government ended the transition period early at this point so that all of these names were removed (Electoral Commission 2016a, 6). The total drop in names on the electoral register since 1 December 2013 was 1.4 million fewer entries on it than the February 2014 register – the last one before IER was introduced (James 2016a).

As Chapter 6 lays out, the transition period was also marked by the establishment of the APPG on Democratic Participation, informed by the research documented in the first half of this chapter. Bite the Ballot organised a National Voter Registration Week leading to 441,696 people registering to vote in a single week of coordinated social action (Bite the Ballot 2019). As Chapter 2 sets out, research does not take place in a hermetically sealed environment – it can be, and should be, interactive with the policy environment. This needs to be considered when the effects of IER are considered, which are set out now.

9.8 Post-implementation effects

The post-implementation survey identified nine key effects of IER.

9.8.1 Opportunities for electoral fraud

The reduction of opportunities for electoral fraud was both the stated aim of the government reform and the anticipated effect of many officials. Quantitative replies provided evidence that IER had achieved this goal. As Table 9.3 illustrates, 77 per cent agreed (with a score of 6–9) that opportunities for electoral fraud were reduced and 68 per cent agreed that the accuracy of the electoral register had improved. Qualitative replies were more sceptical. Some pointed out that electoral fraud of this type was rare to begin with. Most notably, however, many pointed out many other vulnerabilities existed. The check against the DWP database only established that the identity was real, however, it is not a guarantee that their nationality and/or residency entitled them to vote.

'Anyone can register online with someone else's details'

'Checking with the DWP only checks that the person exists it is still down to the ERO to verify if they exist at the property, with it now being on-line more people can register at different properties and if the confirmation letter gets lost in the post or doesn't get delivered the official owners would not know that someone has registered at their property fraudulently.'

'In a sense IER has actually increased the potential for fraud in that previously we would never register anyone unless they could prove residence at an address. Now if they can't be linked to an address any other way we are obliged to seek additional evidence but that can be a passport which of course doesn't bear a person's address! Hence anyone so minded could attempt to register at multiple addresses, pass the DWP identity check and

Table 9.3 Effects of IER on electoral security and the accuracy of the register

%	Don't agree at all					Very much agree			Don't know	Mean	N
	1	2	3	4	5	6	7	8	9		
Opportunities for electoral fraud are reduced	2	0	3	3	14	14	26	27	10	0.7	6.7	270
The accuracy of the electoral register has increased	2	3	6	5	13	13	20	26	9	2	6.4	269
Citizen's confidence in the electoral register has increased	4	4	10	10	27	10	8	6	1	19	4.8	270
Local politician's confidence in the integrity of the electoral register has increased	2	3	7	6	20	16	10	7	4	25	5.5	270

use their passport to support their application when they fail the address check usually done with Council Tax.'

'The documentary evidence stage is just to establish someone's identity, not to prevent fraudulent applications! Cabinet Office have been informed of this, but it is the least of their priorities!'

There was less evidence that this increased accuracy had improved citizen's confidence in the electoral register, however Respondents said that the public rarely gave it much thought and 'didn't care' except, perhaps for when they heard occasional news stories about it. Neither was it felt that local politician's confidence had increased much, as Table 9.3 illustrates. Electoral officials described them as having little understanding of the change. Concerns, as far as they were expressed, were often about the completeness of the register and were often dependent on the party affiliation of the member.

The data also allows us to investigate the socio-geographical distribution of the effects. We might expect that if IER reduced opportunities for electoral fraud, then the effect would be greater in areas where concerns had been raised about electoral fraud. Prior to the implementation of IER, the Electoral Commission published the results of a 'review of electoral vulnerabilities in the UK to identify what could be done to improve confidence in the security of our electoral processes' (Electoral Commission 2014a, 9). This identified 16 of nearly 400 local authority areas where cases of alleged or suspected cases of electoral fraud were especially high and deemed these to be 'at risk'. These were areas that the Commission identified as being:

> often characterised by being densely populated with a transient population, a high number of multiple occupancy houses and a previous history of allegations of electoral fraud . . . these areas are also often home to communities with a diverse range of nationalities and ethnic backgrounds.
> (Electoral Commission 2014a, 16)

Subsequent to this, a research report also found evidence that vulnerabilities for electoral fraud were greater in Bangladeshi and Pakistani communities (Sobolewska et al. 2015). If IER had reduced opportunities for electoral fraud more in the 'at risk' areas, then we might imply support for the hypothesis that these were the causes of electoral fraud and the specific effects of IER in resolving these vulnerabilities.

The data does not seem to support this. Of the 16 'at risk' local authorities, six responded to the survey (Birmingham, Bradford, Coventry, Derby, Peterborough, Walsall). The mean response was similar for this group (6.57) to all other responses (6.7) on the question of whether opportunities for electoral fraud had been reduced.

We can also compare responses in urban areas against those in more rural or sub-urban areas. The local government structure provides a good proxy for this. Metropolitan and London Borough Councils are typically urban areas, densely populated with a transient population. Unitary and District authorities are typically the smaller, more rural authority. A bivariate analysis of the relationship revealed a Pearson's coefficient did not reveal a relationship, however.

Lastly, we can compare electoral officials' responses between those areas which have large Bangladeshi and Pakistani communities. Information is drawn from the 2011 census on the percentage of the population within a local authority area that self-identifies as being Pakistani and Bangladeshi. There appears to be little statistical relationship, however. Bivariate analysis of the relationship between the Pakistani population and a perceived reduction in opportunities for electoral fraud revealed a Pearson's coefficient of –0.031. The value for the Bangladeshi community was –0.011. Neither value was statistically significant. In short, there is no real evidence that this plugged a problem with electoral fraud in these communities, perhaps because any problem was not specific to these areas as first thought.

9.8.2 Effects on completeness and inclusiveness

The second theme of interest was whether the new process would make registration more bureaucratic and negatively affect the completeness of the electoral register. The picture here was more mixed. Respondents were asked whether completeness had declined as a result of the reforms on a scale of 1 to 9. Figure 9.1 shows that there was a very broad distribution in answer to this question with a mean score of 4.9.

Unpacking the qualitative comments helps to interpret this data. Electoral officials stressed that the online registration system had made electoral registration much easier. This was commonly described as 'a massive step forward in the democratic

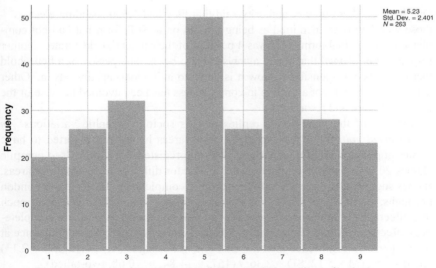

Figure 9.1 The effects of IER on the completeness of the electoral register.

212 *Instruments*

process' and having made the 'process vastly more accessible'. However, there was a heavy caveat, that the process was more complex for those who failed the DWP record check and some groups were finding the process especially difficult.

> The process is difficult for those that have to provide evidence or for vulnerable people such as those in care homes.

Qualitative comments suggested that many electoral officials experienced 'a few' problems with citizens providing identifiers. One response was typical of many, saying that: 'original concerns about the provision of NiNO and DoB have proven incorrect.' However, others said that: 'there is a reluctance to provide NI numbers,' or that:

> Concern isn't about what electoral services departments do with the information. Rather, it has made the collection of the necessary information on the doorstep more difficult with individuals being understandably reluctant to give this to a stranger at the door.

While the online process was thought to have generally made the process smoother, the new two-stage canvass process had made electoral registration more bureaucratic. As one official argued: 'the disengaged now have two processes to disengage with!' Others suggested that:

> It is incomprehensible to many why we would send out a HEF form and not register them from the information provided.

One large northern unitary authority said that they had 7,500 'pending electors' – those who had been identified as being present on a HER form but had not completed an individual form. This was 4 per cent of their potential electorate. Another respondent explained that 'there always used to be the one person in a household that would take responsibility, now it is down to individuals apathy sets in.' Other authorities thought that a decline in completeness has been avoided because of the additional work and resources.

Analysis of the quantitative replies reveals socio-geographic variations. *An urban–rural split* might be expected. Urban areas have been reported to have higher population churns which can make the register more difficult to compile (James 2014a). Table 9.4 compares the means for different local authority areas. It does suggest that there was a higher-drop in completeness levels in the London boroughs, but not in the Metropolitan areas, which, counter-intuitively, was much less affected. An independent-sample t-test was conducted to compare completeness effects for London boroughs and district councils. There was significance at the 90 per cent confidence interval for London boroughs (M = 6.15, SD = 2.13) and districts (M = 5.12, SD = 2.36; t (157) = –1.84, p = 0.68, two-tailed).

The survey also provided information about whether specific groups had been adversely affected more than others. Table 9.5 compares the proportion of people in agreement and disagreement that completeness or accessibility had been adversely affected for specific groups.[8] Answers were very centrally located, and there were many respondents who provided qualitative answers to suggest the case for positive and negative effects for both groups. This divided opinion probably reflects the multiple causal mechanisms in place because of the number of simultaneous reforms undertaken. Overall, it seems that completeness was negatively affected and that students were the principally affected group with a net agreement of +18.5 percentage points. Students were described as being 'notoriously difficult to register, and the requirement to register individually made this significantly harder'. However, many areas were unaffected by a decline in completeness because they had no universities in their local authority, and there was a higher standard deviation compared to other categories. Attainers were also less likely to register because 'as it is their responsibility to register now, rather than their parents' and they 'still do not know their NI numbers which delays their registration'. BME groups were broadly not thought to have been as affected and accessibility for disabled and non-native speakers was not affected either. One respondent remarked that they visited all properties at canvass and have found 'our BME population quite proactive compared to some non BME areas'.

Table 9.4 The effects of IER on completeness by local authority type

Type of authority	Mean	N	Std. deviation
District council	5.1	139	2.4
Unitary authority	5.5	46	2.4
London borough	6.2	20	2.1
Metropolitan district	4.8	29	2.8
Total	5.3	235	2.4

Table 9.5 The effects of IER on the completeness of the electoral register and accessibility of the electoral registration process

Completeness of the register declining		Percentage in agreement	Percentage in disagreement	Net agreement
	Overall	46.8	34.2	12.6
	Attainers	44.1	43.0	1.1
	Young people	40.3	40.3	0.0
	Students	49.5	31.0	18.5
	BME groups	35.3	38.6	−3.3
Accessibility being reduced for				
	Disability	35.7	48.5	−12.8
	Non-native speakers	31.0	50.0	−19.0

9.8.3 Increased costs and administrative burden

The effects on the resources involved in compiling the electoral register were much clearer. Electoral officials were asked whether they had to employ new staff, faced additional IT costs, stationery/postage costs or higher costs in general. Figure 9.2 provides the mean of these responses on a (1–9 scale). All answers were well above the mid-point on the scale (5). The additional stationery and postage costs received the highest score.

In their qualitative comments, respondents most often explained that temporary staff were taken on, especially during 'peak periods' to cover the additional work involved. Some authorities, however, added permanent staff, with one authority employing two additional full-time staff. This was important so that a reasonable level of work was maintained in the team with no one being unreasonably overworked.' In other cases the contracted hours of existing staff were extended or employees 'just had to work longer hours'. The government provided additional funds to local authorities for implementing IER but some expressed concern about what would happen when this transitional funding expired.

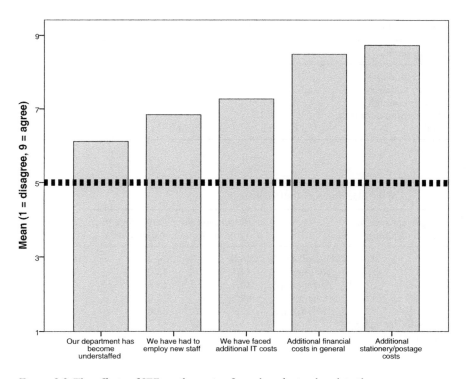

Figure 9.2 The effects of IER on the costs of running electoral registration.

The costs of this will continue after the additional government funding ceases. This is a concern as there is no local funding. The outcome is likely to be that we will be forced to allow the accuracy of the register to decline because we cannot afford the additional resources to maintain it at its current high level of accuracy.

Many officials, who had not been allocated additional staff, argued that this was because the funds were not available, perhaps because of other cuts to their services. The volume of letters that electoral officials had to send out had increased postal costs by an 'astronomical degree'. One official raised concerns that:

> A large number of additional mailouts are now mandatorily required, and as it costs this authority about £100k for each of these it is a major concern how this will be funded in the future.

9.8.4 Workplace conditions and employee outcomes

The survey was unanimous that there were considerable effects on the workplace setting within electoral services and individual employees. As noted above, the existing literature on voter registration reform has tended to focus on the effects on electoral participation and fraud. The electoral officials themselves are given no importance since they are simply part of the faceless bureaucracy that was expected to deliver the outcomes in a machine-like way. Yet the effects on employees matter for two core reasons. Firstly, state employees make up a considerable proportion of the population. The state therefore has a duty of care towards employees. Workers are more than 'units of labour'. They are people, individuals and members of teams and communities whose happiness matters in and of itself. Secondly, the consequentialist case is that employee outcomes matter because they cause other problems. For example, job satisfaction is thought to affect organisational performance, staff turnover and intention to quit (Griffeth, Hom, and Gaertner 2000; Harter, Schmidt, and Hayes 2002; Judge et al. 2001; Saari and Judge 2004; Wegge et al. 2007). For this reason, employee outcomes are given formal weight in the PROSeS method used to assess electoral management set out in Chapter 3.

Measures were developed to identify the effects on a number of key properties of workplace conditions and employee outcomes based on Gould-Williams et al.'s (2014) study of local government employees. The concepts behind each measure are discussed in the next chapter. Each measure was assessed using a 1 to 9-point Likert scale asking respondents whether they agreed with a particular question. An additive index score was created and divided by the number of measures. Cronbach's alpha was calculated to test for the reliability of the new scale where measures were combined and a high reliability was found with values firmly over .8 (see Table 9.6).

Figure 9.3 provides a boxplot of the effects of IER on employee outcomes. The box represents the interquartile range of 50 per cent of the cases. The line in the middle of the box represents the median and the whiskers outline the smallest and

Table 9.6 Measures of workplace conditions and employee experiences

Concept	Measures	Cronbach's alpha
Workplace environment	'Our department has become understaffed.'	–
Work overload	'I have been required to work very intensively.' 'I have been put under pressure to work long hours.' 'I have been required to do too much work to do everything well.'	.879
Civic duty	'Less willing to work beyond your usual hours for no further pay.'	–
Job satisfaction	'Enjoy your job more.' [reversed]	–
Intention to quit	'Think about leaving your job at some point in the last year.'	–
Stress	'Negatively affected your quality of life (e.g. family or social activities).' 'Feeling unable to continue in your job due to work pressures.' 'Confronted with problems that you cannot do much about.'	.807

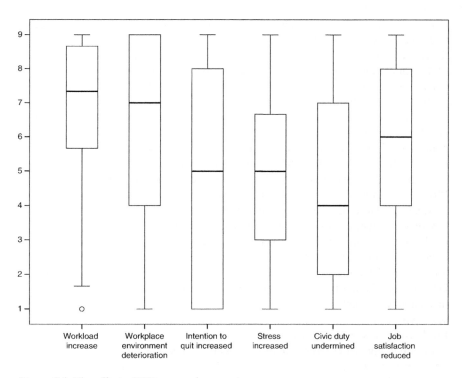

Figure 9.3 The effect of IER on employee outcomes.

highest values. The figure shows that workload and workplace environment was generally negative, with median values above 7. These effects are described in more detail next, in combination with the qualitative comments.

9.8.5 Workload and workplace environment

Many respondents noted that they, or their colleagues, had had their workload increase and had needed to work additional hours during the transition to IER:

> Workloads have increased significantly and consistently – IER is an ongoing process and does not stop at election time!

Some respondents suggested that the increase in workload from the new system might be temporary as there was a process of adjustment or 'a phase of learning and development'. 'Stress points' were also highly seasonal, peaking during the annual canvass or in advance of an election:

> In the run up to the combined General/Local/Parish elections, two members of staff worked in excess of 400 hours each (late nights, weekends and bank holidays), over and above the normal working hours.

Others suggested that while they had managed so far, this was as a result of short-term government funding and that 'we will be significantly understaffed when this post is no longer funded.' As a consequence, other activities were being culled such as 'follow-up visits to non-responding addresses and electors'. A minimalist approach would therefore be taken:

> we have to concentrate on just getting the job done rather than looking at best practice etc. It is reactive rather than proactive with little opportunity to forward plan or review properly.

The working environment was also affecting managerial and staff relations, levels of absenteeism and physical working conditions, as Box 9.1 demonstrates.

Box 9.1 Examples of changed workplace environment as a result of IER

'Colleagues have become less tolerant of each other and distrust the management.'

'Moodiness, arguments and absences have increased noticeably.'

'Very cramped for space to work and storage due to very large forms and double envelopes.'

> 'Staff morale in the department is low due to additional pressures for the same pay.'
>
> 'Taking holidays has also been a near impossible exercise during the last two years.'
>
> 'Tensions between staff members have been increased and absence, particularly through stress related illness, has increased. Morale is low as staff feel a lack of confidence in their abilities caused by constant change on top of heavy workloads.'

9.8.6 Job satisfaction

Some reflected positively that they enjoyed the 'challenge' of IER. Others pointed out that the job was now about 'survival' rather than 'quality' and that the additional work had undermined their enjoyment.

> I still enjoy elections side not so much registration side.

9.8.7 Stress

Stress was much less affected at the aggregate level with a median value of 5. But at an individual level – there were a significant number of people claiming to be adversely affected. Many respondents reported that the job had negatively affected their quality of life.

> 'At peak times, yes. Not leaving the office until midnight during period of high activity did not go down well.'
>
> 'There were some days when I barely saw my family in the run up to May 2015 elections.'
>
> 'I had to visit my doctor for anxiety.'

Some thought that increased stress levels were brought about during pinch points in the transition to IER, such as the software changes in 2014, but while 'it has undoubtedly been very hard' they could now 'see the light at the end of the tunnel'. Software weaknesses and unclear legislation added to stress levels. Stress had also brought about increased staff sickness in some cases:

> Combined with the pressures of elections has increased staff sickness absence which has put additional pressures on remaining staff.

9.8.8 Intention to quit

The median value for intention to quit was also centrally located, but there was a very wide distribution. This suggests that while for many, IER had no impact on their intention to leave their post, it was a major trigger for some. In fact, almost half (48.9 per cent) of respondents selected 6–9 on the scale. One respondent said that 'My wife wanted me to leave!!!!!!' while another said that quitting was not an option because they had a 'wife and two kids to feed'.

9.8.9 Civic duty

Civic duty was much less affected with a median value of 4. As one put it: 'it is a requirement of my job to be willing to work beyond core hours at key points'. For another: 'I would always work additional hours as required to undertake role satisfactorily.' Electoral officials, in general, did not suggest that they were now less likely to work more without pay. This suggests that the levels of civic ethos amongst UK electoral officials was high. However, they equally stressed that it could have been improved and that many had been compensated for their additional work:

> We are professional and have been suitably recompensed and supported. If I was not then there would be issues. The same applies to the whole team.

And, indeed, some did express frustrations that may affect their longer-term willingness to go above and beyond:

> 'Last year I lost 164hrs flexi working hours.'

> 'New canvass process is de-motivating. There is a lack of understanding from council management about the demands of IER both on staff time and on department budgets.'

This, again, reinforces the point that although the averages might be centrally located, the presence of some extreme values on a survey scale can demonstrate that there is a causal process in place.

9.9 Conclusions

This chapter has shown that the traditional academic and policy focus on reforms made to the electoral process have some inherent weaknesses. Reforms to electoral registration and polling processes tend to only be evaluated in terms of whether they reduce opportunities for electoral fraud or increase participation. There are broader consequences on the functioning of organisations, however, including on resources and employees. This case study of the introduction of IER shows that although it was effective in terms of increasing the accuracy of the register and reducing opportunities for electoral fraud (the extent to which there was any fraud, is questionable), it made electoral registration a much more intensive process and had negative effects on employee outcomes. This has academic and policy implications. Both future researchers and policy makers need to be more aware of the broader effects of reforms. Undertaking risk assessments and using bottom-up learning about the likely intended consequences can help to mitigate many of the negative effects that might follow.

Notes

1 There are exceptions, e.g. Garnett 2019a.
2 Prior to this, a central Electoral Commission website only provided an application form that needed to be printed off and posted to the local ERO, whose details were provided if the citizen entered their postcode.
3 For England and Wales. IER began in Scotland from September 2014, following the Scottish Independence Referendum.
4 Registration levels subsequently increased in Northern Ireland after provisions were made for the government to reinstate names on the register and the need for citizens to re-register each year was removed.
5 Northern Ireland was not included in this study.
6 'Retuning Officers' and 'Electoral Registration Officers' were coded as Senior/Strategic. 'Democratic Services Managers' were coded as Upper Management. 'Electoral Services Managers' were coded as Managers. 'Assistant Electoral Services Managers' were coded as Deputy Managers. 'Electoral Services Administrators' were coded as 'Administrative/Clerical'.
7 The implementation was delayed in Scotland to allow for the Scottish Independence Referendum in September 2014.
8 The respondents who selected 1–4 were assumed to disagree – those who chose 6–9 were interpreted to agree.

10 Centralisation

10.1 Introduction

One key issue in any organisation is whether to centralise power, resources and decision making, or decentralise them. Should directions be issued from a central office afar? Or should local officers be allowed to do what they think is best for a given situation? Large multi-national companies, such as fast-food restaurants, might have highly centralised international management teams, who make decisions in the board rooms of high-rise glass towers in metropolitan cites, remote from most local restaurants in which they would never be likely to set foot. Local workers are set target times for tasks such as the production of each meal, or the serving of each customer, so that profit and efficiency are maximised. Prices are set centrally according to various algorithms. These practices contrast drastically to a restaurant owner who might trust her local managers and employees to vary prices to clear stock or catch local tastes. For better or worse, these approaches have major consequences for organisational performance. Electoral officials are not presiding over the cooking of fries and burgers – it's votes and ballot boxes. We should expect that the organisational structure designed to deliver elections could make similar differences. Remarkably, very little research has sought to identify what these are through applied research.

The chapter therefore begins by trying to define centralisation and decentralisation in the sphere of electoral management. It introduces what the field of public administration says about the consequences of (de)centralisation in general, before reviewing the brief literature on centralisation in electoral management. Two simple hypotheses are developed based on this literature. The empirical section of the chapter consists of two studies. The first is a study of the effects of centralising electoral administration in two UK referendums that took place in 2011. The second is a related study of the effects of the same instrument, implemented five years later, in the 2016 UK Brexit referendum.

The chapter therefore advances our knowledge of electoral management design by identifying the effects of attempts to centralise EMB using unique primary data. Introducing measures to centralise elections can generate more consistent services, enable officials to eliminate errors early on, enable new practices and ideas to be shared and ease the implementation for officials. Equally, it can bring about many other side effects such as increased financial costs, absorb staff time, overlook local experience and negatively affect staff morale. Above all, the study points to the temporal nature of these effects. They might recede over time as learning takes place and the meanings attached to the policy instrument shift amongst practitioners. Rather than there being a 'one size fits all', best practice is to craft organisational design to fit local culture and context.

10.2 Defining centralisation and decentralisation

Centralisation in this chapter focusses purely on the internal organisation of electoral management bodies – those state bodies with a formal mandate to play a role in administering elections. In earlier chapters we argued that electoral management isn't in fact undertaken by a single organisation. There are many organisations involved in running elections – even if their role is a rather small one. There are also many non-state actors in civil society, the international community and even political parties that play some de facto role. EMBs are therefore nested into governance relationships, and this chapter's analysis of centralisation only provides part of the story of electoral management – but it is an important one nonetheless.

Within EMBs we can envisage at least two different forms of centralisation and decentralisation. *Organisational* centralisation refers to the number of organisations involved in delivering elections and the power relationships between them. Organisational responsibility can be almost *entirely centralised*. For example, the Zimbabwe Electoral Commission was formed under a Constitutional Amendment in 2009 to conduct and prepare elections for Presidential, parliamentary, metropolitan and provincial elections. There are 10 permanent provincial offices, each headed by a Provincial Elections Officer who reports to the Chief Elections Officer (ZEC 2018). Alternatively, there might be a division of labour between types of elections. In Canada, for example, the national EMB is responsible for national general elections, by-elections and referendums, while separate EMBs retain responsibility for provincial elections. Lastly, there can be a pre-dominantly decentralised system. In Switzerland National EMB is responsible only for policy coordination, because local authorities are in charge of elections.

Geographical centralisation is the extent to which electoral management tasks are geographically dispersed across a polity. Although electoral management might be centralised into one organisation, that organisation might have many offices, as the Australian Electoral Commission does (see Chapter 7). This is made increasingly possible because of the use of IT systems which means that digital records are stored securely on a cloud, while employees can work at one of several offices. Despite the geographic separation, employees might still be united into a single organisation, possibly with a strong chain of command.

Pressures for centralisation and decentralisation in electoral management also map onto broader pressures for constitutional change. The centralisation of administration was a key moment in the formation of states, as a central authority sought to claim legitimate use of force over a territory. Historically, a central method to ensure central control over a polity would include a system of prefectoralism, whereby the national government divided a country up into administrative units and then places an official in charge to manage that jurisdiction. Tactics to ensure compliance might include recruiting officials from outside of a territory, regularly rotating staff or finding methods of supervising local officials (Hutchcroft 2001, 28–9). Recent debates have focussed on a broad move towards organisational decentralisation, in the established democracies at least. *Deconcentration* involves the transfer of particular functions and workloads from the central government to regional or local offices. *Devolution*, meanwhile, involves a more complete transfer of decision-making and accountability settings to a local or regional level (Hooghe, Marks, and Schakel 2008). Trends towards regionalisation and decentralisation have become key themes since the 1980s as new public management reforms have been introduced and demands for self-autonomy have arisen (Marks, Hooghe, and Schakel 2008).

10.3 Existing perspectives on centralising electoral management

Is centralisation better than decentralisation? Or is the opposite so? There has been speculation about whether centralised or decentralised EMBs perform better, but no detailed theorisation or research. Failings in electoral integrity have often been attributed to decentralised management. These claims are predominately in the US where decentralisation is blamed for variations in the voter's experience of election administration, usually for the worse. Gerken (2009b, 1585–6) has suggested that 'localism' has been the cause of many American problems and can make reform difficult to achieve. Pastor has claimed that the US system has been 'decentralized to the point of being dysfunctional' (Pastor 2006, 273).[1] The most cited advantage of centralised systems is consistent experiences for the voter (Guess 2009; International IDEA 2014, 17; Pastor 2004, 2006). However, decentralised forms of election management have also been said to have some advantages. Guess (2009) suggests that they often allow more responsive service delivery for diverse local needs and they enable innovation. International IDEA's *Electoral Management Design* handbook states that they can 'ensure continuity' and 'enhance inclusiveness and transparency in electoral management' (International IDEA 2014, 17).

10.4 Perspectives on centralisation in public management

Broader research from the field of public administration provides insights into how and why bureaucratic centralisation might affect organisational performance, with several different approaches emerging (Brehm and Gates 1999, 1–24). Firstly, a *scientific management school* emerged in the early decades of the twentieth century, seeking to measure inefficiencies in the workplace. It prescribed the better coordination of workers through clear chains of command from the central management, incentives and strict rules to combat these inefficiencies. These Taylorist work processes were criticised, however, for bringing about harsh working conditions for employees. A counter-reaction therefore emerged in the growth of trade union movements in the 1930s. A *human relations school of management* instead proposed more cooperative management practices between employers and labour. Boosting employee morale was seen as important if organisations wanted to be productive (Barnard 1938). Performance would be more likely to be improved by trying to embed the norms of professionalism into organisations, rather than through central command (Friedrich 1940). Herbert Simon (1945) argued that top-down scientific management techniques assumed a level of rationality that central planners (or any humans) were not capable of. The centralised control of bureaucracies was therefore strongly discouraged.

A *bureaucratic discretion school* followed which issued further warnings about centralisation. This approach argued that public officials, or 'street-level bureaucrats', had the capacity to make policies on the grond and decide whether or not to enforce them (Lipsky 1980). The sanctions available to central decision makers were often argued to be ineffective because they were too costly to enforce. Central control was a practical impossibility. However, many authors did not necessarily consider this a problem. 'Street-level bureaucrats' were well positioned to make policy because of their close proximity to the everyday challenges involved with delivering public services. Feldman (1989), for example, describes public officials as being diligent and hard-working. They were therefore not motivated by material rewards and could work autonomous of central direction.

The new public management school that emerged in the 1980s, by contrast, argued that some form of central control of bureaucracy was needed because workers (and supervisors) were assumed to be rational, self-interested actors. The problem that followed was that, as Brehm and Gates noted (1999, 21):

> Some bureaucrats devote extraordinary effort toward accomplishing policy ('work'), where others may expend as much effort deliberately undermining policy objectives of their superiors ('sabotage'). Other bureaucrats may be directing effort towards non-policy goals ('shirking').

New public management theorists therefore sought to develop a range of policy tools that could be used by supervisors to structure the incentives of agents into bringing about compliance, such as targeting rewards and punishments (Bianco and Bates 1990) although the efficacy of these were sometimes questioned (Brehm and Gates 1994; Christopher 2006).

10.5 Research questions and hypothesis

This chapter seeks to answer the question of *what effect does the centralisation of electoral management have?* Two contrasting hypotheses are developed based on the literature discussed above.

Firstly, based on the problems that have been commonly attributed to localism in the US and elsewhere, we should expect some improvements in the quality of electoral services. This position is reinforced by insights from the scientific management school that suggested that a centralised decision maker is well positioned to identify and prescribe best practice for the delivery of elections because of their position of oversight. The central decision maker might also overcome any shirking or sabotage by bureaucrats, if practice is centrally prescribed. Hypothesis 1 is therefore:

- *H1: Centralisation enables more efficient services and better quality services because the EC is able to prescribe better solutions from the centre.*

Based on the arguments of the bureaucratic discretion school, that top-down prescriptions are difficult to enforce and that local officials are often best placed to judge local needs, a second hypothesis is that:

- *H2: Centralisation leads to no change or poorer quality and less efficient services because of a lack of sensitivity to a) local needs and b) the local knowledge of bureaucrats.*

10.6 Study one: centralisation in the 2011 referendums

The UK provides a useful case study for identifying the effects of centralising electoral management because it is an example of a decentralised system where there is variation in local practice and performance. As Chapter 6 outlined, the *process of making* UK electoral law has always been centralised. It is made by Parliament in Westminster.[2] The *process of implementing* election law, however, has always been highly decentralised. Elections have historically been run by Returning Officers (ROs) who are appointed by local authorities. ROs are responsible for the conduct of the poll and have some discretion over the timing of the count. An Electoral Registration Officer (ERO) is responsible for compiling the electoral register. Both ROs and EROs are local government employees but are independent of both central and local government with respect to their electoral duties. They are instead accountable to the courts system as an independent statutory officer and can be prosecuted for being in breach of their duties (Gay 2010). They both draw from local government staff to manage the poll and compile the register.[3]

Between 2000 and 2011, there were common complaints by parliamentarians to the Electoral Commission about variation in practice and performance of local ROs and EROs, illustrated by variations in local registration rates (various private interviews). These complaints led to a performance monitoring scheme being legislated for in 2006 (James 2013). High-profile localised problems became headline news at the 2010 general election, however, as some polling stations developed queues that prevented citizens from casting their vote and officials did not print enough ballot papers (Electoral Commission 2010b). Centralisation was therefore seen as a remedy to local variation in the administration of elections. Officials within the Commission thought that, having improved electoral administration with an earlier performance monitoring scheme, the directions would provide them 'a way of influencing what is done locally' which would allow them to 'report in a more timely fashion and if necessary seek to influence legislative change later on' (private interview, Electoral Commission official, October 2011). The nature of the electoral malpractice was not that electoral officials were acting in a partisan way or engaged in electoral fraud on behalf of political parties. The perceived problem was thought to be variation in the compliance with statutory requirements and overall performance because of uneven resourcing and practice.

The focus of this chapter is on the case study of the implementation of a management system by the UK Electoral Commission for the electoral administration in three referendums: the Welsh devolution referendum in March 2011, the AV referendum in May 2011 and the EU Brexit referendum of 2016.[4] Under the Political Parties, Elections and Referendums Act 2000 the Commission had a number of specific responsibilities and functions in relation to the delivery and regulation of the referendum that it does not have at elections and had not been used before. The Electoral Commission's Chair, Jenny Watson, was therefore the Chief Counting Officer and able to issue directions to EROs and ROs. The use of centralised directions was historically unprecedented in British elections.

The two referendums that took place in 2011 are treated as a single case. This is because these referendums operated using an identical system at a time that was very close to each other and the effects were discussed together in the interviews that follow. The Welsh devolution referendum took place on 3 March 2011 and the AV referendum on 5 May 2011. In both referendums the Commission published a list of directions that it expected officials to implement during the winter of 2010 (see Box 10.1). Local officials were then required to report to the Commission as to whether these directions had been implemented in the run-up to the election. Five checklists were sent out between 28 March

---

Box 10.1   Example directions issued to local officials in preparation for the 2011 referendums, compiled from Electoral Commission (2011a, 2011b)

- A maximum number of electors for each polling station
- A minimum number of staff per polling station
- A requirement to print ballot papers for all electors
- Deadlines for the posting of polling cards and postal ballots
- A requirement to check the personal identifiers on 100% of returned postal ballots rather than 20%, which was law
- A deadline for the verification of ballot boxes and a requirement that counting should begin at 4pm the following day
- Specific wording and layout for the ballot paper, poll cards, postal voting statements and instructions and guidance for voters
- Counting times were centrally defined

and 21 April. Local officials were also required to submit project plans and risk registers. ROs could apply for exceptions of some tasks if compliance was not possible or compliance would introduce further risk in the conduct of the poll, but Electoral Commission approval was required.[5] The Commission provided election officials with PowerPoint briefings for polling workers, flowcharts for postal vote processes and template project plan and risk registers (Electoral Commission 2011a, 115).

10.7 Data and methods

How can the effects of these reforms be identified? Following on from Chapter 9, the approach was to ask those involved in running elections themselves. The logic is that, drawing from theories of implementation, public officials are front-line workers with 'local knowledge' who will have first-hand experience of the reform (Durose 2009, 2011; Lipsky 1980). The effects of such back-office reforms are unlikely to be known and experienced by the citizen. Semi-structured interviews with those who set the standards centrally and those who were involved in managing elections and were subject to the new standards were undertaken.

For study one, four interviews were undertaken with 'elite actors': past and present officials from the Electoral Commission and other key stakeholders. Interviews were also undertaken with 74 local election officials involved in implementing elections. A thematic analysis of the interviews was conducted to identify common challenges. Thematic analysis 'involves the searching across a data set . . . to find repeated patterns of meaning' (Braun and Clarke 2006, 86). The interviews and method were the same as those used in Chapter 9 – the sample and methodology was described there.

10.8 Results

Eight themes were identified from the interviews. The theme definition, subthemes (if appropriate) and the frequency of themes across the interviews are detailed in Table 10.1 and each discussed in turn.

10.8.1 Consistent services

The provision of centralised instructions for election officials removed room for local discretion and therefore produced more consistent services (T1). Some officials thought that this had enabled a better experience for the voter.

> Having that consistent approach, having the same message going out from all authorities is not a bad thing for the electorate, rather than [authority A] giving one message and [Authority B] giving one message.

The most visual of these was the counting times. However, in some local authorities central directions also ensured a minimal level of service to voters and forced

Table 10.1 The effects of top-down directions on electoral management during the 2011 referendums

Theme	Definition	Sub-theme count	Count
T1: Consistent services	Centralised instructions produced uniform services		8
T2: Elimination of errors	Errors in the practices of electoral administrators were identified, prevented or rectified		3
T3: New practices and ideas	Election officials adopted or became aware of new practices		4
T4: Eased implementation	The directions helped officials implement elections		10
- 4a Locating practices	The directions helped officials identify 'good practice' quickly and efficiently	4	
- 4b Early action	Officials took actions earlier than they would have done	3	
- 4c Helped new staff	Directions gave structure and guidance that was valuable for newer staff	3	
T5: Financial costs	Complying with the direction led to increased local costs		43
- 5a Staff	More staff had to be employed	15	
- 5b Ballot papers	More ballot papers had to be printed	9	
- 5c Misc.	Costs increased in general (without the area being specified)	19	
T6: Staff time	Completing and complying with the directions drained staff time		27
- 6a Bureaucratic	The completion process was bureaucratic	9	
- 6b Distraction	The directions distracted staff from completing other tasks	9	
- 6c Duplication	The directions required staff to duplicate tasks already being undertaken	3	
- 6d No time	Staff did not have sufficient time to comply with the directions	6	
T7: Lost local experience or knowledge	The Commission's directions overlooked experience and local knowledge that had been accumulated from many previous elections and adversely affected the voter's experience		42

Centralisation 229

Theme	Definition	Sub-theme count	Count
- 7a Local experience overlooked	The experience of a local electoral official was over-ridden by the need to meet the directions	13	
- 7b Local knowledge overlooked	The electoral officials' knowledge of their local area was overlooked by the need to meet the directions	15	
- 7c Local needs differ	Local needs were perceived to differ from that prescribed by the directions	14	
T8: Staff morale	The Commission's directions reduced the electoral officials' enjoyment of their role in elections and/or reduced staff morale		32
- 8a Job enjoyment declined	The electoral officials' enjoyment of their own job declined	7	
- 8b EC–LEO relations declined	Relations between the electoral official and the Electoral Commission declined as a result of the directions scheme	25	

local authorities to undertake activity that they would not otherwise do. For example, one authority explained that they had not previously had polling station inspectors, but had to under the directions. Another claimed that presiding officers said that the additional polling staff 'made our job a lot easier'. One official suggested that they had begun to prepare for an election earlier than they otherwise would have done. Another suggested that they increased the size of their cards because of the guidance. The move towards being more consistent therefore generally meant doing more for the voter, than less.

10.8.2 Error elimination

The directions allowed for the identification of errors in the run-up to the election and for them to be rectified (T2). A member of Electoral Commission staff explained how one authority initially used the wrong electoral register for the Welsh Referendum; they had used the parliamentary franchise rather than the local government franchise. This had meant that about 900 poll cards were not sent out. As they explained:

> Well we found that out the following day and were able to address it very quickly and make sure that the problem got sorted within 48 hours and

was corrected and it wasn't a problem. Whereas in fact I'm not sure how otherwise that would've been picked up.

The ability to identify such problems increased the Commission's confidence that the referendums would be successfully run:

> Going into the Referendum . . . we had an absolute handle on what had been done and the level of preparation made.

10.8.3 New practices and easier implementation

The directions sometimes provided election officials with new ideas or practices that they perceived to be better for the voter or more efficient (T3). According to one election official 'some of the notices, we quite liked the way they'd done it'.

There was evidence that some election officials found the guidance useful in structuring their work (T4). The directions made identifying the prescribed practice quicker, which can be important when legislation is complex. It was especially useful for new employees, who were less certain of what to do.

> Just the fact that it enables you to make sure you haven't left anything critical out in your plan, because there is so much going on, and all the bits have to all come together on polling day and then the count.

10.8.4 Financial costs

There was significant evidence of increased financial costs involved in the running of the election to meet the centrally defined directions (T5). Election officials generally reported that increased spending did not lead to improved outcomes; rather it simply reduced the efficiency of local services. A requirement to print ballot papers for every elector was reported as unnecessary, when turnout was eventually only 41 per cent, and widely predicted to be low. One election official claimed that he had to increase staffing levels by nearly 20 per cent, which 'has a significant impact on resources, and time on recruitment'. Another authority reported that it had spent roughly £40,000 more on the AV referendum than it otherwise would have done. The new scheme was also more resource-intensive for the Electoral Commission.

10.8.5 Staff Time

Completing and complying with the directions also drained staff time and diverted this from other aspects of the election (T6). An election official explained that there was a significant number of directions and work to complete. This was costly in terms of staff time and also distracted them from their key tasks at the peak 'pinch points' in preparing for an election.

It was a lot of pressure and in the end we didn't respond. Because it was 'Do we respond to this, or do we do this, which has an impact on whether we deliver the election or not?' (Laughter) So it was 'Well we'll deal with the election and we'll worry about that later, shall we?'

One requirement was for election officials to witness the printing of poll cards and postal voting packs. However, many authorities had long-running arrangements with contractors for them to be printed elsewhere in the country, where they had found high levels of quality and economic efficiency. Other election officials said that the standards caused some duplication. For example, one election official described how he had a risk plan for his authority but needed to create another one to satisfy the Commission.

10.8.6 Lost local knowledge

Election officials also suggested that the Commission's directions overlooked the experience and local knowledge that had been accumulated from many previous elections (T7). Variations in local circumstances meant that a one-size-fits-all approach was not the most effective.

> we are the electoral experts at the end of the day, we know our local areas, we know what works, what doesn't work . . . it does vary from authority to authority, because of, you know, geography, if nothing else, and when they try to dictate procedures. . .

The directions forced the solutions to local problems that officials had found and developed over a number of years to be changed. For example, an election official explained how they often faced severe challenges hiring premises for polling stations but had found local solutions. However, the cap of 2,500 electors per station meant that some less appropriate premises had to be hired. One official explained that they had developed a risk register to overcome any local problems but they were forced to not use it and use a centrally defined one which 'wasn't half as good as ours'. Central directions also affected other aspects of election management. Centrally defined counting and declaration times for the AV referendum had knock-on effects for local practices. One RO, who was simultaneously holding local elections, was forced to delay the counting and declaration of local election results until after the AV votes were counted. This meant that for a significant amount of time there were '11 counting stations with nobody doing anything', the declaration was not complete until 5am when officials were tired and more error-prone, and the RO had to deal with 'pissed off [local council] members'.

Some officials noted that the move towards central management reduced local responsiveness.

232 *Instruments*

> The reality is things go wrong every single election and you can't manage all those 300 crises [from the centre] because you just don't know what's going on in a count centre or in a polling station or in a local bypass or a gas explosion...

The changes triggered by the Electoral Commission directions sometimes directly or indirectly adversely affected the citizen's satisfaction. The cap on the number of electors for each polling station led some electoral officials to split their polling stations into two, with electors instructed to go into a room according to their street name which caused some confusion.

Election officials also said that some polling stations were overstaffed as a result of the minimal staffing requirements, which led to comment from members of the public:

> Especially at the present situation when we're having to make cutbacks and justify services, if electors see three people sat in a very quiet station twiddling their thumbs all day, it will be us that they come back to.

10.8.7 Staff morale, job satisfaction and stakeholder relations

Significantly, many election officials noted that the introduction of the performance standards reduced their enjoyment of their role in elections (T8). The introduction of central directions reduced their sense of 'ownership' over their work and demotivated them. One RO raised concerns about what he was being asked to do before the referendum but got a response that made him feel 'dismissed as some sort of thicko from the provinces who just needs to get on and do it and not make a fuss about it'. Another RO said that if the Commission had more powers of direction:

> that would actually remove what for me is some of the interesting parts of being personally responsible for a process.

There was also a broader souring of relations between the election officials, their representative organisation, the Association of Electoral Administrators, and the Electoral Commission. Officials claimed that the Commission's requirements 'grated on a number of people,' were 'quite patronising . . . and a wee bit offensive', were 'a bit irksome' or was:

> 'A bit like teaching your grandmother to suck eggs. Individual councils know their own areas, they know what works for them, what doesn't work for them. And by imposing these directions, they've rubbed a lot of people up the wrong way.'

> 'there was no real appreciation that we're dealing with – in most cases dedicated and professional people in their field.'

Following the referendum the Commission 'kept a low profile . . . because they are not flavour of the month'. The Commission seemed aware of their popularity:

> [W]e're getting the response from some of them 'Oh this is a dictate, we don't like being told how to do things'.

In some authorities, where staff morale may already have been low, and further budget cuts were on the horizon, officials became quite despondent. One explained that:

> I used to really enjoy elections, I used to enjoy everything there was about it. Over the years . . . it has certainly become more and more stressful and after every election I do sort of look at myself or during the election period and think, 'I don't really want to do this, should I just go and get a job. . .' and no disrespect to anybody who stacks shelves in Tesco but, should I just go and do that and get out of this because you struggle to sleep, you've got so many things you've got to do, so many people asking questions, just the whole process has become more and more difficult.

10.9 Study two: centralisation in the 2016 referendum

The second case was the 2016 Brexit referendum where the UK decided to remain or leave the European Union. This provided the Electoral Commission with another opportunity to use its powers of direction. The Electoral Commission had the same statutory powers to influence electoral administration by issuing directions in 2011, but decided to take a slightly different approach. Jenny Watson was again the CCO and Andrew Scallan served as the DCCO. This senior management team referred-back to the 'Referendum Blueprint' – an internal 150-page document that drew lessons from the previous two 2011 referendums, as well as the 2014 Scottish Independence referendum (managed by the Scottish Electoral Management Board). The Commission was aware that there had been 'not universal acceptance of what we had done in 2011' and therefore only wanted to direct on what was necessary:

> That was a journey. In 2011 we were all in a different place in terms of performance standards and what we knew about under performance. We then had several well-run elections where problems were noticeable because they were so few in number. So we felt comfortable focussing only on what was necessary. It focussed more about the relationships that we had with people than the number of directions.
>
> (interview with Jenny Watson, 16 June 2016)

A management board was created made up of senior Electoral Commission officials and RCOs. The scope of directions was formed through that board. Regional

234 *Instruments*

> **Box 10.2 Example directions issued to local officials in preparation for the 2016 referendum, based on Electoral Commission (2016c, 12–13)**
>
> - The notice of the referendum must be published on a date specified by the CCO
> - Ballot papers needed to be printed for all electors
> - A minimum number of staff per polling station
> - Deadline for the dispatch of polling cards and postal ballots
> - Counts to commence at 10pm, immediately after the close of polls
> - The use of 'mini counts' so that votes are collected into smaller self-contained areas
> - Providing the CCO with specified management information
> - The use of Royal Mail sweeps to collect postal votes
> - Use of international business class for overseas postal votes

boards were developed beneath this that acted as sounding boards for the development of any materials and directions. A consultation paper on the direction was then published in the autumn of 2015. Directions were then revised in light of the feedback. Some of the directions were similar to 2011, but there were fewer requests for real-time performance information (see Box 10.2). As with 2011, a process was available to allow COs to apply for exemptions from the directions (Electoral Commission 2016c, 7).

10.10 Data and methods

The second study draws from a survey of counting offers (COs) in local authorities administering the EU Brexit referendum in 2016, undertaken by Alistair Clark and myself.[6] An internet survey was sent to the 380 counting officers (COs), the electoral authorities in Gibraltar and to the Electoral Office of Northern Ireland (EONI). Responses were received from 254 local authority respondents giving a 66 per cent response rate.[7] Scottish Unitaries, London Boroughs and the South West region were slightly over-represented with response rates of 71, 72 and 76 per cent respectively, while the West Midlands and South East regions were slightly below average in responses at 57 and 58 per cent each. An extensive range of qualitative replies were provided in addition to the quantitative replies. These provided a rich source of additional information about the problems faced by COs, mostly explaining the nature of problems experienced in more detail. To add depth to the survey data, 25 semi-structured interviews were conducted with key actors (1 CCO and DCCO, all 11 RCOs and the Chief Electoral Officer for Northern Ireland (CEONI) and a further 12 COs from across Britain), mostly over the telephone. The aim of the interviews was to allow electoral officials to flag important challenges which were not anticipated by the survey. Although the nature of the data is not exactly the same as that used in study one above, owing to time and resource restraints, in combination the data provides an unprecedented temporal view of how the policy instrument changed in nature.

10.11 Results

Table 10.2 summarises views on overall levels of satisfaction among COs with the management structure. This was high since 82 per cent agreed or strongly agreed that it 'worked well'. Interviews with RCOs also suggested that the system seemed to have been successfully adapted from the model used in 2011. They thought that the Chief Counting Officer, Jenny Watson, had made efforts to reach out and speak to COs at local and regional events. This 'had been noticed' in the electoral community. RCOs described themselves as being well supported and drew most of their support from their local teams. In some cases this was strengthened with new, short-term appointments. Many officials were keen to stress that informal networks and relationships were more important than the formal structures in providing support, however. While this was not universally in place, COs also pointed to the importance of peers in other local authorities. 'Structures are fine, but relationships are everything,' said one.

Table 10.3 describes the responses received from COs to a series of questions about the directions. Questions were based on the eight themes identified in study one above. The data allows us to see the overall frequency of the themes across a broader sample of electoral officials. Importantly, the survey demonstrates that the directions were very widely thought to be clear, easy to understand and issued

Table 10.2 Views of the management structure used for the referendum (%)

	Strongly disagree	Disagree	Neither agree nor disagree	Agree	Strongly agree	N
The overall management structure for the referendum worked well	0.4	3.1	14.6	74.0	7.9	254
The overall management structure for the referendum worked better than it does for an election	2.8	26.8	60.2	9.4	0.8	254
The CCO's planning for the referendum was effective	0.8	4.7	19.7	66.1	8.7	254
The RCO's planning for the referendum was effective	–	2.4	11.6	66.9	19.1	251
Rehearsals of the result collation process were useful in helping iron out potential difficulties	2.0	9.9	7.9	62.8	17.4	253

236 *Instruments*

Table 10.3 The effects of the 2016 directions on electoral management

	Strongly disagree	Disagree	Neither agree nor disagree	Agree	Strongly agree	N
The CCO's directions were clear and easy to understand	0.4	1.6	6.7	74.0	17.3	254
The CCO's directions were issued in sufficient time to allow me to prepare effectively for the referendum	0.4	3.6	8.7	70.8	16.6	253
The directions from the CCO made it easier to plan and run the referendum	0.8	7.1	35.2	48.6	8.3	253
The directions from the CCO helped to ensure a consistent experience for voters across local authorities	–	2.4	25.3	62.1	10.3	253
The directions from the CCO helped to prevent errors being made	2.0	17.7	43.7	32.7	3.9	254
The directions focussed on the issues most important for achieving public confidence in the result	0.4	6.7	43.7	44.0	5.2	252
The directions from the CCO involved more financial costs	2.4	15.0	39.9	34.8	7.9	253
The directions from the CCO absorbed staff time	2.4	23.8	35.3	33.3	5.2	252
The directions from the CCO overrode local experience and needs	4.0	32.8	39.1	19.8	4.3	253
I had sufficient opportunity to input during the development of the directions	3.9	22.0	39.8	32.3	2.0	254
The directions from the CCO introduced new ways of working or ideas we haven't thought of before	14.3	44.6	30.7	9.2	1.2	251
The directions from the CCO made me enjoy my job less	15.4	34.8	42.3	5.5	2.0	253

in sufficient time to allow preparation and made it easier to plan and run the referendum. Roughly half of respondents agreed or strongly agreed that the directions focussed on the most important issues for ensuring public confidence in the result. Most (68 per cent) indicated that it was either fairly or very easy to follow the directions. The directions had the positive effects of bringing a consistent experience for the voter (72 per cent agreed or strongly agreed), making it easier for many electoral officials to plan and implement the referendum

(57 per cent agreed or strongly agreed) and, to a lesser extent, prevented errors being made (37 per cent agreed or strongly agreed).

The negative effects included increased financial costs (43 per cent either agreed or strongly agreed), absorbing staff time (38 per cent either agreed or strongly agreed) and overriding local experience (24 per cent either agreed or strongly agreed). Qualitative interviews suggested that many COs felt that the Electoral Commission was over-directive and that the directions given 'are self-evident and just good practice'. As some put it:

> 'The directions covered the key areas but did not allow for local knowledge, team's experience of running elections or give flexibility when local issues arose.'

> 'Pressure for early despatch of postal votes meant extra staffing and [postal vote] issue sessions to be organised.'

Rarely did the directions introduce new ways of working (only 10 per cent either agreed or strongly agreed) or negatively affect staff enjoyment of their roles (only 8 per cent either agreed or strongly agreed).

The use of directions therefore not accepted uncritically and did not add value in every circumstance. They clearly have many positive effects, however. Many qualitative replies suggested that the CCO got the balance better than in 2011 and that the practice of having directions is now more embedded. As one put it:

> We strongly disagreed with the onerous directions imposed by the CCO on the last referendum. The directions used this time were proportional, well written and the CCO should be commended.

10.12 Discussion

To what extent do the empirical findings confirm the hypotheses? There is some evidence to support H1, that the directions led to more efficient and better-quality services because the Commission was able to prescribe solutions from the centre. The first study revealed that more consistent services was thought to lead to perceptions among citizens that services were of better quality (T1). Errors were prevented in some cases (T2). The presence of central directions was useful to officials in learning new practices and ideas (T3) and locating best practice quickly (T4). As Table 10.1 illustrates, the frequency at which these themes were found in the interviews was low. On the one hand, this does suggest that there was relatively little improvement in the quality of electoral management as a result of the scheme. However, a low volume of occurrences of these themes does not equate to importance. Themes such as error prevention (T2) were more commonly found in interviews with the Commission – but they would have been best placed to identify them. More evidence of these positive effects on performance were found in the second study. Only 2.4 per cent of respondents didn't think that greater consistency was achieved; 36.6 agreed or strongly agreed that the directions helped to prevent errors being made. And 56.9 agreed that it made the referendum easier to run, although only a few (10.4 per cent) thought that it had introduced new ideas of ways of working – perhaps partly because the 2016 model was a rerun of 2011 and any innovation had occurred earlier.

There was much more support for H2 in 2011. This hypothesis was pessimistic about the effects of centralisation on the quality and efficiency of electoral services. There was clear evidence that in some cases, electoral services became less economically efficient – a criteria of electoral management quality set out in Chapter 3. Many officials reported unnecessary additional financial costs (T5) so the costs per unit of production would have increased. The interviews showed clear evidence of further polling staff being employed and ballot papers being printed where they were then unused (T5). Data from 2016 provides more information about the frequency of the problems. Again, there is more evidence that the directions increased cost with 42.7 per cent agreeing.

More staff time was taken up by administering the scheme (T6). The Electoral Commission argued that the scheme was not 'an onerous task' (private interview, Electoral Commission official, October 2011) and many officials pointed out that the directions were mostly 'things they should be doing anyway'. Nonetheless, more resources were often required. Even in 2016, after some simplification of the scheme, a large proportion (38.5 per cent) agreed that the directions absorbed staff time. There was evidence that the use of direction overlooked local experience, knowledge and discretion. This is a highly valued commodity for those in the bureaucratic discretion school. A decline in economic efficiency may not be a problem for resource-rich EMBs, but EMBs might be wary of setting minimal standards if resources are scarce if efficiency levels drop. By 2016, this appears to have been less of a problem, with only 21.4 per cent agreed that local knowledge and needs were overridden.

The quality of electoral management was undermined in a further way, however, not previously discussed in the analysis of centralising electoral management. The more holistic set of criteria outlined in Chapter 3 for evaluating electoral management includes job satisfaction because it is of value in and of itself, but because it is also thought to improve organisational performance, staff turnover and intention to quit (Griffeth, Hom, and Gaertner 2000; Harter, Schmidt, and Hayes 2002; Judge et al. 2001). A significant finding from this study was the impact of the directions on staff satisfaction within electoral services (T8). This finding supports the arguments from within the human relations school of management that top-down procedures can undermine workforce motivation, which can affect organisational performance.

It is plausible that some of the themes, particularly the effects on staff time and staff morale, would prove to only have a short-term effect. As election officials become familiar with central directions they may take less time to read through them and assess the changes that are needed. The immediate decline in staff morale might also recover as unhappy officials become used to the new arrangements or leave the profession and are replaced by new ones. These effects might also be partly explained by a poorly designed scheme and therefore could have been avoided in further iterations of the directions. Many directions were sent out very late to election officials because of delays in the passing of the legislation for the referendums. The data from 2016 supports this. Relatively few (7.5 per cent) agreed that the directions made them enjoy their job less. This is not to understate the importance of short-term effects. The directions did create a significant period of time in which staff time was drained and morale was low. In eventuality, the 2011 referendums were characterised by low turnout and the outcome was clear cut. However, in different circumstances this could have created significant problems for the experience of the voter.

It therefore seems important to separate out the *temporal* effects of introducing change in electoral management. Centralisation might accrue certain advantages and disadvantages. However, discussions about EMB reform have so far focussed on the longer-term effects of implementing an ideal-type system be it centralised or decentralised, independent or otherwise. But *implementing change* can bring considerable problems in itself. Poorly managed change at 'pinch points' in the electoral process could produce more dramatic effects. In other words, organisational change can create critical junctures where the performance of EMBs could be adversely affected in the short, but not necessarily longer run. The consequence for theory is that there are some considerable institutional 'lock-in' effects for EMBs. Once institutions are set up in a particular way, there are considerable path dependencies (Mahoney 2000, 512) and reasons to resist reform. It could also politically become very difficult for reformers to implement change.

10.13 Conclusions

Centralising electoral management is one policy instrument which is often proposed to ensure better electoral management. This study, however, shows that organisational centralisation can be a double-edge sword. It can bring a more consistent nationwide experience for the voter, help give local election officials clear and unambiguous instructions in times of uncertainty and allow the centre to pre-empt and respond to some problems in the periphery when it is aware of them. There are, however, some significant advantages to decentralised electoral services and reasons to stick up for localism. Decentralised services can better allow experienced local election officials to use their local knowledge to conduct elections with a higher degree of economic efficiency and responsiveness to local problems. This suggests that we should exert extreme caution in measuring the quality of electoral management by whether local officials met centrally defined standards and subject the standards themselves to scrutiny.

Significantly, the *process* of centralising electoral management introduces risk and challenges for electoral integrity. There are 'transition costs' involved in institutional reform that the literature has hereto not considered and policy makers must beware of. This brings to light the importance of 'lock-in' path dependencies in the choice and design of EMBs. EMB designs are not drawn on a blank canvass. When new EMBs are set up, they are forced to work with those individuals and organisations that have been running elections, often for some time. This brings a wider framework of norms, values and expectations about 'how things are done'. The 'best' choice of EMB may therefore be more contextually dependent than the existing literature acknowledges. It is certainly temporally dependent. Further research will help identify the important characteristics of these contexts that should be borne in mind for institutional designers.

Notes

1 Also see: Pastor (2004).
2 Although some power is now devolved to Scotland.
3 There are some important variations across the UK. In England and Wales the RO and ERO are often the same person working within the same local authority. However, in Scotland, electoral registration is organised by Valuation Joint Boards. There are also different arrangements for Northern Ireland.
4 The same system was used in both referendums. Interviewees in Wales had therefore been subject to the directions scheme twice.
5 A total of 19 exemptions were applied for with only six granted (Electoral Commission 2011a, 121).
6 Alistair Clark and I were recruited as consultants by the Electoral Commission to assess the management of the referendum because the Commission, responsible for running the referendum, felt that there might have been a conflict in interest in also providing an evaluation of its own management. This report was published as: (Clark and James 2016a) and a further study using the data available in: (Clark and James 2019).
7 A little caution is required in interpreting this figure. Some local authorities had two separate members of staff complete the survey and have therefore made duplicate submissions, while in five cases, the response was flagged as covering more than one local authority. Eight local authorities completed two questionnaires, while five responses were made which covered multiple councils involving 11 councils in total. The view of the researchers is that these duplicate/multiple responses largely cancel each other out and that the figures reported are reliable.

11 Training and human resource practices

11.1 Introduction

Advances in technology have often raised questions about whether robots might replace people in many professions. The reality (so far...) is that although technological change has always had major consequences for labour forces and work practices, humans still control robots. Computer programmers write the code that machines perform. A teacher may use technology in the classroom, but they organise the teaching and inspire their pupils. A surgeon uses extensive digital equipment, but the responsibility for performing life-saving operations falls on them.

And so it is with elections. *Humans* decide where to locate and prepare polling stations and how to train their staff. Humans hand out ballot papers to voters, close polling stations and oversee the count. Humans design electronic voting machines and online security protocols and web-forms that citizens need to complete in order to register to vote.

In the previous two chapters this book has showed how electoral management reforms have had many side effects on the *staff* running elections. Introducing major voter registration reforms can introduce considerable stress. Centralising management can lead to a loss of ownership of a job. Yet despite centuries of elections, few scholars have thought to ask questions about the *people* that run elections. Who are they? What are their socio-demographic profiles? How do they feel about their workplace? What consequences does this have for the quality of elections? And what human resource management practices can improve electoral management? This chapter seeks to address that gap through two studies. The first is a survey of UK electoral officials. This allows the characteristics of the permanent workforce to be identified in an established democracy. The second study is a cross-national survey of electoral officials that ran worldwide with responses from EMBs in 51 countries and had responses from 2,029 electoral officials.

The chapter begins by briefly reviewing the literature on EMB workforces before introducing the literature on employee experiences and human resource management from the scholarship from management studies – a domain rarely considered in the study of elections. The methods, theoretical framework and results are sketched out. The key findings are that the UK seems to exhibit many key characteristics of human resource management 'best' practices. There is also evidence from the UK case that participatory training can be effective at improving employee experiences such as reducing levels of stress. The cross-national data shows how a large proportion of employees have not attended training workshops in the five-year period preceding the survey. This is a cause for concern since the analysis provides evidence that training can shape employee experience and have a positive effect on the quality of electoral management too.

11.2 EMB workforces

Existing studies on the staff that deliver elections are limited to only a handful of within-country investigations. The main focus has been on the temporary employees used on polling day – a research theme developed following problems in US elections (Wand et al. 2001). It has been noted that some countries struggle with a short supply of poll workers if they are recruited on a voluntary or low-paid basis (Burden and Milyo 2015). Research has begun to identify the factors that may cause workers to volunteer their time on election day (Cantú and Ley 2017; Clark and James 2016b) and the prevalence of corruption and professionalisation in the Ukrainian workforce (Herron, Boyko, and Thunberg 2017). Local patterns of poll worker recruitment are thought to affect the quality of elections (Goerres and Funk 2019) and descriptive representation has been argued to be important (King 2019). Less is known about the core workforces involved in managing elections, however. The previous chapter illustrated high levels of stress amongst the UK workforce – similar patterns were also reported in the UK immediately before the Brexit referendum when IT problems led to the voter registration system being offline as the deadline passed (Clark and James 2016a). No cross-national studies have explored and compared the characteristics of workforces running elections, however.

11.2.1 The role and effects of employee outcomes

A long-established field of studies called human resource management shows how and why employees matter. This cross-cuts business studies, economic and public sector management. The experiences and feeling that employees have towards their workplace – the employee outcomes – are important in their own right. They are also important, however, for the productivity and performance of an organisation. For this reason, they are central to the study of electoral management and integrity. Six key employee outcomes are described here: stress, work overload, intention to quit, job satisfaction, affective commitment and civic duty.

Stress has been defined as 'a harmful reaction people have due to undue pressures and demands put on them at work' (HSE 2013, 2). Maslach and Jackson (1981, 99) first defined the concept of burnout which involves a 'syndrome of emotional exhaustion and . . . cynical attitudes and feelings about one's clients'. Burnout was found by them to be associated with poorer quality of care, higher turnover and absenteeism, and lower morale. Not all stress is bad. In certain circumstances it can have healthy positive outcomes (Nelson and Simmons 2003).

Nonetheless, most research focusses on the negative effects, noting that organisational performance can be adversely affected with higher levels of absenteeism, increased staff turnover and decreased productivity (European Agency for Safety and Health at Work 2014, 12).

Work overload is thought to be one cause of stress. Higher job demands are thought to lead to burnout, stress, an erosion of organisational commitment, job satisfaction and propensity to quit (Bakker and Demerouti 2007; Hakanen, Schaufeli, and Ahola 2008). There are also links with reduced civic mindedness, demotivation and performance (Gould-Williams et al. 2014).

The *propensity of individuals to voluntarily quit* is often thought to have a negative effect on overall performance. Resources are diverted to recruitment and training new staff, knowledge and expertise is lost. However, it is equally argued that benefits are accrued such as lower payroll, improvement in innovation and reductions in stagnation (Dess and Shaw 2001).

Job satisfaction was defined as 'a pleasurable or positive emotional state resulting from an appraisal of one's job or job experiences' (Locke 1976). This has been found to affect the likelihood that an individual would quit (Tzeng 2002) but also organisational outcomes such as customer satisfaction, productivity, profit, and employee turnover (Harter, Schmidt, and Hayes 2002).

Other employee outcomes are thought to be important mediators in these relationships. *Affective commitment* is the attachment that an employee has to their organisation (Allen and Meyer 1990; Shore et al. 2006); it can mediate burnout and intention to quit (Sharma and Dhar 2016).

Civic duty or public service motivation refers to whether an individual is motivated to working in 'primarily or uniquely in public institutions or organisations' (Perry and Wise 1990, 368). This is thought to be an important mediator between HRMP and employee outcomes including whether they intend to quit, job satisfaction and their affective commitment (Gould-Williams et al. 2014).

11.2.2 Human resource management practices

Human resource management practices (HRMP) are initiatives that are used to improve individual and organisational level performance. They might include de facto procedures on recruitment, training, performance appraisal and pay (Appelbaum et al. 2000). HRMP are thought to be important for organisational performance because they can affect the micro-level behaviour of the individual employee. This, in turn, affects organisational performance such as turnover, productivity, financial returns, survival and firm value (Delery 1998). There are some single country studies linking practices to outcomes such as organisational performance (Melton and Meier 2017; O'Toole Jr and Meier 2003, 2009), but as Gould-Williams and Mohamed noted – this research is rare.

An important theme in the research is that organisational intentions should be separated from the employee's actual experience. Organisations may have great intentions to implement practices set out in formal policy documents. But they may not have the resources, opportunity or ability to do so. As Kinnie et al. (2005,

11) argue: 'the fulcrum of the HRM-performance causal chain is the employees' reactions to HR practices as experienced by them.' Wright and Nishii (2007) argue that the pathway is from (1) intended practices, to (2) actual HR practices, to (3) practices as experiences, to (4) employee outcomes, to (5) employee reactions, to (6) unit level performance.

There is a persistent debate on whether there is a universal set of HMRPs to produce better performance – or whether more bespoke practices are needed for different contexts. A 'best practice' school of thought suggests that there are universal practices that should be adopted in all organisations, in all settings to improve performance. These practices can have an additive effect that creates synergies and 'added value' within organisations. There are many lists of best practices: Pfeffer (1998) presents a list of seven; Arthur (1994) presents four; Boselie, Dietz, and Boon (2005) find 26. A common theme is that complementing 'bundles' of HMRP work well together because synergies occur, but that there are common 'deadly combinations' such as designing the workplace so as to improve teamwork but also rewarding individual performance (Becker et al. 1997). Boxall and Purcell (2011) conclude that 'it is difficult to see the underpinning logic in such a long list of practices'. The 'best practice' model has therefore been subject to critique. There is some scepticism about whether there is a single set of practices that can be used in all contexts. Different sectors, production processes and cultural environments may require employees to be managed differently. A counterveiling 'best-fit' approach is therefore often prescribed.

The most common theory that is used to justify the causal linkage between HRMP and organisational performance outcome is the *Ability, Motivation and Opportunity (AMO)* model. This was first developed by Bailey (1993) and then extended by Appelbaum et al. (2000). It can be considered a 'best practice' toolkit insofar as it argues that the selection of HRMP will improve performance. The logic is that HRMP can develop the *ability* of individuals within organisations by ensuring high-quality recruitment processes and investing in training and skills development. Secondly, the HRMP can increase the *motivation* of employees through good financial incentives and conditions. Intrinsic awards such as employment security, performance reviews and work-life balance can also be important, however. Thirdly, HRMP can provide employees with the *opportunities* to be able to use these skills and motivations within the organisation. In combination, these produce an environment in which positive discretionary effort is higher. Employees have significant discretion in the amount of care and additional time they invest into their job. Boxall and Purcell (2003) argue that the presence of AMO practices is additive. Each antecedent will have a direct and independent effect on performance.

Other human resource practices include *performance appraisals*. Poon (2004), for example, finds that when performance appraisals are not perceived by the employee to be positive, job satisfaction declines. The quality of internal *communication* within organisations has been found to improve performance (Gould-Williams and Mohamed 2010). It has been claimed to be especially important during times of change (Elving 2005) or encouraging supportive workplace environments

(Elving 2005). *Psychological climate is repeatedly found to be important.* Gould-Williams and Mohamed (2010, 656) state that there 'is now growing recognition that employees' experiences at work are affected by organizational characteristics such as support, recognition, fairness, morale, rewards equity and leader credibility'. *Psychological climate* involves 'an individual's experiential abstraction of his/her routine experiences at the workplace, and the consequent sense-making of the same' (Biswas and Varma 2007, 666). It is therefore measured at the individual level and is a different concept to organisational climate or organisational culture. *Discretionary pay* was found by a review of studies to increase performance (Hasnain and Pierskalla Henryk 2012). *Team working* within an organisation has been found to have positive effects on performance to such an extent that Gould-Williams and Mohamed (2010, 671) argued that 'it could be argued that teamworking should be regarded as the "kernel" of HR bundles'.

11.3 Theoretical framework

There is therefore a huge range of characteristics of EMB workforces that have not been examined. This chapter seeks to redress this by centring attention on the inter-relationship between employee outcomes, human resource practice and electoral management quality. Proceeding from the AMO theory, anticipated causal relationships are summarised in Figure 11.1. Policy tools such as AMO practices are thought to shape the employee environment which would include workload and levels of employee support. In turn, this shapes employee outcomes such as job satisfaction, stress and levels of motivation. This all feeds in to shape the level of overall electoral management quality.

11.4 Research questions, methods and hypotheses

This chapter uses two surveys of electoral officials. Firstly, it uses the 2016 survey of UK electoral officials used in Chapter 9 that had 271 respondents. The method

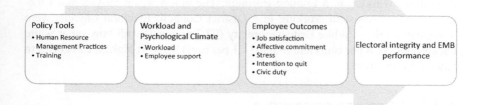

Figure 11.1 The relationship between human resource management and EMB performance.

is described in more detail there. Secondly, data is taken from the ELECT and EMS surveys described in the introduction and James et al. (2019) undertaken in 2016 and 2017. This data is then used to answer some basic descriptive questions:

- Who are the staff that are employed in managing elections? What are their backgrounds and skills? What are their demographic profiles? What are their skills and education?
- What 'HR policies' are in place?

It is then used to test some of the causal linkages in the framework above:

- Do 'best practice HR policies' affect employee outcomes?
- Do 'best practice HR policies' affect overall performance?

11.5 Results

11.5.1 The profile of electoral officials in Britain

Who are the staff that are employed in managing UK elections? What are their backgrounds and skills? What are their demographic profiles? What are their skills and education?

Running UK elections is a part-time profession since not everyone spends all their time on it. Less than half (41.3 per cent) said that their role was entirely devoted to election work. The mean percentage of time spent on elections or electoral registration was 71.5 per cent. This percentage decreased at each level with Senior and Strategic officials spending 60.6 per cent of their time on it, compared to 73.7 per cent of administrative and clerical employees. Employees tended to have high levels of job security. Most employees were on permanent contracts (90.8 per cent). Fixed-term contracts were most common amongst administrative/clerical staff (15.2 per cent). All Senior and Strategic officials were on permanent contracts.

The majority of employees were female (62.0 per cent) and they were most common in all categories of management. The mean age of the overall sample was 44.3 years. The youngest employee was an 18-year-old Electoral Services Apprentice working in a London Borough. The eldest was a 69-year-old Electoral Services Assistant working in a District Council. Electoral officials were overwhelmingly of White British ethnicity (92.3 per cent) with 'any other white background' (1.8 per cent) and Indian (1.1 per cent) the next highest categories to have representation.

11.5.2 UK human resource practices

To what extent were 'best practice HR policies' in place? To fit with the principles of AMO human resource practices, we would expect pay to rise with seniority of responsibility. There was a clear progressive rise in pay in tune with responsibility.

The median pay bands are illustrated in Table 11.1. The median values mask that a very significant proportion of the sample (17.5%) earned between £10,000–£19,999, but do demonstrate that higher management levels are compensated accordingly.

The use of best practice human resource practices would also require an educated and trained workforce. The data does show that the workforce was well educated with everyone reporting having qualifications at GCSE level or above. A very significant proportion had a university degree – even a third (32.0 per cent) of those at administrative and clerical level. Higher positions are associated with higher educational qualification. It is notable, however, that 15 per cent of the senior and strategic officials reported no academic qualification above GCSE level. The highest-qualified group was the upper management group, as Table 11.2 illustrates.

Professional qualifications in electoral administration were also widely held. The Association of Electoral Administrators (AEA) ran courses at four different levels with each course being a pre-requisite for the next (AEA 2016). Table 11.3 ranks the courses in terms of their stages and shows the percentage that had reached each stage. Just under half had taken none of the qualifications (45.4) with most of the other half having taken either the Foundations or Certificate Course (50.2). Overall, the vast majority were members of the Association for Electoral Administrators (88.9 per cent) but very few were members of SOLACE (0.4 per cent).

Table 11.1 Median annual pay for UK electoral officials for 2016

Job title	Median pay band
Senior/Strategic	£50,000–£54,999
Upper Management	£40,000–£45,000
Management	£35,000–£39,999
Deputy Management	£30,000–£34,999
Administrative/Clerical	£20,000–£24,999

Table 11.2 Highest qualification for each level of electoral officials (percentage)

	GCSE/ O'Level	NVQ	A Level	Higher education below degree	Undergraduate degree	Postgraduate degree
Admin/Clerical	28.9	1.0	18.6	14.4	32.0	5.2
Deputy Management	16.7	0.0	8.3	33.3	20.8	20.8
Management	13.6	2.3	15.9	18.2	35.2	14.8
Upper Management	0.0	0.0	5.0	25.0	35.0	35.0
Senior/Strategic	15.4	0.0	15.4	7.7	50.0	11.5

248 *Instruments*

Table 11.3 Percentage of UK electoral officials with AEA qualifications in electoral administration

Lowest level of qualification	Per cent	Cumulative per cent
None	45.4	45.4
AEA Foundations Course	17.0	62.4
AEA Certificate Course	33.2	95.6
AEA Diploma Course	2.6	98.3
AEA Continuing Professional Development Course	1.8	100

11.5.3 Employee experiences are connected

Measures for workload, workplace environment, job satisfaction, intention to quit, stress and civic duty were introduced in Chapter 9, Table 9.6. To what extent are they interconnected? Pearson's correlations were used across these employee outcomes and they demonstrated strong statistically significant relationships. Workload overload, for example, was closely connected to stress ($\beta = .622, p < 0.01$), propensity to quit ($\beta = .400, p < 0.01$), being less willing to do further work beyond an employee's usual hours for further pay ($\beta = .400, p < 0.01$) and to a lesser extent job satisfaction ($\beta = .184, p < 0.01$). Stress was also strongly associated with an employee thinking about quitting their job ($\beta = .674, p < 0.01$).

11.5.4 Participatory training reduces stress levels

The survey upon which this chapter was based was run, as Chapter 9 explained, during a period of time when individual electoral registration (IER) was being implemented. In addition to the general opportunities to undertake qualifications with the Association for Electoral Administrators (AEA) that were provided to electoral officials in the UK, specific training was also offered on IER. Different training mechanisms were provided by SOLACE, the Electoral Commission and Cabinet Office. The latter two were briefings by members of the organisations in which presenters spoke using PowerPoint slides to an audience. The AEA, however, provided a more interactive seminar-based format, which the author had the opportunity to observe at the AEA Conference in January 2015. In these sessions, participants were separated into teams and asked scenario-based questions. They wrote down their answers after a group discussion and then passed the questions onto the next group. Session leaders then facilitated an overall discussion of the questions. PowerPoint presentations were then used to reinforce key points. The proportion of respondents that undertook one of these sessions was: AEA (93.7) SOLACE (13.1), Electoral Commission (72.8), Cabinet Office 75.1, Local authority (49.7).

Did this training have any effect on employee outcomes? No obvious relationships were found in bivariate correlations, so multi-variate OLS models were run. Controls were run for educational qualifications, elections qualifications, income, management level and age. Training did not seem to affect most measures of employee outcomes. However, Table 11.4 reports an OLS model with stress levels

Table 11.4 OLS model where stress is the dependent variable

	Beta	Standard error
Academic qualification	.020	.236
Professional qualification	−.104	.268
Income	−.101	.143
Age	.075	.023
Management level	.337*	.204
AEA training	−.226*	.796
SOLACE training	.025	.825
Electoral Commission training	.591	0.68
Cabinet Office training	−.111	.642
Constant	5.985**	2.522
Adjusted r^2	.123	
N	99	

Beta is the standardised coefficient. *Correlation is significant at the 0.05 level (2-tailed). **Correlation is significant at the 0.01 level (2-tailed).

as the dependent variable. There were few statistically significant predictors, but the model provides evidence that attending an AEA training course did reduce levels of stress as the beta value was −.226, significant at the 0.05 level. Attending sessions from the Electoral Commission and Cabinet Office appeared to make no difference. In other words, more participatory training sessions can make a difference to employee outcomes such as stress when major organisational reform is being run. The effects appear to be relatively small with the overall model only having an r^2 of .123. This might be because of the relatively small N. However, there seems to be a noteworthy effect here. As an aside, it is worth noting that stress levels were positively related with higher management positions.

11.6 The international experience: training affects employee outcomes

Following on from the survey of UK officials that was described above, the survey design was developed and rolled out across multiple countries in the ELECT and EMS surveys (James et. al 2019b). These surveys asked questions about the composition of the workforces, which are described in a sister publication, alongside indexes to measure employee experiences and human resource practices and are therefore not repeated here (James, 2019). However, the ELECT and EMS surveys also included questions about the frequency of training. Respondents were asked whether they had undertaken training workshops within the past five years. Of the 2,079 respondents, exactly 60 per cent had. The provision/take-up of training was negatively associated with the level of democracy measured by V-DEM's electoral democracy index (Coppedge et al. 2017). It was also negatively associated with the level of GDP measured by the World Bank. Quantitative analysis does not explain *why* this is the case – but one explanation might be that established democracies tend to have more stable workforces with employees in post for a longer period of time. Transitional regimes see major investments in

250 *Instruments*

election workforces in advance of an election, but staff then return to other departments, especially if electoral assistance projects end (Maley 2013).

Does the provision of training have any positive effects? Supporting the findings provided in the earlier part of the chapter, there is good evidence that training has a positive effect on employee outcomes. Pearson's correlations were undertaken, and training was found to be associated with lower levels of stress ($\beta = -.097$, $p < 0.01$), a reduced propensity to quit ($\beta = -.142$, $p < 0.01$), improved job satisfaction ($\beta = -.049$, $p < 0.05$) and higher affective commitment ($\beta = -.080$, $p < 0.01$). These effects are small, but there are complex lines of causation so this should not be surprising. Overall, it helps to demonstrate the importance of training for employee outcomes.

11.7 The international experience: training affects performance

Does training have any effects on the quality of electoral management? After all, this is probably the most important dimension of interest. It was not possible to identify this in the UK study described above because there was not an adequate measure of performance available with sufficient number of cases to make quantitative analysis meaningful. At the cross-national level EMB performance can be measured, however, using expert surveys (while noting the limitations of this approach sketched out in Chapter 3). The Perception of Electoral Integrity 6.0 dataset was used (Norris, Wynter, and Cameron 2018). The question taken as the dependent variable was 'The election authorities performed well' which was on a five-point scale. The mean score for elections between 2012–2017 was used.

There was a negative correlation between the provision of training in the past five years and EMB performance using this measure ($\beta = -.307$, $p < 0.01$). This initially seems counter-intuitive. It is important to remember that training is more often found in countries with a lower level of democracy, however. Multi-variate analysis is therefore important. Linear hierarchical regression models were therefore constructed. This analysis can be helpful for identifying the additional explanatory value of adding variables to a model (Gelman and Hill 2006).

An initial model was therefore built consisting of three control variables. Cases were excluded listwise. Firstly, we might expect EMB performance to be higher in democracies. Greater access to information, transparency, press freedom and more rigorous accountability mechanisms should increase EMB performance. The 2016 measure for the electoral democracy index was therefore used from V-DEM 7.1 (Coppedge et al. 2017). Secondly, we might expect EMBs with more resources to be better able to deliver elections (James and Jervier 2017a, also see Chapter 12). GDP per capita data is therefore taken from the World Bank. Thirdly, it is often argued that EMBs with greater institutional autonomy will be better able to run elections as Chapter 7 argued. Data on EMB autonomy is therefore also taken from V-DEM 7.1 (Coppedge et al. 2017).[1]

The models are reported in Table 11.5. In the first model autonomy and polyarchy are statistically significant regressors. When training is introduced in the second

Table 11.5 OLS regressions where the dependent variable is EMB performance measured by the Perceptions of Electoral Integrity survey

	Model 1		Model 2	
	Beta	Standard error	Beta	Standard error
GDP per capita	−.065	.000	.014	.000
Autonomy	.135***	.022	.138***	.020
Polyarchy	.690***	.133	.720***	.123
Training workshops			.276***	.016
Constant	2.469	.064	2.245	.062
Adjusted r^2	.542		.607	
N	1974		1941	

*** Significant at the 0.001 level.

model, this remains the case. Importantly, training has a clear effect in model 2 with β value of .276. The r^2 values are also strong for the models. We therefore have important evidence here that training does improve EMB performance.

11.8 Conclusions

This chapter has argued that the staff who run elections are commonly overlooked in the study of elections. They are overlooked insofar as few studies have considered employee experiences such as levels of stress and propensity to quit to be important areas worth studying. There have been isolated individual national studies identifying some problems in some states – but the focus has tended to be on the temporary polling officials rather than the permanent electoral officials involved. This chapter has sought to advance this line of inquiry by establishing a full menu of workforce characteristics that should be considered in the study of elections. It has provided an original study to chart the characteristics of the UK workforce. In collaboration with the previous chapter, it has shown serious problems with levels of stress during periods of rapid change. It has also provided some evidence that participatory training sessions can make a difference to employee outcomes. The chapter then broadened the study out to the cross-national level to show that levels of training varied enormously worldwide – with many staff having not undertaken a training workshop in the five-year period preceding the surveys. Training, however, alongside other factors such as autonomy and overall level of democracy was shown to affect electoral management quality. Expenditure in training electoral officials is therefore a vitally important measure for improving electoral integrity.

Note

1 The V-DEM question was 'Does the Election Management Body (EMB) have autonomy from government to apply election laws and administrative rules impartially in national elections?'.

12 Austerity and financial investment in electoral management

12.1 Introduction

Funding for public services are often at the heart of election campaigns. Promises of more money for hospitals make for good election pledges; pointing out that the incumbent has cut money to schools can be an equally astute political move. Ironically, money to run elections themselves are not necessarily something that we will find on campaign billboards or manifestos. In fact, as much as the financing of elections might hit the news, the focus might be on how much running the elections 'cost' the public purse rather than the value of investment in them.

Yet, one potential cause of electoral mismanagement is the lack of available resources for electoral officials. Without enough staff and finances there is a strong risk that errors may occur, queues may form at polling stations and citizens may be unregistered. Despite this intuitive logic, there is relatively little information available on the funding that electoral officials receive to test this claim – and few have therefore been able to make the causal linkages. In many countries, the information about how much money is spent on elections is not routinely collected or published. Studies which have attempted to gather this information on a cross-national level have struggled because of hidden costs and different accounting systems and governance structures – they have therefore only been able to make inferences from a limited range of cases.

This chapter sheds new light on this area. It begins with a literature review of what we know about the funding of elections already. Importantly, the focus here is on the funding of the electoral process and not the funding of political parties' campaign expenditure – a related, but separate issue. The chapter consists of two empirical studies. The first provides new data on the funds and source of funds received by EMBs around the world that was collected from original surveys. It demonstrates the huge variety in budget size – but also allows us to identify the effects of austerity. There is evidence that funding cuts can affect the quality of elections. The second study draws from a roundtable discussion of the challenges that electoral officials face in funding elections. The overall conclusion of the chapter is that the funding of elections is an essential but often overlooked aspect of research on electoral management. It is therefore an important policy instrument to improve electoral integrity.

12.2 Existing research on resources and election quality

There has been little scholarly interest in the financing of electoral processes until recently. The landmark publication was the IFES report on the Cost of Registration and Elections (CORE) Project, funded by the UNDP (López-Pintor and Fischer 2005). As that report set out in the introduction, there had not been a 'project of global research exclusively devoted to EMB budget and costs' (López-Pintor and Fischer 2005, 4). The project therefore sought to develop some working definitions for types of costs, identify the sources of funding and evaluate election budgets in 10 countries.

Some important initial findings were made. The project reported that costs varied substantially according to the democratic environment and system of government. Costs were estimated to be lower in stable democracies than transitional and post-conflict democracies. However, in emerging democracies, the institutionalisation of permanent professional staff was leading to cost rises. The use of different electoral rules in federal systems placed an additional financial burden. All countries were experiencing some broader trends towards increasing costs, however. Costs in the areas of personnel and technology were increasing over time, regardless of levels of democratic consolidation. Meanwhile, increasing computerisation was leading to further technological costs. A project of similar geographical coverage has not been attempted since then; however, there have been some useful advances based on studies of individual countries.

Studies have showed how different forms of electoral administration have different costs. Krimmer et al. (2018) compared the costs of different voting methods in the 2017 Estonian local elections and concluded that the administrative costs per vote of online voting were half the price of the second-cheapest option (Election Day Voting). Arguments for adopting internet voting to save money have been made elsewhere (Webroots Democracy 2017). Chapter 9 from this book also contributes towards this literature by revealing how the move from household to individual electoral registration substantially increased costs in the UK.

The determinants of spending within countries have also been explored by Hill (2012) in her 'Public Sector Cost' model. She examines the expenditures in California counties between 1992 and 2008 and identifies how economies of scale and the choice of voting technology can be significant drivers of costs. Meanwhile, Clark (2019) identifies how UK spending is shaped by production costs such as postal voting and polling stations, but also the socio-economic characteristics of local areas, based on data from the 2014 European elections. Politics matters too. Historical accounts of US politics often stress that local elites can seek to manipulate electoral rules for political gain and limiting the supply of polling stations and staff is one tactic to reduce turnout amongst particular populations (Hasen 2012; James 2012; Keyssar 2009; Kousser 1974). Mohr et al. (2019) provide quantitative data to argue that Republican county commissioners in North Carolina, between 1994–2014, spent significantly less on election administration once the county electorate reaches a politically satisfactory Republican majority.

254 *Instruments*

There have been some claims that a lack of resources can lead to poorly run elections in cross-national studies (Birch 2011, 26; Pastor 1999b), studies of American elections (Gerken 2009a; Hale and Slaton 2008; Highton 2006) and UK elections (Clark and James 2016a). Evidence to support this has been sparse. However, (James and Jervier 2017a) show how austerity can lead to cuts in services such as voter outreach work. Clark (2014) provides correlations between the provided to UK local authorities to run elections, and whether they met performance standards.

Conversely, there have also been concerns raised in public debate about inefficiencies within electoral services. Cost efficiency is an important measure of success identified in Chapter 4 of this book. There has been public concern expressed in Scotland about the amount of money that has been paid to Returning Officers to run elections, when they already earn a high salary from their role as Chief Executive. This led to the Scottish Parliament Select Committee on Local Government and Communities (2017) launching an investigation that recommended that Returning Officers should not be paid for their work.

Overall, then, there has been an increase in research in this area – but insights have been limited by the relative paucity of data. A further criticism is that there is often a functionalist logic in determining the drivers of costs and their sufficiency. Costs are modelled statistically based on socio-demographic characteristics and the choice of election administration. They are, this chapter will argue, also the result of social, strategic processes. They are the result of planning, negotiation, the building of relationships between actors. In short, agency. The party–political side of this has been noted, but not the managerial–political dimension. This argument will be developed shortly.

12.3 EMB budgets: a macro-scopic overview

This chapter is firstly able to strengthen the literature by presenting original data on the budgets of many EMBs around the world using the EMS survey (James 2019b) and ELECT survey (Karp et al. 2016).[1] Questions were included in both surveys about the sources of income, who the actors were in approving the budget, the overall annual budget and the overall trends. The surveys were sent to EMBs over email and they nominated an official to complete them on their behalf. It isn't possible to double-check the data provided against other sources since this is not published elsewhere so there are some limitations in reliability. Not all questions in the survey were answered and many countries did not reply. Nonetheless, it is the most complete picture of EMB budgets available and supersedes the existing research.

12.3.1 Budget sizes

A total of 55 EMBs provided data on their annual budget and 20 provided their election year budget. In some cases, EMBs provided both. As the book has already argued, several organisations are often involved in delivering elections. The reported data therefore does not cover the entire cost of electoral management

Austerity and financial investment 255

systems. Data is at the organisational level rather than country level and there might be other EMBs who did not reply. Nonetheless, this is a substantial advance on the range of data collected so far. Data was collected in the local currency and some conversion is needed to enable comparison. The standard practice is to convert into US dollars. It is usually recommended that comparison is best undertaken by converting to a purchase parity rate rather than simply taking exchange rates. Purchase parity rates allow the local costs of goods and services in each country to be accounted for (OECD and Eurostat 2012). The purchasing price parity rate in 2016 against US dollars was taken from the World Bank datasets.[2] Responses in local currencies were then divided by the PPP rate against the US$ in 2016. All data is reported using this converted rate.

The data reveals substantial variations in budgetary levels at different points in the electoral cycle. The EMS survey (but not the ELECT survey) asked respondents to report on the annual budget in the last year that a national election was held in addition to the last year that the survey was undertaken. Budgets were considerably higher during the year of an election. In Poland, for example, the National Electoral Commission had a budget of $216.5m US$ PPP during the election year of 2015, but this dropped to $51.6m in 2016. In Israel the difference was even more marked – from $5.0m (2017) to $63.8m (2015). Yet, in some cases budgets can be very stable. In the Electoral Council of the Netherlands, the budget only rose from $2.3m to $2.6m between 2016 and 2017, despite there being a national election in 2017. The Ministry of the Interior and Kingdom Relations saw a budget reduction in an election year (see Figure 12.1).

Appendix details the full set of data collected. It is immediately obvious that EMBs come with extremely diverse budget sizes. The Commission on Elections in the Philippines, for example, had a budget of $894m, while the General Election Commission of Mongolia had a budget of only $513,537. Variation is to be expected because of the sizes in geographical space and voting age population. Yet allowing for this, fiscal-year budgets can be as much as $33.29 per member of the voting age population, as it was in Costa Rica in 2016. They are similarly high in Rwanda ($27.54) and Panama ($26.53). By contrast the cost in Albania was only $0.76 per person, and $0.07 in Tanzania. Even though the Albanian Central Election Commission and the Tanzanian National Electoral Commission don't implement the whole of the electoral cycle, they are responsible for roughly three-quarters of it, based on their organisations' response to the surveys.

There was some evidence that spending per person was lower in democracies. A comparison of means showed that the mean level of spending per person was $3.63 in 'Free' states using the Freedom House 2016 measure. By comparison the mean spending levels were higher in partially free states ($6.25) and not free states ($12.8). This seems to echo findings reported by López-Pintor and Fischer (2005, 4) that stable democracies' costs would be much lower than transitional and post-conflict democracies, described above.

Despite the large budgets in many organisations, the budgets are usually small as a proportion of overall public expenditure. Table 12.1 details the percentage of overall government expenditure (column 3) and the percentage of expenditure

256 *Instruments*

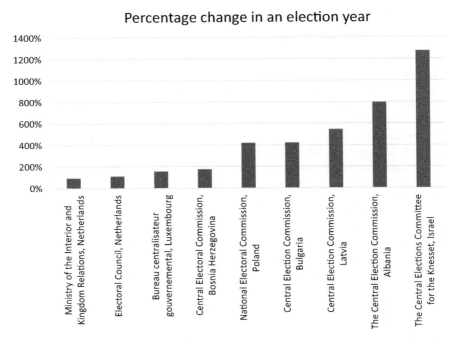

Figure 12.1 Percentage increases in EMB budget from a non-election year to an election year.

on public services (column 4) that the EMB is responsible for. Data was collated from the UN National Accounts Official Country Data[3] on levels of public expenditure in order to do this – and since this dataset is itself limited, we only have data from a small pool of organisations. However, it is striking that investment levels are typically a small proportion of overall government expenditure and the amount spent on public services. Typically, they are well below 1 per cent of expenditure on public services. However, there are some major exceptions such as the Kenyan Independent Electoral and Boundaries Commission, and the Supreme Electoral Tribunal in Costa Rica. It is possible that these extreme values might represent erroneous responses from the EMB or the data held by the UN.

12.3.2 *Budgetary change and its effects*

To identify trends in budgets, and to control for cyclical variations, respondents were asked simply whether their budget had changed overall over the course of the last five-year period.[4] A 5-point scale was used with 'decidedly increased' and 'decidedly decreased' at each end of the scales (see Figure 12.2 and Table 12.2). Data was relatively centrally located. The 'remained about the same' option was

Table 12.1 Percentage of government expenditure and public services expenditure spent on elections

Organisation	Country	% of overall expenditure	% public services budget
Independent Electoral and Boundaries Commission	Kenya	1.9867	
Supreme Electoral Tribunal	Costa Rica	0.8846	22.4252
Central Commission for Election and Referendums	Kyrgyz Republic	0.7165	3.0805
National Electoral Commission	Senegal	0.5130	2.1791
Tribunal Electoral	Panama	0.3527	
Electoral Commission	Malta	0.3338	
State Election Commission of the Republic of Croatia	Croatia	0.2661	1.6068
National Election Commission	Rep. of Korea	0.2561	1.7832
National Electoral Commission	Mozambique	0.0815	0.3288
Electoral Commission	New Zealand	0.0776	
National Electoral Committee	Estonia	0.0508	0.5591
National Electoral Commission	Poland	0.0280	0.3163
National Electoral Commission	Tanzania	0.0225	0.0083
Central Election Commission	Bulgaria	0.0204	0.1987
Central Election Commission	Latvia	0.0146	0.1384
Norwegian Directorate of Elections	Norway	0.0139	0.1355
Central Government Office	Luxembourg	0.0126	0.0698
Central Election Commission of the Russian Federation	Russia	0.1191	1.1751
General Election Commission of Mongolia	Mongolia	0.0103	0.0389
The Central Elections Committee for the Knesset	Israel	0.0070	0.1298
Electoral Authority	Sweden	0.0030	0.0335
Electoral Council	Netherlands	0.0011	0.0166
Central Electoral Board	Spain	0.0003	0.0025
Federal Public Service – Directorate General Institutions and Population – Service Elections	Belgium	0.0000	0.0000

the mode answer in both cases, but there was a tendency towards budgets increasing rather than decreasing. The two organisations to see overall budgets reduced were Slovakia and Bosnia Herzegovina. The most significant increases were reported in Moldova, Albania, Romania and Ecuador.

There was a strong relationship between changes in the overall budget and the training budget, as we might expect. Bivariate analysis returned a positive Pearson's correlation of 0.474, significant at the $p < 0.01$ level. In other words, EMBs making general cuts will make cuts to training.

We might expect that the budgets would be shaped by the overall financial position of the government. Those countries that were expanding government spending might be investing more in elections. Meanwhile, those who were making cuts

258 *Instruments*

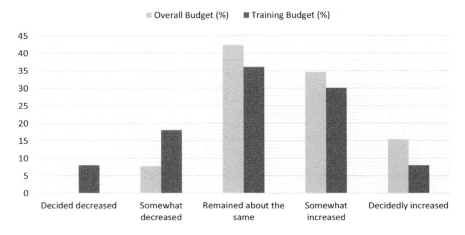

Figure 12.2 Changes in EMB budget size 2011–2016.

Table 12.2 Changes in EMB budget size 2011–2016

	Overall budget (%)	Training budget (%)
Decided decreased	0	8.0
Somewhat decreased	7.7	18.0
Remained about the same	42.3	36.0
Somewhat increased	34.6	30.0
Decidedly increased	15.4	8.0
N	26	50

might be making cuts to EMBs. There is some evidence for this. The proportion of GDP that made up government expenditure was taken from the World Bank in 2011 and 2016.[5] The percentage change over the period was calculated. Pearson's correlations were then calculated between this figure and changes in EMB budgets reported in the surveys. There was a strong correlation between overall change in government expenditure and EMB budgets (.420, significant at $p <$ 0.05 level) which provides some strong evidence for EMB budgets being shaped by broader government austerity drives. Interestingly, there was no relationship found with the budgets for training. This suggests that the overall picture of government finance significantly shapes EMB budgets, but the budgets for specific aspects of EMB work can have much more local drivers.

The data also provides some evidence for the importance of funding for electoral management. Pearson's correlations were also run against changes in the budgets and two measures of EMB performance. A question was taken from the Perceptions of Electoral Integrity 4.5 which asked 'The election authorities performed well'

(Norris, i Coma, et al. 2016). The latest version of the PEI survey was taken at the time when the EMS and ELECT surveys were run. This is a crude measurement of performance (see Chapter 3), but it does provide a parsimonious way of identifying a possible relationship. A correlation of .363, significant at the $p < 0.05$ level (2-tailed), was returned. Funding for elections does indeed therefore affect performance.

12.3.3 Actors and sources of income

If budgets are so important, then it is worth considering who controls them. Data from the same surveys reveal that the legislature is the political actor most commonly involved in approving EMB budgets. Based on data from 72 countries, the legislature is involved in 61.1 per cent of countries. The head of government or executive are involved in 41.7 per cent of countries. Other actors, such as the civil service (4.2), civil society (2.8), judiciary (1.4) and political parties (1.4), are also involved. The two countries that indicated that civil society played a role included Indonesia and Sao Tome and Principe. No further information was included in the survey about how they were involved.

Table 12.3 below demonstrates the most frequently cited sources of income to EMBs. Respondents were asked 'which following institutions provide funds for EMB?' Responses are ranked by the mean score, where 1 indicated 'on a regular basis' and 5 indicated 'never'. Nearly all EMBs receive funding from national governments, with local and regional tiers of government also being not uncommon. International organisations and foreign governments, however, feature prominently in many countries.

12.4 The challenge of funding elections

If funding and investment in the electoral process is so self-important, why is it not provided? What related challenges are there in funding the electoral process?

Table 12.3 Sources of EMB revenue

	Regular basis	Often	Occasionally	Rarely	Never	N	Mean
National governments	95.1%	–	–	1.6%	3.3%	61	1.18
International organisations	7.9%	7.9%	34.2%	13.2%	36.8%	38	3.63
Local governments	8.7%	13.0%	8.7%	4.3%	65.2%	23	4.04
Regional governments	11.1%	11.1%	5.6%	–	72.2%	18	4.11
Foreign governments	–	10.3%	13.8%	6.9%	65.5%	29	4.21
Private donors (philanthropists)	–	4.2%	12.5%	–	83.3%	24	4.63
Private donors (business corporations)	4.3%	–	4.3%	–	91.3%	23	4.74
Civil society organisations	–	8.7%	–	–	91.3%	23	4.86
Political parties	–	–	–	–	100.0%	20	5

One way in which the causal effects of funding can be identified is through the stories of electoral officials themselves. A 'storytelling' session in Stockholm at International IDEA was held in November 2017. Ten senior and experienced practitioners drawn from Africa, North America, Asia and Oceania were invited to share the 'war stories' from their time running elections. The venue of the meeting was International IDEA's Headquarters, located in an eighteenth-century building on Strömsborg,[6] a small islet in central Stockholm, surrounded by bridges carrying a motorway through Stockholm. Some delegates recalled how they were in fact in the same room that was a venue for a meeting in 1996 where ACE was developed with organisations such as the UN and IFES contributing. At that time, the funding of elections was at the top of the agenda, but put into the 'too hard, do later' category delegates explained.

The roundtable effectively provided a focus group with rich information that can shed light on the challenges – information that is rarely captured. The roundtable was recorded by International IDEA. The author, who was present at the roundtable, transcribed the focus group material and undertook a thematic analysis to identify key themes from the interviews. Names of countries, contributors, locations and currencies were removed to ensure anonymity and confidentiality. Quotes were selected very sparingly because of the politically sensitive nature of the discussions.

Ten key themes were identified. One of these was budget cuts. Undoubtedly, wider budget cuts could contribute towards making elections difficult to fund. One delegate recalled how their budget has been cut down to a third of its usual size that year following broader austerity cuts, which was 'more than any other institution of government'. This had major consequences for the delivery of elections:

> It reduces your ability to achieve your strategic objectives. You have a strategic plan but you cannot fulfil it all because of these continual cuts. It is not an electoral year, but there are issues to do with the electoral cycle that we are not able to deal with.

The argument of this chapter, in line with the realist sociological approach to electoral management developed in Chapter 2, is that the overall budget, cuts made to it and its appropriateness for running elections effectively is part of the process of organising elections. A focus purely on quantitative budgetary data misses many of the important social interactions that take place in the financing of elections which shape the complex relationship between budgeting, human relationships and performance outcomes. As one delegate explained, financing elections can be a 'tragi-drama'. The remaining nine themes are described now.

12.4.1 Lobbying purse-string holders

One major challenge is that electoral officials will find themselves competing with other government departments and/or public organisations for resources. In this context, the government upon whom they are dependent for resources, but who will have their own priorities, may not be receptive to demands for money. As Table 12.3 showed, governments and parliaments often have the power to approve budgets. Even where EMBs are supposed to have statutory independence, they remain reliant. Even if they were 'elevated to be a higher constitutional body'

> financial independence was one of the areas where independence has not fully been implemented and we are still linked to the government payment system. We are 100% funded by the government so that creates a dependency.

Elections are often not a high priority for those that decide the budgets.

> A lot of politicians are not particularly interested in talking about elections. . . . For them it is just 'later, later, later – we'll get to it', they know that it has got to be done but it is not a high priority. So trying to get them . . . to actually engage early in discussions about elections costs and budgeting can be challenging.

12.4.2 Statecraft and rent-seeking

The challenge of getting attention and explaining the importance of elections is confounded by the fact that electoral officials will find themselves amongst actors with other motivations in the budgeting for elections. Most obviously, incumbent governments (and opposition parties) will have an eye on their fortunes in forthcoming elections. One delegate explained that in their country the national government funds national elections and there is a different fund for local government elections. However, problems can arise such as 'incumbent holders in the national government can use the local budget in their favour.' Meanwhile, Commissioners might find themselves under pressure from Parliament:

> They can put pressure on the Commission to facilitate and pay for them to meet their constituents and threaten them with an Audit agency if they don't do so.

Further threats include upholding the disbursement of the budget in the Parliament if they don't comply with their needs.

Pressures can also come from elsewhere to spend money in areas that they wouldn't otherwise do. Often EMBs might be encouraged to employ particular groups on election day to achieve broader societal goals. This might include representatives from social movements to consolidate peace and reconciliation, or the unemployed youth to integrate them. While these are admirable goals, some delegates suggested, there were costs involved which are not always appreciated. Likewise, there might also be pressure to employ family or friends. One delegate explained that they had estimated that a system of continuous registration with permanent staff would be cheaper than a system that involved employing short-term workers during six-month periods. But the latter system was often preferred by many because it allowed them to find work for those close to them.

12.4.3 Worker management

Recruiting workers can be especially difficult because the time-bound nature of elections can give employees leverage in any industrial action disputes. Should they decide to strike on the eve of an election, costs might suddenly rise to either replace them or grant them their demands. One EMB explained how they managed to navigate this successfully:

> Obviously we had already invested in training them. We had budgeted for what we would pay them and some of them are government officials and it would have been above their salary – others were unemployed people. We said let them go. They then started filtering back one by one, so we held our bluff. But it was a nightmare as it was the eve of the election.

Another delegate explained how they had experienced staff demanding advance payment for elections.

12.4.4 Contractor negotiation

The fixed short-term nature of elections can leave suppliers in a strong bargaining position. Suppliers, especially if they are few in number, can often take an astute position to bargaining their contracts.

> When the election comes around it is the biggest show in town with [large sums] being spent. Our suppliers understand that because they like to charge a premium. They know that an election must be held, that an election must not be shifted, ballot boxes must be supplied, things must be moved around the country and we get charged an absolute premium.

12.4.5 Procurement processes

Procurement processes are often more complex and more difficult to manage than other government services. As noted above in section one of this chapter, there are much greater needs for resources in electoral years, but 'the government and parliament think that the EMB is like other ministries'. One delegate expressed their frustration that:

> Our first commissioners, when we became democratic decades ago approached Parliament asking for a different type of budget disbursement but to no avail to this day. The budgeting is still the same.

In another case, a delegate explained that:

> 95% of the election budget won't be given to us until the election is called. So we are trying to undertake change and we are also trying to procure materials that will be required for the election but we won't receive the

money until next year. . . . There are also some rules that we have to work to that say that we have to have the money in your account for the items that you are trying to achieve procurement to – otherwise you are breaching purchasing rules.

Policies are therefore unsuitable:

> There are a whole set of government policies, rules and processes which are set in place for government departments, which are operating a business which is nothing like the delivery of an election, yet we are pushed into the same rules, and it doesn't fit.

Further problems might include requirements to undertake competitive tendering processes – because this can often take time and there is no guarantee that contractors will respond.

12.4.6 Unforeseen costs

Elections, no doubt like many other public services, are likely to face many unforeseen costs. If there are not contingency plans in place then this can cause problems with the delivery of elections or for costs to rise. One delegate explained that they had a court challenge on the eve of an election about the use of technology. This resulted in extra-legal costs that were not expected. Nonetheless, that additional cost was relatively small compared to the cost that would have followed with a postponed election:

> If the judgement had gone the other way, what would have been the financial cost of postponing the election and starting again with the printing of ballot papers etc. etc.

The deployment of military forces overseas can also lead to unexpected costs. Military conflicts are by nature unpredictable events where the security of election equipment may require further investment.

> We also had a situation where we had soldiers based in [xx] so we have to provide for foreign voting procedures. We allow them to vote at our missions. We also had a situation where our ballot papers had to be routed through another country in Africa because of the conflict that arose. We found out that our ballot papers were caught in a port and we could not get access to them. So we had a last minute situation where we needed to find extra ballot papers. Fortunately we always print 110% of the ballot papers needed so we had those. But we had to get a military plane to deliver them. That was something unexpected and unplanned.

The late nature of these unexpected costs can also be a multiplier – as noted above, staff and private companies might be able to negotiate a premium on their services or issue a ransom demand. One delegate explained that a recount led to all staff and political parties being 'locked up' in a counting centre for several days with no one able to leave. Costs of providing subsistence for everyone and security for the surrounding area quickly accumulated.

12.4.7 Rising expectations

Expectations have also been rising, delegates explained. There were new pressures, which they recognised and were entirely supportive of, including ensuring that wait times were not excessive and improvements were made to the services for disabled electors. These pressures had not always been present and 'these things add to the cost.' Government was not always willing to share the financial burden and the reputational cost for any defects in service would inevitably be borne by the EMB.

12.4.8 Capacity for strategic thinking

The interplay between contextual situations and electoral officials, structure and agency, shape the challenges in delivering the investment required to run elections effectively. But the scope of electoral officials, as agents, to act strategically can be shaped by their administrative capacity. One delegate explained about 'the lack of capacity of the Commission Secretariat to do the planning and budgeting itself'. Another explained that:

> There are elections almost every year so there is almost no time to build capacity for budgeting. We are moving to simultaneous elections and this might help, but budget wise it might become 'a war rather than a drama'.

12.4.9 The legacies of historical relationships

Electoral officials seeking to fund and run elections may find themselves with a lack of trust, as a result of how their predecessors have run elections. If an EMB or overseas donor had employed staff at a previous election and not paid them, or not settled bills with contractors – then staff and contractors might be reluctant to return to help run future elections. Advance or higher payments might be required as a result of the legacies of historical relationships. The refusal of contractors to bid for a printing contract because of trust issues in one case led to ballot papers being printed overseas at the last minute.

> Once the ballot papers were printed we had to fly them and fly them thousands of kilometres via a military aircraft. We then hit another administrative burden because customs said that you need to bring it through the port first. We were then held up by customs.

12.5 Conclusions

For elections to be run effectively, administrators require resource and capacity, yet concerns have been raised that these have not been provided. These claims have

Austerity and financial investment 265

been difficult to evidence because of a lack of information and transparency about how elections are funded. This chapter has shown that there are considerable variations in the budgets of EMBs around the world. The overall trend is towards higher budgets – more money being required to keep elections running. But this money is much needed because where investment has dropped, the quality of elections is lower.

The realist sociological approach set out in this book requires more analysis than statistical inference. By taking the lessons and stories of practitioners we can learn more about how shortfalls can occur, but also the other challenges in running elections. The chapter has sought a more nuanced understanding of the dynamics behind investing in elections through the use of original 'war-stories' from senior, experienced practitioners from around the world. Austerity, understood as a restriction in the supply of financial resources, to EMBs has a causal effect. But austerity is not the result of a top-down decision, it is the result of a series of dynamic causal mechanisms and relationships. These include insufficient advocacy, listening and networking with budget holders, challenges of statecraft and rent-seeking, negotiation practices with employees and contractors and risk management. There are practical steps that EMBs can take to improve investment in elections. This might include risk management plans, diversification of the suppliers and workforce and simplifying procurement procedures. This is even more evidence that the management of elections matters. And that there are practical policy instruments to improve electoral integrity.

Notes

1 The data is also used in Garnett (2019b)
2 World Bank (2018) 'PPP conversion factor, GDP', https://data.worldbank.org/indicator/pa.nus.ppp, accessed 30 October 2018.
3 UN National Accounts Official Country Data – UNDATA, http://data.un.org/Data.aspx?q=government+expenditure&d=SNA&f=group_code%3a301, accessed 22 October 2018. In most cases data on public expenditure levels was provided for 2016 – but for Senegal, Panama, Mozambique, New Zealand, the latest data available at the time of writing was from 2012, and Russia was 2013. This was therefore used.
4 The question about overall budgets was not included in the ELECT survey, so there is a higher number of responses for data on the training budget.
5 World Bank (2018).
6 Local folklore has it that the building used to be a bar before it was restored for office use. The owners would issue passports for the islet until the Stockholm authorities became annoyed.

Part V

Looking forward

Part V
Looking forward

13 Conclusions

13.1 Introduction

Elections matter. The winners take power of the state apparatus and are gifted the opportunity to use it for social good or ill. It is often the only opportunity that citizens have to boot out leaders and legislators and replace them with their chosen representatives. Ensuring that these elections are well run is therefore essential. The sparsity of research on the electoral management is staggering – and both policy, practice and the citizen have lost out from this.

This book has sought to address this gap by laying down some groundwork frameworks and concepts to inform the comparative study of electoral management and define it as an inter-disciplinary area of study. It has provided original ethnographic stories, comparative case studies and new datasets from around the world. These have generated lessons for how elections should be run and should be studied. This chapter provides a concise summary of the key lessons and then suggests some avenues for future research.

13.2 Methodological lessons

The first set of lessons from this book are definitional. Words and concepts matter. Early scholarship in this area have used concepts such as electoral governance, electoral reform, electoral management bodies, electoral (or election) management board, electoral (or election) management, electoral (or election) administration, electoral (or election) commissions interchangeably and/or without definition (Hartlyn, McCoy, and Mustillo 2008; James 2014d; Mozaffer 2002; Norris 2017c; Pastor 1999a, 1999b; Ugues 2010). Some terminology reflects differences between languages; or the names of organisations colloquially used for EMBs within the countries that academics have been based.[1] However, terms such as 'electoral governance, administration and management' are important in defining what we are studying. The book has sought to distinguish these. Electoral governance is the broader set of power relations between all actors involved in all aspects of the electoral process. It is not just about the design of electoral management bodies – who are simply one of the organisations involved in implementing elections. Electoral management is the study of the implementation of the elections. Crucially, this is not a pure administrative task. The road from law to implementation is a tricky one, laced with political decisions. It involved governance networks, which includes, but is not limited to, EMBs.

Secondly, the book has developed a realist sociological approach to the study of electoral management – and electoral institutions in general. Electoral studies took off in the 1950s and 1960s as part of the behaviouralist revolution – and made a key contribution to establishing it as the mainstream. Questioning the assumptions of this approach and thinking a little more about political science methodology and questions of ontology, epistemology and theories of knowledge is not likely to be at the top of every election scholar's shopping list. But if political science is to inform policy and praxis, rather than be written for its own sake, then deep thinking about the relationship between research and the world it is trying to describe and influence is imperative. As an action point, journal editors and reviewers should be more open to research that uses more diverse methodologies.

Thirdly, the book introduces a new framework for assessing electoral management: the PROSeS framework. Most existing approaches to evaluating elections largely ignore the implementation aspect of elections or they seek to develop quantitative measures. While the latter are very aspirational, and arguably have been achieved within states for a short period to time, it is impossible to develop measures of performance that are not overly reductionist in the data used. Borrowing from theories of public sector management, a new framework is set out that can inform future academic research and practice.

Fourthly, the book has introduced a new approach for answering the question: 'who runs elections?' The answer is not simply the government or an independent EMB, as existing typologies had it, but electoral management governance networks – collaborations of state, civil society and other party actors who come together with each usually playing a role. Electoral management governance networks were therefore defined as the constellation of actors involved in steering and delivering elections, including the micro anthropological practices, beliefs and power relationships between them. The formation of these networks takes different forms and a typology is proposed to allow future comparisons.

Finally, building on work the realist sociological approach, it has offered a distinctive argument about the nature of interventions designed to improve the management of elections. Policy instruments have unintended effects far beyond their original intended aims – both administrative and political (Kassim and Le Galès 2010; Lascoumes and Le Galès 2007). Scholarship on electoral system reform has systematically ignored the side effects of reforms – especially on the cost of elections and staff who run them. A different approach to future research should be undertaken. This should be premised on the idea that voter registration (and other) reforms can have both indirect and direct effects on electoral management performance, using the framework set out in Chapter 3. The direct effects are those which are experienced by the voter because of the reform (Figure 13.1). These are the changes that they experience such as changed deadlines, the requirement to provide information in a particular location or format. The indirect effects of a reform will not necessarily be seen by the voter. They will include the effects on the staff, organisational resources and infrastructure resulting from a reform. All of these

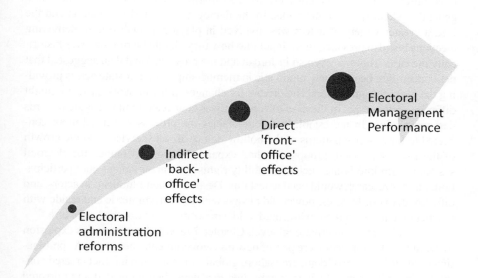

Figure 13.1 The direct and indirect effects of electoral administration (and other) reforms.

may or may not be significantly affected. But if they are, then they will obviously affect electoral management performance because they are taken as measures of success in Chapter 3. They may have further indirect effects on the voter's experience, however, because an organisation with depleted human resources or financial capital may be less able to respond to provide a high-quality service to the voter.

13.3 Key empirical findings

The new frameworks and methodologies used have facilitated new empirical findings in the newly established field of electoral management. On the first theme of performance, the book applied the new PROSeS model to Canada and the UK to reveal many similarities in levels of performance. However, the Canadian system demonstrated much clearer systems of accountability and transparency with resource investment, more convenient services, less frequent service denials to voters, higher satisfaction with citizens. The UK system seems to be delivered more economically and efficiently, has fewer rejected ballots and hasn't exhibited the same accuracy enforcement issues that the Canadian system has – but this might be for a lack of critical examination. A general lesson might be that centralised systems produce greater transparency and accountability – but are financially more costly.

On the second theme of governance networks, Chapters 5 and 6 provided four new case studies on the nature of the governance network involved in running elections. A five fold typology of network structures was introduced ranging from closed statism to a pluralistic collaborative network. Cases were deliberately chosen in the most different of contexts, but there were similarities across the cases. One was a general thickening of the networks. In the democracies of India, Australia and the UK, a greater variety of actors was involved in playing a small role in delivering elections but also provided more input into how they should be run than was historically the case. This was even so in Jordan and the cross-national data suggested that networks might be relatively pluralistic in membership with non-state actors providing the ideas for innovation. The drivers for changes in the network structure might differ by regime type. In the case of Jordan it was connected to the struggle towards democratisation. In the established democracies the processes seemed more connected to longer-term patterns of the hollowing out of state services and the growth of third-sector pressure groups who had expanded beyond demands for electoral system reform into issues such as disability rights and encouraging youth participation. Further research would need to test this. Despite greater pluralism in actors, and different network features, power did always tend to be asymmetric and reside with the incumbent government who could hold a majority or control the legislature.

Meanwhile, at the international level, Chapter 7 revealed an enormous explosion in the range of actors that were part of new transgovernmental networks. A combination of the third wave of democratisation, globalisation and the internet created conditions in which networks were established that were then replicated and mirrored around the world. A new range of soft-power tools became available to international actors trying to improve the quality of elections, even if power did ultimately reside with the national state. These were major transformations in the long history of running elections and new data was introduced demonstrate this development.

The third theme of the book was policy instruments – what could be done to improve electoral management. Voter registration reform is often proposed either to improve over security or participation. Chapter 9 evaluated the effects of introducing individual electoral registration in Britain and demonstrated that it improved the accuracy of the register and reduced opportunities for electoral fraud but had major effects on the cost of the registration process, on personnel, and the completeness of the electoral register. Chapter 10 considered the effects of centralising electoral management and came to similar conclusions. Also examining the effects of reform in Britain it noted how electoral management centralisation can generate more consistent service and reduce errors, but there are efficiency effects, lost local knowledge and staff morale/satisfaction could be undermined. Both chapters have broader academic and policy implications. Future researchers and policy makers need to be more aware of the broader effects of reforms on electoral management quality.

Human resource management strategies were considered in Chapter 11 and the argument was that this was an almost entirely overlooked area of electoral management. It was shown how training can have positive effects on employee experience and the quality of the election. These are intuitive findings – but the chapter made important advances in demonstrating these linkages and also revealed with new international data that 40 per cent of survey respondents around the world had not attended a training workshop in the past five years. Chapter 12 considered financial investment in elections and presented data on levels of spending around the world. Financial austerity, understood as a restriction in the supply of financial resources, to EMBs has a causal effect. But austerity was shown not to always be the result of top-down decisions, but the result of a series of dynamic causal mechanisms such as negotiation, information sharing and strategic planning.

The other lesson from part IV of the book was the temporal nature of reforms. Some effects, whether it is on personnel or the cost of administering elections, might be short term. There are 'transition costs' involved in institutional reform that the literature has hereto not considered and policy makers must beware of. This brings to light the importance of 'lock-in' path dependencies in the choice and design of EMBs. EMB designs are not drawn on a blank canvass. Their institutional architecture is drawn onto a scene of existing relationships, values and expectations about 'how things are done'. The 'best' choice of EMB may therefore be more contextually dependent than the existing literature acknowledges. It is certainly temporally dependent. Further research will help identify the important characteristics of these contexts that should be borne in mind for institutional designers.

13.4 Lessons for policy and praxis

Karl Marx famously wrote that in 1845 'the philosophers have only interpreted the world, in various ways. The point, however, is to change it' (Marx 1888). Following the critical realist approach set out in Chapter 2, which argues that we should be critical of the world with the aim to improve, it follows that we should take lessons for policy and practice and some key recommendations are therefore included in Box 13.1.

Box 13.1   Policy recommendations based on the research findings and new methods from the book

1. Researchers have a duty to play a positive role in promoting improved electoral management.
2. Researchers should be aware of the spatial–temporal nature of research findings and give greater weight to the knowledge of practitioners.
3. The PROSeS model can be used by EMBs and international electoral assistance agencies to identify strengths and weaknesses in electoral management delivery models through systematic comparison.
4. Regular auditing of electoral management can take place at points other than election time, the current main focus of international monitoring work using the PROSeS model.
5. More inclusive governance networks can be built between civil society, government and NGOs to enable knowledge sharing. Parliamentary committees provide one mechanism for this.
6. Electoral management networks can act as an important check on partisan statecraft by political parties and should be strengthened.
7. The international community should also work to build more collaborative networks between academics, civil society and EMBs.
8. Governments, politicians and EMBs should be aware of the importance of investment in electoral management.

> 9 Proposed reforms should include a full risk assessment of the side effects such as to political participation, cost and EMB personnel.
> 10 Policies such as stress management and training should be considered to improve EMB workforce job satisfaction and performance.

13.5 Future research: the tip of an iceberg?

The book noted the relative absence of research on the management of elections and hopes to encourage further studies. There are many obvious research questions that follow. Taking the first theme of the book, methodology, the book set out a realist sociological approach to the study of electoral institutions. This is an alternative to the rational behaviouralist model that has dominated political science so far. The book has followed the principles of the approach and applied it to electoral management, but there is nothing stopping the principles being applied to the study of other electoral institutions. The nature of knowledge, the positionality of the research and the stratified nature of causation could be used to provide entirely different approaches to study old questions. There is much scope for applying this approach to other areas of the electoral cycle.

Secondly, the PROSeS model has been applied to two countries – but there are many more that would benefit from systematic comparison in performance and new insights about their strengths and weaknesses.

Thirdly, the book suggested some core dimensions of governance networks and used four cases interactively with theory to suggest that there might be five ideal types. Having only applied it to four cases, there is obviously a rich opportunity to apply it elsewhere – to see where other countries fit in and consider whether the typology captures the variety of areas. More widely, what governance networks are there for other types of electoral institutions such as finance, electoral reform or just elections in general?

Fourthly, the book suggested that policies designed to improve the implementation of elections could be considered through a policy instrumentation approach. There is a huge opportunity to consider a range of other instruments through this lens.

13.6 Call to action

Elections are thought to be two thousand years old, having been held in ancient Athens, and in Rome to select popes and Holy Roman emperors. Despite this long history, research on electoral management has only just begun. This book has provided new founding concepts and frameworks, and new insights about how they can be improved worldwide. As the reader, whether as an academic, practitioner or campaigner, it's now over to you to take up the mantle, and make improved elections a reality.

Note

1 After writing about 'electoral management boards' for a few years – I conceded to Holly Ann Garnett on this and called them 'bodies'. But it's definitely 'electoral management', not 'election management', Holly. . . .

Bibliography

Alvarez, R. Michael, Lonna Rae Atkeson, and Thad E. Hall. 2012. *Evaluating Elections: A Handbook of Methods and Standards*. New York: Cambridge University Press.
A-WEB. undated. *Proposed Association of World Electoral Election Boards*. South Korea: A-WEB.
AAEA. 1997. *Charter of the Association of Asian Election Authorities*. Philippines: AAEA.
———. undated. *Association of Asian Election Authorities*. AAEA.
Aasland, Aadne, Mikkel Berg-Nordlie, and Elena Bogdanova. 2016. "Encouraged But Controlled: Governance Networks in Russian Regions." *East European Politics*, 32, (2), pp. 148–69.
ACE. 2017. Electoral Cycle. http://aceproject.org/ero-en/topics/electoral-management/electoral%20cycle.JPG/view.
———. 2018a. About ACE. http://aceproject.org/about-en/.
———. 2018b. Election Observation. http://aceproject.org/ace-en/focus/international-election-observation/onePage.
———. 2018c. Electoral Assistance. http://aceproject.org/ace-en/focus/focus-on-effective-electoral-assistance/onePage.
ADR. 2011. Mission and Vision. https://adrindia.org/about-adr/mission-and-vision.
AEA. 2016. Qualifications. www.aea-elections.co.uk/training-qualifications/qualifications/.
———. 2017. *Unaudited Financial Statements for the Year Ending 30 September 2017*. Cannock: Companies House.
Ahlquist, John S., Kenneth R. Mayer, and Simon Jackman. 2014. "Alien Abduction and Voter Impersonation in the 2012 US General Election: Evidence from a Survey List Experiment." *Election Law Journal*, 13, (4), pp. 460–75.
AIADMK. 2014. *Election Manifesto of the All India Anna Dravida Munnetra Kazhagam*.
Allen, Natalie J., and John P. Meyer. 1990. "The Measurement and Antecedents of Affective, Continuance and Normative Commitment to the Organization." *Journal of Occupational and Organizational Psychology*, 63, (1), pp. 1–18.
Alvarez, Michael R., and D.E. Sinclair. 2004. "Who Overvotes, Who Undervotes, Using Punchcards? Evidence from Los Angeles County." *Political Research Quarterly*, 57, (1), pp. 15–24.
Alvarez, Michael R., and Thad E. Hall. 2006. "Controlling Democracy: The Principal-Agent Problems in Election Administration." *Policy Studies Journal*, 34, (4), pp. 491–510.
Alvarez, R. Michael, Lonna Rae Atkeson, and Thad E. Hall. 2007. *The New Mexico Election Administration Report: The 2006 November General Election*. CalTech/MIT.
———. 2012. *Evaluating Elections: A Handbook of Methods and Standards*. New York: Cambridge University Press.

Amegnran, Kokouvi Momo. 2017. "Assessing Electoral Process Challenges through Poll Workers' Performance in Sub-Saharan Africa Togo." Dissertation submitted for examination for PhD, Walden University.

Amis, Jacob. 2016. "Hirak! Civil Resistance and the Jordan Spring." In *Civil Resistance in the Arab Spring: Triumphs and Disasters*, edited by Adam Roberts, Michael J. Willis, Rory McCarthy, and Timothy Garton Ash. Oxford: Oxford University Press.

Andrews, Rhys, George A. Boyne, and Gareth Enticott. 2006. "Performance Failure in the Public Sector." *Public Management Review*, 8, (2), pp. 273–96.

Andrews, Rhys, George A. Boyne, and Richard M. Walker. 2006. "Subjective and Objective Measures of Organizational Performance: An Empirical Exploration." In *Public Service Performance*, edited by George A. Boyne, Kenneth J. Meler, Laurence O'Toole Jr., and Richard M. Walker, 14–34. Cambridge: Cambridge University Press.

Anglin, Douglas G. 1998. "International Election Monitoring: The African Experience." *African Affairs*, 97, (389), pp. 471–95.

Ansell, Chris, and Alison Gash. 2008. "Collaborative Governance in Theory and Practice." *Journal of Public Administration Research and Theory*, 18, (4), pp. 543–71.

Ansolabehere, Stephen, and M. David Konisky. 2005. "The Introduction of Voter Registration and Its Effect on Turnout." *Political Analysis*, 14, (1), pp. 83–100.

Appelbaum, Eileen, Thomas Bailey, Peter Berg, and Arne L. Kallesberg. 2000. *Manufacturing Advantage: Why High-Performance Work Systems Pay Off*. Ithaca, NY: Cornell University Press.

APSA. 2018. Elections, Public Opinion, and Voting Behavior, Section 32. www.apsanet.org/section32.

ArabEMBS. undated. *Establishment of the Organisation of the Arab Electoral Management Bodies*. Secretariat of the organisation of the Arab Electoral Management Bodies.

Archer, Margaret. 1995. *Realist Social Theory*. Cambridge: Cambridge University Press.

———. 1998. "Introduction: Realism in the Social Sciences." In *Critical Realism: Essential Readings*, edited by M.S. Archer, 189–205. London: Routledge.

Arghiros, Daniel, Horacio Boneo, Simon Henderson, Sonia Palmieri, and Therese Pearce Laanela. 2017. *Making It Count: Lessons from Australian Electoral Assistance 2006–2016*. Canberra: Australian Government.

Arirang News. 2013. "World Delegates Launch Association of World Election Bodies Monday." 15 October. www.arirang.co.kr/News/News_View.asp?nseq=152195.

Arthur, Jeffrey B. 1994. "Effects of Human Resource Systems on Manufacturing Performance and Turnover." *Academy of Management Journal*, 37, (3), pp. 670–87.

Associated Press. 2013. Nobody Home: Utah Town Forgets to Hold Election. www.politico.com/story/2013/11/wallsburg-utah-forgets-elections-100193.

———. 2016. Views on the American Election Process and Perceptions of Voter Fraud. http://www.apnorc.org/projects/Pages/HTML%20Reports/views-on-the-american-election-process-and-perceptions-of-voter-fraud-issue-brief.aspx.

Association of Electoral Administrators. 2010. *Press Release – Individual Electoral Registration, Norwich*. Association of Electoral Administrators.

———. 2015a. Elections and Individual Electoral Registration – The Challenge of 2015. https://www.aea-elections.co.uk/wp-content/uploads/2015/07/aea-report-elections-and-ier-challenge-of-2015.pdf.

———. 2015b. History of the Association. www.aea-elections.co.uk/about/history/.

Atkeson, Lonna Rae, Lisa Ann Bryant, Thad E. Hall, Kyle Saunders, and Michael Alvarez. 2010. "A New Barrier to Participation: Heterogeneous Application of Voter Identification Policies." *Electoral Studies*, 29, (1), pp. 66–73.

Atkeson, Lonna Rae, and Kyle L. Saunders. 2007. "The Effect of Election Administration on Voter Confidence: A Local Matter?" *PS: Political Science & Politics*, 40, (4), pp. 655–60.

Atkinson, Paul, and Martyn Hammersley. 1995. *Ethnography*. New York and London: Routledge.

Aucoin, Peter. 2012. "New Political Governance in Westminster Systems: Impartial Public Administration and Management Performance at Risk." *Governance*, 25, (2), pp. 177–99.

Australian Bureau of Statistics. 2018. Australian Demographic Statistics, March. www.abs.gov.au/ausstats/abs@.nsf/mf/3101.0.

Australian Museum. 2017. Bluebottle. https://australianmuseum.net.au/bluebottle.

Badrieh, Belbisi. 2015. *The Organization of Arab Electoral Management Bodies(ArabEMBs)*. Jordan: Arab EMBs Secretariat.

Bagehot, W. 1967 (1876). *The English Constitution*. London: Fontana.

Bailey, Thomas. 1993. *Discretionary Effort and the Organization of Work: Employee Participation and Work Reform since Hawthorne*. Teachers College and Conservation of Human Resources. New York: Columbia University.

Bakker, Arnold B., and Evangelia Demerouti. 2007. "The Job Demands-Resources Model: State of the Art." *Journal of Managerial Psychology*, 22, (3), pp. 309–28.

Barnard, Chester. 1938. *The Functions of the Executive*. Cambridge, MA: Harvard University Press.

Barreto, Matt A., Stephen A. Nuno, and Gabriel R. Sanchez. 2009. "The Disproportionate Impact of Voter-ID Requirements on the Electorate-New Evidence from Indiana." *PS: Political Science and Politics*, 42, (1), pp. 111–15.

BBC News. 2010. Electoral Commission Responds to Polling Problems. http://news.bbc.co.uk/1/hi/uk_politics/election_2010/8666527.stm.

———. 2017. Newcastle-under-Lyme Election Errors: Two Officers Suspended. www.bbc.com/news/uk-england-stoke-staffordshire-42141327.

Beale, Stephen. 2013. *Strengthening Electoral Processes in Jordan*. Jordan: UNDP.

Becker, Brian E., Mark A. Huselid, Peter S. Pickus, and Michael F. Spratt. 1997. "HR as a Source of Shareholder Value: Research and Recommendations." *Human Resource Management*, 36, (1), pp. 39–47.

Beetham, David. 1994. "Key Principles and Indices for a Democratic Audit." In *Defining Democracy*, edited by David Beetham. London: Sage.

Belfrage, Claes, and Felix Hauf. 2016. "The Gentle Art of Retroduction: Critical Realism, Cultural Political Economy and Critical Grounded Theory." *Organization Studies*, 38, (2), pp. 251–71.

Berry, Frances S., Ralph S. Brower, Sang Ok Choi, Wendy Xinfang Goa, HeeSoun Jang, Myungjung Kwon, and Jessica Word. 2004. "Three Traditions of Network Research: What the Public Management Research Agenda Can Learn from Other Research Communities." *Public Administration Review*, 64, (5), pp. 539–52.

Berry, Leonard L., Kathleen Seiders, and Dhruv Grewal. 2002. "Understanding Service Convenience." *Journal of Marketing*, 66, (3), pp. 1–17.

Bertrand, Romain, Jean-Louis Briquet, and Peter Pels. 2007. *Cultures of Voting: The Hidden History of the Secret Ballot*. London: C. Hurst & Co.

Bevir, M., and R.A.W. Rhodes. 2002. "Interpretive Theory." In *Theory and Methods in Political Science*, edited by D. Marsh and G. Stoker. London: Palgrave.

———. 2003. *Interpreting British Governance*. New York: Routledge.

Bharatiya Janata Party. 2014. *Election Manifesto 2014*. New Delhi: BJP.

Bhaskar, R. 1989. *Reclaiming Reality*. London: Verso.

Bhaskar, Roy. 2008. *A Realist Theory of Science*. New York: Taylor & Francis.
———. 2009. *Scientific Realism and Human Emancipation*. Abingdon: Routledge.
Bianco, William T., and Robert H. Bates. 1990. "Cooperation by Design: Leadership, Structure, and Collective Dilemmas." *The American Political Science Review*, 84, (1), pp. 133–47.
Birch, Sarah. 2008. "Electoral Institutions and Popular Confidence in Electoral Processes: A Cross-national Analysis." *Electoral Studies*, 27, (2), pp. 305–20.
———. 2011. *Electoral Malpractice*. Oxford: Oxford University Press.
Birch, Sarah, and Bob Watt. 2004. "Remote Electronic Voting: Free Fair and Secret?" *Political Quarterly*, 75, (1), pp. 60–72.
Biswas, Soumendu, and Arup Varma. 2007. "Psychological Climate and Individual Performance in India: Test of a Mediated Model." *Employee Relations*, 29, (6), pp. 664–76.
Bite the Ballot. 2014. *National Voter Registration Day: February 5th 2014*. London: Bite the Ballot.
———. 2019. Case Studies. www.bitetheballot.co.uk/case-study.
Bjornlund, Eric. 2004. *Beyond Free and Fair: Monitoring Elections and Building Democracy*. Baltimore, MD: John Hopkins Press.
Bjornlund, Eric, David Carroll, Staffan Darnolf, Annette Fath-Lihic, Aleida Ferreyra, Betilde Muñoz-Pogossian, Pippa Norris, and Chad Vickery. 2014. "Lessons from the Ground." In *Advancing Electoral Integrity*, edited by Pippa Norris, Richard W. Frank, and Ferran Martinez i Coma. Oxford: Oxford University Press.
Black, Jerome H. 2000. "The National Register of Electors: Raising Questions about the New Approach to Voter Registration in Canada." *Policy Matters*, 1, (10), pp. 1–126.
———. 2003. *From Enumeration to the National Register of Electors: An Account and an Evaluation*. Vol. 9, Choices. Quebec: Institute for Research on Public Policy.
Blais, A. 2000. *To Vote to Not to Vote: The Merits and Limits of Rational Choice Theory*. Pittsburgh, PA: University of Pittsburgh Press.
Blais, André. 2008. *To Keep or To Change First Past the Post? The Politics of Electoral Reform*. Oxford: Oxford University Press.
Bland, Gary. 2015. "Measuring the Quality of Kenya's March 2013 Election." *Election Law Journal*, 14, (2), pp. 136–47.
Bland, Gary, Andrew Green, and Toby Moore. 2013. "Measuring the Quality of Election Administration." *Democratization*, 20, (2), pp. 358–77.
Bordewich, Chloe, Avery Davis-Roberts, and David Carroll. 2019. International Election Observation. http://aceproject.org/ace-en/focus/international-election-observation/onePage.
Borzel, Tanja A. 1998. "Organizing Babylon – On the Different Conceptions of Policy Networks." *Public Administration*, 76, pp. 253–73.
Borzyskowski, Inken von. 2016. "Resisting Democracy Assistance: Who Seeks and Receives Technical Election Assistance?" *Review of International Organizations*, 11, (2), pp. 247–82.
Boselie, Paul, Graham Dietz, and Corine Boon. 2005. "Commonalities and Contradictions in HRM and Performance Research." *Human Resource Management Journal*, 15, (3), pp. 67–94.
Boutlis, Craig. 2011. *Submission Number 1*. Sydney: JSCEM.
———. 2012. *Submission Number 1*. Sydney: JSCEM.
Bowcott, Owen. 2015. "Judge Who Disqualified Tower Hamlets Mayor Leads Drive to Reform Election Law." *Guardian*, 24 April 2015. www.theguardian.com/law/2015/apr/24/judge-disqualified-tower-hamlets-mayor-reform-election-law-richard-mawrey-electoral-fraud.

Bowler, Shaun, David M. Farrell, and Robin T. Pettitt. 2005. "Expert Opinion on Electoral Systems: So Which Electoral System Is "Best"?" *Journal of Elections, Public Opinion & Parties*, 15, (1), pp. 3–19.

Bowler, Shaun, Thomas Brunell, Todd Donovan, and Paul Gronke. 2015. "Election Administration and Perceptions of Fair Elections." *Electoral Studies*, 38, pp. 1–9.

Boxall, Peter, and John Purcell. 2003. *Strategy and Human Resource Management*. Oxford: Blackwell.

———. 2011. *Strategy and Human Resource Management*. New York: Palgrave Macmillan.

Boyne, George A. 2002. "Concepts and Indicators of Local Authority Performance: An Evaluation of the Statutory Frameworks in England and Wales." *Public Money & Management*, 22, (2), pp. 17–24.

Braiden, Gerry. 2016a. "Anger as Council Chiefs Top Up Annual Pension Pots with One-Off Election Fees." *Sunday Herald*, 30 April. www.heraldscotland.com/news/14463092.Anger_as_council_chiefs_top_up_annual_pension_pots_with_one_off_election_fees/.

———. 2016b. "Reform Calls as Council Chiefs Bag Over £1m in Election Fees in Two Years." *Sunday Herald*, 27 April.

Braun, Virginia, and Victoria Clarke. 2006. "Using Thematic Analysis in Psychology." *Qualitative Research in Psychology*, 3, (2), pp. 77–101.

———. 2012. "Thematic Analysis." In *The Handbook of Research Methods in Psychology*, edited by H. Cooper. Washington DC: American Psychological Association.

Brehm, John, and Scott Gates. 1994. "When Supervision Fails to Induce Compliance." *Journal of Theoretical Politics*, 6, (3), pp. 323–43.

———. 1999. *Working, Shirking, and Sabotage: Bureaucratic Response to a Democratic Public*. Ann Arbor: University of Michigan Press.

Brewer, Gene A. 2006. "All Measures of Performance Are Subjective: More Evidence on US Federal Agencies." In *Public Service Performance*, edited by George A. Boyne, Kenneth J. Meler, Laurence O'Toole Jr., and Richard M. Walker, 35–54. Cambridge: Cambridge University Press.

Bridge. 2019. Statistics. www.bridge-project.org/statistics/.

Brightwell, Ian. 2018. "Online Voting Lessons from (NSW) Australia's iVote Project." Presentation in the House of Commons. https://webrootsdemocracy.org/2018/05/17/online-voting-lessons-from-australias-ivote-project/.

Bryden, Joan. 2018. "Liberals Keen to Push through Voting Reforms Ahead of 2019 Federal Election." *Global News*, 26 March. https://globalnews.ca/news/4106115/voting-reform-canada/.

Budge, Ian. 2000. "Expert Judgements of Party Policy Positions: Uses and Limitations in Political Research." *European Journal of Political Research*, 37, (1), pp. 103–13.

Buller, Jim. 1999. "A Critical Appraisal of the Statecraft Interpretation." *Public Administration*, 77, (4), pp. 691–712.

Buller, Jim, and Toby S. James. 2012. "Statecraft and the Assessment of National Political Leaders: The Case of New Labour and Tony Blair." *The British Journal of Politics & International Relations*, 14, (4), pp. 534–55.

———. 2015. "Integrating Structural Context into the Assessment of Political Leadership: Philosophical Realism, Gordon Brown and the Great Financial Crisis." *Parliamentary Affairs*, 68, (1), pp. 77–96.

Bulpitt, Jim. 1986. "The Discipline of the New Democracy: Mrs. Thatcher's Domestic Statecraft." *Political Studies*, 34, (1), pp. 19–39.

Burden, Barry C., David T. Canon, Kenneth R. Mayer, Donald R. Moynihan, and Jacob R. Neiheisel. 2017. "What Happens at the Polling Place: Using Administrative Data to Look Inside Elections." *Public Administration Review*, 77, (3), pp. 354–64.

Burden, Barry C., and Jeffrey Milyo. 2015. "The Quantities and Qualities of Poll Workers." *Election Law Journal*, 14, (1), pp. 38–46.

Butler, David. 1963. *The Electoral System in Britain Since 1918*. Oxford: Clarendon Press.

Cabinet Office. 2011. *Cabinet Office Elections Policy and Co-ordination Group: Terms of Reference*. London: Cabinet Office.

———. 2013. *Minutes: Elections Policy & Coordination Group*. London: Cabinet Office.

———. 2015. *Funding for New Ways to Encourage Voter Registration*. London: Cabinet Office.

———. 2017a. Minister Holds Inaugural Electoral Summit. www.gov.uk/government/news/minister-holds-inaugural-electoral-summit.

———. 2017b. Minister Hosts 'Call for Evidence' Roundtable to Improve Accessibility of Elections. www.gov.uk/government/news/minister-hosts-call-for-evidence-roundtable-to-improve-accessibility-of-elections.

Calingaert, Daniel. 2006. "Election Rigging and How to Fight It." *Journal of Democracy*, 17, (3), pp. 138–51.

Calingaert, Daniel, Arch Puddington, and Sarah Repucci. 2014. *The Democracy Support Deficit: Despite Progress, Major Countries Fall Short*. Washington DC: Freedom House.

Campbell, Angus, Philip E. Converse, Warren E. Miller, and Donald E. Stokes. 1960. *The American Voter*. New York: John Wiley and Sons.

Cantú, Francisco, and Sandra Ley. 2017. "Poll Worker Recruitment: Evidence from the Mexican Case." *Election Law Journal*, 16, (4).

Carothers, Thomas. 1997. "The Observers Observed." *Journal of Democracy*, 8, (3), pp. 17–31.

———. 2003. *Aiding Democracy Abroad*. Washington DC: Brookings Institution Press.

Carter Center. 1988. *Annual Report 1982–88*. Atlanta, GA: Carter Center.

———. 2013. *The Carter Center's Study Mission Report for Jordan's 2013 Parliamentary Elections*. Atlanta, GA: Carter Center.

———. 2014. *Election Observations and Standards: A Carter Center Assessment Manual*. Atlanta, GA: Carter Center.

———. 2016. *Annual Report 2015–16*. Atlanta, GA: Carter Center.

Carter, Neil, Rudolf Klein, and Patricia Day. 1992. *How Organizations Measure Success: The Use of Performance Indicators in Government*. London: Routledge.

Castells, M. 2000. "Materials for an Explanatory Theory of the Network Society." *British Journal of Sociology*, 51, (1), pp. 5–24.

Catt, Helena, Andrew Ellis, Michael Maley, Alan Wall, and Peter Wolf. 2014. *Electoral Management Design: Revised Edition*. Stockholm: International IDEA.

CBS News. 2008. U.N.: 600,000 Displaced in Kenya Unrest. www.cbsnews.com/news/un-600000-displaced-in-kenya-unrest/.

Cerny, Philip G. 2010. *Rethinking World Politics: A Theory of Transnational Neopluralism*. Oxford: Oxford University Press.

Channel 4 News. 2010. Electoral Commission to Investigate Polling Chaos. *Channel 4 News*, www.channel4.com/news/articles/politics/hundreds+of+voters+turned+away+from+packed+polls/3638632.html.

Chapman, James. 2010. "Eric Pickles Fires the Left-wing Quango Queen Blamed for Election Night Shambles." *Daily Mail*, 8 September. www.dailymail.co.uk/news/article-1310025/Eric-Pickles-fires-left-wing-quango-queen-blamed-election-night-shambles.html.

Cheeseman, Nic. 2008. "The Kenyan Elections of 2007: An Introduction." *Journal of Eastern African Studies*, 2, (2), pp. 166–84.

Chhokar, Jagdeep S. 2018. *Simultaneous Elections: Striking at the Roots of Parliamentary Democracy*. Chennai: Hindu Centre.
Christopher, Hood. 2006. "Gaming in Targetworld: The Targets Approach to Managing British Public Services." *Public Administration Review*, 66, (4), pp. 515–21.
CIA, FBI, and National Security Agency. 2017. *Background to "Assessing Russian Activities and Intentions in Recent US Elections": The Analytic Process and Cyber Incident Attribution*. Washington, DC: CIA.
Claassen, Ryan L., David B. Magleby, J. Quin Monson, and Kelly D. Patterson. 2008. ""At Your Service" Voter Evaluations of Poll Worker Performance." *American Politics Research*, 36, (4), pp. 612–34.
Claassen, Ryan, David Magleby, J. Monson, and Kelly Patterson. 2012. "Voter Confidence and the Election-Day Voting Experience." *Political Behavior*, 35, (2), pp. 215–35.
Clark, Alistair. 2014. "Investing in Electoral Integrity." In *Advancing Electoral Integrity*, edited by Pippa Norris, Richard Frank, and Ferran Matinez I. Coma, 165–88. New York: Oxford University Press.
———. 2015. "Public Administration and the Integrity of the Electoral Process in British Elections." *Public Administration*, 93, (1), pp. 86–102.
———. 2016. "Identifying the Determinants of Electoral Integrity and Administration in Advanced Democracies: The Case of Britain." *European Political Science Review*, 9, (03), pp. 471–92.
———. 2019. "The Cost of Democracy: The Determinants of Spending on the Public Administration of Elections." *International Political Science Review*, 40, (3), pp. 354–369.
Clark, Alistair, and Toby S. James. 2016a. *An Evaluation of Electoral Administration at the EU Referendum*. London: Electoral Commission.
———. 2016b. "Why Volunteer? The Motivations of Polling Station Workers on Election Day." In *Paper for the Political Studies Association Conference*. Brighton.
———. 2017. "Poll Workers." In *Election Watchdogs*, edited by Pippa Norris and Alessandro Nai. New York: Oxford University Press.
———. 2018. "The 2018 Local Elections Poll Worker Survey: New Evidence for Policy Makers." *Arena*, August 2018, pp. 13–5.
———. 2019. "Delivering Electoral Integrity Under Pressure: Local Government, Electoral Administration and the 2016 Brexit Referendum." *Working paper*.
Coles, Kimberley. 2007. *Democratic Designs: International Intervention and Electoral Practices in Postwar Bosnia-Herzegovina*. Ann Arbor: University of Michigan Press.
Collier, Andrew. 1994. *Critical Realism: an Introduction to Roy Bhaskar's Philosophy*. New York: Verso.
Collier, David. 2011. "Understanding Process Tracing." *PS: Political Science & Politics*, 44, (4), pp. 823–30.
Collier, David, Jody Laporte, and Jason Seawright. 2008. "Typologies: Forming Concepts and Creating Categorical Variables." In *Oxford Handbook of Political Methodology*, edited by Janet M. Box-Steffensmeier, Henry E. Brady, and David Collier. Oxford: Oxford University Press.
Commissioner of Elections Canada. 2018a. Charges/Outcomes. www.cef-cce.gc.ca/content.asp?section=charg&document=index&lang=e.
Commisioner of Elections Canada. 2018b. Compliance Agreements. Elections Canada, www.cef-cce.gc.ca/content.asp?section=agr&document=index&lang=e.
Committee on Standards in Public Life. 2007. *Eleventh Report of the Committee on Standards in Public Life: Review of The Electoral Commission*. London: HMSO.

Bibliography

Coppedge, Michael, John Gerring, Staffan I. Lindberg, Svend-Erik Skaaning, Jan Teorell, David Altman, Michael Bernhard, et al. 2017. *V-Dem [Country-Year/Country-Date] Dataset v7.1*. Gothenburg: V-DEM.

Coppedge, Michael, John Gerring, Staffan I. Lindberg, Jan Teorell, David Altman, Michael Bernhard, M. Steven Fish, Adam Glynn, Allen Hicken, Carl Henrik Knutsen, Kelly McMann, Daniel Pemstein, Megan Reif, Svend-Erik Skaaning, Jeffrey Staton, Eitan Tzelgov, Yi-ting Wang. 2014. *Varieties of Democracy: Codebook v3*: Varieties of Democracy (V-Dem) Project.

Cordenillio, Raul, and Andrew Ellis. 2012. *The Integrity of Elections: The Role of Regional Organizations*. Stockholm: International IDEA.

Council of Europe. 2008. *Application to Initiate a Monitoring Procedure to Investigate Electoral Fraud in the United Kingdom*. Strasbourg: Council of Europe.

Crossman, Richard Howard Stafford. 1976. *The Diaries of a Cabinet Minister, Vol. I, Minister for Housing*. London: Hamish Hamilton and Jonathan Cape.

Dacey, Paul. 2005. "Global Perspectives on Associations and Alliances: The Pacific Islands, Australia and New Zealand Electoral Administrators' (PIANZEA) network." Presentation to the Conference of Global Election Organizations and ACEEO General Assembly Meeting, September, Siofok, Hungary.

Dahl, R. 1971. *Polyarchy: Participation and Opposition*. New Haven, CT: Yale University Press.

———. 1989. *Democracy and Its Critics*. New Haven, CT: Yale University Press.

Dahl, Robert A. 1961. "The Behavioral Approach in Political Science: Epitaph for a Monument to a Successful Protest." *American Political Science Review*, 55, (4), pp. 763–72.

Dahl, Robert A. 1956. *A Preface to Democratic Theory*. Chicago, IL: Chicago University Press.

Davies, Jonathan S., Jørn Holm-Hansen, Vadim Kononenko, and Asbjørn Røiseland. 2016. "Network Governance in Russia: An Analytical Framework." *East European Politics*, 32, (2), pp. 131–47.

Davis-Roberts, Avery, and David J. Carroll. 2010. "Using International Law to Assess Elections." *Democratization*, 17, (3), pp. 416–41.

Debre, Maria J., and Lee Morgenbesser. 2017. "Out of the Shadows: Autocratic Regimes, Election Observation and Legitimation." *Contemporary Politics*, pp. 1–20.

Delery, John E. 1998. "Issues of Fit in Strategic Human Resource Management: Implications for Research." *Human Resource Management Review*, 8, (3), pp. 289–309.

Dempsey, Noel. 2017. *Elections: Turnout*. London: House of Commons Library.

Denver, David. 2015. "The Results: How Britain Voted." *Parliamentary Affairs*, 68, pp. 5–24.

Denver, David, Robert Johns, and Christopher Carmen. 2009. "Rejected Ballot Papers in the 2007 Scottish Parliament Election: The Voters' Perspective." *British Politics*, 4, (1), pp. 3–21.

Department, US State, and USAID. 2014. *Strategic Plan 2014–2017*. Washington, DC.

Deputy Prime Minister. 2011. *Individual Electoral Registration*. London: The Stationary Office.

Dess, Gregory G., and Jason D. Shaw. 2001. "Voluntary Turnover, Social Capital, and Organizational Performance." *Academy of Management Review*, 26, (3), pp. 446–56.

Dicey, A.V. 1959 [1885]. *Introduction to the Study of Law and the Constitution*. Eighth Edition. London: Macmillan.

Dolowitz, David, and David Marsh. 1996. "Who Learns What from Whom: A Review of the Policy Transfer Literature." *Political Studies*, 44, (2), pp. 343–57.

Donno, Daniela. 2013. *Defending Democratic Norms: International Actors and the Politics of Electoral Misconduct.* Oxford: Oxford University Press.

Dowding, K. 2001. "There Must Be End to Confusion: Policy Networks, Intellectual Fatigue, and the Need for Political Science Methods Courses in British Universities." *Political Studies*, 49, pp. 89–105.

Dowding, Keith. 1995. "Model or Metaphor? A Critical Review of the Policy Network Approach." *Political Studies*, 43, (1), pp. 136–58.

Downes, Siobhan. 2014. "Thousands Missing from Electoral Roll." *Stuff.co.nz*, 4 August. www.stuff.co.nz/national/politics/10344664/Thousands-missing-from-electoral-roll.

Dunleavy, Patrick, and Christopher Hood. 1994. "From Old Public Administration to New Public Management." *Public Money & Management*, 14, (3), pp. 9–16.

Durose, Catherine. 2009. "Front-line Workers and Local Knowledge: Neighbourhood Stories in Contemporary UK Local Governance." *Public Administration*, 87, (1), pp. 35–49.

———. 2011. "Revisiting Lipsky: Front-Line Work in UK Local Governance." *Political Studies*, 59, (4), pp. 978–95.

Duverger, M. 1951. *Les partis politiques*. Paris: Armand Colin.

ECF-SADC. 2008. *SADC Countries Electoral Profiles*. Botswana: ECF-SADC.

———. 2017. About ECF-SADC. www.ecfsadc.org/index.php/about-ecf-of-sadc.

ECI. 2011a. *491/Media/5/2011*. New Delhi: Electoral Commission of India.

———. 2011b. *Nigerian Election Commissioners Begin Study Visit to India*. New Delhi: Electoral Commission of India.

———. 2012. *Hand Book for Electoral Registration Officers*. Delhi: Electoral Commission of India.

———. 2013. *SVEEP Compendium of Instructions (March 2013)*. New Delhi: Electoral Commission of India.

———. 2016a. *Manual on Polling Stations*. New Delhi: Electoral Commission of India.

———. 2016b. *Proposed Electoral Reforms*. New Delhi: Electoral Commission of India.

———. 2017a. *Mainstreaming of Electoral Literacy through Educational Institutions, Organizations and Communities in India*. New Delhi: Electoral Commission of India.

———. 2017b. *Observer Handbook*. New Delhi: Election Commission of India.

———. 2018a. *Letter the Ministry of Law and Justice*. New Delhi: Electoral Commission of India.

———. 2018b. *Status Paper on Electronic Voting Machines (EVM)*. New Delhi: Electoral Commission of India.

ECNSW. 2010. *Report on the Feasibility of Providing "iVote" Remote Electronic Voting System*. Sydney: ECNSW.

———. 2016. Background. www.elections.nsw.gov.au/voting/ivote/background.

———. 2017. *Annual Report New South Wales Electoral Commission 2016–17*. Sydney: ECNSW.

———. 2018. About Us. http://www.elections.nsw.gov.au/about_us.

ECOWAS. 2018. http://observers.ecowas.int/EN/about.aspx.

EIDHR. 2011. *Delivering on Democracy*. Brussels: EIDHR.

EIP. 2018. Electoral Integrity Project: What We Do. www.electoralintegrityproject.com/what-we-do/.

EISA. 1997. *Annual Report 1996–1997*. Johannesburg: EISA.

———. 2018. About Us. https://www.eisa.org.za/about.php.

Elections Canada. 2011. *Report on the Evaluations of the 41st General Election of May 2, 2011*. Ottawa: Election Canada.

―――. 2015a. *Retrospective Report on the 42nd General Election of October 19, 2015*. Gatineau, QC: Chief Electoral Officer of Canada.

―――. 2015b. *Survey of Election Officers Following the 42nd Federal General Election*. Gatineau: Elections Canada.

―――. 2017a. Description of the National Register of Electors. www.elections.ca/content.aspx?section=vot&dir=reg/des&document=index&lang=e.

―――. 2017b. Elections Canada Quarterly Financial Report 2017–2018: For the Quarter Ended September 30. www.elections.ca/content.aspx?section=res&dir=rep/qua/qua2017b&document=index&lang=e.

―――. 2018a. Advisory Group for Disability Issues. www.elections.ca/content.aspx?section=abo&dir=adv/agdi&document=index&lang=e.

―――. 2018b. Complaints. www.cef-cce.gc.ca/content.asp?section=comp&document=index&lang=e#2.

―――. 2018c. Enforcing the Canada Elections Act. Elections Canada. www.cef-cce.gc.ca/content.asp?section=abo&dir=bck&document=index&lang=e.

―――. 2019. Ways to Vote. www.elections.ca/content.aspx?dir=vote&document=index&lang=e&section=vot.

Electoral Commission. 2003a. *The Shape of Elections to Come*. London: Electoral Commission.

―――. 2003b. *Voting for Change*. London: Electoral Commission.

―――. 2010a. *The Completeness and Accuracy of Electoral Registers in Great Britain*. London: Electoral Commission.

―――. 2010b. *Report on the Administration of the 2010 UK General Election*. London: Electoral Commission.

―――. 2011a. *Referendum on the Voting System for the UK Parliamentary Elections*. London: Electoral Commission.

―――. 2011b. *Report on the Referendum on the Law-Making Powers of the National Assembly for Wales*. Cardiff: Electoral Commission.

―――. 2012a. *Challenging Elections in the UK*. London: Electoral Commission.

―――. 2012b. *The Cost of Electoral Administration in Great Britain*. London: Electoral Commission.

―――. 2012c. *Costs of the May 2011 Referendum on the UK Parliamentary Voting System*. London: Electoral Commission.

―――. 2012d. *Elections, Referendums and Registration Working Group (ERRWG): Terms of Reference*. London: Electoral Commission.

―――. 2013. *Electoral Administration Bulletin #29–15 January 2013*. London: Electoral Commission.

―――. 2014a. *Electoral Fraud in the UK: Final Report and Recommendations*. London: Electoral Commission.

―――. 2014b. *The Quality of the 2014 Electoral Registers in Great Britain*. London: Electoral Commission.

―――. 2015. *The May 2015 UK Elections: Report on the Administration of the 7 May 2015 Elections*. London: Electoral Commission.

―――. 2016a. *Assessment of December 2015 Electoral Registers in Great Britain*. London: Electoral Commission.

―――. 2016b. *The December 2015 Electoral Registers in Great Britain*. London: Electoral Commission.

―――. 2016c. *Part A – Counting Officer Role and Responsibilities*. London: Electoral Commission.

———. 2017a. *Elections for Everyone: Experiences of People with Disabilities at the 8 June 2017 UK Parliamentary General Election.* London: Electoral Commission.
———. 2017b. *Electoral Commission Public Opinion Research – UK Parliament General Election – June 2017.* London: Electoral Commission.
———. 2017c. Public Opinion Surveys. www.electoralcommission.org.uk/our-work/our-research/public-opinion-surveys.
———. 2018a. *Analysis of Cases of Alleged Electoral Fraud in the UK in 2017.* London: Electoral Commission.
———. 2018b. Complaints. Electoral Comission, www.electoralcommission.org.uk/complaints.
———. 2018c. Winter Tracker 2016. www.electoralcommission.org.uk/our-work/our-research/public-opinion-surveys/winter-tracker.
Electoral Commission of India. 2018. About ECI. http://eci.nic.in/eci_main1/the_setup.aspx.
Electoral Management Board of Scotland. 2018. EMB Meeting. www.electionsscotland.info/info/5/electoral_management_board/89/emb_meetings_2017_-_agendas_and_action_notes.
Electoral Reform Society. 2011. *Missing Millions Individual Electoral Registration Roundtable.* London: Electoral Reform Society.
Elgot, Jessica. 2016. "Bite the Ballot Gets Tory Call to Help Boost EU Referendum Turnout." *Guardian.* www.theguardian.com/politics/2016/may/21/bite-the-ballot-gets-tory-call-to-help-boost-eu-referendum-turnout.
Elkins, Zachary, Tom Ginsburg, and James Melton. 2008. "The Comparative Constitutions Project: A Cross-national Historical Dataset of Written Constitutions." *Champaign, IL: University of Illinois at Urbana – Champaign.*
Elklit, Jorgen, and Andrew Reynolds. 2001. "Analysing the Impact of Election Administration on Democratic Politics." *Representation*, 38, (1), pp. 3–10.
———. 2002. "The Impact of Election Administration on the Legitimacy of Emerging Democracies: A New Comparative Politics Research Agenda." *Commonwealth & Comparative Politics*, 40, (2), pp. 86–119.
———. 2005a. "Judging Elections and Election Management Quality by Process." *Representation*, 41, (3), pp. 189–207.
Elklit, Jørgen, and Andrew Reynolds. 2005b. "A Framework for the Systematic Study of Election Quality." *Democratization*, 12, (2), pp. 147–62.
Elklit, Jorgen, and Palle Svensson. 1997. "What Makes Elections Free and Fair?" *Journal of Democracy*, 8, (3), pp. 32–46.
Ellis, Carolyn, Adams, Tony E., and Bochner, Arthur P. 2011. "Autoethnography: an overview." *Historical Social Research*, 36, (4), pp. 273–290.
Elving, Wim J.L. 2005. "The Role of Communication in Organisational Change." *Corporate Communications: An International Journal*, 10, (2), pp. 129–38.
EMN. 2018. About. www.electoralmanagement.com/about/.
ERRN. 2018. Overview. https://law.unimelb.edu.au/centres/errn/about/overview.
Essex University. 2014. *Impact Case Study: Reducing Electoral Corruption in New and Established Democracies.* London: HEFCE.
European Agency for Safety and Health at Work. 2014. *Calculating the Costs of Work-Related Stress and Psychosocial Risks – A Literature Review.* Bilbao and Brussels: European Agency for Safety and Health at Work.
European Union Election Observation Mission. 2008. *Kenya Final Report: General Elections 27 December 2007.* Brussels: European Union Election Observation Mission.
Evans, Mark. 2004. *Policy Transfer in Global Perspective.* Aldershot: Ashgate.

———. 2007. "The Art of Prescription – Theory and Practice in Public Administration." *Public Administration and Public Policy*, 22, (1), pp. 128–52.
Evans, Mark, and Jonathan Davies. 1999. "Understanding Policy Transfer: A Multi-Level, Multi-Disciplinary Perspective." *Public Administration*, 77, (2), pp. 361–85.
Farrell, David M. 2011. *Electoral Systems: A Comparative Introduction*. Basingstoke: Palgrave.
Fascone, Cristina, and Giovanni Piccirilli. 2017. "Towards a Ius Commune on Elections in Europe? The Role of the Code of Good Practice in Electoral Matters in "Harmonising" Electoral Rights." *Election Law Journal*, 16, (2), pp. 247–254.
Feldman, Martha S. 1989. *Order without Design: Information Production and Policy Making*. Stanford, CA: Stanford University Press.
Finer, H. 1932. *The Theory and Practice of Modern Government*. London: Methuen.
Finnemore, Martha, and Kathryn Sikkink. 2005. "International Norm Dynamics and Political Change." *International Organization*, 52, (4), pp. 887–917.
Flyvbjerg, Bent. 2006. "Five Misunderstandings about Case-Study Research." *Qualitative Inquiry*, 12, (2), pp. 219–45.
Friedrich, Carl Joachim. 1940. "Public Policy and the Nature of Administrative Responsibility." In *Public Policy*, edited by Carl Joachim Friedrich and E. S. Mason. Cambridge, MA: Harvard University Press.
Galbreath, David J. 2007. *The Organization for Security and Co-operation in Europe (OSCE)*. Abingdon and New York: Routledge.
Galbreath, David J., and Joanne McEvoy. 2013. "How Epistemic Communities Drive International Regimes: The Case of Minority Rights in Europe." *Journal of European Integration*, 35, (2), pp. 169–86.
Gallagher, Ian. 2010. "How £100k 'Modern Militant' Presided over Voting Shambles." *Daily Mail*, 9 May. www.dailymail.co.uk/news/election/article-1275445/Election-2010-Is-wonder-vote-shambles.html.
Garber, Larry. 1994. *Guidelines for International Election Observing*. Washington, DC: International Human Rights Law Group.
Garnett, Holly Ann. 2014. "Election Management Bodies, Confidence and Voter Turnout." In *Paper prepared for 2014 pre-IPSA Workshop*. Montreal, Canada.
———. 2017. "Open Election Management Bodies." In *Election Watchdogs*, edited by Pippa Norris and Alessandro Nai. New York: Oxford University Press.
———. 2018. "Electoral Management Roles and Responsibilities in Comparative Perspective." In *American Political Science Association Conference*. Boston, MA.
———. 2019a "Evaluating Online Registration: The Canadian Case." *Election Law Journal: Rules, Politics, and Policy*, 18, (1), pp. 78–92.
———. 2019b. "Evaluating Election Management Body Capacity." *International Political Science Review*. 40, (3), pp. 335–353.
Gay, Oonagh. 2010. *Responsibilities of Returning Officers*. London: House of Commons Library.
———. 2013. *The Office of the Deputy Prime Minister*. London: House of Commons Library.
Gelman, Andrew, and Jennifer Hill. 2006. *Data Analysis Using Regression and Multilevel/Hierarchical Models*. New York: Cambridge University Press.
George, Alexander L., and Andrew Bennett. 2005. *Case Studies and Theory Development in the Social Sciences*. Cambridge, MA: MIT Press.
Geoscience Australia. 2018. Area of Australia – States and Territories. www.ga.gov.au/scientific-topics/national-location-information/dimensions/area-of-australia-states-and-territories.

Gerken, Heather K. 2009a. *The Democracy Index: Why Our Election System Is Failing and How to Fix It.* Princeton, NJ: Princeton University Press.

Gerken, Heather K. 2009b. "Shortcuts to Reform." *Minnesota Law Review*, 93, pp. 1582–614.

Gerring, John. 2012. "Mere Description." *British Journal of Political Science*, 42, (4), pp. 721–46.

Glaser, Bonnie E., Karin Mac Donald, Iris Hui, and Bruce E. Cain. 2007. "The Front Lines of Democracy: Who Staffs Polling Places and Does It Matter?" *EARC Working Paper 0704*.

Global Commission on Elections, Democracy & Security. 2012. *Deepening Democracy: A Strategy for Improving the Integrity of Elections Worldwide*. Stockholm: International Institute for Democracy and Electoral Assistance.

Goerres, Achim, and Evelyn Funk. 2019. "Who Counts, Counts: An Exploratory Analysis of How Local Authorities Organise the Electoral Count in Germany's Most Populous State AU – Goerres, Achim." *German Politics*, 28, (1), pp. 61–79.

Goertz, Gary, and James Mahoney. 2012. *A Tale of Two Cultures: Qualitative and Quantitative Research in the Social Sciences*. Princeton, NJ: Princeton University Press.

Golds, Peter. 2014. "Election Fraud, the Scandal Goes On and On." *Conservative Home*, 14 January. https://www.conservativehome.com/localgovernment/2014/01/cllr-peter-golds-election-fraud-the-scandal-goes-on-and-on.htm.

———. 2015. "An Urgently Needed Plan of Action to Stop Electoral Fraud." *Conservative Home*. www.conservativehome.com/platform/2015/05/peter-golds-an-urgently-needed-plan-of-action-to-stop-electoral-fraud.html.

Goodin, Robert E. 1996. "Institutions and their Design." In *The Theory of Institutional Design*, edited by Robert E. Goodin. Cambridge: Cambridge University Press.

Goodwin-Gill, Guy S. 1998. *Codes of Conduct for Elections: A Study Prepared for the Inter-parliamentary Union*. Geneva: Inter-Parliamentary Union.

Gould-Williams, J., and R.B. Mohamed. 2010. "A Comparative Study of the Effects of 'Best Practice' HRM on Worker Outcomes in Malaysia and England local Government." *The International Journal of Human Resource Management*, 21, (5), pp. 653–75.

Gould-Williams, Julian S., Paul Bottomley, Tom Redman, Ed Snape, David J. Bishop, Thanawut Limpanitgul, and Ahmed Mohammed Sayed Mostafa. 2014. "Civic Duty and Employee Outcomes: Do High Commitment Human Resource Practices and Work Overload Matter?" *Public Administration*, 92, (4), pp. 937–53.

Greater Chennai Corporation. 2016. "Arrangements for Poll Briefing of Central Observers."

Greer, Scott L., Iain Wilson, Ellen Stewart, and Peter D. Donnelly. 2014. "'Democratizing' Public Services? Representation and Elections in the Scottish NHS." *Public Administration*, 92, (4), pp. 1090–105.

Griffeth, Rodger W., Peter W. Hom, and Stefan Gaertner. 2000. "A Meta-analysis of Antecedents and Correlates of Employee Turnover: Update, Moderator Tests, and Research Implications for the Next Millennium." *Journal of Management*, 26, (3), pp. 463–88.

Grömping, Max. 2017. "Domestic Monitors." In *Election Watchdogs: Transparency, Accountability and Integrity*, edited by Pippa Norris and Alessandro Nai. Oxford and New York: Oxford University Press.

Gronke, P., P. Miller, and E. Galances-Rosenbaum. 2007. "Early Voting and Turnout." *PS: Political Science and Politics*, 40, pp. 639–45.

Guess, George M. 2009. "Dysfunctional Decentralization: Electoral System Performance in Theory and Practice." Washington, DC: Centre for Democracy and Election Management.

Haas, Peter M. 1992. "Introduction: Epistemic Communities and International Policy Coordination." *International Organization*, 46, (1), pp. 1–35.

Hakanen, Jari J., Wilmar B. Schaufeli, and Kirsi Ahola. 2008. "The Job Demands-Resources Model: A Three-Year Cross-Lagged Study of Burnout, Depression, Commitment, and Work Engagement." *Work & Stress*, 22, (3), pp. 224–41.

Hale, Kathleen, and Christa Daryl Slaton. 2008. "Building Capacity in Election Administration: Local Responses to Complexity and Interdependence." *Public Administration Review*, 68, (5), pp. 839–49.

Hall, Thad E., J. Quin Monson, and Kelly D. Patterson. 2009. "The Human Dimension of Elections: How Poll Workers Shape Public Confidence in Elections." *Political Research Quarterly*, 62, (3), pp. 507–22.

Handley, Lisa, and Bernie Grofman. 2008. *Redistricting in Comparative Perspective*. Oxford and New York: Oxford University Press.

Hanf, Kenneth, and David Porter. 1978. "Local Networks of Manpower Training in the Federal Republic of Germany and Sweden." In *Interorganization Policy Making: Limits to Coordination and Central Control*, edited by Kenneth Hanf and Fritz W. Scharpf, 303–44. London: Sage.

Hansard. 2016a. *Debate Pack Number CDP-00131: Automatic Registration: UK Elections*. London: Houses of Parliament.

———. 2016b. *European Union Referendum: Young Voters*. London: Houses of Parliament.

———. 2016c. *Voter Registration*. London: Houses of Parliament.

Hardman, Helen, and Bruce Dickson. 2017. *Electoral Rights in Europe*. Abingdon and New York: Routledge.

Harris, Joseph P. 1934. *Election Administration in the U.S.* Menasha, WI: George Banta Publishing Company.

Harter, James K., Frank L. Schmidt, and Theodore L. Hayes. 2002. "Business-Unit-Level Relationship between Employee Satisfaction, Employee Engagement, and Business Outcomes: A Meta-Analysis." *Journal of Applied Psychology*, 87, (2), p. 268.

Hartlyn, Jonathan, Jennifer McCoy, and Thomas M. Mustillo. 2008. "Electoral Governance Matters: Explaining the Quality of Elections in Contemporary Latin America." *Comparative Political Studies*, 41, (1), pp. 73–98.

Harvey, David. 1999. "Time-space Compression and the Postmodern Condition." *Modernity: Critical Concepts*, 4, pp. 98–118.

Hasen, Richard L. 2012. *The Voting Wars: From Florida 2000 to the Next Election Meltdown*. Grand Rapids, MI: Yale University Press.

Hasnain, Zahid, and Nick Pierskalla Henryk. 2012. "Performance-Related Pay in the Public Sector: A Review of Theory and Evidence." *World Bank Policy Working Paper*, New York.

Hay, Colin. 1996. *Re-stating Social and Political Change*. Buckingham: Open University Press.

Hay, Colin. 2002. *Political Analysis*. Basingstoke: Palgrave Macmillan.

Heclo, Hugh. 1978. "Issue Networks and the Executive Establishment." In *The New American Political System*, edited by Anthony King, 87–124. Washington, DC: AEI.

Heclo, Hugh, and Aaron B. Wildavsky. 1974. *The Private Government of Public Money: Community and Policy inside British Politics*. London: Macmillan.

Held, David, and Mathias Koenig-Archibugi. 2004. "Introduction." *Government and Opposition*, 39, (2), pp. 125–31.

Held, David, and Anthony McGrew. 2000. *The Global Transformations Reader*. Vol. 94. Cambridge: Polity Press.

Held, David, Anthony McGrew, David Goldblatt, and Jonathan Perraton. 2013. *Global Transformations: Politics, Economics and Culture*. Cambridge: Polity Press.

Hermet, Guy, Richard Rose, and A. Roquie. 1978. *Elections without Choice*. New York: Macmillan.

Hernández-Huerta, Víctor A. 2017. "Judging Presidential Elections around the World: An Overview." *Election Law Journal: Rules, Politics, and Policy*, 16, (3), pp. 377–96.

Herron, Erik S., and Nazar Boyko. 2016. "Conducting Credible Elections under Threat: Results from a Survey of Election Administrators." *Election Law Journal*, 15, (4), pp. 285–301.

Herron, Erik S., Nazar Boyko, and Michael E. Thunberg. 2016. "Serving Two Masters: Professionalization versus Corruption in Ukraine's Election Administration." *Governance*, 30, (4), pp. 601–619.

———. 2017. "Serving Two Masters: Professionalization versus Corruption in Ukraine's Election Administration." *Governance*, 30, (4), pp. 601–19.

Hettne, Björn. 2005. "Beyond the 'New' Regionalism." *New Political Economy*, 10, (4), pp. 543–71.

Highton, Benjamin. 2006. "Long Lines, Voting Machine Availability, and Turnout: The Case of Franklin County, Ohio in the 2004 Presidential Election." *PS: Political Science & Politics*, 39, (01), pp. 65–8.

Hill, Sarah A. 2012. "Election Administration Finance in California Counties." *The American Review of Public Administration*, 42, (5), pp. 606–28.

Hirst, P., and G. Thompson. 1999. *Globalisation in Question*. Cambridge: Polity Press.

Hjern, Benny, and David O. Porter. 1981. "Implementation Structures: A New Unit of Administrative Analysis." *Organization Studies*, 2, (3), pp. 211–27.

HM Government. 2017. *Every Voice Matters: Building A Democracy That Works For Everyone*. London: Cabinet Office.

Hoffmann-Riem, Wolfgang. 2014. "The Venice Commission of the Council of Europe – Standards and Impact." *European Journal of International Law*, 25, (2), pp. 579–97.

Höglund, Kristine. 2009. "Electoral Violence in Conflict-ridden Societies: Concepts, Causes, and Consequences." *Terrorism and Political Violence*, 21, (3), pp. 412–27.

Home Affairs Committee. 1998. *The Fourth Report from the Home Affairs Committee, Session 1997–98, on Electoral Law and Administration*. London: HMSO.

Hood, C. 1995. "The "New Public Management" in the 1980s: Variations on a Theme." *Accounting, Organizations and Society*, 20, (2–3), pp. 93–109.

Hood, Christopher. 1991. "A Public Management for All Seasons?" *Public Administration*, 69, (Spring), pp. 3–19.

Hooghe, Liesbet, Ryan Bakker, Anna Brigevich, Catherine De Vries, Erica Edwards, Gary Marks, Jan Rovny, Marco Steenbergen, and Milada Vachudova. 2010. "Reliability and Validity of the 2002 and 2006 Chapel Hill Expert Surveys on Party Positioning." *European Journal of Political Research*, 49, (5), pp. 687–703.

Hooghe, Liesbet, Gary Marks, and Arjan H. Schakel. 2008. "Operationalizing Regional Authority: A Coding Scheme for 42 Countries, 1950–2006." *Regional & Federal Studies*, 18, (2–3), pp. 123–42.

Hope, Kempe Ronald. 2001. "The New Public Management: Context and Practice in Africa." *International Public Management Journal*, 4, (2), pp. 119–34.

Hope Not Hate. 2015. *Britain's Missing Voters: Individual Electoral Registration and the Boundary Review*. London: Hope Not Hate.

Howarth, George. 1999. *Final Report of the Working Party on Electoral Procedures*. London: Home Office.

HSE. 2013. *Stress and Psychological Disorders in Great Britain*. London: Health and Safety Executive.

Htun, Mala, and G. Bingham Jr. Powell. 2013. *Political Science, Electoral Rules, and Democratic Governance*. Washington, DC: American Political Science Association.

Huber, John, and Ronald Inglehart. 1995. "Expert Interpretations of Party Space and Party Locations in 42 Societies." *Party Politics*, 1, (1), pp. 73–111.

Hutchcroft, Paul D. 2001. "Centralization and Decentralization in Administration and Politics: Assessing Territorial Dimensions of Authority and Power." *Governance*, 14, (1), pp. 23–53.

Hyde, Susan D. 2007. "The Observer Effect in International Politics: Evidence from a Natural Experiment." *World Politics*, 60, (1), pp. 37–63.

———. 2011a. "Catch Us If You Can: Election Monitoring and International Norm Diffusion." *American Journal of Political Science*, 55, (2), pp. 356–69.

———. 2011b. *The Pseudo-Democrat's Dilemma: Why Election Observation Became an International Norm*. Ithaca, NY and London: Cornell University Press.

Hyde, Susan D., and Nikolay Marinov. 2012. "Which Elections Can Be Lost?" *Political Analysis*, 20, (2), pp. 191–210.

ICEO. 2012. 2nd Integrity Coalition for Election Observation Report. http://identity-center.org/en/node/124.

———. 2016. *Integrity Coalition for Elections Observation*. Jordan: Identity Center.

ICMUnlimited. 2016. *Winter Tracking Research 2016: Data Toplines with Narrative*. London: ICMUnlimited.

IEC. 2018. About Us. https://iec.jo/en/content/about-us.

———. undated. Organization Structure- Roles and Responsibilities. https://iec.jo/sites/default/files/IEC-%20About%20Us-%20Organization%20Structure.pdf.

IFES. 1990. *Republic of Haiti General Elections December 16, 1990*. Washington, DC: IFES.

IIDEA. 1995. *Declaration of the Founding Conference of the International Institute for Democracy and Electoral Assistance, February 27–28, 1995*. Stockholm: IIDEA.

———. 2014. *Master of Electoral Policy and Administration: An Overview of the Model Curriculum*. Stockholm: International IDEA.

IMF. 2014. *The Fiscal Transparency Code*. Washington, DC: International Monetary Fund.

INC. 2014. *Your Voice, Our Pledge*. New Delhi: Indian National Congress.

International IDEA. 2014. *Electoral Management Design: Revised Edition*. Stockholm: International IDEA.

———. 2018. *Voter Turnout Database*. Stockholm: International IDEA.

James, Toby, Leontine Loeber, Holly Ann Garnett, and Carolien van Ham. 2017. *Improving Electoral Management: The Organisational Determinants of Electoral Integrity – Research Proposal*. Bucharest: Venice Commission.

James, Toby S. 2010a. "Electoral Administration and Voter Turnout: Towards an International Public Policy Continuum." *Representation*, 45, (4), pp. 369–89.

———. 2010b. "Electoral Modernisation or Elite Statecraft? Electoral Administration in the U.K. 1997–2007." *British Politics*, 5, (2), pp. 179–201.

———. 2011a. "Fewer 'Costs,' More Votes? UK Innovations in Electoral Administration 2000–2007 and Their Effect on Voter Turnout." *Election Law Journal*, 10, (1), pp. 37–52.

———. 2011b. *The Impact of Individual Electoral Registration on British Elections – Evidence to the Political and Constitutional Reform Select Committee*. London: House of Commons.

———. 2011c. "Only in America? Executive Partisan Interest and the Politics of Election Administration in Ireland, the UK and USA." *Contemporary Politics*, 17, (3), pp. 219–40.

———. 2012. *Elite Statecraft and Election Administration: Bending the Rules of the Game*. Basingstoke: Palgrave Macmillan.

———. 2013. "Fixing Failures of U.K. Electoral Management." *Electoral Studies*, 32, (4), pp. 597–608.

---. 2014a. "Electoral Management in Britain." In *Advancing Electoral Integrity*, edited by Pippa Norris, Richard Frank, and Ferran Matinez I. Coma, 135–64. New York: Oxford University Press.

---. 2014b. "Postal Voting and Electoral Fraud: A Reply to Richard Mawrey QC." *Democratic Audit*, 12 March. www.democraticaudit.com/?p=3646.

---. 2014d. "United Kingdom – Electoral Governance in Transition." In *Electoral Management Design: The International IDEA Handbook*, edited by International IDEA. Stockholm: International IDEA.

---. 2015. "Individual Electoral Registration Still Needs a Lot of Work, If It Is Not to Be a Car Crash for British Democracy." *Democratic Audit*, 15 July. www.democraticaudit.com/?p=1036.

---. 2016a. "The Growing Electoral Registration Crisis." *Eastminster*, 24 February. www.ueapolitics.org/2016/02/24/2268/.

---. 2016b. "Neo-statecraft, Historical Institutionalism and Institutional Change." *Government and Opposition*, 51, (1), pp. 84–110.

---. 2017. "How Strong Is the Democratic Integrity of UK Elections? Are Turnout, Candidacies and Participation Maximised?" In *Democratic Audit 2017*, edited by Patrick Dunleavy. London: Democratic Audit.

---. 2019. "Better Workers, Better Elections? The Workforces of Electoral Management Bodies and Electoral Integrity." *International Political Science Review*, 40, (3), pp. 370–390.

James, Toby S., Bite the Ballot, and ClearView Research. 2016. *Getting the Missing Millions Back on the Electoral Register: A Vision for Voter Registration Reform in the UK*. London: All Parliamentary Party Group on Democratic Participation.

James, Toby S., and J. Buller. 2015a. "Statecraft: A Framework for Assessing Conservative Party Leaders." In *British Conservative Leaders*, edited by Charles Clarke, Toby S. James, Tim Bale, and Patrick Diamond. London: Biteback.

---. 2015b. "Statecraft: A Framework for Assessing Labour Party Leaders." In *British Labour Leaders*, edited by Charles Clarke and T. S. James, 15–32. London: Biteback.

James, Toby S., Holly Ann Garnett, Leontine Loeber, and Carolien Van Ham. 2019a. "Electoral Management and Organizational Determinants of Electoral Integrity." *International Political Science Review*, 40, (3), pp. 295–312.

---. 2019b. Electoral Management Survey 1.0. www.electoralmanagement.com

---. 2019. "Electoral Management and Organizational Determinants of Electoral Integrity." *International Political Science Review*, 40, (3), pp. 295–312.

James, Toby S., and T. Jervier. 2017a. "The Cost of Elections: The Effects of Public Sector Austerity on Electoral Integrity and Voter Engagement." *Public Money & Management*, 37, (7), pp. 461–8.

James, Toby S., and Tyrone Jervier. 2017b. *The Cost of Elections Funding Electoral Services in England and Wales*. London: ClearView Research.

---. 2018. "The Higher Education Impact Agenda, Scientific Realism and Policy Change: The Case of Electoral Integrity in Britain." *British Politics*, 13, (3), pp. 312–31.

Jeffrey, Jowwel. 2001. "The Venice Commission: Disseminating Democracy through Law." *Public Law*, p. 675.

Jessop, Bob. 1990. *State Theory: Putting the Capitalist State in Its Place*. Cambridge: Polity Press.

Jessop, Bob. 2000. "Governance Failure." In *The New Politics of British Local Governance*, edited by Gerry Stoker, 11–32. Basingstoke: Palgrave.

---. 2001. "Institutional Re(turns) and the Strategic – Relational Approach." *Environment and Planning A*, 33, pp. 1213–35.

———. 2005. "Critical Realism and the Strategic-Relational Approach." *New Formations*, (56), pp. 40–53.
Johnson, N. 1975. "The Place of Institutions in the Study of Politics." *Political Studies*, 23, pp. 271–83.
Joseph, Jonathan, and Colin Wight. 2010. *Scientific Realism and International Relations*. London: Springer.
JSCEA. 2017. *Third Interim Report on the Inquiry into the Conduct of the 2016 Federal Election: AEC Modernisation*. Canberra: Parliament of the Commonwealth of Australia.
JSCEM. 2005a. *Inquiry into the Administration of the 2003 Election and Related Matters*. Sydney: NSW Parliament.
———. 2005b. *Inquiry into the Administration of the 2003 Election and Related Matters: Report 2*. Sydney: NSW Parliament.
———. 2006. *Inquiry into Voter Enrolment*. Sydney: NSW Parliament.
———. 2008. *Administration of the 2007 NSW Election and Related Matters*. Sydney: NSW Parliament.
———. 2009. *2008 local Government Elections*. Sydney: NSW Parliament.
———. 2012. *Administration of the 2011 NSW Election and Related Matters*. Sydney: NSW Parliament.
———. 2014. *Inquiry into the 2012 Local Government Elections*. Sydney: NSW Parliament.
———. 2016. *Administration of the 2015 NSW Election and Related Matters*. Sydney: NSW Parliament.
Judge, Timothy A., Carl J. Thoresen, Joyce E. Bono, and Gregory K. Patton. 2001. "The Job Satisfaction – Job Performance Relationship: A Qualitative and Quantitative Review." *Psychological Bulletin*, 127, (3), pp. 376–407.
Karp, Jeffrey, Nai Alessandro, Miguel Angel Lara Otaola, and Pippa Norris. 2016. *ELECT*. Sydney: Electoral Integrity Project.
Karp, Jeffrey, Nai Alessandro, Miguel Angel Lara Otaola, and Pippa Norris. 2017. *Building Professional Electoral Management*. Sydney University: Electoral Integrity Project.
Kassim, Hussein. 1994. "Policy Networks, Networks and European Union Policy Making: A Sceptical View." *West European Politics*, 17, (4), pp. 15–27.
Kassim, Hussein, and Patrick Le Galès. 2010. "Exploring Governance in a Multi-Level Polity: A Policy Instruments Approach." *West European Politics*, 33, (1), pp. 1–21.
Kathi, Pradeep Chandra, and Terry L. Cooper. 2005. "Democratizing the Administrative State: Connecting Neighborhood Councils and City Agencies." *Public Administration Review*, 65, (5), pp. 559–67.
Keck, Margaret E., and Kathryn Sikkink. 1999. "Transnational Advocacy Networks in International and Regional Politics." *International Social Science Journal*, 51, (159), pp. 89–101.
———. 2014. *Activists beyond Borders: Advocacy Networks in International Politics*. Ithaca, NY: Cornell University Press.
Kelley, Judith. 2010. "Election Observers and Their Biases." *Journal of Democracy*, 21, (3), pp. 158–72.
———. 2011. *Data on International Election Monitoring: Three Global Datasets on Election Quality, Election Events and International Election Observation*. Ann Arbor, MI: Inter-University Consortium for Political and Social Research.
———. 2012. *Monitoring Democracy: When International Election Observation Works and Why It Often Fails*. Princeton, NJ: Princeton University Press.
Kelley, Judith, and Kiril Kolev. 2010. "Election Quality and International Observation 1975–2004: Two New Datasets." Available at SSRN 1694654.

Kelly, Norm. 2012. *Directions in Australian Electoral Reform: Professionalism and Partisanship in Electoral Management*. Canberra: Australian National University.
Kennedy, J. Ray. 1997. "Clif White's "Centre of Knowledge" a Reality." *Elections Today*, 7, Spring-Summer, (1–2).
Kenny, Christina. 2019. ""Women Are Not Ready to [Vote for] Their Own": Remaking Democracy, Making Citizens after the 2007 Post-election Violence in Kenya." In *Rethinking Transitional Gender Justice: Transformative Approaches in Post-Conflict Settings*, edited by Rita Shackel and Lucy Fiske. Basingstoke: Palgrave.
Keohane, Robert O., and Joseph S. Nye. 1974. "Transgovernmental Relations and International Organizations." *World Politics*, 27, (1), pp. 39–62.
Kerr, Andrew. 2016. "Scottish Election Chief Payouts Inquiry Begins." *BBC News*, 23 November. www.bbc.com/news/uk-scotland-38070879.
Keyssar, Alexander. 2009. *Right to Vote: The Contested History of Democracy in the United States*. Second Edition. New York: Basic Books.
Kickbusch, Jari. 2015. "Estonia E-votes Despite Cyber Security Concerns." *Baltic Times*, 3 April. www.baltictimes.com/estonia_e-votes_despite_cyber_security_concerns/.
Kidd, Richard. 2018. About Me. www.linkedin.com/in/richard-kidd-92017015/.
Kiewiet, D. Roderick, Thad E. Hall, R. Michael Alvarez, and Jonathan N. Katz. 2008. "Fraud or Failure? What Incident Reports Reveal about Election Anomalies and Irregularities." In *Election Fraud*, edited by R. Michael Alvarez, Thad E. Hall, and Susan D. Hyde. Washington, DC: Brookings Press.
King, Bridgett A. 2019. "Descriptive Representation in Election Administration: Poll Workers and Voter Confidence." *Election Law Journal*, 18, (1), pp. 16–30.
King, Bridgett A., and Norman E. Youngblood. 2016. "E-government in Alabama: An Analysis of County Voting and Election Website Content, Usability, Accessibility, and Mobile Readiness." *Government Information Quarterly*, 33, (4), pp. 715–26.
King, G., R. Keohane, and S. Verba. 1994. *Designing Social Enquiry: Scientific Inference in Qualitative Research*. Princeton, NJ: Princeton University Press.
Kinnie, Nicholas, Sue Hutchinson, John Purcell, Bruce Rayton, and Juani Swart. 2005. "Satisfaction with HR Practices and Commitment to the Organisation: Why One Size Does Not Fit All." *Human Resource Management Journal*, 15, (4), pp. 9–29.
Kinzer, Bruce L. 2007. *J.S. Mill Revisited: Biographical and Political Explorations* New York: Palgrave Macmillan US.
Kirkland, Christopher, and Matthew Wood. 2017. "Legitimacy and Legitimization in Low Turnout Ballots." *Government and Opposition*, 52, (3), pp. 511–31.
Kjaer, Anne Mette. 2011. "Rhodes' Contribution to Governance Theory: Praise, Criticism and the Future Governance Debate." *Public Administration*, 89, (1), pp. 101–13.
Klijn, Erik-Hans. 2008. "Governance and Governance Networks in Europe: An Assessment of Ten Years of Research on the Theme." *Public Management Review*, 10, (4), pp. 505–25.
Klijn, Erik-Hans, and Joop Koppenjan. 2012. "Governance Network Theory: Past, Present and Future." *Policy & Politics*, 40, (4), pp. 587–606.
Kousser, J. Morgan. 1974. *The Shaping of Southern Politics: Suffrage Restrictions and the Establishment of the One-Party South, 1880–1910*. New Haven, CT: Yale University Press.
Krimmer, Robert. 2018. Roots. www.e-voting.cc/en/about-us/roots/.
Krimmer, Robert, David Duenas-Cid, Iuliia Krivonosova, Priit Vinkel, and Arne Koitmae. 2018. "How Much Does an e-Vote Cost? Cost Comparison per Vote in Multichannel Elections." Paper presented to the E-Vote 2018, Third International Joint Conference E-Vote-ID 2018, October 2–5, Bregenz, Austria.

Bibliography

Labour Party. 2015. *Labour Party Manifesto 2015: Britain Can Be Better*. London: Labour Party.
Lai, Adrian. 2013. "Staff May Have Failed to Use Indelible Ink Properly: EC." *New Straits Times*, 13 May. www.nst.com.my/latest/staff-may-have-failed-to-use-indelible-ink-properly-ec-1.268714.
Larkins, David. 2017. "Elections Manitoba Recommends Doing Away with Enumeration." *Winnipig Sun*, 9 October. https://winnipegsun.com/2017/10/09/elections-manitoba-recommends-doing-away-with-enumeration/wcm/4a8f40c0-5d41-4fd6-b77d-006499eeac04.
Lascoumes, Pierre, and Patrick Le Gales. 2007. "Introduction: Understanding Public Policy through Its Instruments – From the Nature of Instruments to the Sociology of Public Policy Instrumentation." *Governance*, 20, (1), pp. 1–21.
Law Commission. 2011. *Eleventh Programme on Law Reform*. Vol. 330. London: Law Commission.
Law Commission of India. 2015. *Electoral Reforms*. New Delhi: Government of India.
Le Galès, Patrick. 2016. "Performance Measurement as a Policy Instrument." *Policy Studies*, 37, (6), pp. 508–20.
Leca, Bernard, and Philippe Naccache. 2006. "A Critical Realist Approach to Institutional Entrepreneurship." *Organisation*, 13, (5), pp. 627–51.
Lehoucq, F.E. 2003. "Electoral Fraud: Causes, Types and Consequences." *Annual Review of Political Science*, 6, pp. 233–56.
Lever, Annabelle. 2007. "Mill and the Secret Ballot: Beyond Coercion and Corruption." *Utilitas*, 19, (03), pp. 354–78.
Levitsky, Steven, and Lucan A. Way. 2002. "The Rise of Competitive Authoritarianism." *Journal of Democracy*, 13, (2).
———. 2010. *Competitive Authoritarianism: Hybrid Regimes after the Cold War*. Cambridge: Cambridge University Press.
Levitt, Justin. 2014. "A Comprehensive Investigation of Voter Impersonation Finds 31 Credible Incidents Out of One Billion Ballots Cast." *Wonkblog: The Washington Post*. www.washingtonpost.com/blogs/wonkblog/wp/2014/08/06/a-comprehensive-investigation-of-voter-impersonation-finds-31-credible-incidents-out-of-one-billion-ballots-cast/.
Lijphart, A. 1971. "Comparative Politics and the Comparative Method." *American Political Science Review*, 65, pp. 682–93.
Lijphart, Arend. 1996. "The Puzzle of Indian Democracy: A Consociational Interpretation." *American Political Science Review*, 90, (2), pp. 258–68.
———. 1999. *Patterns of Democracy*. London: Yale University Press.
Lindberg, Staffan. 2006. *Democracy and Elections in Africa*. Baltimore, MD: Johns Hopkins University Press.
Lindblom, C. 1977. *Politics and Markets: The World's Political-Economic Systems*. New York: Basic Books.
Lion, Patrick. 2013. "Electoral Commission Apologises for Loss of 1375 Votes in Knife-Edge WA Senate Recount, Orders Inquiry." *The Australian*, 31 October. www.theaustralian.com.au/news/electoral-commission-apologises-for-loss-of-1375-votes-in-knifeedge-wa-senate-recount-orders-inquiry/story-e6frg6n6-1226750581460?nk=84fbb0bdf2af4471b7dbd3f40474be25.
Lipsky, Michael. 1980. *Street Level Bureaucracy*. New York: Russell Sage Foundation.
Local Government and Communities Committee. 2017. *Payments to Returning Officers in Scotland*. Edinburgh: Scottish Parliamentary Corporate Body.

Local Government Association of NSW and Shires Association of NSW. 2009. *Inquiry into the 2008 Local Government Elections.* Sydney: NSW Parliament.

Locke, E. A. 1976. "The Nature and Causes of Job Satisfaction." In *Handbook of Industrial and Organizational Psychology*, edited by M. D. Dunnette, 1297–349. Chicago, IL: Rand McNally.

Loeber, Leontine. 2017. "The Use of Technology in the Election Process: Who Governs?" Paper presented at the Building Better Elections Workshop, Organised by the Electoral Management Research Network at the ECPR Conference, Oslo, September 2017.

López-Pinter, Rafael. 2000. *Electoral Management Bodies as Institutions of Governance.* Washington, DC: United Nations Development Programme.

López-Pintor, Rafael. 2000. *Electoral Management Bodies as Institutions of Governance.* Washington, DC: United Nations Development Programme.

López-Pintor, Rafael. 2011. "Assessing Electoral Fraud in New Democracies: A Basic Conceptual Framework." Washington DC International Foundation for Electoral Systems: White Paper Series Electoral Fraud.

López-Pintor, Rafael, and Jeff Fischer. 2005. *Cost of Registration and Elections (CORE) Project.* New York: UNDP.

Lowe, David. undated. Idea to Reality: NED at 30. http://www.ned.org/about/history/#1.

Lowe, Josh. 2017. "Netherlands Abandons Electronic Vote Counting Amid Hacking Fears." *Newsweek*, 3 June. www.newsweek.com/dutch-election-electronic-voting-hacking-russia-france-macron-trump-clinton-564198.

Lowenstein, Daniel Hays, Richard L. Hasen, and Daniel P. Tokaji. 2001. *Election Law*: Durham, NC: Carolina Academic Press.

Lowndes, V. 2002. "Institutionalism." In *Theory and Methods in Political Science*, edited by D. Marsh and G. Stoker, 90–108. Basingstoke: Palgrave Macmillan.

Lowndes, Vivien, Lawrence Pratchett, and Gerry Stoker. 2001. "Trends in Public Participation: Part 1 – Local Government Perspectives." *Public Administration*, 79, (1), pp. 205–22.

———. 2006. "Diagnosing and Remedying the Failings of Official Participation Schemes: The CLEAR Framework." *Social Policy and Society*, 5, (2), pp. 281–91.

Lührmann, Anna. 2018. "United Nations Electoral Assistance: More Than a Fig Leaf?" *International Political Science Review*, 40, (2), pp. 181–96.

Lukes, Steven. 2005. *Power: A Radical View.* Second Edition. Basingstoke and New York: Palgrave Macmillan.

Lynch, Colum. 2005. "U.S. Troops' Role in Iraqi Elections Criticized." *Washington Post*, 27 January. www.washingtonpost.com/wp-dyn/articles/A39753-2005Jan26.html??noredirect=on.

Mac Donald, Karin, and Bonnie Glaser. 2007. "From Locomotive to Bullet Train: Street-Level Implementation of E-Voting." Paper presented at the prepared for presentation at the 2007 Annual Meeting of the Midwest Political Science Association.

Mahoney, James. 2000. "Path Dependence in Historical Sociology." *Theory and Society*, 29, (4), pp. 507–48.

———. 2010. "After KKV: The New Methodology of Qualitative Research." *World Politics*, 62, (1), pp. 120–47.

Mahoney, James, and Kathleen Thelan. 2010. "A Theory of Gradual Institutional Change." In *Explaining Institutional Change: Ambiguity, Agency and Power*, edited by James Mahoney and Kathleen Thelan, 1–37. New York: Cambridge University Press.

Maley, Michael. 2013. "International Election Observation: Coming Ready or Not?" In Lecture in the Senate Occasional Lecture Series at Parliament House, Canberra, on 6 December.

Malinowski, Bronislaw. 1922. *Argonauts of the Western Pacific.* London: Routledge.

Bibliography

Marks, Gary, Liesbet Hooghe, and Arjan H. Schakel. 2008. "Patterns of Regional Authority." *Regional & Federal Studies*, 18, (2–3), pp. 167–81.

Marsh, David, and Martin Smith. 2000. "Understanding Policy Networks: towards a Dialectical Approach." *Political Studies*, 43, pp. 4–21.

Marsh, David, Martin J. Smith, and Dave Richards. 2003. "Unequal Plurality: Towards an Asymmetric Power Model of British Politics." *Government and Opposition*, 38, (3).

Martínez i Coma, Ferran, and Carolien van Ham. 2015. "Can Experts Judge Elections? Testing the Validity of Expert Judgments for Measuring Election Integrity." *European Journal of Political Research*, 54, (2), pp. 305–25.

Marx, Karl. 1888. *Ludwig Feuerbach and the End of Classical German Philosophy*. Die Neue Zeit.

Maslach, Christina, and Susan E. Jackson. 1981. "The Measurement of Experienced Burnout." *Journal of Organizational Behavior*, 2, (2), pp. 99–113.

Massicotte, Louis, Andre Blais, and Antoine Yoshinaka. 2004. *Establishing the Rules of the Game*. London and Toronto: Buffalo and University of Toronto Press.

McAnulla, Stuart. 2006. "Challenging the New Interpretivist Approach: Towards a Critical Realist Alternative." *British Politics*, 1, pp. 113–38.

MEDSL. 2018. *Elections Performance Index*. Boston, MA: MEDSL.

Meier, Kenneth J., Jeffrey L. Brudney, and John Bohte. 2002. *Applied Statistics for Public Administration*. Orlando, FL: Harcourt College.

Melton, Erin K., and Kenneth J. Meier. 2017. "For the Want of a Nail: The Interaction of Managerial Capacity and Human Resource Management on Organizational Performance." *Public Administration Review*, 77, (1), pp. 118–30.

Memo98. 2019. About Us. http://memo98.sk/p/o-nas.

Miiro, Hadija. undated. *Donor Strategy for Electoral Assistance*. Stockholm: International IDEA.

Minnite, Lorraine C. 2010. *The Myth of Voter Fraud*. Ithaca, NY: Cornell University Press.

Mockabee, Stephen T., J. Quin Monson, and Kelly D. Patterson. 2009. *Study of Poll Worker Training in Butler and Delaware Counties, Ohio for the March 4, 2008 presidential primary Election and in Bexar and Travis Counties, Texas for the November 4, 2008 General Election*. Center for the Study of Elections and Democracy.

Mohr, Z., Joellen V. Pope, M. Kropf, and M. Shepherd. 2019. "Strategic Spending: Does Politics Influence Election Administration Expenditure?" *American Journal of Political Science*, 63, (2), pp. 427–438.

Moravcsik, Andrew. 2004. "Is There a 'Democratic Deficit' in World Politics? A Framework for Analysis." *Government and Opposition*, 39, (2), pp. 336–63.

Moynihan, Donald P. 2004. "Building Secure Elections: E-Voting, Security, and Systems Theory." *Public Administration Review*, 64, (5), pp. 515–28.

Mozaffer, Shaheen. 2002. "Patterns of Electoral Governance in Africa's Emerging Democracies." *International Political Science Review*, 23, (1), pp. 85–101.

Mozaffer, Shaheen, and Andreas Schedler. 2002. "The Comparative Study of Electoral Governance – Introduction." *International Political Science Review*, 23, (1), pp. 5–27.

Munck, Gerardo L. 2009. *Measuring Democracy: A Bridge between Scholarship and Politics*. Baltimore, MD: Johns Hopkins Press.

Murray, Judy. 2012. "Absent Voting, the Help America Vote Act of 2002, and the American Overseas Voter: An Analysis of Policy Effectiveness and Political Participation." PhD Thesis, University of Newcastle.

NCHR. 2011. The Final Recommendations of the Jordanian Alliance for Reforming the Legal Framework of the Electoral Process. http://www.nchr.org.jo/.

———. 2017. The National Centre for Human Rights (NCHR) Launches the EU Support to Civil Society in Jordan Project. www.nchr.org.jo/User_Site/Site/View_Article.aspx?type=2&ID=1515.

Ndletyana, Mcebisi. 2015. *Institutionalising Democracy. The Story of the Electoral Commission of South Africa: 1993–2014*. Pretoria: Africa Institute of South Africa.

Nelson, Debra L., and Bret L. Simmons. 2003. "Eustress: An Elusive Construct, an Engaging Pursuit." *Emotional and Physiological Processes and Positive Intervention Strategies*, 3, 265–322.

Neufeld, Harry. 2013. *Compliance Review: Final Report and Recommendations*. Ottawa: Elections Canada.

Norris, Pippa. 2013a. "Does the World Agree about Standards of Electoral Integrity? Evidence for the Diffusion of Global Norms." *Electoral Studies*, 32, (4), pp. 576–88.

———. 2013b. "The New Research Agenda Studying Electoral Integrity." *Electoral Studies*, 32, (4), pp. 563–75.

———. 2014. *Why Electoral Integrity Matters*. New York: Cambridge University Press.

———. 2015a. "What Works? Evaluating Electoral Assistance." In *Introductory Paper for the Electoral Integrity Project pre-APSA Workshop on "What Works: Strengthening electoral integrity" on 2nd September 2015, Grand Hyatt, San Francisco*, edited by Pippa Norris.

———. 2015b. *Why Elections Fail*. New York: Cambridge University Press.

———. 2017a. 'It's Even Worse Than the News about North Carolina: American Elections Rank Last among All Western Democracies'. *LSE US Centre*: 8 January. http://blogs.lse.ac.uk/usappblog/2017/01/08/its-even-worse-than-the-news-about-north-carolina-american-elections-rank-last-among-all-western-democracies/.

———. 2017b. *Strengthening Electoral Integrity: The Pragmatic Case for Electoral Assistance* New York: Cambridge University Press.

———. 2017c. "Transparency in Electoral Governance." In *Watchdog Elections: Transparency, Accountability and Integrity*, edited by Pippa Norris and Alessandro Nai. New York: Oxford University Press.

———. 2019, "Conclusions; The New Research Agenda Studying Electoral Management." *International Political Science Review*, 40, (3), pp. 391–403.

Norris, Pippa, Nai Alessandro, Holly Ann Garnett, and Max Grömping. 2016. *Perceptions of Electoral Integrity: The 2016 American Presidential Election*. Boston, MA and Sydney: Electoral Integrity Project.

Norris, Pippa, Holly Ann Garnett, and Max Grömping. 2016. Electoral Integrity in all 50 US States, Ranked by Experts. www.vox.com/the-big-idea/2016/12/24/14074762/electoral-integrity-states-gerrymandering-voter-id.

Norris, Pippa, Ferran Martinez i Coma, and Max Grömping. 2015. *The Year in Elections, 2014*. Sydney and Harvard Universities: Electoral Integrity Project.

———. 2016. *The Year in Elections, 2015*. Sydney and Harvard Universities: Electoral Integrity Project.

Norris, Pippa, Ferran Martinez i Coma, Max Grömping, and Alessandro Nai. 2016. Perceptions of Electoral Integrity, Version 4.5.

Norris, Pippa, and Ronald Inglehart. 2018. *Cultural Backlash: The Rise of Authoritarianism-Populism*. New York: Cambridge University Press.

———. 2019. *Cultural Backlash: The Rise of Authoritarianism-Populism*. New York: Cambridge University Press.

Norris, Pippa, and Andrea Abel van Es. 2016. *Checkbook Elections?: Political Finance in Comparative Perspective*: Oxford: Oxford University Press.

Norris, Pippa, Thomas Wynter, and Sarah Cameron. 2018. Perceptions of Electoral Integrity, (PEI-6.0).
NSW Government. 2009. *Response to the Report of the Joint Standing Committee on Electoral Matters*. Sydney: NSW Government.
———. 2014. *Response to the Joint Standing Committee on Electoral Matters*. Sydney: NSW Government.
———. 2016. *Government Response to the Joint Standing Committee on Electoral Matters*. Sydney: NSW Government.
———. 2018. *Joint Standing Committee on Electoral Matters*. Sydney: NSW Government.
NSW Parliament. 2017. *Electoral Bill 2017: Second Reading Debate*. Sydney: NSW Parliament.
O'Leary, Cornelius. 1962. *Elimination of Corrupt Practices in British Elections, 1868–1911* London: Clarendon Press.
O'Malley, Eoin. 2007. "The Power of Prime Ministers: Results of an Expert Survey." *International Political Science Review*, 28, (1), pp. 7–27.
O'Toole Jr, Laurence J., and Kenneth J. Meier. 2003. "Plus ça Change: Public Management, Personnel Stability, and Organizational Performance." *Journal of Public Administration Research and Theory: J-PART*, pp. 43–64.
———. 2009. "The Human Side of Public Organizations: Contributions to Organizational Performance." *The American Review of Public Administration*, 39, (5), pp. 499–518.
O'Donnell, Guillermo A. 2001. "Democracy, Law, and Comparative Politics." *Studies in Comparative International Development*, 36, (1), pp. 7–36.
OAS. 1962. *Annual Report of the Secretary-General 1962*. Washington, DC: Pan American Union.
———. 2010. *Seventh Inter-American Meeting of Electoral Management Bodies: Increasing Access to Electoral Processes*. Washington, DC: OAS.
Oberschmidt, Randolf. 2001. "Ten Years of the Office for Democratic Institutions and Human Rights – An Interim Assessment." *Helsinki Monitor*, 12, pp. 277–90.
ODPM: Housing, Planning, Local Government and the Regions Committee. 2014. *Postal Voting: Seventh Report of Session 2003–04*. London: HMSO.
OECD. 2017. General Government Deficit. https://data.oecd.org/gga/general-government-deficit.htm.
OECD, and Eurostat. 2012. *Eurostat-OECD Methodological Manual on Purchasing Power Parities (2012 Edition)*. Luxembourg: European Commission.
Office for Democratic Institutions and Human Rights. 2005. *United Kingdom of Great Britain and Northern Ireland General Election 2005 Assessment Mission Report*. Warsaw: OSCE/ODIHR.
Office of the Deputy Prime Minister. 2004. *Seventh Report of Session 2003–04: Postal Voting* London: ODPM: Housing, Planning, Local Government and the Regions Committee.
Office of the Deputy Prime Minister: Housing, Planning, Local Government and the Regions 2005. *Joint First Report*. London: HMSO. https://publications.parliament.uk/pa/cm200405/cmselect/cmconst/243/24302.htm vols.
Ohanyan, Anna. 2012. "Network Institutionalism and NGO studies." *International Studies Perspectives*, 13, (4), pp. 366–89.
Ohmae, K. 1990. *The Borderless World*. London: Collins.
Orozco-Henríquez, J. 2010. *Electoral Justice: The International IDEA Handbook, International Institute for Democracy and Electoral Assistance*. International IDEA: Stockholm.
Osbourne, D., and T. Gabler. 1992. *Reinventing Government* Reading, MA: Addison-Wesley.
OSCE. 1975. *Helsinki Final Act*. Helsinki: OSCE.
———. 2010. *Election Observation Handbook*. Helsinki: OCSE.

———. 2015a. *Canada Parliamentary Elections, 19 October 2015: OSCE/ODIHR Election Assessment Mission Final Report*. Warsaw: OSCE/ODIHR.

———. 2015b. *Recommendation of the Council on Budgetary Governance*. Vienna: OSCE.

OSCE/ODIHR. 2015a. *OSCE/ODIHR Election Assessment Mission Final Report: Canada Parliamentary Elections, 19 October 2015*. Warsaw: OSCE.

———. 2015b. *United Kingdom of Great Britain and Northern Ireland General Election, 7 May 2015*. Warsaw: OSCE/ODIHR.

———. 2016. *Handbook on the Follow-up of Electoral Recommendations*. Warsaw: OSCE/ODIHR.

Ostrom, Elinor. 1973. "The Need for Multiple Indicators of Measuring the Output of Public Agencies." *Policy Studies Journal*, 2, pp. 85–91.

Pal, Michael. 2016. "Electoral Management Bodies as a Fourth Branch of Government." *Review of Constitutional Studies*, 21, (1).

———. 2017. "Canadian Election Administration on Trial: 'Robocalls', Opitz and Disputed Elections in the Courts." *King's Law Journal*, 28, (2), pp. 324–42.

Palacio, Myrtle. 2003. *The Association of Caribbean Electoral Organization (ACEO)*. Mexico City: Global Electoral Organisation Network.

Parkinson, John. 2001. "Who Knows Best? The Creation of the Citizen-initiated Referendum in New Zealand." *Government and Opposition*, 36, (3), pp. 403–22.

———. 2004. "Why Deliberate? The Encounter between Deliberation and New Public Managers." *Public Administration*, 82, (2), pp. 377–95.

Parks, Roger B. 1984. "Linking Objective and Subjective Measures of Performance." *Public Administration Review of International Political Economy*, 44, pp. 118–27.

Parliament of Canada. 2018. Participate Parliament of Canada. www.ourcommons.ca/en/participate.

Pastor, Robert A. 1999a. "A Brief History of Electoral Commission." In *The Self Restraining State: Power and Accountability in New Democracies*, edited by Andreas Schedler, Larry Diamond, and Marc F. Plattner. Boulder: Rienner.

———. 1999b. "The Role of Electoral Administration in Democratic Transitions: Implications for Policy and Research." *Democratization*, 6, (4), pp. 1–27.

———. 2004. "America Observed." *The American Prospect*, 20 December. http://prospect.org/article/america-observed.

———. 2006. "The US Administration of Elections: Decentralized to the Point of Being Dysfunctional." In *Electoral Management Design: The International IDEA Handbook*, edited by Alan Wall, Andrew Ellis, Ayman Ayoub, Carl W. Dundas, Joram Rukambe, and Sara Staino, 273–6. Stockholm: International IDEA.

Patomäki, Heikki, and Colin Wight. 2000. "After Postpositivism? The Promises of Critical Realism." *International Studies Quarterly*, 44, (2), pp. 213–37.

Patron, Russel. 2018. "4,000 People Unable to Cast Ballot in Local Elections Due to "Chaotic" Voter ID Scheme." *iNews*, 4 May.

Pawson, Ray, and Nick Tilley. 1997. *Realistic Evaluation*. London: Sage.

Pawson, Ray. 2006. *Evidence-Based Policy*. London: Sage.

Penrose, John. 2015. *Vision for Electoral Registration: Speech by John Penrose*. Policy Exchange: Cabinet Office.

Perrow, Charles. 1984. *Normal Accidents: Living with High-Risk Technologies*. New York: Basic Books.

Perry, James L., and Lois Recascino Wise. 1990. "The Motivational Bases of Public Service." *Public Administration Review*, 50, (3), pp. 367–73.

Peters, B. Guy. 1999. *Institutional Theory in Political Science: The 'New Institutionalism'* London: Pinter.

———. 2005. *Institutional Theory in Political Science: The 'New Institutionalism*. Second Edition. London & New York: Continuum.
Pevehouse, Jon, and Inken von Borzyskowski. 2016. "International Organisations in World Politics." In *The Oxford Handbook of International Organizations*, edited by Jacob Katz Cogan, Ian Hurd, and Ian Johnstone. New York: Oxford University Press.
Pfeffer, Jeffrey. 1998. *The Human Equation: Building Profits by Putting People First*. Cambridge, MA: Harvard Business Press.
Phadnis, Ashwini. 2016. "EC Cancels Polls to Aravakurichi, Thanjavur Assembly Seats." *The Hindu*, 28 May. www.thehindubusinessline.com/news/ec-cancels-polls-to-aravakurichi-thanjavur-assembly-seats/article8659939.ece.
Pickles, Eric. 2016. *Securing the Ballot: Report of Sir Eric Pickles' Review into Electoral Fraud*. London.
Pinto-Duschinsky, Michael. 2014. *Electoral Commission*. London: Policy Exchange.
Piven, Frances Fox, and Richard A. Cloward. 1988. *Why Americans Don't Vote*. New York: Pantheon Books.
———. 2000. *Why Americans Still Don't Vote*. New York: Beacon Press.
Political and Constitutional Reform Committee. 2011. *Individual Electoral Registration and Electoral Administration*. London: House of Commons.
Poon, June M.L. 2004. "Effects of Performance Appraisal Politics on Job Satisfaction and Turnover Intention." *Personnel Review*, 33, (3), pp. 322–34.
Popper, Karl. 1959. *The Logic of Scientific Discovery*. London: Hutchinson.
Pressman, Jeffrey L., and Aaron Wildavsky. 1973. *Implementation*. Berkeley: University of California Press.
Przeworski, Adam. 1999. "Minimalist Conception of Democracy: A Defence." In *Democracy's Value*, edited by Ian Shapiro and Casiano Hacker-Cordon. Cambridge: Cambridge University Press. [Reprinted in Robert A. Dahl et al (eds) The Democracy Sourcebook].
PTI. 2018. "Association for Democratic Reforms Report: 48 MP, MLAs Have Declared Cases of Crime against Women." *Indian Express*, April 19.
Pugh, Martin. 1978. *Electoral Reform in War and Peace 1906–18*. London: Routledge.
Putnam, H., and J. Conant. 1990. *Realism with a Human Face*. Cambridge, MA: Harvard University Press.
Quraishi, S.Y. 2014. *An Undocumented Wonder: The Great Indian Election*. New Delhi: Rupa Publications India.
QuraishiPatidar, Vijay, Ajay Jha, and S.Y. Quraishi. 2014. "India: The Embodiment of EMB Independence." In *Electoral Management Design: Thee International IDEA Handbook*, edited by Helena Catt, Andrew Ellis, Michael Maley, Alan Wall, and Peter Wolf. Stockholm: International IDEA.
Qvortrup, Matt. 2005. *A Comparative Study of Referendums: Government by the People*. Manchester: Manchester University Press.
Radcliffe-Brown, Alfred Reginald. 1964. *The Andaman Islanders*. New York: Free Press.
Radcliffe, Mark. 2018. Mark Radcliffe: Public Linkedin Profile. www.linkedin.com/in/markradcliffe/.
Rae, Douglas W. 1967. *The Political Consequences of Electoral Laws*. New Haven, CT: Yale University Press.
Ramesh, R. 2011. "Historical Perspectives of the Electoral Reforms in India." *Proceedings of the Indian History Congress*, 72, pp. 1325–36.
Ramia, Gaby, Roger Patulny, Greg Marston, and Kyla Cassells. 2017. "The Relationship between Governance Networks and Social Networks: Progress, Problems and Prospects." *Political Studies Review*, p. 1478929917713952.

Raynor, Gordon, and Holly Watt. 2010. "General Election 2010: Electoral Commission Accused Over 'Third world' Ballot." *The Telegraph*, 7 May. www.telegraph.co.uk/news/election-2010/7689014/General-Election-2010-Electoral-Commission-accused-over-third-world-ballot.html.

Reif, Linda C. 2000. "Building Democratic Institutions: The Role of National Human Rights Institutions in Good Governance and Human Rights Protection." *Harvard Human Rights Journal*, 13, pp. 1–289.

Renwick, Alan. 2010. *The Politics of Electoral Reform: Changing the Rules of Democracy*. Cambridge: Cambridge University Press.

Reske-Nielsen, Finn. 2017. *Independent Final Evaluation of the EU-UNDP project: Support to the Electoral Cycle in Jordan: 2012–2017*. New York: UNDP.

Rhodes, R. A. W. 1994. "The Hollowing Out of the State – The Changing Nature of the Public-Service in Britain." *Political Quarterly*, 65, (2), pp. 138–51.

———. 2011. *Everyday Life in British Government*. Oxford: Oxford University Press.

Rhodes, R. A. W., and David Marsh. 1992. "New Directions in the Study of Policy Networks." *European Journal of Political Research*, 21, (1–2), pp. 181–205.

Rhodes, R.A.W. 1986. *The National World of Local Government*. London: Unwin Hyman.

———. 1997. *Understanding Governance*. Buckingham: Open University Press.

Rhodes, RAW. 2006. "Policy Network Analysis." In *The Oxford Handbook of Public Policy*, edited by M. Moran, M. Rein, and R.E. Goodin. Oxford: Oxford University Press.

Rhodes, R.A.W. 1990. "Policy Networks a British Perspective." *Journal of Theoretical Politics*, 2, (3), pp. 293–317.

Richard, Pierre J., Timothy M. Devinney, George S. Yip, and Gerry Johnson. 2009. "Measuring Organizational Performance: Towards Methodological Best Practice." *Journal of Management*, 35, (3), pp. 718–804.

Ripley, Randall B., and Grace A. Franklin. 1984. *Congress, the Bureaucracy, and Public Policy*. Homewood, IL: Dorsey Press.

Rogers, David, and David Allred Whetten. 1982. *Interorganizational Coordination: Theory, Research, and Implementation*. Ames, IA: Iowa State Press.

Rogin, Josh. 2017. "State Department Considers Scrubbing Democracy Promotion from Its Mission." *Washington Post*.

Rumble, Carol. 2008. *Submission to the Inquiry into Administration of the 2007 NSW Election and Related Matters*. Sydney: NSW Parliament.

Saari, Lise M., and Timothy A. Judge. 2004. "Employee Attitudes and Job Satisfaction." *Human Resource Management*, 43, (4), pp. 395–407.

Sabatier, Paul A. 1986. "Top-Down and Bottom-Up Approaches to Implementation Research: A Critical Analysis and Suggested Synthesis." *Journal of Public Policy*, 6, (01), pp. 21–48.

SADC. 2019. SADC Overview. www.sadc.int/about-sadc/overview/.

Sanders, David. 2010. "Behavioural Analysis." In *Theory and Method in Political Science*, edited by David Marsh and Gerry Stoker. Basingstoke: Palgrave Macmillan.

Savigny, Heather. 2007. "Ontology and Epistemology in Political Marketing Keeping It Real?. " *Journal of Political Marketing*, 6, (2 and 3), pp. 33–47.

Sayer, Andrew. 1984. *Method in Social Sciences*. First Edition. Sussex: Hutchinson University Library.

———. 2000. *Realism and Social Science*. London: Sage.

———. 2010. *Method in Social Sciences*. Revised Second Edition. Abingdon: Routledge.

Schatz, Edward. 2009. "Ethnographic Immersion and the Study of Politics." In *Political Ethnography: What Immersion Contributes to the Study of Power*, edited by Edward Schatz. Chicago, IL and London: University of Chicago Press.

Schedler, Andreas. 2002. "The menu of manipulation." *Journal of Democracy*, 13, (2), pp. 36–50.

Schedler, Andreas. 2012. "Judgment and Measurement in Political Science." *Perspectives on Politics*, 10, (1), pp. 21–36.

———. 2013. *The Politics of Uncertainty: Sustaining and Subverting Electoral Authoritarianism*. Oxford: Oxford University Press.

Schlozman, Daniel, and Ian Yohai. 2008. "How Initiatives Don't Always Make Citizens: Ballot Initiatives in the American States, 1978–2004." *Political Behavior*, 30, (4), pp. 469–89.

Schmeets, Johannes Josephus Gerardus. 2002. *Vrije en eerlijke verkiezingen in de OVSE-regio?: De ontwikkeling van een meetinstrument*: [Sl: sn].

Schmidt, Adam. 2010. "Indonesia's 2009 Elections: Performance Challenges and Negative Precedents." In *Problems of Democratisation in Indonesia: Elections, Institutions and Society*, edited by Edward Aspinall and Marcus Mietzner, 100–21. Canberra: Australian National University Press.

Schumpeter, J. 2003[1942]. *Capitalism, Socialism, Democracy*. New York: Harper.

Schwedler, Jillian. 2003. "More Than a Mob: The Dynamics of Political Demonstrations in Jordan." *Middle East Report*, (226), pp. 18–23.

Select Committee on Political and Constitutional Reform. 2011. *Individual Electoral Registration and Electoral Administration*. London: The Stationery Office.

———. 2014. *Voter Engagement in the UK*. London: The Stationery Office.

———. 2015. *Voter Engagement in the UK: Follow Up*. London: The Stationery Office.

Select Committee on Political and Constitutional Reform. 2015. *Voter Engagement in the UK*. London: The Stationery Office Limited.

Senecal, Jeanette. 2007. "Election Day Front Line: Poll Workers." *The National Voter*, June 2007, pp. 6–7.

Seymour, Charles. 1915 [1970]. *Electoral Reform in England and Wales*. London: David & Charles Reprints.

Sharma, Jyoti, and Rajib Lochan Dhar. 2016. "Factors Influencing Job Performance of Nursing Staff: Mediating Role of Affective Commitment." *Personnel Review*, 45, (1), pp. 161–82.

Shore, Lynn M., Lois E. Tetrick, Patricia Lynch, and Kevin Barksdale. 2006. "Social and Economic Exchange: Construct Development and Validation." *Journal of Applied Social Psychology*, 36, (4), pp. 837–67.

SIGI. 2018. Building Capacity. http://sigi-jordan.org/en/?page_id=770.

Simon, H.A. 1945. *Administrative Behaviour*. New York: Free Press.

Simpser, Alberto. 2013. *Why Governments and Parties Manipulate Elections: Theory, Practice, and Implications*. New York: Cambridge University Press.

Sjoberg, Fredrik M. 2014. "Autocratic Adaptation: The Strategic Use of Transparency and the Persistence of Election Fraud." *Electoral Studies*, 33, pp. 233–45.

Slaughter, Anne-Marie. 2009. *A New World Order*: Princeton: Princeton University Press.

Sloam, James and Matt Hen. 2018. *Youthquake 2017: The Rise of Young Cosmopolitans in Britain*. Basingstoke: Palgrave.

Smart, Christopher. 2015. "The Hamlet of Wallsburg Hasn't Forgotten the 2013 Election It Didn't Hold." *Salt Lake Tribune*, August 31. http://archive.sltrib.com/article.php?id=2870856&itype=CMSID#gallery-carousel-446996.

Smartmatic. 2018. Our History. www.smartmatic.com/about/our-history/.

Smets, Kaat, and Carolien van Ham. 2013. "The Embarrassment of Riches? A Meta-Analysis of Individual-Level Research on Voter Turnout." *Electoral Studies*, 32, (2), pp. 344–59.

Smith, Cat. 2018a. "Despite Shameful Tory Rhetoric, Voter ID Pilots Proved Nothing." *The Times*, 15 June.
Smith, Chloe. 2018b. "Labour's Scaremongering Was Wrong, Voter ID Really Did Work." *The Times*, 7 June.
Smith, M.J. 1999. *The Core Executive in Britain*. London: Palgrave Macmillan.
Snyder, Michael R. 2013. "For Want of a Credible Voter Registry: Do Problems in Voter Registration Increase the Likelihood of Electoral Violence?" *Josef Korbel Journal of Advanced International Studies*, Summer, pp. 27–58.
Sobolewska, Maria, Stuart Wilks-Heeg, Eleanor Hill, and Magna Borkowska. 2015. *Understanding Electoral Fraud Vulnerability in Pakistani and Bangladeshi Origin Communities in England. A View of Local Political Activists*. Manchester and Liverpool: Centre on Dynamics of Ethnicity.
Standing Committee on Procedure and House Affairs. 2017. *BILL C-23: An Act to Amend the Canada*. Ottawa: Parliament of Canada.
Stewart III, Charles. 2006. "Residual Vote in the 2004 Election." *Election Law Journal*, 5, (2), pp. 158–69.
Stewart, John. 2006. "A Banana Republic? The Investigation into Electoral Fraud by the Birmingham Election Court." *Parliamentary Affairs*, 59, (4), pp. 654–67.
Stone, Diane. 2008. "Global Public Policy, Transnational Policy Communities, and Their Networks." *Policy Studies Journal*, 36, (1), pp. 19–38.
Strange, Susan. 1996. *The Retreat of the State: The Diffusion of Power in the World Economy, Cambridge Studies in International Relations*. Cambridge: Cambridge University Press.
Suiter, Jane, Farrell, David M., and Eoin O'Malley. 2014. "When Do Deliberative Citizens Change Their Opinions? Evidence from the Irish Citizens' Assembly." *International Political Science Review*, 37, (2), pp. 198–212.
Sukma, Rizal. 2009. "Indonesian Politics in 2009: Defective Elections, Resilient Democracy." *Bulletin of Indonesian Economic Studies*, 45, (3), pp. 317–36.
Superior Court of Justice. 2012. Wrzesnewskyj v. Attorney General (Canada), 2012 ONSC 2873.
Szolnoki, Zsolt. 2016. "The First 25 Years – The ACEEEO's History." In *ACEEEO 25 – Development of Electoral Systems in Central and Eastern Europe Since 1991*, edited by Zsolt Szolnoki, Márta Dezső, and Zoltán Pozsár-Szentmiklósy, 7–23. Budapest: Association of European Election Officials.
Tapsoba, Moussa Michel. 2005. "Experience of the Association of African Election Authorities (A.A.E.A.) in Terms of Installing Network." www.aceeeo.org/sites/default/files/PDF/presentation_of_conference/2005/Tapsoba_angol.pdf.
Teague, Vanessa, and Rajeev Gore. 2015. *Inquiry into the 2015 NSW State Election*. Sydney: NSW Parliament.
The Commonwealth. 2017. The Commonwealth Electoral Network." http://thecommon-wealth.org/commonwealth-electoral-network.
The Democracy Program. 1983. *The Commitment to Democracy: A Bipartisan Approach*. Washington, DC: IFES.
The Hindu. 2010. "Swamy for Expert Panel on Secure EVMs." *The Hindu*, 13 February.
Throup, David W. 2008. "The Count." *Journal of Eastern African Studies*, 2, (2), pp. 290–304.
Toffoli, José Antonio Dias. 2016. "Brazilian 20-years Experience in E-voting." In 13th European Conference of Electoral Management Bodies, Bucharest, 15 April.
Truman, David Bicknell. 1951. *The Implications of Political Behavior Research*. New York: Social Science Research Council.

Tuccinardi, Domenico. 2014. *International Obligations for Elections*. Stockholm: International IDEA.
Tzeng, Huey-Ming. 2002. "The Influence of Nurses' Working Motivation and Job Satisfaction on Intention to Quit: An Empirical Investigation in Taiwan." *International Journal of Nursing Studies*, 39, (8), pp. 867–78.
U.N. Electoral Assistance Division et al. 2005. *Declaration of Principles for International Election Observation and Code of Conduct for International Election Observers*. New York: United Nations.
U.S. Commission on Civil Rights. 2001. *Voting Irregularities in Florida during the 2000 Presidential Election*. Washington, DC: U.S. Commission on Civil Rights.
Uggen, C., and J. Manza. 2002. "Democratic Contraction? Political Consequences of Felon Disenfranchisement in the United States." *American Sociological Review*, 67, (6), pp. 777–803.
Ugues, Antonio. 2010. "Citizens' Views on Electoral Governance in Mexico." *Journal of Elections, Public Opinion & Parties*, 20, (4), pp. 495–527.
———. 2014. "Electoral Management in Central America." In *Advancing Electoral Integrity*, edited by Pippa Norris, Richard W. Frank, and Ferran Martinez i Coma, 118–34. New York: Oxford University Press.
UN. 2019. Types of Assistance. https://dppa.un.org/en/elections#Types%20of%20Assistance.
UN General Assembly. 1948. *The Universal Declaration of Human Rights*. New York: UN General Assembly.
United Nations. 1991. *Enhancing the Effectiveness of the Principle of Periodic and Genuine Elections: Report of the Secretary-General*. New York: United Nations.
———. 1994. *A/49/675*. New York: United Nations General Assembly.
United Nations Secretary-General. 2015. *Strengthening the Role of the United Nations in Enhancing the Effectiveness of the Principle of Periodic and Genuine Elections and the Promotion of Democratization: Report of the Secretary-General*. New York: United Nations General Assembly.
University of Liverpool. 2014. The Integrity of UK Elections: Electoral Malpractice and the State of the Electoral Registers. https://re.ukri.org/research/ref-impact/.
US Electoral Assistance Commission. 2014. *The 2014 EAC Election Administration and Voting Survey Comprehensive Report: A Report to the 114th Congress*. Silver Spring, MD: US Electoral Assistance Commission.
van Biezen, I. 2004. "Political Parties as Public Utilities." *Party Politics*, 10, (6), pp. 701–22.
Van de Walle, Nicolas. 2003. "Presidentialism and Clientelism in Africas Emerging Party Systems." *The Journal of Modern African Studies*, 41, (2), pp. 297–321.
van Ham, Carolien. 2014. "Getting Elections Right? Measuring Electoral Integrity." *Democratization*, pp. 1–24.
van Ham, Carolien, and Staffan Lindberg. 2015. "When Guardians Matter Most: Exploring the Conditions under Which Electoral Management Body Institutional Design Affects Election Integrity." *Irish Political Studies*, 30, (4), pp. 454–81.
van Ham, Carolien and Garnett, Holly Ann. 2019. "Building impartial electoral management? Institutional design, independence and electoral integrity." *International Political Science Review*, 40, (3), pp. 313–334.
Venice Commission. 2002. *Code of Good Practice in Electoral Matters: Guidelines and Explanatory Report*. Strasbourg: Venice Commission.
———. 2015. Supporting Co-operation between Electoral Bodies in the Arab World. www.venice.coe.int/WebForms/pages/?p=03_05_Arab_EMBs&lang=EN.

———. 2017a. *14th European Conference of Electoral Management Bodies: Operational Electoral Management Bodies for Democratic Elections*. Strasbourg and St Petersburg: Venice Commission.
———. 2017b. "The Commission's Activities." www.venice.coe.int/WebForms/pages/?p=01_activities&lang=EN.
———. 2017c. Tunisia – Independence of Electoral Administrations – Arab EMBs Workshop and 2nd General Assembly. www.venice.coe.int/webforms/events/?id=2355.
———. 2017d. The Venice Commission of Council of Europe. www.venice.coe.int/WebForms/pages/?p=01_Presentation&lang=EN.
Venice Commission, and ArabEMBS. 2015. *Memorandum of Understanding*.
Visser, Maartje De. 2015. "A Critical Assessment of the Role of the Venice Commission in Processes of Domestic Constitutional Reform." *The American Journal of Comparative Law*, 63, (4), pp. 963–1008.
Vonnahme, Greg, and Beth Miller. 2013. "Candidate Cues and Voter Confidence in American Elections." *Journal of Elections, Public Opinion & Parties*, 23, (2), pp. 223–39.
Waarden, Frans. 1992. "Dimensions and Types of Policy Networks." *European Journal of Political Research*, 21, (1–2), pp. 29–52.
Walker, Peter. 2018a. "England Voter ID Trial 'a Solution in Search of a Problem'." *Guardian*, 29 April.
———. 2018b. "Voter ID Trials 'Risk Disenfranchising Vulnerable People'." *Guardian*, 6 March.
Wall, Alan, Andrew Ellis, Ayman Ayoub, Carl W. Dundas, Joram Rukambe, and Sara Staino. 2006. *Electoral Management Design: The International IDEA Handbook*. Stockholm: International IDEA.
Walshe, Kieran, Gill Harvey, Paula Hyde, and Naresh Pandit. 2004. "Organizational Failure and Turnaround: Lessons for Public Services from the For-Profit Sector." *Public Money & Management*, 24, (4), pp. 201–8.
Wand, Jonathan N., Kenneth W. Shotts, Jasjeet S. Sekhon, Walter R. Jr. Mebane, Michael C. Herron, and Henry E. Brady. 2001. "The Butterfly Ballot Did It: The Aberrant Vote for Buchanan in Palm Beach County, Florida." *American Political Science Review*, 95, (4), pp. 793–810.
Webroots Democracy. 2017. *Cost of Voting: Estimating the Impact of Online Voting on Public Finances*. London: Webroots.
———. 2018. About. https://webrootsdemocracy.org/people/.
Wegge, Jürgen, Klaus-Helmut Schmidt, Carole Parkes, and Rolf Van Dick. 2007. "Taking a Sickie: Job Satisfaction and Job Involvement as Interactive Predictors of Absenteeism in a Public Organization." *Journal of Occupational and Organizational Psychology*, 80, (1), pp. 77–89.
White, Isobel, and Andrew Parker. 2009. *Speaker's Conferences*. London: House of Commons Library.
Wight, Colin. 2007. "A Manifesto for Scientific Realism in IR: Assuming the Can-opener Won't Work!" *Millennium*, 35, (2), pp. 379–98.
———. 2012. "Critical Realism: Some Responses." *Review of International Studies*, 38, (1), pp. 267–74.
Wilkinson, Steven I. 2006. *Votes and Violence: Electoral Competition and Ethnic Riots in India*. Cambridge: Cambridge University Press.
Wilks-Heeg, Stuart. 2008. *Purity of Elections in the UK: Causes for Concern*. York: Joseph Rowntree Trust.
———. 2009. "Treating Voters as an Afterthought? The Legacies of a Decade of Electoral Modernisation in the United Kingdom." *Political Quarterly*, 80, (1), pp. 101–10.

Bibliography

———. 2012. *A Literature Review for the Cabinet Office Electoral Registration Transformation Programme*. London: Cabinet Office.

Wilks, Stephen, and Maurice Wright. 1987. *Comparative Government-Industry Relations: Western Europe, the United States, and Japan*. Oxford: Clarendon Press.

Wilson, W. 1956. *Congressional Government: A Study in American Politics*. Cleveland, OH: World Publishing.

Wingrove, Josh. 2014a. "Conservative MP Retracted Voter-Fraud Story after Complaint to Elections Canada." *The Global and Mail*, 25 February, updated 25 March 2017. www.theglobeandmail.com/news/politics/conservative-mp-retracted-voter-fraud-story-after-complaint-to-elections-canada/article17079771/.

Wingrove, Josh. 2014b. "Scholars Denounce Conservatives' Proposed Fair Elections Act." *The Globe and Mail*, March 19. www.theglobeandmail.com/news/politics/scholars-denounce-conservative-governments-proposed-fair-elections-act/article17561354/.

Wolchok, Scott, Eric Wustrow, J. Alex Halderman, Hari K. Prasad, Arun Kankipati, Sai Krishna Sakhamuri, Vasavya Yagati, and Rop Gonggrijp. 2010. "Security Analysis of India's Electronic Voting Machines." In *Proceedings of the 17th ACM conference on Computer and Communications Security*, 1–14. Chicago, IL: ACM.

Wolfinger, Raymond E., Benjamin Highton, and Megan Mullin. 2005. "How Postregistration Laws Affect the Turnout of Citizens Registered to Vote." *State Politics & Policy Quarterly*, 5, (1), pp. 1–23.

Wolfinger, Raymond E., and Steven J. Rosenstone. 1980. *Who Votes?* New Haven, CT: Yale University Press.

World Bank. 2018. *World Development Indicators*. New York: World Bank.

Wright, P.M., and L.M. Nishii. 2007. *Strategic HRM and Organizational Behavior: Integrating Multiple Levels of Analysis, Center for Advanced Human Resource Studies*. Ithaca, NY: Cornell University, School of Industrial and Labor Relations, Center for Advanced Human Resource Studies.

Yanow, D. 2004. "Translating Local Knowledge at Organisational Peripheries." *British Journal of Management*, 15, (1), pp. 9–25.

ZEC. 2018. ZEC Functions. Zimbabwe Electoral Commission.

Appendix
EMB budget sizes

Country	Organisation	Fiscal annual budget (US$ PPP)	Election year budget (US$ PPP)	Voting age population	Annual budget per eligible elector	Election year budget per eligible elector	Election year	Proportion of electoral cycle
Afghanistan	Independent Election Commission of Afghanistan	8,560,119		16,208,255	0.53			80
Albania	The Central Election Commission	2,064,057	16,414,591	2,356,975	0.88	6.96	2015	75
Argentina	National Electoral Directorate	348,735,833		31,996,332	10.90			25
Bahamas	Parliamentary Registration Department	2,475,248		184,000				
Belarus	Central Commission of the Republic of Belarus on Elections and National Referenda		41,347,118	7,797,893		5.30	2016	
Belgium	Federal Public Service – Directorate General Institutions and Population – Service Elections	3,750		8,206,762	0.00			10
Bhutan	Election Commission of Bhutan	3,399,638		467,896	7.27			100
Bosnia Herzegovina	Central Electoral Commission	9,851,429	17,111,429	3,014,585	3.27	5.68	2014	55
Bulgaria	Central Election Commission	4,347,826	18,260,870	5,864,631	0.74	3.11	2016	45
Burkina Faso	Independent National Electoral Commission	1,244,496		9,100,031	0.14			50
Costa Rica	Supreme Electoral Tribunal	121,286,889		3,643,021	33.29			80

(*Continued*)

(Continued)

Country	Organisation	Fiscal annual budget (US$ PPP)	Election year budget (US$ PPP)	Voting age population	Annual budget per eligible elector	Election year budget per eligible elector	Election year	Proportion of electoral cycle
Croatia	State Election Commission of the Republic of Croatia	52,493,640	52,493,640	3,564,675	14.73	14.73	2015	50
Dominica	Electoral Office	484,456		40,812	11.87			55
Ecuador	Tribunal Contencioso Electoral	5,978,806		11,579,443	0.52			15
Estonia	National Electoral Committee	4,037,596		1,046,458	3.86			40
Finland	Ministry of Justice		16,426,093	4,079,928		4.03	2015	
Hungary	National Election Commission		160,742,997	8,043,818		19.98	2014	
Indonesia	Election Commission for West Java Province	95,497,096		168,300,873	0.57			95
Iraq	Independent High Electoral Commission	312,623,226		21,877,107	14.29			70
Israel	The Central Elections Committee for the Knesset	5,013,193	63,852,243	5,591,000	0.90	11.42	2015	80
Jordan	Independent Electoral Commission	6,250,000		4,793,499	1.30			65
Kenya	Independent Electoral and Boundaries Commission	400,421,507		25,374,082	15.78			85
Kyrgyz Republic	Central Commission for Election and Referendums			3,682,303				90
Kyrgyz Republic	State Registration Service		4,802,790	3,682,303		1.30	2016	60
Latvia	Central Election Commission	1,311,340	7,143,420	1,767,172	0.74	4.04	2014	20
Luxembourg	Bureau centralisateur gouvernemental	1,251,348	1,941,011	396,354	3.16	4.90	2013	
Malawi	Malawi Electoral Commission	17,022,518		8,173,669	2.08			70
Malta	Electoral Commission	9,296,667	10,000,000	337,540	27.54	29.63	2013	65
Mauritius	Office of the Electoral Commissioner	5,297,181		978,887	5.41			65

Country	Body					
Mexico	National Electoral Institute	2,012,134	85,801,675	0.02		85
Moldova	Central Electoral Commission	20,188,425	2,804,089	7.20	7.20	2016	65
Mongolia	General Election Commission of Mongolia	513,537	2,071,968	0.25		65
Mozambique	National Electoral Commission	2,594,340	11,850,615	0.22			80
Netherlands	Ministry of the Interior and Kingdom Relations	3,862,195	13,664,324	0.28	0.27	2017	
Netherlands	Electoral Council	2,317,073	13,664,324	0.17	0.19	2017	30
New Zealand	Electoral Commission	21,768,707	3,444,750	6.32			65
Norway	Norwegian Directorate of Elections	10,396,952	4,172,659	2.49	2.49	2017	5
Palestine	Central Elections Commission						70
Panama	Tribunal Electoral	24,193,548	2,338,207	10.35			90
Peru	National Elections Jury	12,500,000	20,909,390	0.60			50
Philippines	Commission on Elections	894,520,764	61,728,990	14.49			95
Poland	National Electoral Commission	51,602,222	31,568,464	1.63	6.86	2015	55
Rep. of Korea	National Election Commission	727,666,596	40,193,279	18.10			80
Romania	Permanent Electoral Authority	78,417,647	17,810,217	4.40	4.40	2016	30
Russia	Central Election Commission of the Russian Federation	669,424,098	114,473,081	5.85	5.85	2016	60
Rwanda	National Electoral Commission	16,355,369	5,918,583	2.76			70
Saint Lucia	Saint Lucia Electoral Department	97,802	123,629	0.79			60
Sao Tome and Principe	National Electoral Commission	69,844	85,885	0.81			5
Senegal	National Electoral Commission	24,807,182	7,596,246	3.27			70
Slovakia	State Commission on Election and Control of Funding of Political Parties	13,245,988	4,455,753		2.97	2016	

(Continued)

(Continued)

Country	Organisation	Fiscal annual budget (US$ PPP)	Election year budget (US$ PPP)	Voting age population	Annual budget per eligible elector	Election year budget per eligible elector	Election year	Proportion of electoral cycle
Spain	Office of the Electoral Census	5,303,030		39,691,061	0.13			
Spain	Ministry of the Interior		197,987,980	39,691,061		4.99	2016	
Spain	Central Electoral Board	829,577		39,691,061	0.02			50
Suriname	Independent Electoral Council	410,959		397,915	1.03			10
Sweden	Electoral Authority	3,846,154		7,962,006	0.48			45
Taiwan	Central Election Commission			18,906,005				65
Tanzania	National Electoral Commission	1,693,886		24,994,742	0.07			75
Timor-Leste	National Commission of Elections	7,812,500		701,368	11.14			60
Trinidad and Tobago	Elections and Boundaries Commission	24,962,976		940,813	26.53			70
Zimbabwe	Zimbabwe Electoral Commission	28,846,154		5,696,780	5.06			70

Source: Author based on data in EMS and ELECT surveys.

Index

Note: **Boldface** page references indicate tables. *Italic* references indicate figures and boxed text.

Abdallah II, King 152
Ability, Motivation and Opportunity (AMO) model 244
academics and electoral management bodies 192–3
academic surveys 51–3
accessibility 60, 82, 112, 114, 142, 153, 179, 206, 213
accountability 13, 44, 63, 72–3
accuracy of services/rules 6–8, 76
ACE Project 42
actual domain 25–6, **26**
Ad-Hoc Committee on Electronic Democracy 179
administrative environment 34–5
Advisory Group for Disability Issues 72
affective commitment 243
agency 29–30, 92–3
agency model 22
agora 161
Ahmedabad 132
Alderman, Keith 110
Allen, Graham 112, 115–16
All-Party Parliamentary Group 112–13, 120
Alvarez, R. Michael 33
America First platform 165
American Voter, The 22
Andaman Islanders 57
Andrews, Rhys 34, 36
Anglo School 95–100, *96–7*
Annan, Kofi 13
Ansell, Chris 100
apartheid 47
appraisals, performance 244–5
APSA 13
Arab EMBs 149, 152–3, 171
Arab Spring 152, 155, 171, 184

Arthur, Jeffrey B. 244
assessing election quality *see* performance; PROSeS framework
Association of Asian Election Authorities (AAEA) 171
Association for Democratic Reforms (ADR) 132
Association of Electoral Administrators (AEA) 107, 112, 116, 119–20, 123, 201, 247–8
Association of Electoral Bodies of Central America and the Caribbean (Tikal Protocol) 169–70
Association of Electoral Officials (A-WEB) 172
Association of European Electoral Officials (ACEEEO) 152, 170
Association of South American Electoral Organizations (Quito Protocol) 170
asymmetric network **154**, 156
asymmetric power 162–3
AusAID 136
Australian Centre of Disability Law and Homelessness 137
Australian Commonwealth Electoral Legislation Amendment Act (1983) 136
Australian Electoral Commission (AEC) 136, 139, 187
automatic registration 208

back-office efforts 199, 227
Bagehot, Walter 19
ballot papers, rejection of 68–9, 79
Ban Ki Moon, 172
Barry, Colin 136
Baxter, Joe 168
Beetham, David 13, 43–4, 46, 58, 62

312 Index

behaviouralism 20–3
Belbisi, Badrieh 149, 172
big data 22
Birch, Sarah 22, 37, 49, 53, 104, 109
Bite the Ballot 108–9, 112–13, 120–1, 208
Bland, Gary 37, 51–3
blog posts 121–2, 208
Boon, Corine 244
Borzel, Tanja 95, 99
Boselie, Paul 244
bottom-up policy 55
Boxall, Peter 244
Boyne, George A. 34, 36, 60–1, 63, 69–70
Braun, Virginia 204–5
Brehm, John 224
Brexit referendum 80, 234
BRIDGE (Building Resources in Democracy, Governance and Elections) project 187–8
bridging practices 162
British East India Company 131
Brown, Gordon 115
budgets of EMBs 64, 254–9, *256*, **257**, *258*, **258**
Burden, Barry C. 55
bureaucratic discretion school 224
business-oriented networks 162
Butler, David 19, 104

Cabinet Office 111
Canada: comparison with UK in applying PROSeS framework 71–85, 271; online electoral registration in 75; Standing Committee on Procedure and House Affairs 72; 2015 election 72
Carothers, Thomas 165
Carter Center 168, 184
'cash bonuses' 74
causation 27–9
central compliance 48
Central Election Commission of Russia 179
centralisation: defining 222–3; discussion of empirical findings confirming hypotheses 237–9; electoral management and 224–5; empirical findings of studying 237–9, 272; geographical 222; human relations school of management and 224; new public management and 224; organizational 222; overview 221–2, 239–40; in public management 223–4; research questions/hypothesis 224–5; scientific management school and 223–4; in 2011 referendums 225–7, *226*, **228–9**, 229–33; in 2016 referendum 233–7, *234*, **235**, **236**
Centre for National Renaissance 133
Cerny, Phil 163
certifying task 8
Chief Electoral Officer 74
citizens: satisfaction of 81–4; as stakeholders 70–71; surveys of 49–50, *50*
civic duty 219, 243
Civic Institute for Democracy (KOCEI) 173
civil rights, guaranteed 44
civil society: actors 112; groups 54; as stakeholder 71
Clark, Alistair 48–9, 109–10, 253
Clarke, Victoria 204–5
Clegg, Nick 107
clientelistic political culture 99
Clinton, Bill 110
closed statist systems 154–5, **154**
Cloward, Richard 110
co-authored blogs 122
Code of Good Practice in Electoral Matters 45, 185
collaborative governance 95, 176
Committee for Standards in Public Life 201
Commonwealth Electoral Network (CEN) 169
Commonwealth Ministerial Action Group (CMAG) 169
comparative governance networks: case study selection 125, *126*, **126**, 127; comparison of cases 152–4, **153**; India (2000–2016) 127–35; Jordan (2009–2017) 147–52; methodology 125, 127; New South Wales (2004–2018) 135–46; overview 15, 125, 158–9; proposed governance network types 154–6, **154**; vertical connections and 152–3, **153**
Comparative Study of Electoral Systems (CSES) 49
Competence Center for Electronic Voting and Participation 174
completeness of electoral register 67–8, *68*, 77–8, *78*, 211–14, *211*, **213**
compliance, central 48
concepts and evidence of performance, existing: conceptualisations of electoral management quality 42–9; data sources for measuring performance 49–57; issues in evaluating performance, philosophical/methodological 34–6;

methods for measuring performance, growing 36–7, **38–41**, 42; overview 15, 33–4; structure-agent relationship 35, *35*
concepts and evidence of performance, existing; *see also* performance
Conference of Electoral Management Bodies 194
confidence in democratic institutions 13, 70–71
conflict and electoral management 13
Constitution Act (1902) 145
constitutional formal-legal analysis 44–5
contestation: governance networks and 102; India's governance networks and 131–3, 153–4; international governance networks and 181–3; Jordan's governance networks and 150–1, 153–4; New South Wales's governance networks and 139–44, 153–4; UK governance networks 114–17
contested statist systems **154**, 155
contexts, shifting 93
contingency 65, 74, 92–3
contingent causation 29
contractor negotiation 262
convenience 65–6
Cooperative Threat Reduction programme 165
Corbyn, Jeremy 122
Cordenillio, Raul 163
core tripartite system of government civil servants 110
cost of elections, also see: budgets of EMBs
cost per unit of service production 80–81
Cost of Registration and Elections (CORE) 64, 253
costs, unforeseen 263–4
cross-continental organisations: cultural challenges and 187; electoral management and 166–9, **167**, 185–7, 189–90; Europe and 168–9; financial reliance and 191–5; international governance networks and 166–9, **167**, 184–95; knowledge building and 187–8; legal review and 189; 'naming and shaming' and 189–90; network building and 188–9; polices and, developing common 184–5; rise in 166; standards and, defining 184–5; tactics/strategies of 184–95; United Nations and 166–8; US foreign policy and 168; Venice Commission and 169

Crossman, Richard 57
cultural challenges 187

Dahl, Robert 20–1, 43–4
Database of International Electoral Expert Speakers (DIEES) 164
Davies, Jonathan S. 99
decentralisation 221–3
decision-making powers 134
decision-making processes 7, *61*, 62–3, 101
Declaration of Principles for International Election Observation 189–90
deconcentration 223
de facto power 20, 92–3
de jure power 20
de jure process 6, 44, 133
delivery partnerships 102, 153
Democracy Index 6
democratic ideals 13, 61
democratic institutions, confidence in 13, 70–71
democratic society 44
democratic theory 43–4
denial of voting 69, 80
Designing Social Enquiry (King, Keohane, and Verba) 21
devolution 223
Dietz, Graham 244
Dimbleby, David 4
diplomacy, personal 193
discretionary pay 245
disenfranchising electors 117
dissemination process 25
domains of reality 25–7, **26**
domestic observer reports 54
Donno, Daniela 42
donor governments 183–4
Dowding, Keith 96, 99
Durose, Catherine 55–6

economy-efficiency-effectiveness (3Es) model 60
efficiency 67
Election Administration Systems Index (EASI) 51–2
Election Administration and Voting Survey 54
Election Law (journal) 14
election monitoring 189–90
elections: complexity of 3–4; EMBs' role in 89; fair 44, 49, *50*; free 44; funding for 65, 74, 252, 259–64; implementation of 7–8; importance of 269; people

314   *Index*

running 15; public participation in 72; resourcing of 140–1; violence and 3, 69, 129; *see also* fraudulent practices; performance; PROSeS framework
Elections Canada 72, 76
Elections, Referendums and Registration Working Group (ERRWG) 111
Elections and Registration Working Group 110
Electoral Act (2017) 145
electoral administration 7
electoral assistance 185–7
Electoral Assistance Division (EAD) 171
Electoral Commission of India (ECI) 127–8, 130–2, 134
Electoral Commission of Kenya 3
Electoral Engineer (Norris) 179
Electoral Forum of the South African Development Community countries (ECF of SADC) 170
electoral fraud *see* fraudulent practices
electoral governance 6–7; *see also* governance networks
Electoral Institute for Sustainable Democracy for Africa (EISA) 170, 187
Electoral Integrity Project (EIP) 174
electoral justice 7
electoral malpractice 22
Electoral Malpractice (Birch) 37
electoral management: centralisation and 224–5; certifying task in 8; confidence in democratic institutions and 13; contributions of book to 16–7, 269; cross-continental organisations and 166–9, **167**, 185–7, 189–90; data sources *16*; defining 101, 269–70; democratic ideals and 13; electoral governance and 6–7; empirical findings from studying, key 271–3; funding for 252; future research on 270, 274; GDP per capita and 10, *11*; by geographic region 10, *12*; as global issue 15; implementing 7–8; importance of 3–5, 10–13; interdisciplinary approach to 13–14, *14*; methodological lessons from studying 269–71; monitoring task in 8; as multi-disciplinary field 13–14, *14*; organizing task in 8; overview 4–5; policy lessons from studying 273, *273–4*; problems with 37; professional associations and 13–14; public accountability and 13; rule-making and 6–7; security, peace and conflict and

13; as sub-field of political science 5–6, **5**; terminology, clarifying 6–7, 269; variation in, worldwide 8, *9*, 10; *see also* electoral management bodies (EMBs); financial investment in electoral management
electoral management bodies (EMBs): academics and 192–3; Arab 149, 152–3, 171; budgets of 64, 254–9, *256*, **257**, *258*, **258**; capacity, global rise in 51, *51*; collaboration of 95; contexts and, shifting 93; evaluating 34; focus on 6; formal-legal structures of 22; globalisation and 93–4; hollowed out 94–5; human resource management and performance of 244, *245*, 250–1; human resource management of workforces and 242–5; implementation of elections and 7–8, 20; individual actions and 92–3; informal relations and 92; interorganisational relations and 90–2; legal analysis and 46; national 172–3; officials 172–3; as open politics 101; other governance networks and 156–8, *157*; political context and, misreading 93; revenue sources for 259, **259**; role of in elections 89; tasks in electoral process of 90–2, *91*; technical data 54–5; transparency in 48; *see also* governance networks
Electoral Management Design handbook (IDEA) 20, 90, 187, 223
Electoral Management Network 174
Electoral Management Survey 148–9
Electoral Office of Northern Ireland (EONI) 234
electoral officials 55–7
Electoral Reform Society (ERS) 104, 108–9, 113, 116, 120–1, 208
Electoral Registration and Administration Act (2014) 208
Electoral Registration Officers (EROs) 73, 106–7, 225
Electoral Regulation Research Network 174
electoral studies 5–6, **5**
Electorates and Elections Act (1912) 140
electronic poll books 144
electronic voting machines (EVMs) 132–3
ELECT surveys 249
Elklit, Jørgen 37, 174
Ellis, Andrew 163
El Salvador 165
EMB officials 172–3

Index 315

empirical domain 25, **26**
empirical findings of studying electoral management, key 271–3
EMS surveys 249, 255
enforcement of rules 66, 76
Enticott, Gareth 36
epistemic communities 162
equity 70
Estonia 253
ethnographic methods 28–9, 57
Etobicoke Centre (Canada) 76
European Commission-United Nations Development Task Force on Electoral Assistance 149
European Conference of Electoral Management Bodies in Romania 194
European Court of Human Rights 189
European Union Election Observation Mission 3
Every Voice Matters Tour 112
expectations, rising 264
expert surveys 51–3

failures at steering and rowing 35–6
Farage, Nigel 122
Fascone, Cristina 15
Feldman, Martha S. 224
fieldwork process 24–5
Financial Administration Act 73
financial investment in electoral management: austerity and 254, 260, 265; budget cuts and 260; budgets of EMBs 254–9, *256*, **257**, *258*, **258**; contractor negotiation and 262; costs and, unforeseen 263–4; expectations and, rising 264; funding elections and 252, 259–64; historical relationships and, legacies of 264; lobbying purse-string holders and 260–1; overview 252, 264–5; procurement processes and 262–3; realist sociological approach and 265; research on, existing 253–4; revenue sources for EMBs 259, **259**; statecraft/rent-seeking and 261; strategic thinking and, capacity for 264; themes from roundtable/'storytelling session' in Stockholm and 260–4; worker management and 262
financial reliance 191–5
Financial Transparency Code, The 64
Finer, Herman 19
Finnemore, Martha 184
Fischer, Jeff 168, 188, 255

Foreign Assistance Act (1961) 165
formal effectiveness 76
formal-legal institutionalism 19–20, 22, 29, 92–3
Forum of Election Management Bodies of South Asia (FEMVoSA) 171
fraudulent practices: individual electoral registration and 209–11; levels of 68; localised studies of 46–7; measuring, difficulty of 46; New South Wales's governance networks and 143–4; performance and 46–7; stakeholders' concerns about 83
Freedom House 2016 measure 255
Freedom Support Act 165
front-line workers 36
funding elections 65, 74, 252, 259–64
future research 274

Gabler, T. 94
Garnett, Holly Ann 20, 30, 37, 48, 52, 55, 75, 174, 194, 274
Gash, Alison 100
Gates, Scott 224
Gauja, Anika 139
geographical centralisation 222
Gerken, Heather 6, 223
Gerring, John 30
gerrymander 53
Global Commission on Elections 13
globalisation 93–4, 161–3
Goertz, Gary 21
Goodwin-Gill, Guy S. 189
Gould-Williams, Julian S. 215, 243, 245
governance networks: agency and contingency 92–3; alternative approach 100–2; boards 90; collaborative 95; contestation and 102; contexts and, shifting 93; contributions to electoral management and 270; critique of 90–5; delivery partnerships and 102; dimensions of, new 102; electoral management bodies and 156–8, *157*; empirical findings of studying, key 271–2; globalisation and 93–4; hollowed out 94–5; informal relations 92; inter-organisational complexity and relations 90–2; overview 15, 89, 102–3; policy networks and 95–100; power an 102; types 101–2, 154–6, **154**; *see also* comparative governance networks; international governance networks; *specific country*

governance school 95–6, 99–100
Gray, Bill 171
Great Reform Acts 19
Green, Andrew 37
Green, Antony 139
Guidelines for International Election Observing (International Human Rights Law Group) 189
Gyimah, Sam 117

Harris, Joseph P. 19
Hartlyn, Jonathan 22
Harvard University workshop (2013) 23
Hawke Labour government 144
Heclo, Hugh 96
Hill, Sarah A. 253
Hirst (No.2) case 185
historical case studies 28
historical relationships, legacies of 264
Hjern, Benny 100
Holden, Angela 113
Hope Not Hate 203
household electoral registration (HER) 202
Howard Liberal-Nationals Coalition Government 144
Howarth Committee 108, 115, 120
human relations school of management 224
human resource management: affective commitment and 243; civic duty and 243; discretionary pay and 245; electoral officials' profile and 246, *247*, **247**, **248**; of EMB workforces 242–5; empirical findings of studying 272; employee experiences and, connectedness of 248; employee outcomes and 242–3, 249–50; individuals volunteering to quit and 243; international experience 249–51; job satisfaction and 243; methodology for studying 245–6; organisational performance and 244, *245*; overview 241–2, 251; performance appraisals and 244–5; performance of EMBs and 244, *245*, 250–1; practices 243–7; psychological climate and 245; research questions for studying 245–6; results of studying 246–9; stress of workers and 242–3, 248–9, 251; team working and 245; theoretical framework for studying 245, *245*; UK practices 246–7; work overload and 243
Hungarian National Election Office 170
Hyde, Susan 53

Iemma, Morris 145
impartiality in decision-making processes 62, 72
Independent Electoral Commission (IEC) 147, 150
Index of Electoral Malpractice 53
Indian Institute of Management (IIM) 132
India's governance networks (2000–2016): civil society involvement and 130; commercial sector and 130; contestation and 131–3, 153–4; delivery partnerships and 153; ECI and 127–8, 130–2, 134; integration of 127–31, 153; membership 127–31; parliamentary system and 127; power diffusion and 133–5, 154
indicators, absence or poor use of 36
individual electoral registration (IER) in UK: administrative burden of 214–15; changes in, simultaneous 202; civic duty and 219; completeness of electoral registration and 211–14, *211*, **213**; costs of, increased 214–15, *214*, 253; data quality/management and 207; empirical findings of studying, key 272; employee outcomes and 215, *216*, 217; fraudulent practices and 209–11; impact of 109, 205–7, 272; inclusiveness and 211–14; intention to quit by workers and 218–19; job satisfaction of workers and 218; knowledge about, existing 202–4; local government resources and 207; methodology of studying 204–5, **205**; negotiating 208; overview 201–2, 219–20; participation rates and 205–7; post-implementation effects 209–19, **209**; spillover/displacement effects and 207; stress of workers and 218; themes in studying 205–7, **206**; urban-rural split and 212; voter confidence and 205; workload and 217; workplace conditions and 215, **216**, 217; workplace environment and 217, *217–18*
informal relations 92
inputs-outputs-outcomes (IOO) model 60–1, 70
Instituto Nacional Electoral Mexico 179
Integrity Coalition for Election Observation (ICEO) 150
Inter-American Union of Electoral Organizations (UNIORE) 170
interest intermediation school 95–100, *96–7*
international civil servants 162

Index   317

International Forum for Democratic Studies (IFDS) 188
International Foundation for Electoral Systems (IFES) 23, 64, 151, 168
international governance networks: bridging practices and 162; collaboration and 176; consensus and 181–3; contestation and 181–3; cross-continental organisations 166–9, **167**, 184–95; donor governments and 183–4; globalisation and 161–3; integration of 175–81; interaction among 175–81; international speakers dataset 177, **178**, 179–81, **179**, **180**, *181*; language barriers and 176; membership 164–75, **167**; methodology of studying 164; national EMBs/EMB officials 172–3; national governments and 164–6; other actors 173–5; overview 15, 160–1, 195–6, **195**; power and, asymmetric 162–3; public policy and, global 161–3; qualitative interviews and 175–7; regional associations of practitioners 169–72; resources of 183–95, **195**; tactics/strategies of 183–95, **195**; transnational policy networks and 161–3; types 162; work on, existing 163
International Institute for Democracy and Electoral Assistance (IIDEA) 43, 45, 90, 169, 188, 223
internationalised public sector officials 162
international speakers dataset 177–81
internet voting 142–3
inter-organisational complexity/relations 90–2
inter-organisational service 100
issue networks 97, **98**

James, Toby S. 8, 49, 98, 246
Janak Singh vs. Ram Das Rai and Others (2003) 129
Janata Party 133
Jessop, Bob 26–7, 100
job satisfaction of workers 243
Johnson, Nevil 19
Joint Standing Committee on Electoral Matters (JSCEM) 136–7, 139–41, 145–6, 153
Jordanian Alliance for Electoral Reform (JAER) 150
Jordanian Council of Representatives 147
Jordanian Day of Rage 152

Jordan's governance networks (2009–2017): Arab EMBs and 149, 152–3; contestation and 150–1, 153–4; delivery partnerships and 153; historical perspective of 147; integration of 152, 153; membership 147–9; policy networks and 147–9; power diffusion and 151–2, 154
Joseph Rowntree Reform Trust 109, 201

Kabaki, Mwai 3
Kalaldeh, Khaled 152
Kassim, Hussein 98
Kelley, Judith 53, 190
Kelly, Norm 144
Kennedy, Lord 120
Kennedy, Ray 148
Kenya 3, 13
Keohane, R. 21, 42
King, Bridgett A. 49
King, G. 21, 42
Kingsley, Jean-Pierre 181
Klijn, Erik-Hans 100–1
knowledge: cross-continental organisations and building 187–8; gaps in expert 52–3; local 55–6, 231–2; networks 162; realist sociological approach and nature of 23–5, 29
Koppenjam, Joop 100
Korean Electoral Commission 172
Krimmer, Robert 174, 253

language barriers 52, 176
Leca, Bernard 28
legal analysis/review 46–7, 189
legitimacy of funding 64, 74
Lindberg, Staffan 22
linguistic problems 52, 176
Lobbying Bill 113
lobbying purse-string holders 260–1
localism 223
local knowledge 55–6, 231–2
Loeber, Leontine 174, 194
López-Pintor, Rafael 20, 174, 193, 255
Lührmann, Anna 185–6
Lynch, Paul 145

Mahoney, James 21
Maley, Michael 136, 146, 173
Marsh, David 97, 99
Martinez i Coma, Ferran 52–3
Marx, Karl 273
mature governmental network **154**, 155–6

318   *Index*

mature independent network 156
Mawrey, Richard 108
McCoy, Jennifer 22
mechanistic bridging practices 162
methodological approach 15; *see also* realist sociological approach
methodological lessons 269–71
Mexico 179
Miller, Beth 50
Mill, J. S. 46
mimetic bridging practices 162
minimalist approach 43
Minnitte, Lorraine 47
Missing Millions, The, campaign 113, 122
mixed methods 30
Mohamed, R.B. 243, 245
Mohr, Z. 253
monitoring task 8
Moore, Toby 37
Motor Voter registration 208
Moynihan, Donald P. 36
multiple bridging practices 162
Murray, Judy 110
Mustillo, Thomas M. 22
Myth of Voter Fraud, The (Minnitte) 47

Naccache, Philippe 28
'naming and shaming' 189–90
National Center for Human Rights 149
National Committee on Women's Affairs 149
National Council of Hungarian Ethnic Minority 179
National Democratic Institute (NDI) 168
national EMBs 172–3
National Endowment for Democracy (NED) 165, 168, 188
national governments 164–6, 183
National Register of Electors 75, 77
National Voter Education Committee (NVEC) 148
National Voter Registration Act (1993) 110, 200
National Voter Registration Day 121
network building 188–9
network types 162
new institutionalism 20
New Public Management (NPM) 94, 224
New South Wales Disability Discrimination Legal Centre (NSWDDLC) 141
New South Wales Electoral Commission 127, 140–1, 145

New South Wales's governance networks (2004–2018): contestation and 139–44, 153–4; delivery partnerships and 153; fraudulent practices and 143–4; integration of 152, 153; internet voting and 142–3; membership 136–7, **138**, 139; parliamentary system and 135; postal voting and 143; power diffusion and 144–6, 154; resourcing of elections and 140–1; tactics/strategies of 144–6; 2015 elections and 144; voter participation and 141–2
New South Wales and Victoria Electoral Commission 174
Nishii, L.M. 244
normative bridging practices 162
norms/standards, international 45–6
Norris, Pippa 22, 46, 48–9, 174, 179, 184, 194
Northern Ireland 106, 234

Obama, Barack 165
objectivity 34
observable political phenomena 21–2
observer reports 53–4
Office for Democratic Institutions and Human Rights (ODIHR) 168
Office of the United Nations High Commissioner for Human Rights 167
Ohanyan, Anna 162
old institutionalism 19–20
O'Leary, Cornelius 19
oligopolies 94–5
OLS model 248–9, **249**, **251**
online transparency 48–9
Operation Black Vote 116
organisational centralisation 222
organisational performance 244, *245*
Organisation of Arab Electoral Management Bodies (ArabEMBs) 149, 152–3, 171
Organisation for Security and Co-operation in Europe (OSCE) 168
Organization of American States (OAS) 169
organizing task 8
Osbourne, D. 94
overhead organisations 19

Pal, Michael 20
Paris Charter (1990) 168
Parliamentary Assembly of the Council of Europe (PACE) 185

Parliamentary Electorates and Elections Act (1912) 145
Parliamentary Select Committees 112–13
parties as stakeholders 71
Pastor, Robert 6
Peacebuilding Fund 168
peace and electoral management 13
People with Disabilities Australia (PWD) 141
Perception of Electoral Integrity Index (PEII) 51, 250
Perceptions of Electoral Integrity survey 8
Perelli, Carina 182
performance: administrative environment and 34–5; appraisals 244–5; citizen surveys and 49–50, *50*; compliance and, central 48; constitutional formal-legal analysis and 44–5; democratic theory and 43–4; domestic observer reports and 54; electoral officials and 55–7; expert/academic surveys 51–3; failure of steering and rowing and 35–6; fraudulent practices and 46–7; human resource practices and organisational 244; legal analysis and 46–7; measuring, growing methods for 36–7, **38–41**, 42; norms/standards, international 45–6; objectivity and 34; observer reports and 53–4; online transparency and 48–9; organisational 244, *245*; overview 15, 58; researcher ethnography and 57; service provision 48–9; sociological mass perceptions and 47–8; structure-agent relationship and 35, *35*; technical EMB data and 54–5; *see also* concepts and evidence of performance, existing; PROSeS framework
Permanent Electoral Authority of Romania 179
Perrow, Charles 36
personal diplomacy 193
Pfeffer, Jeffrey 244
Physical Disability Council of New South Wales 143
Piccirilli, Giovanni 185
Pickles, Eric 116
Pinto-Duschinsky, Michael 110
Pitcaithly, Mary 107
Piven, Frances Fox 110
pluralism, methodological 101
pluralistic collaborative network **154**, 156
policy communities 97, **98**

policy instruments 15–16; *see also specific type*
policy lessons/recommendations 273, *273–4*
policy networks: Anglo School and 95–100, *96–7*; criticisms of 98–9; dimensions of 97; governance and 95; governance networks and 95–100; governance school and 95–6, 99–100; issue networks and 97, **98**; Jordan's 147–9; policy communities and 97, **98**; typologies 97, **98**
Political and Constitutional Reform Select Committee (PCRSC) 112, 115–16, 121, 208
Political Parties and Election Act (PPE) (2010) 201
Political Party Liaison Council (PPLC) 148
political rights, guaranteed 44
politicking 163
Polity 10
poll books, electronic 144
polyarchy 43
Poon, June M.L. 244
Popper, Karl 21
Porter, David O. 100
positivist empirical approaches 26
postal voting 115, 143, 201
power: *de facto* 20, 92–3; *de jure* 20; governance networks and 102; India's governance networks and diffusion of 133–5, 154; international governance networks and asymmetric 162–3; Jordan's governance networks and diffusion of 151–2, 154; New South Wales's governance networks and diffusion of 144–6, 154; UK governance networks and 117–22
practice, lessons for 273
pressure groups 71
Price Waterhouse Coopers 76
probity in decision-making processes 62, 72
procedural approach 43
process design in PROSeS framework *61*, 62–3, 71–3
procurement processes 262–3
PROSeS framework: applying 71–85, 274; Canada-UK comparison 71–85; contributions to electoral management and 270; decision-making processes 62–3; democratic ideals and 61, *61*; dimensions 62, **62**; matrix 61–2, *61*, 66; overview 15, 59, 84–5; process

design *61*, 62–3, 72–3; public administration assessment and 60–1; resource investment *61*, 64–5, 73–4; service outcomes *61*, 66–9, 76–81, *77*; service output quality *61*, 65–6, 74–6; stakeholder satisfaction *61*, 70–71, 81–4
psychological climate 245
public accountability 13, 44
public administration assessment 60–1
public management, centralisation in 223–4
public participation in decision-making processes 63
public participation in elections 72
Public Sector Cost model 253
Pugh, Martin 19
Purcell, John 244

qualitative interpretation 58
qualitative research 21
quality of elections *see* performance; PROSeS framework
quantitative analysis 30, 249
quitting, propensity of individuals to volunteer for 243

Ratcliffe, Mark 139
real domain 26, **26**
realist sociological approach: behaviouralism and 20–3; causation and 27–9; consequences of 29–30; context and 27–8; contingent causation and 29; contributions to electoral management and 270; description and, value of 30; dissemination process and 25; domains of reality and 25–7, **26**; fieldwork process and 24–5; financial investment in electoral management and 265; formal-legal institutionalism and 19–20, 29; knowledge and, nature of 23–5, 29; learning relationship between subject and object in 24–5; literature, existing 19–23; mixed methods and 30; outcomes and 27–8; overview 15, 18–19; researcher positionality and 29; social phenomenon and, measuring 28–9; structure-agent relationship and 29–30, 35, *35*; *verstehen* and 28, 30
'Referendum Blueprint' 233
regional associations of practitioners 169–72
regional differences 176

regular blog posts 121
regulative bridging practices 162
Reinforcing Democracy in the Americas project 168
Reinventing Government (Osbourne and Gabler) 94
rejection of ballot papers 69, 79
Rennard, Chris 107–8
rent-seeking 261
Representation of the People Act (1918) 19, 104–5
Representation of the People Act (1951) 134
research ethnography 57
researcher positionality 29
Resolution 46/137 on Enhancing the Effectiveness of the Principle of Periodic and Genuine Elections 166
resource distribution and UK governance networks 117, **118**, 119–22
resource investment in PROSeS framework *61*, 64–5, 73–4
resourcing of elections 140–1
Returning Officers (ROs) 73, 106–7, 225
Reynolds, Andrew 37, 174
Rhodes, Rod A. W. 97
Robocall scandal 80
Rock and Enrol project 121
Rogers, David 100
Romanian Permanent Electoral Authority 173, 188
Rosenstone, Steven J. 200
Ruane, Chris 107
rule implementation 7
rule-making 6–7, 100
Russian Conservative Party of Entrepreneurs and Others v. Russia (2017) 185

Saiah, Emad Al 149, 172
satisfaction 81–4
Sayer, Andrew 24, 27, 201
Schatz, Edward 29
Schedler, Andreas 37
scientific management school 223–4
Scottish Independence Referendum Act (2013) 107
Scottish Parliament Select Committee 254
security and electoral management 13
service denial 69, 80
service outcomes in PROSeS framework *61*, 66–9, 76–81, *77*
service output quality in PROSeS framework *61*, 65–6, 75–6

Index 321

Seymour, Charles 19
Shires Association 137, 140, 143
Sidorczuk, Oliver 109
Sikkink, Kathryn 184
Simon, Herbert 224
Simpster, Alberto 37
Skidmore, Chris 112
Slaughter, Anne-Marie 162
Smith, Chloe 113, 116
Smith, Martin 99
Smith, Rodney 139
Sobolewska, Maria 46–7
social democratic agenda 191
social phenomenon, measuring 28–9
sociological mass perceptions 47–8
SOLACE (Society of Local Authority Chief Executive and Senior Managers) 107, 112, 120
South Africa 47
South Korea 172–3
South Korean National Election Commission 172
staff satisfaction 82–3
staff as stakeholders 71
stakeholders: fraudulent practices and, concerns about 83; satisfaction in PROSeS framework 61, 70–71; staff as 71
statecraft 261
Stone, Diane 161
storytelling/roundtable session in Stockholm, themes from 260–4
strategic learning 29
strategic relational approach (SRA) 26–7
strategic thinking, capacity for 264
Straw, Jack 108
street-level bureaucrats 224
Strengthening Electoral Processes in Jordan (SEPJ) 147–8
stress of workers 242–3, 248–9, 251
structure 29–30
structure-agent relationship 29–30, 35, *35*
substantive approach 43
sufficiency 64
Summers, Mike 113
Support for Eastern European Democracy (SEED) 165
Supreme Court of India 133, 135
surveys, expert/academic 51–3
sustainability of funding 64–5, 74, 151
SVEEP (Systematic Voters' Education and Electoral Participation) scheme 130
Switzerland National EMB 222
Sydney Town Hall 144

Tanzania 255
Teague, Vanessa 139
team working 245
technical EMB data 54–5
Tham, Joo-Cheong 174
#TheAmendment campaign 120
Title IX of Foreign Assistance Act 165
training *see* human resource management
Transatlantic Business Dialogue 162
transgovernmental network of actors 15; *see also* governance networks
transnational advocacy networks 162
transnational policy professionals 162
transparency 48–9, 64, 74
Trudeau, Justin 83
Truman, David 21
Trump, Donald 165, 184
Trustee Council 166
Tunisia 152
2011 referendums: costs of, financial 230; data 227; directions issued to local officials and *226*, **228–9**; error elimination and 229–30; implementation and, easier 230; job satisfaction and 232–3; local knowledge and, lost 231–2; methodology of studying 227; new practices and 230; overview 225–7; results of studying 227–33; services and, consistent 227, 229; staff morale and 232–3; staff time and 230–1; stakeholder relations and 232–3; themes, overview 227, **228–9**
2016 referendums: CCO's responses to questions/instructions 235–7, **236**; costs of, financial 237; data 234–5; directions issued to local officials and *234*, 236–7, **236**; management structure's views 235, **235**; methodology of studying 234–5; overview 233–4; results of studying 235–7, **235**, **237**; views of management structure used for 235–6, **235**

UK: comparison with Canada in applying PROSeS framework 71–85, 271; Department of International Development 174; Electoral Advisory Board 111; Electoral Commission 72–3, 82, 109, 111–12, 114–16, 119–20, 123, 203, 227, 231–3, 248; human resource practices 246–7; online electoral registration in 75; 2010 elections in 4; voter turnout in parliamentary general elections 76–7, *77*; *see also* individual

electoral registration (IER) in UK; UK governance networks
UK governance networks: contestation and 114–17; integration among 110–14, *111*; interaction of 110–14, *111*; membership 105–10; methodology of studying 105; overview 15, 104–5, 122–3; power and 117–22; resource distribution and 117, **118**, 119–22
unforeseen costs 263–4
United Nations and cross-continental organisations 166–8
United Nations Development Programme (UNDP) 20, 64, 147–8, 151, 167, 253
United Nations Educational, Scientific and Cultural Organization (UNESCO) 167
United Nations Entity for Gender Equality and the Empowerment of Women 167
United Nations National Accounts Official Country Data 256
Universal Declaration of Human Rights 45, 184
urban-rural split 212
US: foreign policy 168; military intervention in Afghanistan and Iraq 184; 2000 Presidential election 3–4, 14, 69, 200; 2016 Presidential election 52
USAID funding 165

Valuation Joint Boards 74
value of description 30
Van Ham, Carolien 22, 37, 52–3, 174, 194
Varieties of Democracy (V-DEM) Index 51, 126–7, 249
Venice Commission 44–5, 152, 169, 185, 189, 194
Verba, S. 21, 42
verstehen 28, 30
Vickery, Chad 22–3
violence, election 3, 70, 129
Vonnahme, Greg 50
voter fraud 83; *see also* fraudulent practices
voter registration reform: back-office effects and 199; changes and, simultaneous 202; electoral management and, effects on 270–1, *271*; overview 199–200, 219–20; temporal nature of 273; UK individual electoral registration and 201–8; voting technologies and 199–201; *see also* individual electoral registration (IER) in UK
voter turnout 67
Voter Turnout Database (International IDEA) 67–9
Voter Verifiable Paper Audit Trail (VVPAT) 133
Voting Age Population (VAP) 81
voting technologies, research on 200–1

Walker, Richard M. 34
Wallace, Anna 113
Walshe, Kieran 34–5
Watson, Jenny 4, 119, 233, 235
Watt, Bob 109
Weber, Max 28
Webroots Democracy 113
Weinstein, Allen 168
Welsh Referendum 229
Wen, Roland 139
Whetten, David Allred 100
White, F. Clinton 168
Wildavsky, Aaron B. 96
Wilson, Woodrow 19
Wolfinger, Raymond E. 200
Women Solidarity Institute 149
worker management 262
work overload 243
World Bank 249
World Values Survey 81
Wright, P.M. 244

Yannow, Dvora 56
Youngblood, Norman E. 49
Younger, Sam 110, 119
Youth Action & Policy Association (YAPA) 141

Zimbabwe Electoral Commission 222